VB Oracle 8 Programmer's Reference

Dov Trietsch

John Mason

Wrox Press Ltd. ®

VBScript Programmer's Reference

Published by Wrox Press Ltd
Arden House, 1102 Warwick Road, Acock's Green, Birmingham B27 6BH, UK
Printed in USA
ISBN 1-861001-78-9

Trademark Acknowledgements

Wrox has endeavored to provide trademark information about all the companies and products mentioned in this book by the appropriate use of capitals. However, Wrox cannot guarantee the accuracy of this information.

Credits

Author
Dov Trietsch

Editors
Catherine Alexander
Tony Davis

Contributing Author
John Mason

Development Editor
Dominic Lowe

Technical Reviewers
Aaron Abdis
Steve Fowler
Philip B. Janus
John Mason
Sumit Pal
Manish Shah
Amy Sticksel
Beverley Treadwell

Project Manager
Sophie Edwards

Design / Layout
Tom Bartlett
Mark Burdett
William Fallon
Jonathan Jones
John McNulty

Additional Material
Aaron Abdis
Steve Fowler

Index
Alessandro Ansa

Cover Design
Chris Morris

Managing Editor
Joanna Mason

Illustrations
William Fallon

Contributing Author

John Mason

John P. Mason, MCSD, was born November 6, 1967 in Norfolk, Virginia. He is married to Kimberly A. Mason, and they live in Chesapeake, Virginia. He has worked as a computer professional for over ten years and is currently employed by Unisys where he is both a Principal Programmer/Analyst and a Team Leader. Unisys is an international corporation that often provides highly technical manpower (consultants) on various contracts and subcontracts for government and commercial organizations. He is currently working for a client on software that schedules sets of deliverables in cross-functional business units at multiple geographical sites, with customers around the world.

John is a Microsoft Certified Solution Developer (MCSD). His current interests include scalable, high-availability, distributed applications, and XML. Outside the field of Software Development, his interests include reading, complex computer-based strategy games, Toastmasters International, and keeping up-to-date with the frontiers of science.

Acknowledgments:

I would like to thank the many fine people at WROX press for the opportunity to write for such a cutting-edge company. Special thanks are in order for Tony Davis, Technical Editor and Sophie Edwards, Project Manager for their help. I also owe a tremendous debt of gratitude to my wife, Kimberly, for her support and her understanding as I put many hours into this project on top of an already ambitious schedule at work.

About the Author

Dov Trietsch

Dov Trietsch has been a professional Programmer/Analyst for over thirty non-consecutive years. The break in the continuum happened when he was demoted to VP of a life insurance company. He is still trying to make up for this transgression. He has been involved in many forms of data storage and retrieval systems, culminating in RDB in general and Oracle in particular. He has also worked in various user interfaces. He keeps himself at the forefront of the technology by a relentless pursuit of self-education, which leaves little time for his favorite pastimes of theater, music, and fine literature. When not writing, learning, or vacationing, he helps his clients build web-enabled applications using VB, VBScript, Oracle, IIS, ASP, MTS, Java Script, and ADO.

Dedication

To my wife, Batia, who stuck with me through thick and mostly thin, and to our daughter, Irith, whose help was instrumental in writing this book.

Acknowledgments

Writing this book gave me the greatest satisfaction of my professional life. Never before have I devoted so much time and effort to any one project or cause. I am grateful to all the people who made it possible, especially the editors and reviewers at WROX who made sure of the quality and truth of every statement and helped me finish the project on time. Among them, I would like to extend special thanks to Dominic Lowe, who started the process, and Catherine Alexander and Tony Davis, who so expertly and patiently guided me in its final shaping.

I am also grateful to my clients, who suffered my writing absences and continue to seek my help and advice. I developed most of my methodology of VB and Oracle deployment while building software for clients, which is also how this book was conceived.

Last but not least, I thank my daughter, Irith -- a technical writer and translator -- who shared the writing. I supplied the words, and she contributed the punctuation.

I hope that you, the reader, will find the book instructive and useful. If you do, then I have done my duty well, and at the end of the day that is all that counts.

Table of Contents

Chapter 2: Queries and Data Manipulation Using SQL   49

Chapter 4: Object Oriented Programming, Data Classes and Data Access Technologies   135

Section II - Using OO4O and Oracle

Chapter 5: An OO4O Application   151

Chapter 6: Using Parameters with OO4O   177

Chapter 7: Optimizing the OO4O Connection and Data Classes   187

Section III - Using ADO and Oracle

Chapter 9: An ADO Application 237

Chapter 10: Using Parameters with ADO 255

Chapter 11: Optimizing the ADO Connection and Data Classes 275

Chapter 12: An ADO Reference 285

Section IV - PL/SQL, Stored Procedures and Transactions

Chapter 13: PL/SQL, Stored Procedures and Triggers   311

Chapter 14: A Practical Application Using Transactions and Stored Procedures 353

Section V - Moving on up - N-Tier Solutions

Introduction

VB is the king of RAD. There are at least three million VB programmers in the industry. Half the development efforts undertaken by business are done in VB; almost all are done in one relational database or another. Oracle is the king of RDB. There is no other commercial RDB that can handle as much information as well and as fast, or scale as well both vertically or horizontally. Many of the new web businesses trust their precarious survival to Oracle. Yet there are hardly any books or articles that cover both VB and Oracle. This book is designed to fill the void.

Filling a literary void is not the only purpose of this book, of course. There is a definite need for programmers who can write robust software that allows businesses to store and dispense pertinent and correct information, a need for programmers who can deploy such software quickly. Knowledge and experience are the key to fast and robust deployment; this book will give you both.

Practical exercises in Oracle, SQL, and PL/SQL will enrich your database knowledge. Practical exercises in building VB applications in ADO and Oracle Objects for OLE (OO4O) will enrich your VB vocabulary and strengthen your OOP muscle. Finally, a complete guide to SQL, PL/SQL, Oracle Objects for OLE, and ADO will serve you as a desk reference. All this in one concise book to help you make the most of your most important resource - the time you need for development.

About the Book

The demand for programmers well versed in both Oracle and VB is rising. This book will help the VB practitioner gain the knowledge and skills required for working with Oracle databases. It covers:

- ❑ SQL in general, with an emphasis on the Oracle dialect (including extensive exercises)
- ❑ PL/SQL – The Oracle database internal language used to write stored procedures and triggers (including extensive exercises)
- ❑ An introduction to data access methods in general and how to access Oracle via:

> ❑ ADO (ActiveX Data Objects) – the Microsoft flagship of Universal Data Access (UDA)
>
> ❑ Oracle Objects For OLE (OO4O) -- The Oracle answer to DAO, RDO and ADO

The book goes through a series of VB exercises, each done once with OO4O and again with ADO. It then draws these together by guiding the reader through a mini HR application using OO4O and ADO. The reader is instructed on how to build the application, with and without the use of stored procedures. As a result, the reader will be able to use all the techniques of VB and Oracle and make informed decisions about the development of business applications. Finally, we look at building middle-tier business and data objects with Oracle.

The book provides a comprehensive reference to both ADO as it is used with Oracle, and Oracle Objects for OLE. Each is contained in its own section for speedy and easy learning.

So let's take a brief look at each section of the book:

Section I. The Fundamentals - an Overview of Oracle, VB, SQL and Data Access.

We are introduced to the concepts we will use later in the book. These chapters double up as a reference section and a practical plethora of code examples.

Chapter 1. An overview of **Oracle and VB**. This covers why we would want to use VB and Oracle together, and goes on to explore Oracle, its **architecture**, history and the **versions** and products available. We go on to compare **SQL Server** and **Access** to Oracle and the necessary considerations before moving to Oracle. The chapter finishes with the **installation** of Oracle on Windows 95 and NT; an exploration of the database tables used in the book and our **first program**, using the ADO data control.

Chapter 2. This covers the **Data Query Language (DQL)** and the **Data Manipulation Language (DML)**. We start by exploring a simple version of the DQL SELECT statement; and then learn to use the WHERE, ORDER BY and GROUP BY clauses, as well as arithmetic operators and functions, with the SELECT statement. This section ends with a look at complex queries, including nested queries, joins, aliases and using the SET operator.

We finish the chapter with a look at transactions and the DML statements - DELETE, UPDATE and INSERT - with practical examples of using these to modify data.

Chapter 3. This continues our exploration of SQL with a look at the **Data Definition Language (DML)** statements - CREATE, ALTER and DROP - and how we can use these with databases, tables and sequences. We continue to examine the database tables of the book and the scripts we can use to create them. Further highlights include a look at: Oracle **data types**, **constraints**, **indexes** and **views**.

Chapter 4. This chapter provides a summary of the principles of **Object Orientated Programming (OOP)**, including a simple application showing how we can apply these to the VB data classes. This overview of important concepts ends with a look at various **data access methods** that can be used to connect VB to Oracle.

Section II - Using OO4O and Oracle

This section combines theory and hands on practice - beginning with a look at the basics of OO4O. We then develop a complete application in stages. At the end we have a quick reference chapter which consolidates everything we have learnt and develops our knowledge further.

Chapter 5. Our introduction to **OO4O**. We start with a look at a simplified version of the OO4O **object model**; and continue with our first practical look at OO4O. In this program, we create a Dynaset to hold the records from one of our database tables and examine ways of navigating and modifying them.

Chapter 6. We build on our knowledge of OO4O and the program from the previous chapter, by examining the practical use of **parameters** with OO4O.

Chapter 7. Again we expand our knowledge of OO4O by adding **transaction control** and **triggers** to our program.

Chapter 8. Here we summarize our current knowledge of OO4O and expand on it with an extensive **reference section**. This covers the all the **objects** of the full OO4O object model, with their **methods** and **properties**.

Section III - Using ADO and Oracle

These next few chapters follow a similar structure to the above four, but are now examining **ADO**. We begin with a look at the basics of ADO. To further our knowledge we then build a program in segments, introducing new concepts with each chapter. At the end we have a quick reference chapter which consolidates everything we have learnt and provides additional knowledge. Thus we learn through both theory and hands-on practice.

Chapter 9. We start with an introduction to the simplified ADO **object model**. As in Chapter 5, we continue by building a new practical example. We create a Recordset which will receive the results of a simple SELECT statement against one of our database tables. We then use various methods of this Recordset to modify and navigate the data.

Chapter 10. We continue to follow our OO4O code by looking at how we can use **parameters** with ADO.

Chapter 11. Again, we build on our ADO knowledge by adding **transaction control** and **triggers** to our program.

Chapter 12. We finish our look at ADO by summarizing what we have learnt and develop this with a **reference section**. We examine the full object model, covering the **methods** and **properties** of each object as they are relevant to Oracle, the **Parameters Collection** and **error handling**.

Section IV - PL/SQL, Stored Procedures and Transactions

By now, we have a solid knowledge of using Oracle with VB via both OO4O and ADO. This section culminates in the actual building of an application that maintains four database tables. But first, we will look at PL/SQL - the language of stored procedures and triggers.

Chapter 13. A practical overview of the principles of **PL/SQL**. We start with some simple examples and by examining the different **data types** available. We then learn to use **loops**, arrays, PL/SQL **cursors**, **stored procedures**, functions, **packages** and tables - returning the latter of these to VB via ADO and OO4O. To end we examine REF CURSORS, creating **triggers** and **error handling**. As well as the numerous practical examples, this doubles up as an excellent reference section for PL/SQL.

Chapter 14. We now combine all our knowledge together in a wide-ranging **application**. This application is built in four ways. Firstly, we use OO4O and ADO with **transaction control** to guarantee data integrity. We then repeat this using **stored procedures**, again for both OO4O and ADO.

Section V - Moving on up: N-Tier Solutions

Chapters 15, 16 and *17* will take everything we have learnt so far and apply it to **multi-tier development**. We'll use an example business case to discuss building middle tier business and data objects in Visual Basic with Oracle as the database server. Finally, we will see how to use components with **Microsoft Transaction Server** (**MTS**).

What You Need to Use This Book

To be able to fully use the book, the reader needs:

- ❏ VB 6.0 Professional or (preferably) Enterprise Edition

- ❏ ADO 2.1

- ❏ Access to an Oracle (8.03 and up) database. A 30-day trial copy of Personal Oracle is available on line at www.oracle.com. You may also get a 30 day trial copy on a CD for the price of shipping and handling. To order call 1-800-Oracle1 (1-800-672-2531).

- ❏ Oracle Object For OLE (OO4O) version 2.2 and up. Comes with the Oracle CD or the download of the trial version. Alternatively, ask your network manager or your Oracle DBA.

Conventions Used in This Book

I've used a number of different styles of text and layout in the book, to help differentiate between different finds of information. Here are some of the styles I've used and an explanation of what they mean:

> **These boxes hold important, not-to-be forgotten, mission-critical details that are directly relevant to the surrounding text.**

Background information, asides and references appear in text like this.

❑ **Important Words** are in a bold font

❑ Words that appear on the screen, such as menu options, are in a similar font to the one used on screen, for example, the Tools menu

❑ All object names, function names and other code snippets are in this style: SELECT

Code that is new or important is presented like this:

```
SELECT CustomerID, ContactName, Phone
FROM Customers
```

Whereas code that we've seen before or has little to do with the matter being discussed, looks like this:

```
SELECT ProductName FROM Products
```

In Case of a Crisis...

There are a number of places you can turn to for help if you encounter a problem:

❑ Useful books and web sites are listed in Appendix C

❑ For how to get support from WROX, see Appendix G

Section I

The Fundamentals – an Overview of Oracle, VB, SQL and Data Access

Introducing Oracle and VB

Why would we want to combine Oracle and VB? Oracle is the relational database of preference in the corporate world. It is deployed in more businesses than any other RDB. Oracle works on every computing platform available to us – from the PC to the Mainframe and across every shade of Unix. This means that Oracle scales better. Scaling, as you know, may be done in two ways: horizontally, deploying more and more servers of the same kind, or vertically, deploying a bigger and bigger server. When you can deploy many of the biggest you obviously scale best. Oracle is also a forerunner of the in-memory databases and has been memory centered since its beginning. The popularity of Oracle as a purveyor of relational database engines is constantly growing. In these days of e-commerce, businesses must have highly reliable and highly scalable databases and they are turning to Oracle.

VB is the rapid application tool of choice and like Oracle enjoys a plurality of preference. This means that there will be more magazine articles, books and third-party tools available, making it easier to master the technology and solve problems. By now the number of VB programmers has surpassed the number of COBOL programmers. Ever since the advent of VB 3.0 and ODBC in 1993 it became easier and easier to deploy data-centric applications using VB as the front end. Lately, because we can create (somewhat) multithreaded COM objects using VB, we are starting to see VB as a viable server-side programming tool. The advent of ASP in 1996 and the ability program it with VB Script gives a great boost to VB's popularity. It is this capability for producing flexible sophisticated software that makes VB so ideal as a front end to Oracle.

We're going to learn how to use these two technologies together. Each chapter contains real examples. You can repeat them on your computer, or you can take my word for it. I hope you opt for the more active approach. In fact, when you finish reading this chapter the active way, you will have already produced a simple yet useful VB and Oracle program.

I've just finished an unscientific survey of the New York City job market. One popular online job site has posted 1575 request for jobs involving Oracle. During the very same week they have also posted 1126 jobs for Sybase, 835 jobs for SQL Server, 470 for DB2, and significantly lesser numbers to the rest of the field. The respective number of requests also involving VB (in other words, Oracle and VB, Sybase and VB, etc.) was 175, 93, 198, and 32. There is a higher demand for VB and SQL Server than for VB and Oracle, but the gap is narrowing. Again, why VB and Oracle? That's where the jobs are!

Previous Visual Basic support for Oracle has been less than ideal. However, this situation has been continuously improving as new versions of VB are released.

❑   Until Visual Basic 3 there was no support for remote databases. With this version, access to Oracle was provided via DAO. This didn't (and still doesn't) support many Oracle-specific features.

❑   With version 4, RDO was introduced, which was the first ODBC method to support some of the necessary features, but things were still not perfect.

❑   Now we have VB 6 and ADO, which provides greater support for Oracle-specific syntax than any other product except for OO4O (Oracle Corporation's own data-access method, based on DAO).

❑   In addition to supporting ODBC data sources, VB6 also comes with a native OLE DB provider for Oracle; and database design tools that work well against an Oracle database.

With these advances and the continuing improvements in OO4O, the outlook has never been brighter for VB and Oracle!

The History of Oracle

Larry Ellison and others formed Oracle Corporation in 1977 as a small start-up company called Relational Software Incorporated (RSI) to develop the world's first relational database – Oracle.

Oracle originally came out with a prototype, Oracle 1.0, with the first actual release being version 2. Version 3 saw the company's name change to Oracle Corporation. Surprisingly, it was not until version 5 that client/server architecture was supported. With Oracle8 there have been further architectural developments with the introduction of the Network Computing Architecture (NCA) concept, discussed later in the chapter.

So that we provide useful information on developing Visual Basic and Oracle solutions we are going to only talk about examples from Oracle 7.3 to the latest version Oracle 8. We have chosen 7.3 because that was when integration of Oracle and Visual Basic 4.0 started.

Following are some of the enhancements that came with version 7.3:

❑ Major performance gains in the processing of SQL operations, such as "anti-joins" including the NOT IN condition, and the evaluation of the OR condition.

❑ Enhanced the use of views in applications development by allowing unambiguous INSERT, UPDATE, and DELETE operations on views involving multi-table joins, providing additional flexibility.

❑ Index rebuilds can now execute faster, because the existing index is used, rather than the base table itself. Since the index is much smaller then the base table, executing time is substantially reduced.

❑ Support for partition views. A partition view allows a table, usually a core application table, to be broken into multiple partitions ("sub-tables") and then presented to the application as one table by using the UNION ALL view. Since the partitions are independent of each other, application developers can query just the data they want.

With Oracle 8.0 came major improvements for the data management of an object-relational paradigm. Though most of Oracle 8i's improvements have been made for the support of Java development, Oracle 8i completes the object data management the 8.0 release began. LOB (large objects) data types can now operate into partitioned tables, and temporary LOBs are available to improve performance.

The Oracle Database Architecture

Oracle is a **DataBase Management System** (**DBMS**) that supports the largest number of databases found in today's development arena. Where most DBMS meet their limitations, Oracle does just fine maintaining potentially hundreds of gigabytes of information. In addition to supporting large amounts of data Oracle can support large numbers of concurrent users.

Oracle has both physical and logical structures within its architecture. These structures follow the relational model; hence Oracle is a **Relational DataBase Management System** (**RDBMS**). A relational database is made of tables of data, in which individual rows can quickly be identified and accessed. Tables may be related to each other – hence the term relational – by having one or more columns that they share. Here is a disturbing example of such a relationship. The IRS and the Census bureau both use the Social Security Number (SSN) to identify you. The two databases share this column, and could thus be connected. Luckily this is illegal, yet this illegality does not lessen my worries.

Physical and Logical Structures

The **physical structure** of the database constitutes the operational system files that store the information about the database and its data. Within Oracle the physical structure consists of three types of system files: one or more data files, two or more redo log files; and one or more control files.

We are not going to go into detail about the physical structure. Simply, the data file(s) store the data, the redo log files record all changes made the data, and the control file(s) records the physical structure of the database.

In Oracle-speak, a **database** is the collection of files that store the data. In order to get the database up and running it needs to make use of memory structures (which we will discuss briefly a little later in the chapter), and other processes, in order to allow a user to interact with the data. In this case, we speak of an **instance**.

The **logical structures** of Oracle dictate how the physical space of the database is used. These structures consist of the following:

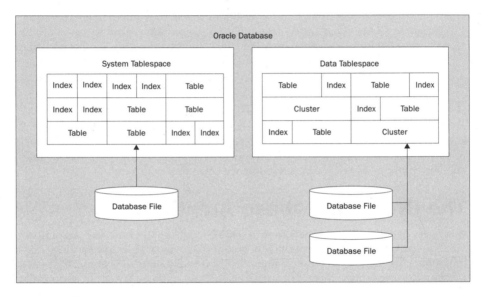

Note that the database objects are separated into different storage spaces (tablespaces). A DBA would probably, for example, store all the tables used by one application in their own separate storage space. We will now look at the database objects in this diagram (and others) in more detail.

Tablespaces

A **tablespace** is the largest logical structure within Oracle. A database is typically divided into one or more tablespaces. One or more data files are created for each tablespace to physically store the data of the logical structures within that tablespace.

Schemas

A **schema** is a virtual partition of the database. Schemas may be user partitions (User Schema) or application partitions (Application Schema). In the latter case we simply create a pseudo-user named after the application and give the application developers unlimited access to the schema.

There is an example user schema supplied with Oracle, which you can log on to with a user ID of scott and a password of tiger. You'll only be able to work with objects that have been defined in the scott schema. All other objects will be invisible.

Tables in the data dictionary cache are always available (see later in this chapter), but they will only describe the objects for which you have been granted permission. In our case only scott schema objects will be described. We can easily give any user the privilege of using any schema. We can also easily disallow users from seeing other schemas. All this is done by granting and revoking privileges, and is reflected in the USER_ROLE_PRIVS table of the data dictionary cache.

The DBA (or anybody with a similar privilege) is the only person who can view and manipulate database objects in all the schemas at once. If you've installed your own Personal Oracle, you actually have DBA privileges in the database. If you do your exercise at work, you probably have rights that stop at just one schema of the database. The scott schema is sufficient for all you'll need to do in this book.

The schema is comprised of logical structures that directly refer to the database's data. These structures include: **tables**, **views**, **stored procedures**, and **indexes**. There is no link between a schema and a tablespace. That is to say that a schema can exist across multiple tablespaces.

Tables

A **table** is the basic unit of the storage of data in an Oracle database. Tables consist of **columns** and **rows**. These columns are defined with data types for storing data. Once the table is defined data can be entered in as rows. Tables can be queried against to retrieve data.

An important concept is that that of the ROWID. This is a database wide unique identifier that cannot be edited. No two rows in the whole database have the same ROWID. Oracle does not let you Update or Delete a row for which you don't have a ROWID. The underlying reason is that the database is one big hash of data and that the search mechanism is based on hashing algorithms.

Views

A **view** is a 'stored query', consisting of a pre-compiled SQL SELECT statement. The user does not see a difference between a view and a database table, and may use the view's column names in other SQL statements. In this respect they are a close equivalent of Microsoft Access Queries. We normally use views to hide information from unauthorized users. In such a case, a view consists of some, but not all, of a table's columns, and the user has permission to use the view but not the underlying table. When nesting multiple queries, views come in handy to encapsulate data into one view.

Views are virtual tables. They do not store actual data; rather they contain data from the table for which the query is built. Like tables views can be queried against.

Indexes and Clusters

An **Index** is a collection of unique values for each of the rows, by which we can identify the row and fetch it quickly. Most of the time the index is made of the values in a single column or the concatenation of two or more columns. A prime example will be an index made of Social Security Numbers.

Indices are created to help increase performance when retrieving data from a table. This is achieved in Oracle using some or all of the table's indices to retrieve information based on your query. It is the Oracle SQL engine that determines what index (indices) to use.

Indices can be created on one or more rows in a table. As new records are added to the table they are likewise added to the index. Because indices are separated from the tables, they can be added or dropped with out harming the data within the table.

Be careful with your index strategy; adding too many indices defeats the purpose of indices themselves. Also note that, when removing an index, a query against that column may be actually slower than if an index had never existed.

Clusters are a method of increasing performance on table queries by physically storing commonly linked tables together. The linked columns in the tables in a cluster are called a **cluster key**. Cluster keys are themselves indexed so that rows of the cluster can be retrieved more quickly.

Based on the SQL query placed against a clustered table, this too can also improve performance. If the SQL is joining tables existing in the same cluster, the tables are retrieved from a single Oracle disk I/O operation. Data stored in a clustered table is queried in the same manner a non-clustered table is.

Similar to how tables are stored together in a cluster for performance, likewise rows can reside within a **hash cluster** to increase performance. Rows that reside in a hash cluster are physically stored in the table based on their hash value.

Procedures and Functions

Business rules can be defined on the data tier of your system with the use of **procedures** and **functions**. Procedures and functions are developed using SQL statements within PL/SQL code. It is PL/SQL that provides the procedural programming, and generates dynamic SQL. These procedures can be called from with an application to return recordsets.

Packages

Packages are used to group similar procedures, functions, and variables into a single Oracle object. This eases the maintenance of your business rules, and increases performance of function calls from within procedures.

Stored Procedures

A **stored procedure** is a pre-compiled program written in PL/SQL that performs an operation on data stored in the Database.

> *Stored procedures are considered to be pre-compiled, although in fact the database converts them to p-code – an intermediate level code that does not need to be parsed. Raw SQL, on the other hand, needs to be parsed again and again.*

The most common usage of stored procedures is in formulating business rules. n-tiered client/server advocates claim that such business rules should reside in a middle tier rather than in the database. Maybe, but the ability to perform it in the database is definitely welcome. Using stored procedures in the database for business rules enhances performance. Business rules generally involve many tables and rows. If we have to do them in a separate tier, we have to hold a long conversation with the database, most times across the network. This is time and resource consuming.

Triggers

Triggers are defined to ensure that data is maintained in such a way that it retains its integrity. If we were to have a record in a table, the child table, that is dependent on a record entry in another table, the parent table, we would not want to delete the entry in the parent table, because it would cause an orphan record in the child table. That is to say that we could not effectively use the data in the child table because the parent was destroyed.

Like stored procedures, triggers are pre-compiled, but while we explicitly invoke stored procedures, triggers are invoked automatically as responses to events such as adding a new row, and deleting or updating existing rows. Triggers can be defined to execute on one of three events: INSERT, UPDATE, or DELETE. Should a constraint violation exist, Oracle will rollback the transaction as if it never transpired.

A good place for a Trigger is in audit trails where we track who and when has changed a vital piece of information. Another is to guarantee the referential integrity of the database beyond the mere requirements of foreign keys.

> *The simplest form of referential integrity is a foreign key. When one table references another, it is normally done by pointing to a field in the referenced table. We expect this field to exist. We force the issue by declaring it to be a foreign key. If we need a more complex referential integrity we must maintain it by some procedure that we code. A trigger is the best place to put such code.*

Sequences

A **sequence** is a persistent object (it always remembers its state and will go on as if it has never been stopped even after the server goes down) that generates numbers according to a prescribed order. The most common ones are counters. These are used most of the time, to guarantee that each row added to a table has a unique identifier (key).

Synonyms

A synonym is an alias for any Oracle object. Synonyms are usually employed when you want to transparently map the logical location of an oracle object.

Synonyms can be both public and private. Public synonyms are owned by the user group named PUBLIC and is exposed to every user within that database. A Private synonym is contained in the schema of a specific user, and its scope is only exposed to that user or the user's grantees.

The Oracle System Architecture

Now that we have just completed talking about the storage aspect of Oracle, let's discuss the processing aspect to Oracle.

Just as important as understanding the storage concepts of Oracle is understanding the memory structures and processes. There are several key memory structures that are associated with Oracle: the **System Global Area (SGA)** and the **Program Global Area (PGA)**.

System Global Area

The SGA is a shared memory area of Oracle that contains data and control information for an instance of Oracle. For every Oracle instance there is a SGA, which all users work within. Because all users access the database via this SGA it is important that it be given the resources (memory) necessary to support the amount/frequency of data I/O. These days it is not uncommon to have 512MB to 1024MB of RAM in an Oracle server machine.

The SGA itself is made of memory structures. These structures are called **buffers**. Buffers are fixed size memory structures that are defined when that instance of Oracle is started. Let's look at the various types of buffers:

The **Shared Pool** is an area of the SGA that maintains the shared memory constructs. This is made up of the **Library Cache** and the **Data Dictionary Cache**.

The library cache consists of several components that can be accessed by all users. The Shared SQL Area of the library cache is where SQL cursors are maintained.

> *A **cursor** is a pointer to the memory associated with a specific SQL statement. When we issue a SQL statement, Oracle implicitly creates a cursor to maintain our results. In PL/SQL we can procedurally create and destroy cursors.*

Let's look at the data dictionary cache in a bit more detail.

The Data Dictionary Cache

The objects that we've discussed in this chapter define the structure of our database. Oracle gave us a convenient way to look at that structure – the data dictionary tables. A data dictionary is a combination of read-only table and views that provide reference information about the database. This data dictionary stores information about physical and logical structure in our database. In addition to this information it also maintains user accounts, table constraints, and space allocation to schemas. The data dictionary is created when the database is created, and as objects are added to the schema, the dictionary maintains this information.

We will use the data dictionary tables in our first application, later in this chapter.

The tables of interest are (details of their structure can be found in Appendix D):

❑ USER_OBJECTS - where all the objects (tables, columns, indexes, sequences and stored procedures etc.) are listed and described

❑ USER_TABLES– where the tables are described

❑ USER_TAB_COLUMNS– where the table columns are described

❑ USER_SOURCE– where the code for the stored procedures is held

❑ USER_SEQUENCES– where all the Sequences are described

❑ USER_INDEXES– where the index/table relationship is kept

❑ USER_ROLE_PRIVS – where a user can see his or her roles and privileges

The other main areas are the **Database Buffer Cache** and the **Redo Log Buffer**. The first of these is where data resides that has not yet been updated to disk. The second one holds a journal of all the changes made to the database.

The Program Global Area

The PGA in Oracle has nothing to do with golf. It is a memory buffer that contains all the data and control information for the server processes. Whenever a server process is started, it will reside with the PGA. These process are identified on several ways:

Client Process

A client process is created to maintain an application program such as an Oracle tool.

Server Process

A server process is responsible for maintaining the communication between a client process and Oracle. If a user was to issue a SQL statement that does not already reside within the SGA, it is the server process that reads the proper data file, and loads data into the SGA.

Background Process

The background processes work behind the scenes to help monitor and maintain Oracle. These would include the system monitor, the process monitor, the archiver, and the database writer just to name a few.

Network Computing Architecture (NCA)

We discussed the concept of multi-tier architecture in the introduction to this book. Oracle's implementation of this is known as Network Computing Architecture (NCA). As the name implies it is an architecture developed by Oracle for building and integrating applications in a Network Computing (NC) environment. As the World Wide Web is a NC environment, the NCA is ideal for the deployment of Client/Server applications over the Internet or an intranet. This creates the opportunity for powerful new e-commerce solutions.

The model is similar to those presented previously, but with the emphasis on the middle and back-end tiers. Thus we have a thin client for the presentation layer, an application server for the business rules and a database server for data storage and manipulation. These will be discussed in more detail later when we look at the components of NCA.

Standards

First let's discuss the main open standards on which NCA is based - CORBA 2.0 and HTTP/HTML. These standards allow independent programs to work together and fit into the architecture regardless of who developed them. Developers can mix and match components to create top-notch applications that deliver real business benefits.

CORBA 2.0

The CORBA (Common Object Request Broker Architecture) standard is a specification developed by a consortium called the Object Management Group (OMG) that includes over 600 companies from all areas of the computer industry. This defines a distributed architecture with an open channel through which objects from multiple vendors, running on different operating systems can communicate. This allows the exchange of information between CORBA-compliant applications. For this communication an Internet Object Request Broker has been defined, which uses the TCP/IP network protocol as its transport layer.

This is discussed further in Chapter 15.

HTTP/HTML

Hypertext Transfer Protocol (HTTP) is the TCP/IP protocol used on the World Wide Web to define the communication between servers and browsers and designed to transfer documents at a fast rate. Hypertext Markup Language (HTML) is the language used to define web pages.

Web browsers use HTTP to communicate and HTML to define what they will be displaying. Both of these are necessary for the distribution of information over the Internet.

Components

The key components of NCA are:

- ❑ NCA compliant applications
- ❑ Cartridges
- ❑ Protocols

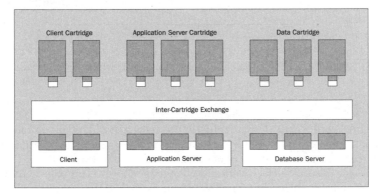

Applications

Applications are the most visible part of the NCA, as they are what the user will work with. As discussed above, these are composed of a thin client, an application server and a database server.

Client

This is a thin client and could be any one of the following:

- ❑ Web browser
- ❑ Java-based client
- ❑ Network Computer

A thin client is used because the client only provides the user interface; the business logic is kept in the application server.

Application Server

The application server is the middle-tier of our application that acts as a platform for reusable business logic, taking responsibility for code that would otherwise reside on the client or the database server. This enables the lightweight thin client discussed above.

It is essentially a web server that supports cartridges for HTTP/HTML applications. Cartridges are plug-in products that can be run on top of the server software to extend the base applications (these will be discussed more in a bit).

Database Server

This is known as the Oracle Universal Server as it should be capable of handling any type of data. Oracle8 has been designed to fill this role in two ways: additional features and additional flexibility. One of the most important aspects of this is its ability to handle data items up to 4GB. This is especially useful nowadays, as data types can be any of the following:

❑ Video

❑ Audio

❑ Text

❑ Spatial data

Cartridges

As mentioned earlier cartridges are plug-in products that can be run on top of the server software to extend the base applications. They are component-based software, which can be written in a variety of languages, such as Java, Visual Basic, C++, SQL, etc. Cartridges use an Interface Definition Language (IDL), a language neutral interface, to identify themselves to other objects in the NCA.

Cartridges can be used on the client, application server or database server. In each case the cartridge must be installed and registered before use.

The cartridge itself also uses an object bus called the Inter-Cartridge Exchange (ICX), which enables cartridges distributed across a network to communicate with each other.

Protocols

These are the standards on which NCA is based. These include TCP/IP, CORBA 2.0 and HTTP/HTML as discussed above.

Accessing Data Using SQL

The primary medium for accessing data from Oracle is **queries**. Queries are defined with the use of **Structured Query Language (SQL)** statements.

SQL is the language by which we talk to relational databases. There are various flavors of SQL, but most – Oracle included – adhere to the common core of **ANSI SQL**. Oracle enhances its SQL with PL/SQL functions. SQL Server uses its own enhancements namely Transact SQL, and Access allows us to use Access Basic or in later versions VBA. The basic structure of SQL permeates all three (and other lesser-known) versions.

I assume that you have some knowledge of SQL, especially of the SELECT statement. We will touch on SQL at various levels of detail throughout the book. Here we are going to define the various parts of Structured Query Language or SQL.

A SQL statement is string of text that gives Oracle the instructions of what, where, and how information should be retrieved from the database. A simple SQL statement would look like this:

```
SELECT Field1 FROM Table1
```

The minimum requirements from a SQL statement are that you specify what you want (Field1) and where it is (Table1).

VB Developers need also to be concerned with the following five main categories of SQL statements:

- ❑ **Data Query Language (DQL)** consists of one statement – SELECT. Originally (and officially) DQL does not exist. A query is considered to be a part of the Data Manipulation Language (DML). It is, however, both customary, and convenient to make the distinction.

- ❑ **Data Definition Language (DDL) Statements** create, maintain and destroy database objects and to set the relations between tables. These relationships are established by creating constraints – of which foreign keys are the most common form – and triggers. These are discussed in Chapter 3. They are also used to maintain rights and privileges.

- ❑ **Data Manipulation Language (DML) Statements** manipulate the database with the use of INSERT, UPDATE, and DELETE of rows in a table. These are discussed in Chapter 2.

- ❑ **Transaction Control Language (TCL) Statements** manage changes made to the database by the DML statements with the use of COMMIT, ROLLBACK, and SAVEPOINT. These are discussed in Chapter 2.

- ❑ **Embedded SQL Statements**, with the use both DDL and DML statements, are used to control statements in PL/SQL. These include OPEN, CLOSE, FETCH, and EXECUTE. These are discussed in Chapter 13.

PL/SQL

PL/SQL is a **Procedural Language** used to write programs inside the Oracle Server. It is an almost complete programming language especially built to work with the database objects. It is useful for writing stored procedures and triggers.

PL/SQL brings procedural logic to database querying by incorporating the capacity of creating dynamic SQL. With the use of IF...THEN and WHILE...LOOP logic a developer can author a procedure or function that builds SQL on the fly based on any given number of input parameters.

The advantage to PL/SQL is that is can be used to maintain business rules on the server side of a multi-tiered systems architecture. Doing so will also increase system performance because SQL statements do not have to be built on the client machine, and then sent to the database via the network and ODBC.

Table Constraints

NOT NULL

When a table column is specified with the NOT NULL constraint it prohibits the insertion of records where that column's data value is NULL.

UNIQUE

This is a constraint rule applied to a column to insure that the column contents for all records are unique. An index is automatically created on this column.

PRIMARY KEY

A column with this rule is implicitly indexed by Oracle, and can only consist of unique values and cannot be NULL.

FOREIGN KEY

Because Oracle is an RDBMS, tables can be associated with one another with or across schemas. These associations are made with the use of foreign keys in a child table, to the primary key in a parent table.

CHECK

A CHECK constraint allows you to develop and employ sophisticated constraint rules. These rules consist of evaluating the values of a column or set of columns in a record to ensure they meet the CHECK constraint. In the event they do not meet the rule, the DML statement is rolled back.

Which Version of Oracle?

Oracle comes in many versions. Some run on mainframes, others on the various shades of Unix, and still others run on the various versions of Windows. Oracle8 is the latest version of the Oracle Server line of products. The different versions available are:

❑ **Personal Oracle**: The one we use extensively in this book. It is the PC/Desktop version of the Oracle database server, with which you can work on a stand-alone or networked PC and write or test code against an Oracle database. One of the advantages of Personal Oracle is that code that is written against a Personal Oracle database requires no change when you point the code at your enterprise's Oracle Server.

❑ **Oracle8 Server**: This is a low-cost, work-group level database, which includes the basic features.

❑ **Oracle8 Enterprise Edition**: This is the full version with advanced features. This edition includes Advanced Replication, and you can, at extra cost, move up to Oracle Parallel Server.

- ❑ **Oracle Lite**: This is a lightweight, low-cost, high performance client database designed for mobile and embedded applications.

- ❑ **Oracle8i**: The first relational database to integrate Java programs, web sites, and Internet content; specifically designed as an Internet development and deployment platform.

- ❑ **Oracle8i Lite**: The Internet platform for mobile computing. Requiring less than 1 MB of system memory and less than 5MB of hard-disk space, this is the smallest object-relational database available.

The Personal Oracle that I recommend that you install on your PC, is almost every bit as featured as the Enterprise Edition that you may run on your server. The difference, though, is only in the administrative capabilities, and this book is not going to deal with them much. You can develop industrial strength applications on your Personal Oracle and then port them to any other vehicle. I recommend it simply because you can get a free 30 day demo so that you can program at home. The others are much more expensive.

Oracle, regardless of version, is not as fully featured, from the developer point of view, as SQL Server and even Access are. Oracle Navigator – the Oracle-supplied Windows development tool – is primitive when compared to the rich environment of SQL Server. I'll touch on the Navigator, but I personally prefer to design my databases using DDL in SQL*PLUS – the Oracle regular window. For fancy design jobs you'll probably have to resort to third party tools such as Erwin or Rational Rose.

You'll have the opportunity to install Personal Oracle on your computer and use it. Some of you will use the book in your offices. You may, or may not be able to install Oracle on your office computer. This depends entirely on your employer's policies. Those of you who use Oracle as their business database of choice may be able, with the DBA's permission, to follow the book on the office database. If that is the case, make sure that you are doing it in a test database and in a user account especially set for this purpose. This way you won't be able to wreak havoc.

The Oracle database is a server application. Oracle may be deployed in many ways. When you install Personal Oracle on a PC you run both the client and the server on the same machine, but in two different process spaces. When you run on the test database in your office, the Oracle database is still running on a server, but the server and the client run on different machines. This does not make any difference in the way we use the programs in this book. In both cases the database and the client programs run on different process spaces and use the same (hidden) interface to communicate with each other.

Oracle comes with a test database and DBAs tend to leave it in place. This is normally set as the ExampleDB and has scott as its user and tiger as the password. This is the user schema in which this book assumes that you work. If you install Personal Oracle you will also use the scott/ tiger account but the database of this schema is nameless.

How does Oracle Compare to Access and SQL Server?

When deciding when to use Access, SQL Server, or Oracle, there are primarily three major decisions that need to be answered:

- ❏ What can I afford?
- ❏ How much data will I have?
- ❏ How many users will I have?

Following is a table showing some of the considerations:

Access	*Low* number users / *Moderate* frequency of transactions **or**
	Moderate number of users / *Low* frequency of transactions
SQL Server	*High* number users / *Moderate* frequency of transactions **or**
	Moderate number of users / *High* frequency of transactions
Oracle	*High* number users / *High* frequency of transactions

Access is a great DBMS for prototyping your Visual Basic application. For those developers who do not like using the database design interface of VB6.0; Access's table development tools make the development of your application's design and development almost effortless.

Moving to Oracle

What do we need to consider when moving from Access/SQL Server to Oracle?

Microsoft Access

Migrating from Access to Oracle is covered in detail in Appendix B. The following are points that should be considered:

- ❏ Access SQL syntax is not entirely compatible with Oracle
- ❏ Access does not include stored procedures, whereas Oracle does
- ❏ Oracle table names should be uppercase with no spaces, Access is less pedantic
- ❏ Where Access uses a counter column, Oracle uses sequences
- ❏ Oracle does not include the reports, code modules, and queries seen in Access. These will have to be moved to VB equivalents.

SQL Server

While SQL Server is an active server like Oracle is, Oracle is quite different to SQL Server. The following should be considered when moving to Oracle:

❑ Oracle does not include the concept of a master database

❑ As you will have seen above, the Oracle architecture is quite different to that of SQL Server. A main difference is the use of a user schema rather than logging directly into the database.

❑ SQL Server uses T-SQL; Oracle uses PL/SQL

❑ Oracle automatically uses transactions, which have to be committed with the COMMIT statement; in SQL Server transactions have to be declared, but are committed by default.

❑ Where SQL Server (like Access) uses a counter column, Oracle uses sequences

❑ SQL Server supports temporary tables, Oracle does not

❑ SQL Server has a much larger set of fundamental data types

❑ Functions differ between the two, and some many not have an equivalent

❑ SQL Server stored procedures return a recordset if you carry out a SELECT command; Oracle supports this only through **cursor variables**.

Oracle has a series of migration tools, which make it easier to migrate up to Oracle. There is an import utility that should be used to import flat files created with SQL Server's DTD.

Connecting VB to Oracle

VB offers a very rich user interface. We may even use it to generate web classes. Better yet, Microsoft is now building its ASP-Plus, which will allow us to use compiled VB (not just VB Script) inside the IIS server applications. In this book you'll learn to use the Oracle database in conjunction with VB. Obviously this opens a world of possibilities to use this richest of databases in client/server applications and all the way to e-commerce applications and beyond.

There are many ways in which a VB program can utilize an Oracle database. We are going to learn three of them in depth:

The Oracle Data Control (ORADC)

ORADC behaves like the familiar VB data control, or the ADO Data Control. The difference is that because the ORADC is a wrapper around OO4O, it is especially built to connect to an Oracle database. Using ORADC is the best way to write 'quick and dirty' code for an Oracle database. You'll be able to make a program querying the database in minutes.

Oracle Objects For OLE (OO4O)

This is Oracle's own set of lightweight, loosely connected objects with which we can talk to the Oracle database. It is the least known of the Oracle tools, which may explain why it is so seldom used. I have stumbled upon it in the Oracle magazine where the author taught us how to use it in conjunction with Excel, and have used it ever since. It seems that Oracle does not bother to push it and Microsoft, obviously, is not pushing it either. OO4O is the simpler of the two approaches and will be discussed first. The ORADC – the Oracle Data Control, which we'll use in this chapter – is built around OO4O. You'll use OO4O directly (unhidden in the ORADC) as early as in Chapter 3.

ActiveX Data Objects (ADO)

Most Oracle VB development is done with ADO. ADO is the newest of the Microsoft's tools used to connect to a great variety of data sources. It is a set of lightweight, loosely connected objects and is a great improvement over its predecessors – RDO and DAO. ADO with Oracle requires a somewhat more elaborate effort than OO4O and it will be used in Chapters 9 to 11 after we've learned the SQL action queries (DML) in Chapter 2.

Before this introductory chapter is over, you'll install Oracle on your computer, load the sample database and code and run a small program utilizing the ADO version of the data control.

SQL*NET (Net8)

If you are using Personal Oracle, you will have your own personal copy of the database on your machine and will have no need for SQL*NET. It is the software layer that enables a client machine to access Oracle across a network, or enable two or more computers running Oracle to exchange data through a network, regardless of the network protocols available. You may well have heard of the Listener process, which runs on the database server and "listens" for and handles connection requests from your VB program. This is similar to the HTTP listener process on a Web server.

For further information on this topic, I would refer you to the technet website : www.technet.Oracle.com.

Installing the Oracle Database

Before you install the database you must first acquire it. Oracle may be reached on the web at www.Oracle.com or by phone at (800) ORACLE1. A 30-day demo of Personal Oracle is available in the US, and arrives 2 or 3 days after you've ordered it. You may want to invest in a full version of the same program. You may purchase a version without any support, or pay more for a year of unlimited support on a Toll Free line (Toll free in the US and Canada). You may also download the demo absolutely free. This is feasible if you have a high-speed connection, otherwise order it by mail. The download is 180 MB and will take forever and a day.

Once you have the software, insert the CD into your reader. If you are on Windows 95 or 98, just wait for the startup screen to appear and follow the very simple instructions. Select all the standard options. You'll have plenty of time later, when you are an expert, to install it the way you see fit.

If you use NT or have downloaded the software, simply double-click on the setup.exe and follow the same simple instructions, as below:

Installing Oracle 8 Enterprise Edition on NT

System Requirements

Don't even attempt an installation with less than 96 MB of memory. 128 MB is strongly recommended. A full installation, without the help files requires close to 600 MB of hard disk.

Installation

This screen appears after inserting the Oracle 8i CD:

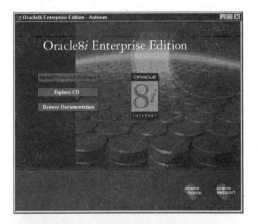

Click Install/Deinstall Products:

Click Next

When the following screen appears allow all the choices of home directory and Path to remain as recommended:

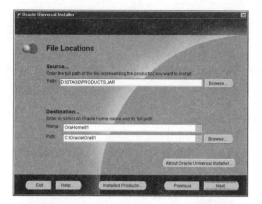

Click Next:

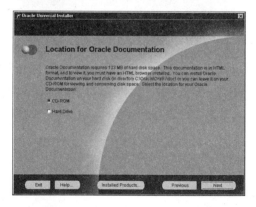

Select Oracle8i Enterprise Edition 8.1.5.0.0 (Full installation) and click Next:

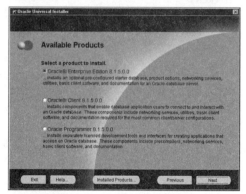

I have a huge disk (26 GB) and prefer to have the documentation and help file on the Hard Drive. Select CD-ROM if your drive is relatively small, or already close to full. If you have room, put documents on the hard drive. And whatever you do, click Next.

The system will display the form below. In it you are asked for a **Global Database Name** and a **SID**. The **SID** is the system identifier and will be automatically set to the first part (preceding the period) of the database name. I happen to like the word **MY**, but many people set their system to **TEST** and this is the most likely name of the test database in your office:

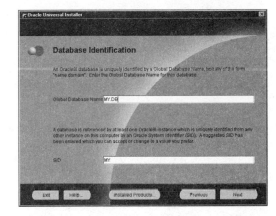

The system will install the services and issue two accounts. One is the **INTERNAL** account, the other is the **SYS account**:

I suggest that you print this screen, then click **OK**.

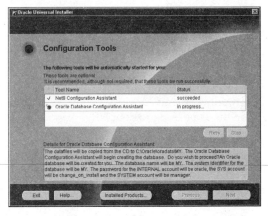

Hurray!

If for any reason you need to reinstall, as I have it might be a bit hairy. Here is what happened to me. I had my removable disk active at the time of the installation and I did not notice that the installation proceeded to load onto it (it was the D: drive). So I tried to reinstall. But now the installation demanded the D: drive and would not install on C. I ended up going to the Registry where I removed the complete Oracle folder. To do so:

- ❏ Click the Start button, then the Run and type Regedit

- ❏ Click on the + next to HKEY_LOCAL_MACHINE

- ❏ Then on the + next to Software

- ❏ Now click on ORACLE and delete the whole entry. Don't delete anything else!

Oracle changes the registry in the first few seconds of an install, and does not ever change it again, no matter what. It will always try to install the same way again and again. Once you made a choice you're stuck. This is stupid, but a fact. Uprooting ORACLE completely is the only solution for a clean reinstallation.

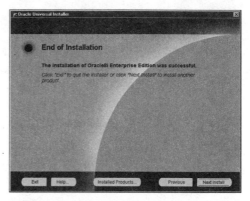

You are going to be much better off if you make some desktop shortcuts. These are very easy to make. Start a Windows Explorer and click your way into the C:\Windows\StartMenu sub-directory. Now select the program group in which the desired program resides. In our case this is Programs\Oracle For Windows 95. Click on it as well:

Now right-click on the SQL Plus 8.0 icon and select Create Shortcut from the dropdown menu. Drag the newly created shortcut to your desktop. While you're at it, do the same thing to your VB6.

That's it! You are now ready for the adventure ahead. In order to establish our database tables in the Scott schema and load them with data we are going to execute some SQL scripts. We will do this from the SQL*PLUS window, so we should look at that now.

The SQL*PLUS Environment

Many of our daily tasks such as creating and modifying tables, running scripts, and performing queries are done in SQL*PLUS – the standard Oracle environment in which you run SQL and PL/SQL. It exists in every platform and provides consistent behavior across platforms. This is comforting on one hand, but very disturbing on the other. In order to perform equally in all platforms, Oracle made it perform as it would in the most primitive of these platforms – that of a dumb terminal. This is very much the equivalent of editing a DOS or Unix command line.

When you start SQL*PLUS it will ask you to sign in. If you're running on a test database at work, ask your DBA for a username/password combination. If you installed the free trial version of Personal Oracle, use the name scott and the password tiger. You may also have to fill in the Host String Text Box. This is where you enter the database name. If you are running in your Personal Oracle leave this field empty. A space in this textbox is not the same as an empty. To make sure, double click on the field and press the Delete key.

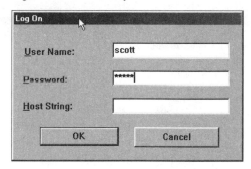

When you're signed in, you'll be in the SQL*PLUS window, and able to type your commands at the **SQL>** prompt. This is the command line, where the cursor is put and where you type your next command.

It is very inconvenient to edit the command line. If you mistyped, you won't be able to cut and paste on the line. You can, however, cut complete areas of the SQL*PLUS window and paste them into a text editor such as NotePad, where you may edit the command line and then paste it back into the SQL*PLUS window for execution.

You may also run scripts. Scripts are pre-edited and hopefully pre-tested successions of commands. We run Scripts from files. Here is the "run script" command:

```
@FileName;
```

FileName is the name of the script file. Notice the semi-colon – this is the instruction to execute the command.

Oracle is very unforgiving. Here is what happens when you point to a file name that includes spaces. I created a very simple script with a single SQL statement: SELECT * FROM USER_OBJECTS and put it in C:\My Documents\OracleBook\Test.sql. Because the Directory My Documents contains a space in its name and the Oracle command line reads only to the first space, we get the enigmatic message:

unable to open file "c:\My.SQL"

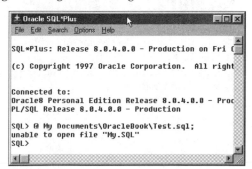

This, by the way, is also a good reason not to use spaces in filenames at all. As a rule no filenames should have spaces; especially if they have the possibility of going cross platform. Why did Microsoft name the directory My Documents instead of MyDocuments?

Once the file name (path) is enclosed in double quotes, the script runs as prescribed. This is a UNIX like behavior and shows us the true origin of SQL*PLUS.

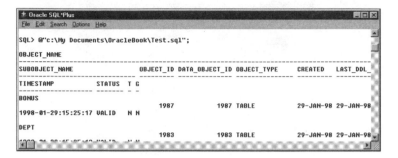

When a command is finished, the SQL*PLUS window has the cursor ready for a new command. Commands may occupy many lines and you are welcome to use the enter key to start new lines. New lines are marked with a line number. SQL*PLUS runs the command only when it finds a semicolon at its end. To actually run the command, type a semicolon and press the **ENTER** Key. This is shown below:

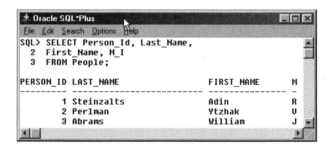

When we get to PL/SQL in Chapter 13, you'll learn about using a forward slash '/' as a terminator as well.

Installing the Sample Tables

In this book we are going to learn sophisticated database enquiries, inside and outside VB, so we need a good set of sample tables. You can follow the SQL just by eyeballing the tables in the text, but nothing beats actually seeing it in action. I have created a few scripts that complement this book. The scripts may be downloaded from the WROX site – **www.wrox.com**.

The four scripts are as follows:

- ❑ ClearIt.sql – which removes everything
- ❑ CreateIt.sql – creates all tables and sequences
- ❑ Populate.sql – loads the data
- ❑ Bookinit.sql – the previous three scripts combined – it does the lot (in the above order!)

Don't worry about the inner workings of these scripts just yet. All will be revealed in Chapters 2 and 3. We will also wait until Chapter 2 to discuss the structure of these tables and the relationships that exist between them. Suffice it to say that they are the core tables for a Human Resources application and, as such, contain such employee-related information (for example, name, job title, current salary etc.).

Loading the sample tables is easy. After you've signed on to Oracle – either on Personal Oracle as we did above, or in a test database at work, where you have your sign-on instructions from the DBA – just execute the BookInit.sql script. For example:

SQL> @ C:\VBOracleBook\Chapter1\Bookinit.sql;

Download the script into your hard drive and run it in SQL*PLUS. I assume that you parked it in the download directory on the C: drive. If it is elsewhere, just type the proper path in the window. The script will create tables, indexes, and sequences. It will then populate the tables with the data that we'll use throughout the book.

It is very difficult to even see the results of your queries in SQL*PLUS. This is especially so when the fields are long and many (by the way, our sample tables were designed to work well even in the SQL*PLUS environment). Try running the query: SELECT * FROM USER_OBJECTS (one of the data dictionary tables). The results are really difficult to read:

To be easier on the eye, we're going to write a little program with which we'll view results in a much more pleasant and controllable environment. This is the first program in which you'll combine VB and Oracle. Before we finally get down to it though, a quick word about notation and saving your work.

Notation and Conventions

The book is made of two major elements: Oracle and VB. They come from different companies, and we all know that these companies are not the best of friends. The two camps do not agree on much and notation is the smallest of their disagreements.

When in Oracle we'll do as the sibyls do.

Each of the Oracles of ancient Greece had a prophetess or a sibyl. Two of the sibyls have a place of honor in Michelangelo's Sistine chapel. They are the Oracles of Delphi and Cuma (La Delphina & La Cumaea).

We are going to name the various Oracle objects such as tables and columns using capitalized meaningful names, and we are going to separate `Multi_Word` names with underscores – for example, `Last_Name`. Oracle limits object names to 30 characters. This means that every now and then we'll have to resort to abbreviations.

When we say 'capitalized' we mean that each word starts with a capital letter and continues in small letters. This is the way you treat proper names and words at the head of a sentence. CAPS will mean that the whole word is in capital letters.

When in VB, we'll use Hungarian notation for `Multi_Word` names, for example, `Last_Name`. Each word is capitalized and the spaces between words are compressed. There are no length limitations and we'll use abbreviations only when they are a part of the language. `ID` for identification is one such case, `MI` for middle initial is another. In VB and Hungarian notation it is also common to type variables by prefixing the capitalized names with a variable type identifier shorthand. I use single character shorthand as much as I can. Here are a few:

Character	Data Type
s	String
l	Long
i or n	Integer
d	Date
v	Variant
t	User Defined Type (UDT)

Other data types will be identified by a three-character prefix, as will all the VB controls

Character	Data Type
txt	TextBox
sgl	Single
dbl	double
cbo	dropdown Combo
lst	dropdown list

More notational convention will be discussed when needed.

Saving your Work

From this point and on, you'll be asked to perform various programming tasks. Some will involve VB. Others will be done in the Oracle environment. You'll do well to save the fruits of your labor. I save all the code that is used here in a directory called VBOraBook. I also save the work of each chapter in a subdirectory named for the chapter. The code used in this chapter is saved in C:\VBOraBook\Chapter1.

I recommend that you take a similar approach.

Our First Useful Program

Our first program is a quick and easy one to produce. We will use the ADO Data Control (ADODC) bound to the MSHDataGrid control as a means to accessing and displaying the data. We will execute some simple in-built SQL statements to retrieve data from the data dictionary tables (as a means of investigating the structure of our database). We will also take a first look at the data in our HR tables. As a small flourish, we will make use of the MoveComplete event and the RecordCount property of the ADODC in order to display the number of records returned from the Oracle tables.

Before we proceed, a caveat. A simple program such as this may encounter problems dealing with large objects (LOBs). Every table in the database that uses a default value for a column, as our People table does, will have this problem. Later in the book (Chapter 8 for OO4O and Chapter 12 for ADO) you will see how to program around this using the GetChunk method, but to introduce this now would take away from the fun of coding this program.

The problem with LOBs is also is the reason I've chosen the ADODC over the Oracle Data Control. The above problem is much more pronounced using the latter and I have found the program very prone to crashing. However, for those still intrigued, I will point out the code differences after we have finished with the ADODC.

It is time to let us start VB (hopefully by double clicking your desktop shortcut!). Open a new Standard EXE project. Change the name of the form to frmView and its caption to View Oracle tables.

The first thing we need to do is to set a reference to the ADO DLL. Navigate to **Project |References | Microsoft ActiveX Objects 2.1 Library** and check this box.

Let's now add the ADODC to our VB toolbox. Go to the **P**roject menu and select **C**omponents. When the **C**omponents form appears, scroll down and check the **Microsoft ADO data Control 6.0 (OLEDB)** box:

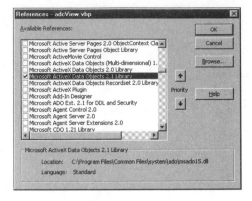

Click **OK** and the data control will appear in your toolbox. Place a control on your form and go to the property box. We now rename the control `adcView`. I use `adc` as the prefix identifying ADO data controls. Now scroll down the property box until you get to the `ConnectString` property. We are going to build the Connection String, so click on the ellipsis button.

You will see the **Property Pages** screen. Click on the **Build...** button and you will arrive at the **Data Link Properties** screen. We are going to connect through the Microsoft OLE DB Provider For Oracle so select that option in the **Provider** tab and click **Next**.

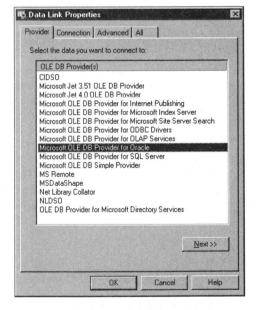

In the **Connection** tab we must enter our connection details. In this book we use the `scott` schema so our username is **scott** and the password is **tiger** (if you are in the office use the name/password combination given to you by the DBA). We can leave the server name blank – we only have one database in the system and it defaults to it. In most work places, the DBA has set a few databases. You should only exercise in a database set by the DBA exclusively for testing.

Your connection string, if you are using the `scott` schema, should look as follows:

```
Provider=MSDAORA.1;User ID=scott;Persist Security Info=False
```

Now let us define a record source for the control. In the first instance we are going to use the `USER_OBJECTS` data dictionary table. Go to the `RecordSource` property; click on the ellipsis button and in the **Command Text (SQL)** section type:

```
SELECT * FROM USER_OBJECTS
```

Now add a new control to the toolbox. This is the Microsoft Hierarchical FlexGrid control (add it to your toolbox from the **Project|Components** menu). Drag the **FlexGrid** control onto the form, make it large like the one in the picture below, and name it `grdView`. Your form may now look something like this:

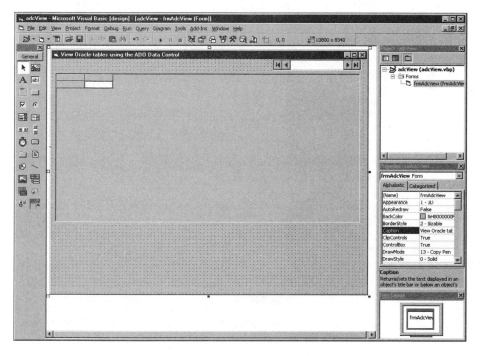

We need to bind the grid to the data source so go to the grid's property box and down to the `DataSource` property and click in it. Only one `DataSource` is currently available – **adcView** – and it shows in the dropdown combo. Click on it.

Of course, the real data source is the database table. The ADODC is basically a "conduit" for our data.

Next enable the grid's `AllowUserResizing` property by setting it to 1. This allows column resizing. Our work is only half done, but we can actually see some results. Run the project and in a few seconds you'll get this result:

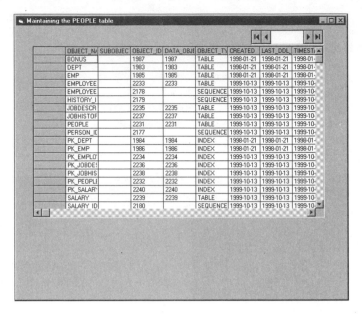

What you see are all the objects in your schema conveniently arranged in a grid. I'm sure you'll agree that this is a much nicer way of viewing the data!

We will use this program to investigate the structure of our database even further so let's make some improvements. First, we will add a dropdown combo for the program where we will list a few pre-coded SQL statements. When we want to run any of them, we'll select it in the combo, which will automatically change the adcView's `RecordSource` property to the selected SQL statement. We then load the new data by calling the `Refresh` method of the data control (which causes it to re-read the database) in the click event of an "execute" button.

Add a dropdown combo to the form. Stretch it for the whole width of the form, just underneath the grid. Name it cboSQL. Change its Text property to say **cboSQL** as well.

Next we add a command button and call it cmdExecute. Change its Caption to read **&Execute** and yet another command button: cmdExit with the Caption **&Exit**. The screen now looks more or less like this:

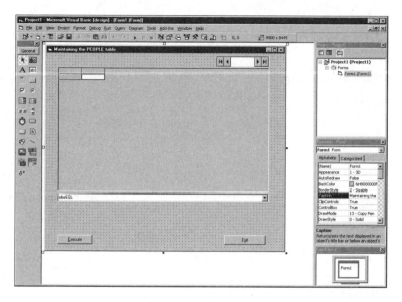

It is now time to add some code to the program so open the code window for the form. We are going to add items to the combo in the `Form_Load` event routine. We add `SELECT` statements that give us access to the data dictionary tables of Oracle.

> *The DBA can get such information to span the whole database. For us, the limitation to the schema is fine.*

The first seven lines of the insertion name the major players of the data dictionary, as described previously. We set USER_TABLES as the "default":

```
With cboSQL
    .AddItem "SELECT * FROM USER_TABLES"
    .AddItem "SELECT * FROM USER_OBJECTS"
    .AddItem "SELECT * FROM USER_TAB_COLUMNS"
    .AddItem "SELECT * FROM USER_SEQUENCES"
    .AddItem "SELECT * FROM USER_INDEXES"
    .AddItem "SELECT * FROM USER_ROLE_PRIVS"
    .AddItem "SELECT * FROM USER_SOURCE"
    .AddItem "SELETC INDEX_NAME, TABLE_NAME, UNIQUENESS " & _
        "    FROM USER_INDEXES"
    .ListIndex = 0
End With
```

Note that we have included the USER_ROLE_PRIVS table where we can find out our roles and privileges. Oracle allows the DBA to assign various users different roles. A role is a set of permissions or privileges that the user has. One user may only be able to SELECT or read a few tables, another may also be able to UPDATE a few tables. The privileges are given as a list of tables and actions. The actions are SELECT, UPDATE, INSERT, and DELETE. Each user may have many roles. The DBA has unlimited privileges over all the objects in the database.

Many programs are written to behave according to the user's role. For instance, if a manager signs on, she may delete records, while others cannot. As we have said before all this can be achieved by a smart DBA limiting unauthorized users to just views.

Anyway, back to our program, which is almost ready. All it needs is some "Action" Code.

Double click the `cmdExecute` button. Add the following code to the `cmdExecute_Click` routine:

```
Private Sub cmdExecute_Click()
    On Error GoTo RefreshError
    adcView.RecordSource = cboSQL.Text
    adcView.Refresh
    Exit Sub
RefreshError:
    MsgBox "Error Number: " & Err.Number & " Mesage is: " & Err.Description
End Sub
```

Basically the text in the combo box will be applied to the `RecordSource` property of the control and the data control will be refreshed.

Finally just add one line to the `cmdExit_Click` routine to allow users to exit elegantly. It should say:

```
Unload Me
```

Run the program again and select freely from lines of the combo. After each selection click the Execute button and see what you get. You may, of course rearrange the grid to your liking. Make one column wider, another narrower and so on. The program is now useful for the investigation of the data dictionary.

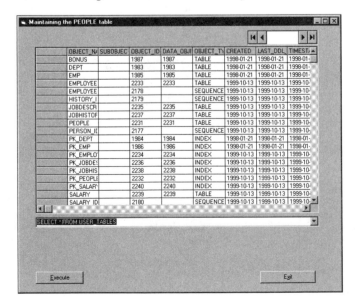

Another improvement will make it a nice general tool for querying the database. We are going to add a multi-line text box to the form, where we'll be able to edit the SQL and therefore execute our own commands. Any SQL statement that we select from the combo will be copied into this text box. We will modify the `cmdExecute` code so that we will populate the `RecordSource` with the text box rather than the combo and then refresh the data control. In the interim between selecting a statement from the combo and executing it, the user can edit the SQL; or even write his own by typing valid SQL commands into the multi-line text box.

Add a large text box to the form. Make it stretch as wide as the combo and from below the combo to just above the command buttons. Name it `txtSQL` and set its text property to an empty string (Null String). Go to the `MultiLine` property and select **True**.

Now we'll change some of the code. In the `cmdExecute_click` routine change the line

```
adcView.RecordSource = cboSQL.Text
```

To say:

```
adcView.RecordSource = txtSQL.Text
```

Finally, add the following two routines to the form:

```
Private Sub cboSQL_Change()
  txtSQL.Text = cboSQL.Text
End Sub

Private Sub cboSQL_Click()
  txtSQL.Text = cboSQL.Text
End Sub
```

These guarantee that any selection made on the combo is copied to the text box.

To make life even easier, add another command button to the form. Name it `cmdClear` and let its caption be **&Clear**. Now double-click on it and in the `cmdClear_Click` sub insert the line:

```
txtSQL.Text = ""
```

When you click the button you'll have a *Tabula Rasa*, or a clean slate, on which to compose a valid SELECT statements, which you may then run by clicking the **Execute** button.

Since we are adding the capability of editing the dropdown selection, we may add some useful prewritten yet incomplete selections, which will refine our ability to interrogate the data dictionary tables. These selections include the WHERE clause which allows us to "home in" on exactly the data we require (see Chapter 2 for full details).

Remember, we should always strive to send as little data across a network as possible.

In some cases, the WHERE is followed by two single quotes. You'll be able put a literal between those single quotes to complete the statement, and then execute it. I find the following additions very useful:

```
.AddItem "SELECT * FROM USER_OBJECTS WHERE " & _
    "OBJECT_TYPE = '''"
.AddItem "SELECT * FROM USER_OBJECTS WHERE " & _
    "OBJECT_TYPE = 'PROCEDURE'"
.AddItem "SELECT * FROM USER_OBJECTS WHERE " & _
    "OBJECT_NAME = '''"
.AddItem "SELECT * FROM USER_TAB_COLUMNS WHERE " & _
    "TABLE_NAME = '''"
.AddItem "SELECT COLUMN_NAME, DATA_TYPE, " & _
    "DATA_LENGTH, DATA_PRECISION, DATA_SCALE, " & _
    "NULLABLE FROM USER_TAB_COLUMNS " & _
    "WHERE TABLE_NAME = '''"
.AddItem "SELECT * FROM USER_SOURCE WHERE NAME = '''"
```

What you insert between the single quotes is case sensitive. The table name in the normal SQL statement is not case sensitive, as is the case with all the Oracle object names, but inside the quotes they are case sensitive, and must be in caps. The reason is that in these statements the object names are just data, and Oracle data is case sensitive.

Of course, now that we have the text box we can simply type in any valid command we please so we can access our HR tables.

I've run the program using SELECT * FROM People in the text box. This is not one of the pre-written commands in the dropdown combo. Here is the result:

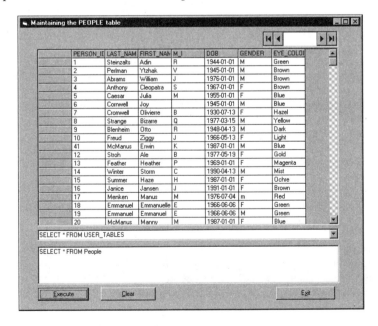

We'll use this program time and again. It is one of our query tools. The other is the SQL*PLUS window. We'll also use the pre-written SQL statement in the combo again, to gain extra knowledge about the structure of our tables and the values of our sequences.

Before you move on, save the program's .VBP file and its form and .frx (form extension) files in the Chapter1 subdirectory of VBOraBook. The following section will show the equivalent code using the OO4O data control.

A View Program Using the OO4O Data Control

When we are using the OO4O data control, as well as OO4O itself, making the connection string is easy. OO4O "talks" directly to Oracle's native API (the Oracle Call Interface – OCI). We do not need to go through OLE DB (or ODBC). The Connect string is simply the schema name followed by a forward slash and then by the password. Thus in our case it is simply: scott/tiger (if you are in the office use the name/password combination given to you by the DBA).

Immediately below the Connect string you find that DatabaseName property. If you have installed the Oracle demo leave this property blank – we only have one database in the system and it defaults to it. In most work places, the DBA has set a few databases. You should only exercise in a database set by the DBA exclusively for testing. Check with your DBA and use the name she gives you as DatabaseName property.

Our "Action" Code in the cmdExecute_Click routine is slightly different:

```
Private Sub cmdExecute_Click()
    On Error GoTo RefreshError
    odcView.Recordset.SQL = txtSQL.Text
    odcView.Recordset.Refresh
    Exit Sub
RefreshError:
    MsgBox "Error Number: " & Err.Number & " Mesage is: " & Err.Description
End Sub
```

We apply our command to the SQL property of the Recordset object. This will change the RecordSource property of the control and run the new query. Because the grid is bound to the data control it will be refreshed as well.

As you can see, we change the RecordSource property of the control indirectly by changing the odcView.Recordset.SQL property. This is an idiosyncrasy. Object Oriented Programming advocates polymorphism – telling us to reuse familiar forms whenever possible. So why do we have to set the SQL one way at design time and another at run time? Beats me! Worse, this is actually a double transgression! As we have already stated, the ORADC is a wrapper around OO4O. OO4O does not have Recordset objects only Dynaset objects.

In our Form_load routine, we cannot select the USER_TAB_COLUMNS table. The Oracle data control simply cannot handle the LOBs in this table:

```
'.AddItem "Select * from USER_TAB_COLUMNS"
```

Data Controls allow us to write quick and dirty programs to access and modify database data – if we were to alter a value in our bound grid and moved to the next record, the data in the database would be automatically updated. They are ideal for quick prototyping and for small work groups. However, data integrity and performance issues (among others) mean that they are rarely used for serious development. Don't expect to write mission critical programs using them!

Let's finish this chapter by briefly investigating two more tools that the programmer has at his or her disposal to investigate the database.

Oracle Navigator

The Oracle Navigator is a program that allows you to perform many of the DBA functions in a GUI environment. You can create and modify tables, add users and maintain their privileges, even write stored procedures and triggers. It may be found in the Oracle 8 Personal Edition Group:

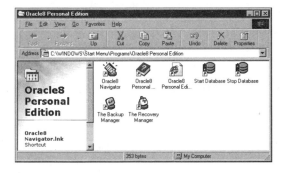

It may also be started from the Start button as part of that group. Once in you'll see a divided screen that looks much like the familiar Windows Explorer screen:

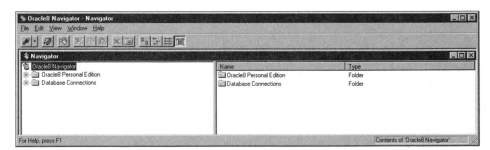

Click On the Plus (+) next to the Oracle8 Personal Edition folder on the left. Then Click on the Blue Local Database icon. The database will load (if it was not already loaded by another process) and this is what the screen will look like:

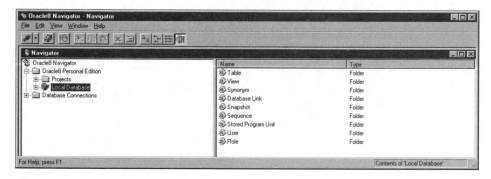

I prefer to work with the left side of the screen whenever I can. If you click on the Plus (+) next to the **Local Database** icon the structure on the right will also be positioned underneath the icon and indented to the right:

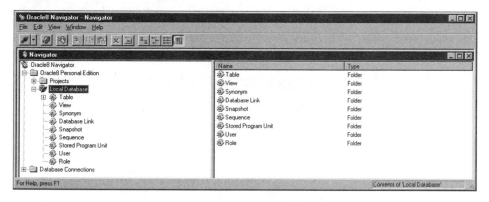

Note that the Table icon is also expanded. Now when you click on any item a subsidiary list appears on the right. Right clicking on any such item brings a dropdown menu to view, of which the **Properties** selection is the most important one. If the item is a table, then the most important action is the **Open**.

When you select a **Table**'s **Properties** from the right click dropdown menu, as I did here for the **People** table, you'll get the **Properties** form. Click on the **Design** tab to get the equivalent of the DESC command.

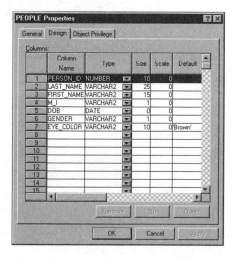

I'll come back to the Navigator when we discuss building triggers and stored procedures. For now, just stay in the Navigator and mosey around on your own. See how things work. In most cases it is better than the program you've just finished, but here is where our program is definitely better:

Click on **Sequences** in the left window, and then double click any of the sequences in the right. This is what you'll get:

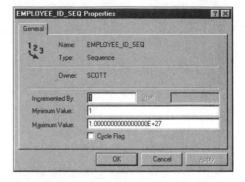

Which is not really much. Now go to the **OraView** program, select and execute the SELECT * FROM USER_SEQUENCES and this is what you'll get:

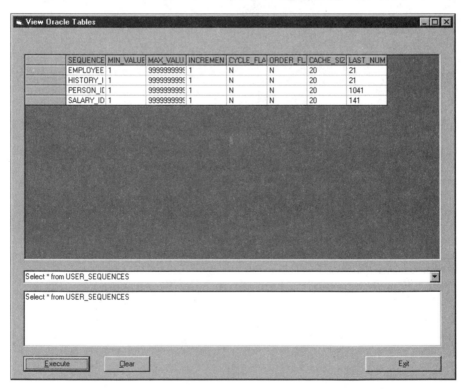

This is much better. You can even tell what the last number in each sequence is, and you don't need to do it for every sequence alone. I rest my case!

Even Microsoft gave us a better tool. This is Microsoft InteDev. I'll give you a short guided tour of its data project. You'll be able, by trial and (hopefully not mostly) error, to continue the tour on your own. You'll need a System DSN so that you may connect to our Oracle database. This System DSN will also serve us well later. Here is how we build it.

The Visual InterDev Data Project

Visual InterDev has a built in project that allows you to view any ODBC-enabled data base.

> As this implies, in order to use this you must set up a Data Source Name (DSN) – which I called msOra – using the Microsoft ODBC For Oracle driver. If you do not know how to do this, please refer to Chapter 5.

Visual InterDev actually uses ADO to help you navigate any database you are connected to. As you'll soon discover, it offers many things that Oracle Navigator does and some that it does not. It also lacks a few features. The core functionality is almost identical, but I prefer the Microsoft Interface.

Start the VID and open a New Database Project:

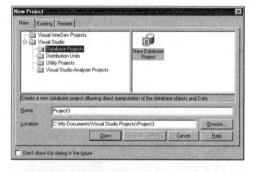

Click on the Machine Data Source tab of the form and select your newly created msOra:

Click **OK**. Now enter the `tiger` password in the next input box and press **OK** again. You may need to press **OK** twice.

Now Click on the (+) next to the SCOTT (**msORA**) in the **Data View** panel on the lower right corner of the screen and then on the (+) next to **Tables**. Click again on the (+) next to **PEOPLE**. This is what you get:

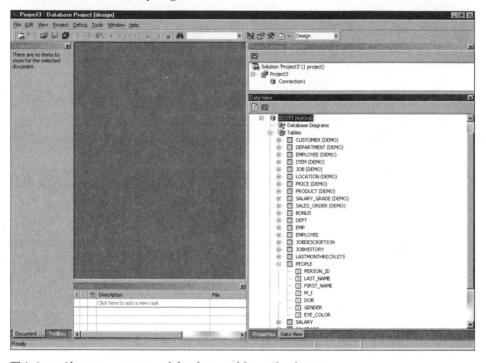

This is a nifty tree structure of database, table, and columns.

Now right click the `People` table and select **design**. Rearrange the windows and voilà here is the table described. Click **Open** and get the table content. After some rearrangement of the windows and the Grid columns here is what we can see:

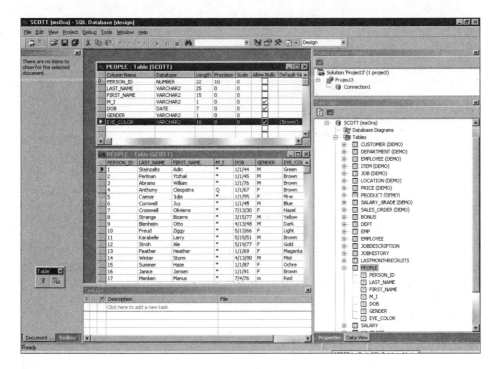

Notice that some table names are followed by (DEMO). These are tables in the DEMO schema have the same names as tables in the scott schema. Continue from here on your own. Happy discovery!

There is still another easily available option of viewing the Oracle Database. Use Access to link the Oracle tables. This will be described in Appendix B.

Summary

We have had a brief tour of the architecture of an Oracle database. It was by no means comprehensive but, hopefully, covered the details that a VB programmer needs to know.

You've now installed Oracle and loaded the demo data tables. You've also written a simple yet useful VB program that runs on Oracle. This program is a more convenient way to view the Oracle data. In the next chapters we'll continue to use this program to view various queries.

Bear in mind, however, that OO4O and ADO prove to be much better tools. I use data controls only when I need to produce a 'quick and dirty' program in a few minutes.

You've also been introduced to the Oracle Navigator. This is a tool that you may use in place of SQL*PLUS. It is not featured enough to really replace SQL*PLUS and I hardly ever use it. Another option is to use Visual InterDev's Data project.

2

Queries and Data Manipulation Using SQL

Ask, and it shall be given you; seek, and ye shall find.

In this chapter, we will discuss how to retrieve, analyze and modify the data in the Oracle database using Structured Query Language. SQL is a powerful, full-featured language and it is the one that every relational database system understands. We can describe SQL functionality in terms of four sub-languages:

❑ **Data Query Language** (DQL): this is the SQL SELECT command, used to retrieve data from the database.

❑ **Data Manipulation Language** (DML): a set of SQL commands used to modify existing rows of data in the database tables (for example, INSERT, UPDATE and DELETE)

❑ **Data Definition Language** (DDL): SQL commands that create, alter or drop database objects. Essentially, DDL consists of the CREATE, ALTER and DROP commands, covered in Chapter 3.

❑ **Data Control Language** (DCL): used to provide database security and assign privileges to users.

Officially, DQL does not exist. A query is considered to be a part of the DML. It is, however, both customary and convenient to make the distinction.

As Visual Basic programmers, it is very important that we understand how to harness the power of DQL in our applications. In modern multi-user client-server applications it is very important that we write efficient database queries that allow us to retrieve the data we want quickly, without putting undue strain on the database. Also, we must always strive to minimize the load on the network by only requesting the specific data required. There are many ways in which we can connect Visual Basic to the Oracle database. The most prevalent method uses ActiveX Data Objects (see Chapters 9 - 12). This is a thin layer of code that encapsulates both the new OLE-DB and the ODBC Application Programming Interfaces (the ODBC is actually supported through an OLE-DB provider especially made for it). Oracle adds its own Oracle Objects For OLE (OO4O), which we use in Chapters 5 - 8. In both cases, a SQL SELECT statement defines the contents of the Recordset object (Dynaset object in OO4O).

In the first part of this chapter we cover the basics of SQL and use the SELECT statement, in conjunction with various clauses, to retrieve specific data from a database table and perform simple data manipulation tasks on the selected data. We will then take this knowledge a step further and review some more advanced features of SQL. Due to the inherent design of a relational database we will commonly need to bring data from many tables together and display the data in a single result table. In particular, we will discuss how to use joins and subqueries to achieve this.

In theory, the VB programmer will have less need to use DML. For simple applications, we can utilize the Delete, Update and AddNew methods of the Recordset object. If we have a client-server application that accesses a production database, the SQL modification commands will be encased in complex stored procedures to safeguard data integrity. These objects are usually stored on the database server and will, along with DDL and DCL, be the preserve of the DBA. Even if we, mere programmers, are allowed to design and define the database – we won't do it using VB.

However, it is very important that we have a feel for what the DML commands can do and how they do it. Thus, in the final part of this chapter we will enter the domain of the DBA to investigate DML statements and how we can use them to manipulate our data.

The more you know the better off you are, so I urge you to read all of these chapters.

A Brief SQL Overview

SQL (Structured Query Language) is a language used to query, define and maintain a relational database. Using SQL, you can update information in database tables, create or change the structure of the database and query the database to retrieve information. SQL-99, more commonly known as SQL3, is the new ANSI standard that defines the core elements of SQL, updating the previous formal release of the industry standard, SQL-92. SQL3 is compatible with SQL-92 except in a few areas, a discussion of which is beyond the scope of this book.

SQL-92 was a watershed event. For the first time ANSI, in cooperation with ISO, tried to create a large enough core of the language to allow for vendor blind database development. To this day, not a single vendor has implemented any of the standards completely, but some, like Oracle are close. In this chapter we deal only with the Oracle dialect of SQL. It differs only slightly from the standards, as long as you don't use functions.

Large database servers provide procedural extensions to the industry standard. The syntax of the keywords is typically the same, but additional, powerful built-in functions are added to make our data manipulation tasks easier. **PL/SQL** is an "extended" language supported by Oracle, and will be discussed in Chapter 13. Another example is Transact-SQL, supported by Microsoft SQL Server and Sybase databases.

The first thing to note about SQL is that it is a **nonprocedural** or **declarative** language. This means that instead of specifying *how* to perform a particular task, we simply tell SQL *what* we want to achieve and let the Database Management System (DBMS) decide the best way to go about it. SQL is referred to as a set-oriented language. It gives us access to all the tables in the database in one go and returns data in a spreadsheet-style recordset - basically a table with a set of rows (analogous to records) made up of various columns (analogous to fields).

SQL allows us to search and manipulate data in databases using logical expressions, called **search conditions**. Almost every programming language uses Boolean logic – based on the two values, TRUE and FALSE, and on the three basic operators AND, OR and NOT.

SQL, however, uses a three-valued logic based on the values TRUE, FALSE and UNKNOWN. So how, when database field values are compared, does the UNKNOWN logical value arise? The answer lies in the presence of null field values.

What Are Null Values?

A **null value** is the way the database says, "I don't know! I haven't received any value for this field yet." Why not use a blank for character fields or a zero for numeric fields instead, you may ask. The answer is that a relational database must have a way of differentiating between a "blank" value and an unanswered one. If you participate in a survey and are asked about your income, you may answer or skip the question. If you're between jobs, your income is zero. If you skip the question your income is null. When we discuss DDL in the next chapter, you'll see that we may bar certain columns from containing null values. We may also assign default values to unanswered (unassigned) fields. Bear in mind that an unexpected null value can cause invalid or unexpected results, or even crash a program.

If a null value is compared to a definite value (or even another null) the resulting logical value is UNKNOWN. Since it is not possible to say what the null stands for, it is not possible to say if the comparison is TRUE or FALSE. We will encounter null values several times as we progress through the SQL chapters.

SQL Notation

As with any programming language, knowledge of the language syntax is necessary in order to understand its definition. In this chapter, and in other places in the book where syntax is discussed, we'll use a standard format for the presentation of SQL command syntax. Adherence to certain conventions, in this manner, aids the identification of the various elements of each command:

❑ Optional items will be enclosed in square brackets: [optional] These may be embedded to show options within options as in:

```
ColumnName DATA_TYPE[(a [,b])]
```

Which means that after the keywords DATA_TYPE you may insert (a) or (a, b) or nothing at all.

❑ SQL reserved words (such as SELECT) will be displayed in uppercase and in code in text font.

❑ Element names in the syntax (supplied by the programmer) will be enclosed in angle brackets, for example: <TableName>

❑ Delimited Lists. I use the term Comma Delimited list quite frequently. A delimited list is a succession of items separated by a Delimiter. In a Comma Delimited list the delimiter is a comma. Delimited lists have the delimiter between consecutive items, but not before the first item or following the last item. Here are a few examples:

A, B, C – is a comma delimited list of three items

A\B\C – is a back-slash delimited list of three items. In all versions of Windows and DOS a path is a backslash delimited list of directories.

We use four types of constants:

❑ **NULL**

❑ **Numeric constants**. These will be italicized and used with or without decimals, as dictated by the context.

❑ **Date and time constants**. These chapters use the Oracle default date format, which is 'DD-MON-YYYY' and enclosed in single quotes, for example, '14-JUL-1999'. When date and time are combined we'll use 'DD-MON-YYYY: HH: MI: SS', for example, '14-JUL-1999:17:53:16' which stands for 5:53 and 16 seconds PM on Bastille day, 1999. When the time of day is not specified Oracle defaults to 12:00:00 AM.

This is important to remember when using a date with the WHERE clause, which is discussed later. When a date is specified, Oracle searches for rows in the date column with exactly the same time and date. If only the date is entered, the time defaults to 12AM. Only rows with this exact time and date will be returned - that won't be many! (This can be worked around by using the TRUNC function, described later, which truncates the time portion of the date column).

❑ **Character constants** are enclosed in single quotes, for example, `'Sparta'`.

SQL commands may run as a single line of code or may be broken out into multiple lines. For more complex statements, multiple line code is much easier to read and understand and this format is always used in this book. The code may also be indented if it aids understanding of the syntax.

Now, finally, let's get to the SQL...

Database Queries – The SELECT Statement

The `SELECT` command enables us to read information stored in the database. We'll start by discussing the command in its simplest form and add more capabilities as we go along.

> You can execute the SQL commands in this chapter from either the View program we developed in Chapter 1 (as I did) or from SQL*PLUS. If you choose the latter, remember to include a semicolon at the end of the code.

If you wish to execute the code in this chapter it is probably a good idea to synchronize your database with mine. The intricacies of SQL are explained mostly by example, and we want our results to agree. You gain a much deeper understanding of the language when you know what to expect, and why you are going to get it. To achieve this, run the three scripts:

```
ClearIt.sql,
CreateIt.sql, and
Populate.sql
```

in order from your `SQL*PLUS` window. This will recreate the original 21-row People table and all of its subsidiaries.

When all the scripts have been run execute the command `COMMIT;` (alternatively you may start the session with the `SET AUTOCOMMIT ON` command.)

The simplest form of the `SELECT` statement deals with reading raw information from a single table and simply specifies the columns we wish to retrieve and the table from which we wish to retrieve them:

```
SELECT <ColumnList> FROM <TableName>
```

The `TableName` element is the name of a table in the database and `ColumnList` is one of two options:

Firstly, an asterisk (*) can be used. This denotes that you want to retrieve every column in the specified table. For example, the following code will fill the data grid with all columns from the `SALARY` table:

```
SELECT * FROM SALARY
```

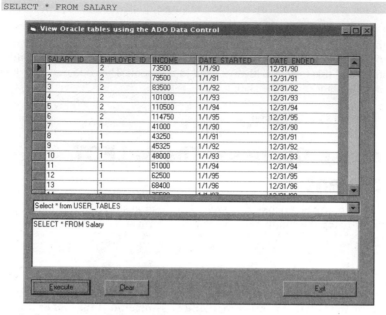

Alternatively, a comma delimited list of column names that you want to select can be used. Each column name must be defined in the table, for example, Last_Name, First_Name, Gender. Note that a comma does not follow the last item in the list. For example, the following code will only return two columns from the PEOPLE table:

```
SELECT First_Name, Last_Name FROM People
```

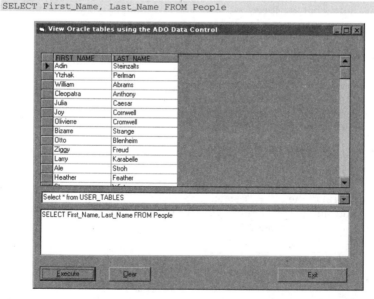

Note that this is actually a table. This simplest form of the SELECT statement probably does more than we first expected. We must be able to refine the results a bit if we want it to be useful. We can achieve that by appending selection criteria to our basic SELECT statement.

The greater the number of fields returned, the more memory that must be allocated to store the data and the slower our application will run. If we're retrieving a very large number of records, even a single field can push the memory envelope, especially if that field is storing a large image. In client-server systems, transferring large recordsets from your database to our application is time-consuming and can result in excessive, and often unnecessary, network traffic.

The WHERE Clause

In order to refine the returned table we tell the database to search for further criteria. In order to do this we append a WHERE clause to the end of the statement. This clause will be added just before the end of the statement and following a space:

```
SELECT <ColumnList> FROM <TableName> WHERE <Condition>;
```

A Condition may take various forms, all of which can be evaluated to a Boolean value. The simplest is a column name followed by a comparison operator followed by another column name or a constant. The comparison operators we can use are listed below:

Operator	Description
=	Is equal to
<	Is less than
<=	Is less than or equal to
>	Is greater than
>=	Is greater than or equal to
! =	Is not equal to
<>	Is not equal to

For example, if we want to view data for all female employees, we could execute the following statement:

```
SELECT Last_Name, First_Name FROM People WHERE Gender = 'F'
```

LAST_NAME	FIRST_NAME
Anthony	Cleopatra
Caesar	Julia
Cromwell	Olivierre
Freud	Ziggy
Stroh	Ale
Feather	Heather
Summer	Haze
Janice	Jansen
Emmanuel	Emmanuelle
McManus	Manny

The WHERE clause applies a search condition to the records gathered by the SELECT statement. In the above example, the WHERE clause navigates through all the records in the People table (this isn't strictly true in all cases, for example, if the criteria column is indexed, but that is outside the realm of the current discussion) and applies the search condition Gender='F' to them. Only those records that test TRUE are displayed. If the search condition returns a FALSE or UNKNOWN (due to the presence of a null value – unlikely in this case!) value for a record then that record will not be displayed.

> **Note that we did not actually have to select the Gender column in order to use it as the criterion in our command.**

We can use Boolean logic to append multiple search conditions to the WHERE clause. The Boolean reserved words are NOT, AND, and OR. If Boolean expressions are not enclosed in parentheses they are performed in their order of precedence, which is NOT, AND, and finally OR. For example, if we want a list of all male employees born in 1967 or later we should issue the following statement:

```
SELECT Last_Name FROM People WHERE Gender = 'M' AND DOB > '31-DEC-1966'
```

LAST_NAME
▶ Abrams
Strange
Winter
McManus

If you examine the People table closely you will notice that the young **Mr. Menken** is missing from our result table. This is because his gender was misspelled when the data was entered into the table and marked as 'm' rather than 'M'. In Oracle, the process of comparing characters in a column to a string literal is case sensitive. This is not true in Access or SQL Server, both of which started in the Windows on Intel boxes (Wintel) environment. Oracle has its origin in Unix.

Oracle gives us many string manipulation functions that can be used inside SQL. We'll immediately introduce two of them: UPPER and LOWER. As you probably guessed, UPPER (string) simply converts all the alphabetic characters in the string to uppercase. LOWER, of course, converts them to lowercase.

> **These are Oracle-only functions. Access, like VB uses the UCase(String) and the LCase(String) instead.**

Thus we can execute the following statement to retrieve the full result set:

```
SELECT Last_Name FROM People WHERE UPPER(Gender) = 'M' AND DOB > '31-DEC-1966'
```

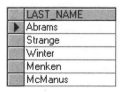

LAST_NAME
▶ Abrams
Strange
Winter
Menken
McManus

Of course, ideally, Mr. Menken's gender should have been correctly entered into the database in the first place. In the next chapter we shall see how this mistake could have been avoided by applying a CHECK constraint.

Before we move on, let's have a look at a more complex statement involving all three Boolean operators:

```
SELECT First_Name, Last_Name FROM People
WHERE NOT (Eye_Color = 'Yellow' OR Eye_Color = 'Gold' OR Eye_Color = 'Ochre')
AND Gender = 'F'
```

Here we have retrieved data for female employees who have any eye color other than yellow, gold or ochre:

FIRST_NAME	LAST_NAME
Cleopatra	Anthony
Julia	Caesar
Olivierre	Cromwell
Ziggy	Freud
Heather	Feather
Jansen	Janice
Emmanuelle	Emmanuel
Manny	McManus

You may want to experiment with statements such as these. Remove the brackets and view the resulting table. Remove the NOT operator. Get a feel for how these statements are executed.

When the selection criteria become more involved, there are a few other operators available to us that can simplify, and increase the flexibility of, such statements.

The NULL Operator

The NULL operator can be used to find all records where the value in a selected column is null. The NULL operator works in conjunction with the IS keyword (use of '= NULL' is not permitted). Thus, we may search for the current job description for each employee:

```
SELECT Employee_ID, Job_Code FROM JOBHISTORY WHERE Date_Ended IS NULL
```

EMPLOYEE_ID	JOB_CODE
1	CEO
7	CIO
10	MRC
4	MRS
9	CO
3	CSM
12	CO
6	COO

We can also use IS NOT NULL (instead of '<> NULL', which is not allowed).

The IN Operator

Instead of using clauses that repeat the Boolean OR, we may use the IN operator, which searches for a column value in a set of other column values:

```
IN <List>
```

Here, again, the List is comma delimited with each item. Thus, the following statement will produce the same result as the last one:

```
SELECT First_Name, Last_Name FROM People
WHERE Eye_Color NOT IN ('Yellow', 'Gold', 'Ochre')
AND Gender = 'F'
```

We can also use NOT IN to provide information about rows we *don't* want.

The BETWEEN Operator

The BETWEEN operator works hand-in-hand with the AND operator. Instead of looking for specific values, using the IN operator (or complex OR clauses) we can retrieve values within a certain range:

```
SELECT Last_Name FROM People WHERE Person_ID BETWEEN 15 AND 18
```

The BETWEEN operator is always inclusive so Person_ID values of both 15 and 18 will be selected:

PERSON_ID	LAST_NAME
15	Summer
16	Janice
17	Menken
18	Emmanuel

Again, we can use NOT BETWEEN to select all of the people in the table apart from those listed above.

However, try not to use negative criteria (NOT IN, NOT BETWEEN) unless you really have no choice. The best selection criteria are the simplest. Also, use of the NOT operator to search indexed columns can give you a performance hit. The database engine stores indexed columns in sorted form and can find particular values very quickly. If you use a negative criterion in your statement then the selection process is performed by reading through the unsorted rows, which is a much longer process.

Last but not least is another operator that can prove useful but that should be used sparingly.

The LIKE Operator

The LIKE operator works as a regular expression parser on character fields. It uses the percent sign (%) as the wildcard for any string and the under score (_) as the wildcard for a single character. Thus, the following statement will select all last names starting with an 'A':

```
SELECT First_Name, Last_Name FROM People WHERE Last_Name LIKE 'A%'
```

FIRST_NAME	LAST_NAME
William	Abrams
Cleopatra	Anthony

The following statement would retrieve all last names exactly 3 characters long that start with an 'A' (none will be selected!):

```
SELECT First_Name, Last_Name FROM People WHERE Last_Name LIKE 'A__'
```

The LIKE operator should be used sparingly because it tends to resolve the selection process by reading the whole table. This is not always true, however: if Last_Name is indexed, Oracle (and some other database engines) is smart enough to resolve the LIKE 'A%' using the index. Unfortunately, placing a wildcard at the beginning of a search string, such as LIKE '_A%' is different. Here the index can not be used and the complete table will be scanned, placing a heavy burden on the server.

The following statement may be good for doing the New York Times crossword puzzle, but is not a statement a responsible programmer issues:

```
SELECT Word FROM Dictionary WHERE Word LIKE '_a_x___'
```

The ORDER BY Clause

The ORDER BY clause is a useful report feature. You will almost certainly have noticed that the queries we have implemented so far have returned rows in no particular order (generally, they are returned in the order they were entered into the database, or according to what index the server used). The ORDER BY clause, which goes at the very end of any SELECT statement, is applied to a specific column (or columns) to sort the rows into ascending or descending order. Let's look at an example that we've already used:

```
SELECT Last_Name, First_Name FROM People WHERE Gender = 'F'
ORDER BY Last_Name
```

By default, ORDER BY sorts the rows in ascending order:

LAST_NAME	FIRST_NAME
Anthony	Cleopatra
Caesar	Julia
Cromwell	Olivierre
Emmanuel	Emmanuelle
Feather	Heather
Freud	Ziggy
Janice	Jansen
McManus	Manny
Stroh	Ale
Summer	Haze

As you can see, this makes it much easier to find any particular name. In order to sort in descending order (Z to A) add DESC to the command:

```
SELECT Last_Name, First_Name FROM People WHERE Gender = 'F'
ORDER BY Last_Name DESC
```

SQL and Arithmetic

SQL allows the use of operators in the SELECT statement. The basic arithmetical operations: addition (+), subtraction (−), multiplication (*) and division (/) can be performed on numerical column values. The concatenation operator (| |) can be used to bring together strings.

If you wish to raise a number to a power, it is best to use the POWER function

As an example of the use of arithmetic operators, consider the following. If we want to know how much Ms. Caesar is going to make next year, after a 10% increase we can use the following statement:

```
SELECT Income * 1.1 FROM Salary
WHERE Employee_ID = 1 AND Date_Ended IS NULL
```

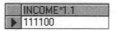

INCOME*1.1
▶ 111100

Note that we use the `NULL` operator so that we retrieve only her most recent position. The column is automatically given an alias (`INCOME*1.1`) – in some databases, such as SQL Server, an alias name would need to be explicitly stated. Of course, we can also do this in Oracle, using the `AS` keyword, in the way that follows:

```
SELECT Income * 1.1 AS YR2000INCOME FROM Salary
WHERE Employee_ID = 1 AND Date_Ended IS NULL
```

We can concatenate multiple column values, with a hard-coded comma and space (this will include a comma and a space in addition to the combined phrases) between each column value. If necessary, the `TO_CHAR` function, described later, can be used to convert any data type to character data type.

```
SELECT Last_Name || ', ' || First_Name || ', ' || M_I AS Full_Name FROM People
WHERE Gender = 'F'
```

This will produce the following table:

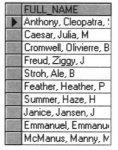

FULL_NAME
▶ Anthony, Cleopatra, :
Caesar, Julia, M
Cromwell, Olivierre, B
Freud, Ziggy, J
Stroh, Ale, B
Feather, Heather, P
Summer, Haze, H
Janice, Jansen, J
Emmanuel, Emmanuⁱ
McManus, Manny, M

We could do the last examples as easily in VB as in SQL. So which is better? There is no general answer to this, though in our case I choose VB. We have to do the operation on each and every row that we return. This means that we do not gain any decrease in traffic. But doing the manipulation in VB saves server time. When the manipulation is a part of an aggregate result, I tend to do it in SQL – or on the server.

Using Functions with Oracle SQL

SQL is almost a programming language and the over-zealous authors, in order to get it closer to fully-fledged, loaded it with mathematical and string functions. Oracle is particularly rich in these functions because Oracle promotes the philosophy of very thin clients and very hefty servers (they have been the greatest proponents of the Network Computer and have even proposed to produce the device). The general syntax of a function is:

```
FUNC [(Arg1, Arg2,   ArgN)]
```

The functions we cover in this section operate on each row in a column individually. Remember, like anything else in SQL, if the argument to a function is a column, then unless we use restrictive WHERE conditions, the function will operate on every row in that column

Certain functions, known as Aggregate or Group functions, operate on groups of rows. These will be discussed in greater detail later in this chapter.

Some functions such as SYSDATE, which returns the current server date and time, have no arguments, and thus no parentheses, while others may accept one or more arguments, as in UPPER(Last_Name). For example, the following statement returns the Last_Name column values in upper case.

```
SELECT First_Name, UPPER(Last_Name) FROM People WHERE Gender = 'M'
```

FIRST_NAME	UPPER(LAST_NAME)
Adin	STEINZALTS
Ytzhak	PERLMAN
William	ABRAMS
Joy	CORNWELL
Bizarre	STRANGE
Otto	BLENHEIM
Larry	KARABELLE
Storm	WINTER
Emmanuel	EMMANUEL
Erwin	MCMANUS

Oracle databases include a table called dual (we will find out more about it in Chapter 6), which is automatically available to every user. It contains one column, called dummy (data type: VARCHAR2) and one row, with a value of x. We can use it in queries to test all of these functions, without the need to build sample tables (essentially, it allows us to view information that is not contained in a real table). The general syntax is as follows:

```
SELECT FUNC(<ArgumentList>) FROM dual
```

This allows us, for example, to use Oracle SQL as a calculator. Here we compute the Cosine of 180 degrees. The angle is given in Radians. 3.141592654 is PI, and thus 180 degrees.

```
SELECT COS (3.141592654) FROM dual
```

Also, we can retrieve the current date and time from the server:

```
SELECT SYSDATE FROM dual
```

SYSDATE
20/10/99 16:36:26

If you run the command from
SQL*PLUS, you will see an interesting
difference:

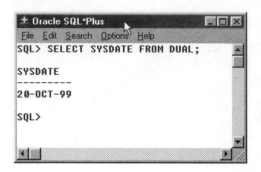

Even though SYSDATE has the time built in it does not show in here. The reason is that
the system uses the default date format – DD-MON-YY. To get the time as well use the
TO_CHAR function, which is similar to the VB Format function.

```
SELECT TO_CHAR(SYSDATE, 'DD_MON_YY:HH:MI:SS:a.m.') FROM dual
```

Some of these functions, in their Oracle form, are listed below. I find it convenient to
divide the various functions into the following categories: Mathematical, String, Date,
Conversion and General.

As usual, when the argument has the word 'List' in it, it means a comma-delimited
list. And a final note, these functions work on columns as well as on hard coded
values. When used in procedures they also work on variables.

The majority of the code examples here can be run from the dual table (except where
another table is already stated):

```
SELECT <code example> FROM dual
```

For example:

```
SELECT TAN(45*3.14159/180) FROM dual
```

For some of the date functions (MONTHS_BETWEEN, ROUND and TRUNC), it is necessary
to use a conversion function, for example:

```
SELECT ROUND
TO_DATE('10-JUL-1999:13:51:16','DD-MON-YY:HH24:MI:SS'))
FROM dual
```

```
SELECT MONTHS_BETWEEN
(TO_DATE('02-FEB-1996','DD-MON-YYYY'), TO_DATE('01-JAN-1996','DD-MON-YYYY') )
FROM dual
```

The Mathematical Functions

Function	Description
ABS(n)	Returns the absolute value of a number.

Function	Description
ACOS(n)	-1<=n<=1, Returns the arc cosine (the angle whose cosine is n) of n. The returned angle is given in Radians, in the range 0 to PI. To convert to degrees multiply by 180/PI().
	ACOS(.5) is 1.047197551197 Radians (that's 60 degrees)
	ACOS(-0.5)*180/3.14159 equals 120 (degrees)
ASIN(n)	-1<=n<=1, Returns the arc sine (the angle whose sin is n) of n. The returned angle is given in Radians in the range -PI/2 to PI/2. To convert to degrees multiply by 180/PI().
	ASIN(.5) is 0.5235987755983 (that's 30 degrees).
	ASIN(-0.5)*180/3.14159 equals -30 (degrees)
ATAN(n)	n<=1, Returns the arc tangent (the angle who's tangent is n) of n. The returned angle is given in Radians in the range -PI/2 to PI/2. To convert to degrees multiply by 180/PI().
	ATAN(1) is 0.7853981633974 (that's 45 degrees).
	ATAN(1)*180/3.14159 equals 45 (degrees)
ATAN2(n,m)	Same as ATAN(m/n). Returns the arc tangent of two values.
CEIL(n)	Returns the smallest integer greater or equal to n.
COS(n)	Cosine of n (n is in Radians). If the angle is in degrees, multiply it by PI()/180 to convert it to Radians.
	COS(60*3.14159/180) equals 0.5, the cosine of 60 degrees
COSH(n)	Hyperbolic Cosine of n.
EXP(n)	Exponent applied to the base e to the power of n.
	To calculate powers of other bases, use the exponentiation operator (^).
	EXP is the inverse of LN, the natural logarithm of number.
	EXP(1) equals 2.718282 (the approximate value of e)
FLOOR(n)	The largest integer less than or equal to n.
LN(n)	The Natural Logarithm of n (n>0).
LOG(b,n)	Returns the Log base b of n. b>0, n>0.
MOD(m,n)	The remainder of m/n (m, n, and MOD are all integers).
POWER(m,n)	m raised to the power of n (m^n)

Table Continued on Following Page

Function	Description
ROUND(m[,n])	Rounds the number m to n places right of the decimal point. When n is negative it rounds left of the decimal point. When n is omitted it returns an integer (zero decimal places). ROUND(15.111) is 15 ROUND(15.111,2) is 15.11 ROUND(15.111,-1) is 20. Can you see why? (Hint: ROUND(14.987,-1) is 10).
SIGN(n)	Returns 0 if n=0, -1 if n<0, 1 if n>0.
SIN(n)	Sine of n (n is in Radians). If the angle is in degrees, multiply it by PI()/180 to convert it to Radians. SIN(30*3.14159/180) equals 0.5, the sine of 30 degrees
SINH(n)	Hyperbolic Sine of n.
SQRT(n)	The Square Root of n (n >=0). If number is negative, SQRT returns the #NUM! error value.
TAN(n)	Tangent of n (n is in Radians). If the angle is in degrees, multiply it by PI()/180 to convert it to Radians. TAN(45*3.14159/180) equals 1
TANH(n)	Hyperbolic Tangent of n (n in Radians).
TRUNC(n[,d])	Truncates a number n to d decimal places. Integer if d is 0 or missing.

The String Functions

Function	Description
ASCII(x)	Returns a number which is the ASCII code of the character x.
CHR(n)	The inverse of ASCII. Given a number n (0-255) it returns a character.
INITCAP(s)	Returns the string with the first character of each word in caps.
INSTR(S1, S2[,n[,k]])	S1 starting at position n, is searched for the kth occurrence of S2, if found the position is returned, else INSTR returns 0. If n is negative, the search begins with the characters at the end of the string and searches backwards.

Function	Description
LENGTH(s)	The number of characters in s. All trailing spaces are included.
LOWER(s)	All the characters in s are converted to lower case. If we want to have only the first letter of the Last_Name column values (People table) to be in uppercase we can do: INITCAP(LOWER(Last_Name))
LPAD(s,n[,p])	Makes s a certain length, n, by adding a set of pad characters, p, to the left of the string. If p is omitted it is padded with spaces. If s is longer than n characters, only n characters are returned and no padding is done. For example: LPAD('Johns', 10, '.') yields: '.....Johns'
LTRIM(s[,set])	The optional set defaults to a single space. The function scans the string s for characters that are in the set. If the leftmost character is in the set it is removed and the process continues with the remaining string. Once the leftmost character of the string is not in set, the process stops. For example: LTRIM('mymyMy Name', 'my') yields 'My Name' LTRIM('mymyMy Name', 'My') yields 'mymyMy Name' LTRIM(' My Name') yields 'My Name'
NVL(e1,e2)	Returns e2 if e1 IS NULL, e1 otherwise. This allows you to assign your own meaning to NULL.
REPLACE(s,p[,r])	Any occurrence of pattern p in string s is replaced by string r. When r is omitted, all occurrences of p are removed. For example: REPLACE('Jrnum and Jiley', 'J', 'Ba') yields 'Barnum and Bailey'
RPAD(s,n[,p])	Makes s a certain length, n, by adding pad characters, p, to the right of the string. If p is omitted it is padded with spaces. If s is longer than n characters, only n characters are returned and no padding is done. For example: RPAD('Johns', 10, '.') yields: 'Johns.....'

Table Continued on Following Page

Function	Description
RTRIM(s[,set])	Similar to LTRIM but works from the right end of the string. RTRIM('My Namemymy', 'my') yields 'My Name'
SOUNDEX(s)	SOUNDEX is an algorithm that groups words that sound alike (like string s). It is a good way to find a person whose name is Smyth when we look for Smith. The function returns the 4 digit SOUNDEX number produced by the string. SELECT Last_Name FROM People WHERE SOUNDEX(Last_Name) = SOUNDEX('cesar') will return Caesar.
SUBSTR(s,m[,n])	Cuts off the substring of s, starting in position m and being n characters long (m=0 is the same as m=1). If m is negative the position is counted backwards from the last character of s. If n is omitted the selection goes all the way to the last character of s. If n is 0 a NULL is returned. To keep matters simple, use integers for m and n. Let's say that s is 'ABCDEFGHIJ' then: SUBSTR(s,5) is 'EFGHIJ' SUBSTR(s,-5) is 'FGHIJ' SUBSTR(s,-5,3) is 'FGH'

Function	Description
TRANSLATE(s,from,to)	TRANSLATE is a positional formatter. Each character in the s string is looked at. It then checks the from string to see if that character is there. If it is, the corresponding (occupying the same position) character in the to string is substituted for the character in s string. The from string can contain more characters than the to string, but not vice versa. If from is longer than to, the corresponding to character is NULL, thus the resulting string may be shorter than the original. If to is the empty string, and this is dangerous, the result of TRANSLATE is that all the characters in from are removed from the result. Again let s be 'ABCDEFGHIJ': TRANSLATE(s, 'BDE', 'bde') yields 'AbCdeFGHIJ' TRANSLATE(s, 'BDE', 'b') yields 'AbCFGHIJ' TRANSLATE(s, 'bde', 'QQQ') yields 'ABCDEFGHIJ' Why?
UPPER(s)	All the characters in s are converted to uppercase - same as VB's Ucase. UPPER('abcde') is 'ABCDE' UPPER('a123q') is 'A123Q'

The Date functions

Function	Description
ADD_MONTHS(d, n)	Adds n months to the date d. ADD_MONTHS('01-JAN-1999', 4) yields '01-MAY-1999'
GREATEST(d1, d2, d3 ...)	Picks the latest of a list of dates.
LAST_DAY(d)	Returns the last day of the month of d. you can get 28, 29, 30 or 31 depending on the month and year. LAST_DAY('10-FEB-2000') yields 29.

Table Continued on Following Page

Function	Description
MONTHS_BETWEEN(d1,d2)	The number of months between the two dates (d2-d1). If d1 is later than d2 the result is positive. If d2 is later, the result is negative. MONTH_BETWEEN('02-FEB-1996', '01-JAN-1996') Is 1.03226. Why? It is 1 and 1/31 months.
NEW_TIME(d,z1,z2)	Converts the date and time from one time zone, z1, to another, z2. Zones must be one of a selected list such as: EST/EDT (Eastern Standard/Daylight Time) GMT (Greenwich Mean Time) etc.
NEXT_DAY(d, dayname)	Returns the date of the first dayname (must be one of the names of the weekdays) following d. NEXT_DAY('01-JUL-1999', 'TUESDAY') will yield: '06-JUL-1999'
ROUND(d[,fmt]	fmt is one of 'HOUR', 'DDD' for day, 'MONTH', 'YEAR', and many other esoteric rounding formats signifying the granularity of the rounding. The date is rounded (not truncated) to the nearest chunk. When fmt is omitted:'DDD' is assumed. The date is rounded to 12am (midnight, the beginning of the day) if time of day is before noon, otherwise rounds up to the next day. ROUND('10-JUL-1999:13:51:16') yields '11-JUL-1999' ROUND('10-JUL-1999', 'MONTH') yields '01-JUL-1999' ROUND('10-JUL-1999', 'YEAR') Yields '01-JAN-2000'

Function	Description
SYSDATE	Accepts no arguments. This is always selected from DUAL and returns the current date and time of the server. Use SYSDATE whenever you need to put a timestamp into a row. Using the VB function NOW inserts the workstation's time. It is better to use the common time and date kept in the Oracle server.
TRUNC(d[,fmt])	Similar to ROUND, only it truncates to the proper time unit.
	Again when fmt is omitted the date is truncated to a day (DDD) unit. It is truncated to 12am (midnight) for any time up to and including 11:59:59pm - compare this to the ROUND function.
	TRUNC('10-JUL-1999:13:51:16')
	yields '10-JUL-1999'
	TRUNC('10-JUL-1999', 'YEAR')
	Yields '01-JAN-1999'

Conversion Functions

Here we convert data from one type into another. Many of the functions just convert to Oracle internal forms such as ROWID. Others convert between various international character codes. We'll just look at the most common conversions:

Function	Description
TO_CHAR(d[,fmt[,nls]])	Converts a DATE to VARCHAR2 according to the format (fmt) and national language standard (nls). When nls is omitted we default to the language in which the session is conducted.
	When fmt is omitted the conversion is to the standard format of 'DD-MMM-YYYY'.
	SELECT TO_CHAR(DOB) FROM People
	WHERE Person_ID = 1
	yields '01-JAN-1944'
	SELECT TO_CHAR(DOB, 'MONTH DD, YYYY')
	FROM People WHERE Person_ID - 1
	Yields 'January 1, 1944'

Table Continued on Following Page

Function	Description
TO_CHAR(n[,fmt[,nls]])	Converts a number to VARCHAR2 according to the optional fmt and the optional language standard.
	Language standards govern the decimal symbol (point in the USA, comma in Europe), the group separator between groups of 3 digits (comma in the USA, point in Europe), and the currency code. Omitting it defaults to the settings in the current session – which is good enough for me.
	Omitting the format converts to a number without group separators.
	In the format:
	G is used for group separator
	D is used for decimal point
	L is used for currency. This includes support for the Euro from version 8.1.5 onwards.
	MI denotes a trailing minus sign
	V multiplies number by 10n where n is number of digits to right of V
	TO_CHAR(-10000, 'L99G999D99MI')
	Yields $10,000.00-
TO_DATE(s[,fmt[,nls]])	Converts a character string to an Oracle internal date.
	TO_DATE('10-JUL-1999')
	Yields '10-JUL-99'
	This will work because it uses the default date format. If in any other form, add a format as a second argument.
	TO_DATE('JANUARY 11, 1492', 'MONTH DD, YYYY')
	Yields '11-JAN-92'
TO_NUMBER(n[,fmt[,nls]]	The format lets the program understand the number. This is a superfluous function. Oracle understands numbers by the sessions default nls anyway.

General Functions

Function	Description
GREATEST(List)	Returns the greatest member of the list. Each member may be an expression. The list's members have to be of the same type. Oracle cannot compare apples to mangos
	You can compare any type of number to any type of number. You can also compare dates, dates without a time are assumed to be at 00:00 military time.
LEAST(List)	Returns the smallest member of the List. The same type restrictions as for GREATEST apply here
USER	Returns the name of the user currently logged on. USER is a pseudo-column and, as such, can be queried in SELECT statements, but can not be updated.

Function Execution: Visual Basic or Oracle?

Visual Basic includes a counterpart for every function listed in this chapter, except for SYSDATE and USER. These counterparts do not necessarily share the same names, only function (purpose). We can perform these functions either in the database or in our Visual Basic program and we have to make an intelligent and informed decision as to where will be most effective. Obviously, the answer depends on you particular architecture and particular application. I can, however give you a few guiding rules of thumb:

❑ Remember that your physical system consists of Personal Computers, a network, and servers.

❑ Network and servers are public resources.

❑ The slowest link in the system is, most likely, the network. This is especially true if you use the Internet.

❑ The real measurement of performance is response time. Do anything you can to minimize it.

❑ Be a good netizen. Conserve public resources (network and servers).

All this leads to the following conclusions:

❑ Conserve network traffic as much as possible by minimizing the amount of information you request, and by minimizing the number of roundtrips required in the acquisition and storage of this information.

❑ All things being equal, do as much as you can on the personal computer. This rule applies to all the mathematical, string, date and conversion functions we've encountered so far, except SYSDATE and USER, which do not have a counterpart in Visual Basic. If a computation is to be done on each row that is returned, save server time and do it on the PC. If the computation is done to do some kind of a summary, save on traffic and do it in SQL on the server.

Here is an example. I want to see how much each employee will make if I give a 10% raise across the board, but I do not want to actually change it in the database. I'll do it in two ways. One is to take each salary and multiply it by 1.1, then pass it to the client. The other is to pass the salary to the client, who will multiply it by 1.1. Which is better? Obviously the latter is. The traffic is the same, but the server does less. Public resources are preserved.

❑ Last, but not least, always do your Math before you do your Arithmetic, and they are not the same! This rule applies equally well to client or server. I want to see how much it will cost me to raise each salary by 10%. It would be better to do the summation in the server and send just the sum across the network. Here, again we can investigate two of the ways in which this can be achieved. One is to multiply each salary by 1.1 and then sum, the other is to sum, then multiply by 1.1. Obviously the latter is better, because instead of multiplying many times, we do it just once. It will be even better if this single multiplication is done on the client. Where does Math enter here?

$$A * X + B * X + \ldots Q * X = (A + B + C + \ldots + Q) * X.$$

Simple Algebra goes a long way. By the way, if I already passed each individual salary to the client (as I did in the previous example) I don't need to ask the server the question about the total. I already have the info and I can calculate it in the VB. This reduces server and network work.

Aggregate functions, which we are going to study next, are a rule by themselves. They were designed to run in SQL.

Group or Aggregate Functions

The functions we dealt with in the previous sections operate on individual rows. Often, however, we don't need the level of detail that a simple SELECT statement provides and would rather see a summary of the data so that we may make educated business decisions. For this purpose, SQL provides us with **Aggregate functions**, which act on groups of rows. The data in the rows is processed in a specific manner and the result displayed in a single row answer. They are most powerful when used in conjunction with the GROUP BY and HAVING clauses.

The following sections will describe the seven ANSI standard aggregate functions.

AVG

This function returns the average of all values in a specific column:

```
AVG(Column_Name)
```

The following statement will tell us the average value in the Income column of the Salary table:

```
SELECT AVG(Income) FROM Salary
```

Well, the answer is: 46550.658. This average is of dubious value, because the question is not really meaningful– the salaries are listed for years ranging from 1990-1999 and there are several entries for each employee, as salaries have changed year-on-year. Alas, this is not a book about data analysis and the SQL statement gives you the exact answer to the dubious question.

COUNT

Returns the number of rows in which the value is not a null:

```
COUNT(Column_Name)
```

Thus the following command returns a count of seven:

```
SELECT COUNT(Date_Ended) FROM JobHistory
```

We can also use COUNT(*) as a row counter, which counts all of the rows, including nulls:

```
SELECT COUNT(*) FROM JobHistory
```

This returns a count of 15 – there are 15 rows in the table. How many men in the People table? Here's how we find out:

```
SELECT COUNT (*) FROM People WHERE Gender IN ('M', 'm')
```

And the answer is 11.

MAX and MIN

These functions return the maximum and minimum of all values in a specified column, respectively. Note that they do not identify the row(s) in which this value occurred – we'll return to this point when we discuss subqueries.

The following statement will find the date of birth of the youngest person in the People table:

```
SELECT MAX(DOB) FROM People
```

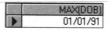

This is all very well, but who is this person? Can we construct a single query to find out? In the next section we're going to deal with subqueries. You'll find the answer there.

Of course, we can find the oldest person in a similar manner:

```
SELECT MIN(DOB) FROM People
```

STDDEV

Returns the standard deviation (square root of the VARIANCE - see below) of all values in a specified column:

```
STDDEV(Column_Name)
```

SUM

Returns the sum of all the values in a specified column:

```
SUM(Column_Name)
```

We can calculate the sum total of all incomes as follows:

```
SELECT SUM(Income) FROM Salary
```

The result is 1,768,925. However, as when we found for the average value on the `Income` column, the result is actually meaningless. What if I try to answer meaningful questions, such as: What is the sum of salaries for 1999?

Then, I have to compose a very complex statement to accommodate complex situations. What if somebody had a salary change mid year? What about people whose salary last changed prior to 1999? What about people who left our employ in the middle of the year? And so on. You are better off doing this sort of calculation in your VB program. You'll do even better to import the raw table into a spreadsheet, where you can do very complex math on the data and where you can use the same data again and again for all sorts of different computations and what ifs. If the query is fixed and run only as is, then the server is better. You should even go as far as composing a stored procedure in place of the query (that might be too complex) and run it in the server.

The following statement, however, will garner possibly meaningful information – we can calculate the expected total payroll for 1999 (assuming that we're not going to have any salary increases, nor do we expect any changes in personnel):

```
SELECT SUM(Income) FROM Salary WHERE Date_Ended IS NULL
```

VARIANCE

Computes the variance of all values in the column:

```
VARIANCE(Column_Name)
```

The variance is the mean square distance from the average, corrected for the loss of degrees of freedom. Again, we cannot go into statistical analysis in this book. Unless you're careful, the results you get will be meaningless.

The GROUP BY Clause

The group functions always return an answer in the form of a table of one row. On many occasions we need to separate the aggregate results into groups. For instance, it would be useful to be able to find both the youngest male and female from the `People` table. For just such a purpose the fathers of SQL have invented the GROUP BY clause. The GROUP BY clause is often (though it does not have to be) followed by an ORDER BY clause. The following is example syntax (note the square brackets around the ORDER BY clause):

```
SELECT <GroupFunction>(Column_Name1) FROM <TableName>
GROUP BY Column_Name2
[ORDER BY Column_Name2];
```

As a first example, say we wanted to find the most common eye color in the `People` table. The following command would do the trick:

```
SELECT Eye_Color, COUNT(Eye_Color) FROM People
GROUP BY Eye_Color
ORDER BY Eye_Color
```

EYE_COLOR	COUNT(EYE_COLOR)
Blue	4
Brown	5
Dark	1
Gold	1
Green	3
Hazel	1
Light	1
Magenta	1
Mist	1
Ochre	1
Red	1
Yellow	1

Generally, the RDMBS will first group together rows with the same value in the `Eye_Color` column. The COUNT function will then perform an aggregate calculation for each of these groups.

Let us now find the birth dates of the youngest in each gender in our `People` table:

```
SELECT MAX(DOB), Gender FROM People
GROUP BY Gender
ORDER BY Gender
```

MAX(DOB)	GENDER
1/1/91	F
4/13/90	M
7/4/76	m

Oops! How can we have three different genders? The typing error in Mr. Menken's Gender Field is giving us trouble. As you will recall, this caused a little trouble previously but we circumvented it using the UPPER function. Circumvention is nice, but correct data is nicer. Unless you write a reference book and need interesting examples, don't let bad data stay in your tables. Correct it as soon as you discover it.

Last but not least, There is yet another clause that you may use with group functions. This is the HAVING clause. This clause is the equivalent of the WHERE clause, but for use with group functions instead of single rows (why are they different? Beats me!). Let's see it in action (and at the same time prevent Mr. Menken from disturbing our results again):

```
SELECT MAX(DOB), Gender FROM People
GROUP BY Gender HAVING Gender IN ('M','F')
ORDER BY Gender
```

A WHERE clause can be used with GROUP BY clause, placed in front of the GROUP BY to determine which rows are included in the groups.

```
SELECT DOB, Gender FROM People
WHERE DOB > '31-JUL-1975'
GROUP BY Gender, DOB HAVING Gender IN ('M','F')
ORDER BY Gender
```

This works in a similar way to the previous piece of code. It selects the eight youngest people (those born after 31-JUL-1975) and then excludes Mr. Menken.

The WHERE clause can also be used to solve another problem. How would we include the last names of the two youngest people? To do this we need to be able to form a subquery using the WHERE clause, discussed in the next section. Then all will be revealed...

Group functions are best performed at the server. It is interesting that all the other functions we've encountered in this chapter are Oracle specific, while the group functions are plain-vanilla SQL. This is not the reason why I suggest performing aggregate functions in the database. The reason is that aggregating at the server dramatically reduces the amount of traffic, as we only pass a single row rather than many. When we later learn to use ADO, we'll see another excellent reason to use functions (but not aggregates) in VB.

So far in this chapter we have discussed how to use SQL to read the rows and columns from a single table. This is SQL in its simplest form; it is, however, complex enough. In the next chapter we'll learn how to use SQL to retrieve data from two or more related tables.

Complex Queries

Normal databases are so named because the resulting tables are independent of each other. This is akin to the Cartesian coordinate system, in which the axes are independent of each other because they are perpendicular – or normal – to each other. A complete piece of information is like a point in space. The point in space is defined by its X, Y and Z coordinates (or more if the space is of a higher dimension). Thus, the information is defined by an appropriate combination of data from 'perpendicular' tables.

For our sample tables we started with the `People` table. The employees are a subset of this table and that's why the `Employee` table is just a collection of IDs. We also created a third independent table of job descriptions and tied it all together with the `JobHistory` table.

In order to find the last name of the current CEO, we have to look for the `Employee_ID` in the `JobHistory` table where the `Job_Code` is `CEO` and the `Date_Ended` column contains a `NULL`. This leads us to an `Employee_ID` value of one. We now go to the `Employee` table to get the `Person_ID` of this employee and find that it is five. With this piece of information in hand, we look at the `People` Table and find the desired last name, `Caesar`.

How does that compare to coordinates? We tell the traveler to go North (on the `JobHistory` table) until a place that is marked `CEO` and `NULL` is encountered. The traveler is then told to look for a clue in the mailbox. The clue says: Travel West (On the `Employee` table) for 1 mile (`Employee_ID = 1`) and look for a clue there. There the clue is: Climb to the 5th floor (Go to `Person_ID = 5`) and look for the final clue under the mat. This is where the word `Caesar` is finally found. Traversing the relational database is like playing 'Treasure Hunt'! Obviously SQL has to measure up to the task of performing such hunts.

There are two major ways in which SQL performs such tasks: using subqueries and using table joins.

Subqueries

A **subquery** is a query within a query, or a `SELECT` statement within another SQL statement, that will allow us to perform our "treasure hunt". The second `SELECT` is enclosed in parentheses and follows the `WHERE` or `IN` keywords. The nested query may pass only one column to the parent query. However, depending on how you structure the query, it may return a single row or multiple rows.

Let's start with a subquery that returns a single row. We are going to build a single subquery that allows us to find out the last name of the current CEO. Let's build up the subquery in steps:

Step 1
Find out the `Employee_ID` of the current CEO:

```
SELECT Employee_ID FROM JobHistory
WHERE Job_Code = 'CEO' AND Date_Ended IS NULL
```

Step 2
Find out the `Person_ID` that corresponds to the CEO's `Employee_ID`. In order to do this we nest our first query within a second query. The inner (or nested) query is executed first and passes its result to the outer query:

```
SELECT Person_ID FROM Employee
WHERE Employee_ID =
    (SELECT Employee_ID FROM JobHistory
        WHERE Job_Code = 'CEO' AND Date_Ended IS NULL)
```

Step 3

To get to the desired `Last_Name` we need to take the query one step further:

```
SELECT Last_Name FROM People
WHERE Person_ID =
    (SELECT Person_ID FROM Employee
       WHERE Employee_ID =
          (SELECT Employee_ID FROM JobHistory WHERE Job_Code =
             'CEO' AND Date_Ended IS NULL))
```

Theoretically there is no limit to the number of levels in a SubSelect, but performance degrades rather quickly. As a rule of thumb, we should not go beyond three levels. This rule is also good for our sanity –it is very difficult to keep track, in our minds, of anything much deeper.

Generally, we can treat the SubSelect like a regular `SELECT` statement. We can even use group functions within it.

> **There is one exception to this: for no obvious reason, you cannot use the BETWEEN keyword in a nested query.**

A subquery does not necessarily have to hunt for data on different tables. Here is how we would find the name of the youngest person in the `People` table using SQL – a query that involves a subquery on a single table and uses the `MAX` group function to boot!

```
SELECT Last_Name, First_Name FROM People WHERE DOB =
    (SELECT MAX(DOB) FROM People)
```

The answer is…

LAST_NAME	FIRST_NAME
Janice	Jansen

Nested `SELECT` statements do not always return a single value (row) and, furthermore, we cannot expect all the SubSelects to return a single value either. In the above example we only have one CEO, but we employ two computer operators (CO). What will happen if we change the query to:

```
SELECT Last_Name FROM People
WHERE Person_ID =
    (SELECT Person_ID FROM Employee
       WHERE Employee_ID =
          (SELECT Employee_ID FROM JobHistory
             WHERE Job_Code = 'CO' AND Date_Ended IS NULL))
```

This query will encounter an error:

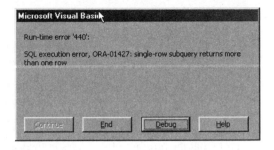

So what do we do if we want the last names of the computer operators? By making a small change to the structure of the statement, incorporating the IN keyword, we can build a subquery that will work for both single row and multi-row cases:

```
SELECT Last_Name FROM People
WHERE Person_ID IN
    (SELECT Person_ID FROM Employee
        WHERE Employee_ID IN
            (SELECT Employee_ID FROM JobHistory
                WHERE Job_Code = 'CO' AND Date_Ended IS NULL))
```

The resulting table is as follows:

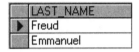

Remember the question we asked regarding how to include the last names of the youngest people for each gender in the People table? Here is the code - note that we still exclude Mr. Menken!

```
Select Last_Name, DOB, Gender FROM People
WHERE (DOB, Gender) IN
(Select MAX(DOB), Gender FROM People
GROUP BY Gender HAVING Gender IN ('M','F'))
```

LAST_NAME	DOB	GENDER
Winter	13/04/90	M
Janice	01/01/91	F

Joins

We've discussed how to use a SELECT statement within a SELECT statement in order to get information from more than a single table. Another way to achieve such results, and more, is to Join multiple tables in a single query. While a query with a subselect displays columns only from the top table, joins can display columns from every table involved. Joins allow us to bring together multiple tables in one result set using a SELECT statement. The following statement, is an example of joining two tables in a query and would display all columns for both the Employee and the JobHistory tables:

```
SELECT * FROM Employee, JobHistory
```

Using joins in this manner, without restricting conditions, is dangerous because they can produce huge result sets. A join is actually a **Cartesian product** of the tables involved. We normally associate a product with multiplication. Cartesian products (named after Rene Descartes, the father of analytical geometry) work on sets.

For example, the product of the two sets {1,2,3} and {1,2} is the set of pairs:

{<1,1>,<1,2>,<2,1>,<2,2>,<3,1>,<3,2>}.

Note that the number of elements in the Cartesian product is indeed the product of the number of elements in the two sets. In mathematical terms, the cardinality of the product is the product of the cardinalities (isn't that a mouthful?!). Joining two tables without restrictions produces a joined table in which the number of rows (cardinality) is the product of the number of rows in each individual table involved in the join. Thus, our previous statement will produce a table of 12*15 = 180 rows. This is not what we normally want, and this is where the WHERE clause helps us out.

Using the WHERE Clause in Joins.

The general syntax for standard table joins is as follows:

```
SELECT <ColumnList> FROM <TableList> WHERE <Condition>
```

ColumnList is comma delimited, with each item but the last followed by a comma. The same applies to TableList. The Condition in the WHERE clause essentially defines the relationship between the two tables to be joined. For example, consider the following statement:

```
SELECT *
FROM Employee, JobHistory
WHERE Employee.Employee_ID = JobHistory.Employee_ID
```

Here we require the system to limit its selection to matching pairs only. In other words, a row is only selected if a particular Employee_ID value exists in both the Employee table and the JobHistory table. This will limit the selection to:

Employee_ID	Person_ID	History_ID	Employee_ID	Job_Code	Date_Started	Date_Ended
1	5	3	1	CIO	1/1/1990	12/31/1994
1	5	4	1	COO	1/1/1995	12/31/1998
1	5	5	1	CEO	1/1/1999	NULL
2	1	1	2	COO	1/1/1990	12/31/1992
2	1	2	2	CEO	1/1/1993	12/31/1995
3	2	13	3	CSM	7/1/1992	NULL
4	3	11	4	MRS	1/1/1990	NULL
6	4	15	6	COO	1/1/1999	NULL

Employee_ID	Person_ID	History_ID	Employee_ID	Job_Code	Date_Started	Date_Ended
7	8	6	7	CO	1/1/1990	12/31/1990
7	8	7	7	CSM	1/1/1991	06/30/1992
7	8	8	7	PA	7/1/1992	12/31/1994
7	8	9	7	CIO	1/1/1995	NULL
9	10	12	9	CO	1/1/1991	NULL
10	9	10	10	MRC	1/1/1990	NULL
12	19	14	12	CO	7/1/1992	NULL

If, for example, a new employee joins and we add that person to the Employee table (Employee_ID = 13) but haven't got round to adding them to the JobHistory table, then that row would not be included in the result set.

> **In SQL Server, you can achieve the same effect using the INNER JOIN syntax, which is not supported in Oracle.**

Note that we use qualifiers where column names in two tables are identical, as is the case in the Employee_ID column. We explicitly identify a column with a particular table by using a period between the table name and the column name:

```
Table_Name.Column_Name
```

There is no need to use qualifiers if the column names are different and some people would argue that it would be much easier if we used different column names in different tables. This would require us to use synonyms, though, and we'd start running out of those rather quickly. It would also put an unnecessary burden on our memories. We're much better off using polymorphism. We name items according to their content and usage, and we qualify them by their origin.

This gives a new twist to the way we define the ColumnList. The ColumnList is a comma-separated list of qualified columns. A qualified column is of the form:

```
[TableName.]ColumnName | *
```

The vertical bar signifies the OR operator. Thus we have the column list as a (*) or, alternatively, as a comma delimited list of optionally qualified (that's what the square brackets signify) columns. The * can also be used to define the TableList.

Previously, we saw how to construct a subquery to provide us with the name of our computer operators. Now let's see how we do the same thing using table joins. Again, we will approach this in a step-by-step manner.

Step 1

Following our previous scheme, our first task is to obtain the appropriate
Employee_ID values from the JobHistory table:

```
SELECT Employee_ID
FROM JobHistory
WHERE Job_Code = 'CO' AND Date_Ended IS NULL
```

EMPLOYEE_ID
9
12

Step 2

When constructing our subquery previously, we passed the Employee_ID values to
an outer query and used them to obtain the appropriate Person_ID values from the
Employee table. Here, however, we simply join the two tables and apply the correct
condition in the WHERE clause:

```
SELECT JobHistory.Employee_ID, Employee.Person_ID
FROM JobHistory, Employee
WHERE JobHistory.Employee_ID = Employee.Employee_ID
AND Job_Code = 'CO' AND Date_Ended IS NULL
```

Notice that we now qualify our column names. The result looks like this:

EMPLOYEE_ID	PERSON_ID
9	10
12	19

Step 3

In the final step, we join all three tables to get at the desired Last_Name values:

```
SELECT JobHistory.Employee_ID, Employee.Person_ID, Last_Name
FROM JobHistory, Employee, People
WHERE Employee.Person_ID = People.Person_ID
AND JobHistory.Employee_ID = Employee.Employee_ID
AND Job_Code = 'CO' AND Date_Ended IS NULL
```

The result looks like this:

EMPLOYEE_ID	PERSON_ID	LAST_NAME
9	10	Freud
12	19	Emmanuel

Let's now have a look at a keyword that will allow us to answer some interesting
queries.

The DISTINCT Keyword

The JobHistory table has multiple entries for some members of the Employee table,
a single entry for some and no entry at all for others. The last ones are of particular
interest. Why should we have a row in the Employee table that describes someone
who has never worked for us? Beats me, but it serves as a great example for the next
few sections.

Consider the following directives:

- ❑ Give me a list of our current employees
- ❑ Give me a list of all employees who have ever worked for us
- ❑ Give me a list of people in the Employee table who have actually never worked for us (we need to sort this out!).

We are going to find out how to provide this information.

Obtain a List of Current Employees

This is a fairly straightforward task. It is clear that, in the JobHistory table, any employee still working for the company will have a NULL value in the Date_Ended column. We then join tables to work back to the employees' names. Thus:

```
SELECT Last_Name
FROM JobHistory, Employee, People
WHERE Date_Ended IS NULL
AND Employee.Employee_ID = JobHistory.Employee_ID
AND Employee.Person_ID = People.Person_ID
ORDER BY Last_Name
```

LAST_NAME
▶ Abrams
Anthony
Blenheim
Caesar
Emmanuel
Freud
Perlman
Strange

Obtain a List of All Employees Who Have Ever Worked for the Company

If an employee is included in the JobHistory table, with a job code and start and end dates, then they must have worked for the company at some stage! So this is also a straightforward task – we simply get rid of one line of code:

```
SELECT Last_Name
FROM JobHistory, Employee, People
WHERE Employee.Employee_ID = JobHistory.Employee_ID
AND Employee.Person_ID = People.Person_ID
ORDER BY Last_Name
```

LAST_NAME
▶ Abrams
Anthony
Blenheim
Caesar
Caesar
Caesar
Emmanuel
Freud
Perlman
Steinzalts
Steinzalts
Strange
Strange
Strange
Strange

Well, all the correct names are there (trust me!) but this table is not very helpful. The problem is, as noted earlier, that some people have performed several different jobs for the company and so have multiple entries in the `JobHistory` table. Thus the names of these people appear several times in our result set. This problem is very easy to solve:

```
SELECT DISTINCT Last_Name
FROM JobHistory, Employee, People
WHERE Employee.Employee_ID = JobHistory.Employee_ID
AND Employee.Person_ID = People.Person_ID
```

We now clearly see that one name has been added to our table, that of **Steinzalts**:

LAST_NAME
Abrams
Anthony
Blenheim
Caesar
Emmanuel
Freud
Perlman
Steinzalts
Strange

The `DISTINCT` keyword merely disregards duplicated column values. Note also, that the `ORDER BY` clause is now redundant because use of the `DISTINCT` clause returns the rows in ascending order. However, if you want the results displayed in descending order you can add the last line back in as:

```
ORDER BY Last_Name DESC
```

Now let's tackle the third directive. There are several ways to go about this and we'll look at the most elegant way first, in the process introducing the concept of an outer join.

Outer Joins

The joins we have considered so far have been regular joins. In SQL Server and Access they are also known as Inner Joins. Rows are only included in the joined table if a matching column value exists in each separate table. Consider the following statement

```
SELECT Employee.Employee_ID, Employee.Person_ID, JobHistory.Job_Code
FROM Employee, JobHistory
WHERE Employee.Employee_ID = JobHistory.Employee_ID
```

A row will only be included in the joined table if an `Employee_ID` column value in the `Employee` table also exists in the `JobHistory` table:

EMPLOYEE_ID	PERSON_ID	JOB_CODE
2	1	COO
2	1	CEO
1	5	CIO
1	5	COO
1	5	CEO
7	8	CO
7	8	CSM
7	8	PA
7	8	CIO
10	9	MRC
4	3	MRS
9	10	CO
3	2	CSM
12	19	CO
6	4	COO

However, as we know, employees are included in the `Employee` table who have never worked for the company. Thus there will be no corresponding `Employee_ID` column value in the `JobHistory` table and these rows will not be included in the joined table. In this instance, of course, it is precisely these people in which we are interested. Make the following small adjustment to the previous section of code:

```
SELECT Employee.Employee_ID, Employee.Person_ID, JobHistory.Job_Code
FROM Employee, JobHistory
WHERE Employee.Employee_ID = JobHistory.Employee_ID (+)
```

You will see that we have three entries with a null value in the `Job_Code` column:

EMPLOYEE_ID	PERSON_ID	JOB_CODE
2	1	COO
2	1	CEO
3	2	CSM
4	3	MRS
5	6	
6	4	COO
7	8	CO
7	8	CSM
7	8	PA
7	8	CIO
8	7	
9	10	CO
10	9	MRC
11	13	
12	19	CO

Congratulations, you have just executed an **outer join** command. The `Employee` table is chosen as the primary table. Any rows in this table without matches in the `JobHistory` table stay in the results. When there was no corresponding `Employee_ID` value in the `JobHistory` table, the query returned a null value in the `Job_Code` column.

Note that every column in a table designated as an outer join table must have the (+) after the column name; and that no two outer join tables can be joined to each other.

> Note that at this stage we did not use the `DISTINCT` keyword in the query. It would not have done us any good anyway because where there are multiple entries per employee, each has a different (distinct) `Job_Code`.

Now that we have a joined table with null values in the Job_Code column, for the lazy sloths who have never worked for the company, we can use this to get at their names, in the usual fashion:

```
SELECT Last_Name, People.Person_ID, Employee.Employee_ID
FROM Employee, JobHistory, People
WHERE Employee.Employee_ID = JobHistory.Employee_ID (+)
AND JobHistory.Job_Code IS NULL
AND Employee.Person_ID = People.Person_ID
```

LAST_NAME	PERSON_ID	EMPLOYEE_ID
Cornwell	6	5
Cromwell	7	8
Feather	13	11

Access gives us the keywords LEFT JOIN or RIGHT JOIN for the same purpose. Access' syntax does not follow the ANSI SQL standard, but Oracle's does.

Outer joins are not a common occurrence. In a well-designed database we would not have any dangling records in the first place (they are only included in our tables for demonstration purposes!). I also do not recommend using any Oracle dialect in SQL if ADO is to be used in your VB program as the database conduit (see Chapter 10).

Combining a Join with a SubSelect

It is possible to create a hybrid of a SubSelect and a join. This is a SubSelect where the inner SELECT statement is a join. The following hybrid statement provides an alternative route to the names of our computer operators:

```
SELECT Last_Name
FROM People
WHERE Person_ID IN
    (SELECT Employee.Person_ID
        FROM Employee, JobHistory
            WHERE Employee.Employee_ID = JobHistory.Employee_ID
                AND Job_Code = 'CO' AND Date_Ended IS NULL)
```

I don't normally use such hybrids, but the hybrid serves to show that you can mix and match. With the introduction of a new keyword, EXISTS, we find we also have an alternative route to finding the names of the people included in the Employee table who have actually never worked for the company.

The EXISTS Keyword

Let's start with the simple statement that will retrieve the Employee_ID values of all people who *have* worked for the company at some stage:

```
SELECT DISTINCT Employee.Person_ID
FROM Employee, JobHistory
WHERE Employee.Employee_ID = JobHistory.Employee_ID
```

This statement may also be written using the EXISTS keyword:

```
SELECT DISTINCT Employee.Person_ID
FROM Employee, JobHistory
WHERE EXISTS
    (SELECT * FROM JobHistory
        WHERE Employee.Employee_ID = JobHistory.Employee_ID)
```

This adds an unnecessary level of complexity to the SQL, but it works. It becomes useful, in our example, only when we use it in the negative form to find out who in the Employee table has *never* worked for us:

```
SELECT DISTINCT Employee.Person_ID
FROM Employee, JobHistory
WHERE NOT EXISTS
    (SELECT * FROM JobHistory
        WHERE Employee.Employee_ID = JobHistory.Employee_ID)
```

Resulting in:

PERSON_ID
6
7
13

We simply put this into a bigger statement to produce the names:

```
SELECT Last_Name
FROM People
WHERE Person_ID IN
    (SELECT DISTINCT Employee.Person_ID
        FROM Employee, JobHistory
            WHERE NOT EXISTS
            (SELECT * FROM JobHistory
                WHERE Employee.Employee_ID = JobHistory.Employee_ID))
```

The result should look like this:

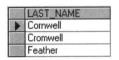

LAST_NAME
Cornwell
Cromwell
Feather

Using Aliases

The following statement is considered by some people to be too long (!):

```
SELECT Employee.Person_ID
FROM Employee, JobHistory
WHERE Employee.Employee_ID = JobHistory.Employee_ID
AND Job_Code = 'CO' AND Date_Ended IS NULL
```

They prefer to use shortcuts:

```
SELECT A.Person_ID
FROM Employee A, JobHistory B
WHERE A.Employee_ID = B.Employee_ID
AND Job_Code = 'CO' AND Date_Ended IS NULL
```

This is indeed somewhat shorter (and could be much shorter if the original statement were longer and more complex). What happened here is that we gave each table an alias by following each `Table_Name` in the `Table_List` with a space and another name (an alias). Thus, the `Employee` table is given the alias `A` and the `JobHistory` table the alias `B`. We then use these new aliases to qualify the column names in the `WHERE`, `SELECT`, `ORDER BY` and `GROUP BY` clauses.

In this circumstance, I am not a proponent of this trick. What do we gain? A few keystrokes. What do we lose? Readability. In SQL, as in VB programming, we normally write a statement but once, and maintain it for a very long time. The short-term gain of halving the keystrokes could cost us years of frustration because when we next read the statement its purpose will no longer be clear to us.

As we touched on briefly earlier in the chapter, we can also use aliases in column names:

```
[TableName.]ColumnName[ [AS] NewName]
```

If an alias is made up of two or more words and contains spaces, it must be enclosed in double quotes. Here are some examples:

```
EmployeeID AS EID, PersonID AS PID

EmployeeID AS "Employee ID", PersonID AS PID

EmployeeID EID, PersonID AS PID

EmployeeID, PersonID AS PID
```

When you work in the Oracle environment – SQL* PLUS – the results of the query are displayed as a succession of rows and columns. The top row contains the column names, the row below this places hyphens under each column name, then the selected rows come underneath these two. If we use an alias, then this will appear on the top line rather than the column name. If we have used complex or cryptic column names in our database, then using aliases will help to give the query a clearer meaning.

Aliasing may also be necessary when we use the UNION operator (as you will see in the following sections).

The DECODE Function

The DECODE function is a way of, well, decoding an expression. In the JobHistory table we have column values such as COO, MRC. Say you were producing a table for a report - would everybody know what these acronyms meant?

> *Fortunately for us, of course, we could simply obtain the information from the* JobDescription *table, but this may not always be the case.*

The general syntax for the DECODE function is as follows:

```
DECODE(Column_Name, Code1, Description1 [,Code2, Description2,] [,Code3,
Description3,] …,else)
```

It works like this:

```
SELECT Employee_ID,
    DECODE (Job_Code, 'CO', 'Operator',
                      'COO', 'President',
                      'CEO', 'Chairman',
                      'CIO', 'Chief Information Officer',
                      'CSM', 'Computer Shift Manager',
                      'MRC', 'Clerk',
                      'MRS', 'Supervisor',
                      'PGM', 'Programmer',
                      'PA', 'Analyst') Job_Title
FROM JobHistory
WHERE Date_Ended IS NULL
ORDER BY Employee_ID
```

The result is:

EMPLOYEE_ID	JOB_TITLE
1	Chairman
3	Computer Shift Mana
4	Supervisor
6	President
7	Chief Information Offi
9	Operator
10	Clerk
12	Operator

Note that Job_Title (outside the closing bracket of the DECODE function) acts as an alias for the new column in the result set. If we left it out, our Job_Title column would be named:

DECODE (Job_Code, 'CO', 'Operator',...

And this is a very funny column name.

Combining Queries with Set Operators

There is yet another family of complex queries which we use to combine the results of multiple queries. We do this using the following set operations

❑ UNION

❑ UNION ALL

❑ INTERSECT

❑ MINUS (the DIFFERENCE operator in ANSI SQL)

I would express the difference between a UNION query and a join as follows:

❑ Joins allow us to combine related tables of dissimilar structure

❑ UNIONs allow us to combine unrelated tables of similar structure

The syntax for a UNION query may look something like the following:

```
SELECT ColumnList1
FROM TableName
UNION [ALL]
SELECT ColumnList2
FROM TableName2
```

Each of the combined SELECT statements is in effect a temporary table. In effect we are combining these tables **vertically** (whereas joins can be thought of as combining tables horizontally).

As such, the tables must have identical data types on the columns chosen for the UNION (or UNION ALL, or INTERSECT, or MINUS) and each query involved in the UNION must produce the same number of columns.

In set theoretical terms:

A UNION of two sets is a set with all the members (elements) of each set, with each member counted once:

{a,b,c,d,e,f} UNION {c,d,e,f,g} produces {a,b,c,d,e,f,g}.

SQL (but not set theory) allows members to be counted twice (i.e. duplications) in the UNION ALL operation:

{a,b,c,d,e,f} UNION ALL {c,d,e,f,g} produces {a,b,c,d,e,f,c,d,e,f,g}

INTERSECT is used to find the members who belong to the two sets:

{a,b,c,d,e,f} INTERSECT {c,d,e,f,g} produces {c,d,e,f}

While UNION, and INTERSECT are commutative (which means that the order in which the sets are presented is not important) MINUS is directional. MINUS selects the elements in the minuend that are not in the subtrahend to produce the difference. The difference contains elements of the minuend:

{a,b,c,d,e,f} MINUS {c,d,e,f,g} produces {a,b}

but:

{c,d,e,f,g} MINUS {a,b,c,d,e,f} produces {g}.

To summarize (in SQL terms):

- ❑ UNION produces all the distinct rows that are in either SELECT statement, with each row appearing but once. The resulting rows are implicitly sorted.

- ❑ UNION ALL simply appends one table underneath the other, thus allowing duplicates.

- ❑ INTERSECT produces the distinct rows that are in the first table as well as in the second table.

- ❑ MINUS produces the distinct rows in the first table that are not in the second table.

Let us revisit three simple queries that we have encountered in this chapter:

- ❑ SELECT Last_Name FROM People

  WHERE Eye_Color NOT IN('Yellow', 'Gold', 'Ochre')

- ❑ SELECT Last_Name FROM People

  WHERE Eye_Color IN('Yellow', 'Gold', 'Ochre')

- ❑ SELECT Last_Name FROM People

The third query is equivalent to the UNION ALL of the first two queries and produces 21 names:

```
SELECT Last_Name FROM People
WHERE Eye_Color NOT IN('Yellow', 'Gold', 'Ochre')
UNION ALL
SELECT Last_Name FROM People
WHERE Eye_Color IN('Yellow', 'Gold', 'Ochre')
```

The order in which the names appear is different since the UNION ALL returns the one set followed by the other. Now, try to run the same statement as a mere UNION, and the result will be rather different:

```
SELECT Last_Name FROM People
WHERE Eye_Color NOT IN('Yellow', 'Gold', 'Ochre')
UNION
SELECT Last_Name FROM People
WHERE Eye_Color IN('Yellow', 'Gold', 'Ochre')
```

This code produces just 19 names and they are sorted alphabetically:

LAST_NAME
▶ Abrams
Anthony
Blenheim
Caesar
Cornwell
Cromwell
Emmanuel
Feather
Freud
Janice
Karabelle
McManus
Monken
Perlman
Steinzalts
Strange
Stroh
Summer
Winter

This is because the UNION operator, like its set theory equivalent, is returning each member just once, and SQL added to it an implied ORDER BY. This is the equivalent of:

```
SELECT DISTINCT Last_Name FROM People
```

Can we use such statements in place of the wasteful NOT IN? Yes but it does not help:

```
SELECT DISTINCT Last_Name FROM People
WHERE Eye_Color NOT IN ('Yellow', 'Gold', 'Ochre')
```

Will produce the same results as:

```
SELECT Last_Name FROM People
MINUS
(SELECT Last_Name FROM People WHERE Eye_Color IN ('Yellow', 'Gold', 'Ochre'))
```

This stands to reason because the statement NOT IN means the whole, take away those who are IN. But running the query this way is still as time consuming. We still did not escape spanning the whole table.

SQL is a language. As such you have to adhere to its rules. Even so there is no way to stop people from executing ill-advised queries. Here are two queries, each acceptable on its own:

```
SELECT Last_Name FROM People
```

```
SELECT First_Name FROM People
```

Now let's try to MINUS them:

```
SELECT Last_Name FROM People
MINUS
(SELECT First_Name FROM People)
```

Where each statement alone made sense the combination is really meaningless.

The result set looks like this:

LAST_NAME
Abrams
Anthony
Blenheim
Caesar
Cornwell
Cromwell
Feather
Freud
Janice
Karabelle
McManus
Menken
Perlman
Steinzalts
Strange
Stroh
Summer
Winter

Note that the table has only 18 entries. If you look carefully you'll notice that we've lost the Emmanuel family – it is also a first name - and one of the McManus siblings because MINUS produces a distinct list.

Again, SQL is a very rich and powerful language, allowing us to solve the same problem in many ways, but it also powerful enough to lead you astray. Be careful what ye ask for it might be given unto you.

We now know how to slice and dice the information in the database. For most of humanity this is more than enough. If you are satisfied with just using SQL for queries you may even want to stop here and move on to the next Chapter. However, readers who wish to use ADO will definitely need to know how to modify database data using Data Manipulation Language (DML). Using ADO with Oracle requires you to use the ADO Command object for simple manipulations that you should have been able to do in the Recordset object, and that may be done in the OO4O Dynaset object.

Even if you don't think you need the Data Manipulation Language now, I strongly urge all of you to stay the course. You're always better off knowing more.

Data Modification Using SQL

DML is comprised of three basic statements:

❑ DELETE – Used to remove rows from tables

❑ INSERT– Used to add new information rows to a table

❑ UPDATE – Used to change existing rows

If you wish to continue executing code from your VB program, you will have to make a small refinement to the DataGrid control to allow the insertion, updating or deleting of records. To do this, right-click on the DataGrid and select **Properties** and then check the AllowAddNew and AllowDelete check boxes. Bear in mind though that this is a simple program, not really designed for these operations. When you execute DML from this program you will receive a message warning you that "The operation requested by the application is not allowed if the object is closed", followed by an error message "Application-defined or object-defined error". However, the command *will* be executed!

Personally, for this sort of data manipulation, I find it easier and quicker to execute these commands from SQL*PLUS, and this philosophy is adopted from here in. However, feel free to use your VB program!

The DELETE Statement

Information that was viable and current yesteryear may no longer be relevant today. It clutters the database and causes a waste of space and a reduction in speed. We need to be able to trim it out or archive it. This is where the DELETE statement helps. SQL allows us to delete rows from tables and gives us the power to delete all the rows at once or to delete them one by one. Its syntax is very simple:

```
DELETE FROM <TableName> [WHERE <Condition>];
```

Issue this command with care. You might delete the entire contents of tables (the table structure will still be there, it will just be empty). If the optional WHERE clause is missing, or written such that all records match the clause, all the rows in the table will be removed.

Let's look at the employee table. As you remember from earlier Employee_ID 5 does not have a JobHistory (he's never worked for us). Let's remove his record from the table:

```
DELETE FROM Employee WHERE Employee_ID = 5;
```

This is a fine surgical removal of a single record. I also showed you earlier how to use the NOT EXISTS keyword. We will now use this for the removal of all the rows in the Employee table for people who have never worked for us. Here is how this is done:

The SELECT statement:

```
SELECT DISTINCT Employee.Employee_ID FROM Employee, JobHistory
WHERE NOT EXISTS
(SELECT * FROM JobHistory
WHERE Employee.Employee_ID = JobHistory.Employee_ID);
```

Returns two Employee_IDs: **8** and **11** (A minute ago it would have returned 3 such IDs, but we've just deleted Employee_ID = 5).

Let us use this statement as a subquery for the WHERE clause in the DELETE statement:

```
DELETE FROM Employee
WHERE Employee_ID IN
(SELECT DISTINCT Employee.Employee_ID FROM Employee, JobHistory
WHERE NOT EXISTS
(SELECT * FROM JobHistory
WHERE Employee.Employee_ID = JobHistory.Employee_ID));
```

This will remove the 2 offending rows from the table.

Here is the total operation and its results. Note that Employee_IDs 5, 8, and 11 no longer exist, as evidenced by the SELECT * FROM EMPLOYEE statement below:

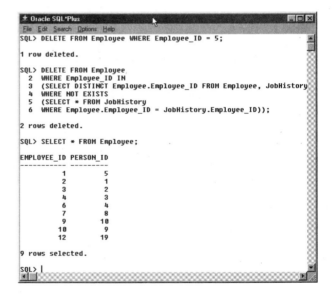

Here is an interesting twist. Oracle is different compared to most other database providers like SQL Server and Access, where each DML action is executed immediately.

In SQL Server you can request for a group of statements to be carried out in a transaction. Access does not support transactions at all, and would have removed the rows immediately. It even warns you that this is a one way street and that once done the rows are lost forever.

Transactions

Oracle gives you the opportunity to regret your last actions. So before we plunge into the other DML statements, we're going to discuss the concept of **transactions**.

Oracle just deleted the 3 rows from your personal copy of the database. If many people are using the database simultaneously, each works in his private workspace. The rows that you've just deleted still exist in the database, but are locked. This means that other users cannot get to them until you release them, but they are still there!

By issuing the DELETE statement (and similarly for the UPDATE and INSERT statements we will discuss later), we have made a change to the database, but this has not been made permanent. Any changes we have made are not visible to any other user except ourselves.

The changes made are considered to be part of a transaction, which is a sequence of SQL statements that Oracle treats as a single unit. The statements involved in a transaction either succeed together or fail together (you can almost hear the Three Musketeers: "All for one and one for all") and all the changes will be made permanent at the same time. Let us consider an every day example:

In a banking environment, customers will want to move money from one account to another. This, in fact, involves two operations: taking the money from the first account and placing it into the second. If the first operation was successful, but the second was not, the customers would not be very happy, and would soon move to another bank. A transaction wraps these two events together such that they both work or neither works.

Oracle automatically starts a transaction when you execute your first DML statement either at the start of a session, or immediately after the previous transaction. This transaction will then need to be committed to make the changes to the database permanent.

How, then, do we do this? We use one of the Transaction Control Language (TCL) statements: COMMIT. If we follow our DELETE with:

```
COMMIT;
```

The changes become effective and the deleted rows no longer exist.

A user need not always explicitly issue the COMMIT statement. Under the following circumstances statements are automatically committed:

❑ Starting an Oracle session with SET AUTOCOMMIT ON causes each line afterwards to be automatically committed (there is also no need to add semicolons on the end of session commands).

❑ Issuing a DDL (Data Definition Language) statement, such as CREATE TABLE, causes an automatic commit and because a commit is a session command, it commits your DML as well. Be careful not to mix and match your DML with DDL. If you want to do both in one session, do the DDL first. I always do DDL and DML in separate sessions.

❑ DML done within ADO, Oracle Objects for OLE, Access (Oracle through Access), or a Data Control commits automatically unless it is done in a transaction.

How do we retract an erroneous deletion? By using another TCL statement: ROLLBACK. This command:

```
ROLLBACK;
```

undeletes the rows from your private copy and releases the lock you've held on the 3 rows, thus allowing the other users to see them.

An important concept with the ROLLBACK statement is the SAVEPOINT command. This is a marker you can set within your transaction to which you may ROLLBACK. Savepoints allow you to ROLLBACK parts of your current transaction, using ROLLBACK TO SAVEPOINT <savepoint name>. This would result in the following:

❑ Only statements executed after the savepoint are rolled back

❑ The specific savepoint is preserved, but all savepoints created after this one are lost

❑ Any tables and rows that have acquired locks since that savepoint are released, but all locks acquired previous to the savepoint are kept

❑ The transaction is still active; it can be continued

Savepoints are useful within long transactions. Assume the number of people who had never worked for us was larger. We could run a large series of deletes to remove them; if we used savepoints and then made an error, we would not have to resubmit every statement.

A transaction also ends when you do one of the following:

❑ Execute a DDL command. If the current transaction contains any DML statements, this transaction is committed, and the DDL statement is executed as a new transaction.

❑ Exit your SQL*PLUS session or VB application (the transaction will be committed)

❑ Abnormally terminate your SQL*PLUS session or VB application (the transaction will be rolled back)

In an Oracle SQL*PLUS session all of your actions are done in a transaction state.

One of the reasons Oracle hit it big was that it allowed the system to work with a much higher number of locked records than other early RDBs (particularly DB2). This, by the way is still true. The higher the number of locks the system tolerates the better, of course, but it is never limitless. Once it overflows its lock capacity, the system freezes (you'll be notified and asked to commit or rollback). Long before this happens it starts to show sluggish performance.

Other vendors solve the problem by a 'No regrets' policy. This means that if you don't declare your next actions to be a transaction, you cannot ROLLBACK. Oracle, on the other hand, considers your session to be a transaction, from the moment you sign on to the moment you log off. This can put a heavy burden on the system and requires the users to behave responsibly. We are professionals and in our case there is no excuse to lack of responsibility.

So what do we do? We COMMIT early and frequently and ROLLBACK as soon as we can (if need be); making sure that transactions are kept as short and fast as possible. If we overlook committing our changes, we will eventually end up with users accessing data that is rather different from the current data, which we have been continuously changing. This will decrease data integrity and, eventually, we will not be able to manipulate the locked rows.

The INSERT statement

There are many ways to add new information to a table. For huge amounts of information that does not as yet reside in the database, I prefer to use the Oracle's SQL*LOADER utility, which we are not going to discuss in this book. This utility is normally used just once, at the time we start a new database, or convert from another vendor's database, or from a pre-existing flat file. You may also add new rows through an ADO Recordset or an OO4O Dynaset, but the INSERT statement is the way to do it directly.

The INSERT statement's syntax is one of two flavors:

Single Row INSERT

The first form of the INSERT statement just creates one row. The syntax is:

```
INSERT INTO <TableName> [(<ColumnList>)] VALUES (<ValueList>);
```

Where ColumnList is a comma-delimited list of column names, and ValueList is a comma-delimited list of values. ColumnList is optional. This statement allows us to INSERT a *single* row.

The order in which we list (or not) the columns has to correspond exactly with the order of the values. The values have to correspond exactly with the column's data-type. Let's look at two examples:

```
INSERT INTO People
VALUES (Person_ID_SEQ.NEXTVAL, 'Marvelous', 'Marvin', 'H', '01-JAN-1951', 'M',
'Brown');
```

We are using the pseudo column Person_ID_SEQ.NEXTVAL as the value of the PERSON_ID field in the inserted row. This guarantees that the column will remain unique as is required because it is the primary key.

This statement will insert a new person into the People table. Because the statement does not include a ColumnList, we had to give a value to every column. How do we know the order of the columns? We issue a DESCRIBE command (DESC for short):

```
DESC People;
```

Which describes each column in the table, and lists them in the order they were created.

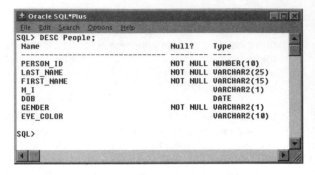

Note that the DESC statement does not show you the full information about the table. Conspicuously missing are the primary key and default constraints (these are discussed further in the next chapter, DDL).

The statement below uses column names:

```
INSERT INTO People (Person_ID, Last_Name,
First_Name, M_I, DOB, Gender)
VALUES (Person_ID_SEQ.NEXTVAL, 'Marvelous',
'Marvin', NULL, '01-JAN-1951', NULL);
```

This results in an error. Why an error? When we defined the table we did not allow NULLs in the Gender column.

```
+ Oracle SQL*Plus                                            _ □ X
File  Edit  Search  Options  Help
SQL> INSERT INTO People (Person_ID, Last_Name,
  2  First_Name, M_I, DOB, Gender)
  3  VALUES (Person_ID_SEQ.NEXTVAL, 'Marvelous',
  4  'Marvin', NULL, '01-JAN-1951', NULL)
  5  ;
INSERT INTO People (Person_ID, Last_Name,
            *
ERROR at line 1:
ORA-01400: cannot insert NULL into ("SCOTT"."PEOPLE"."GENDER")

SQL> |
```

We correct it and issue it again, this time with a proper gender:

```
INSERT INTO People (Person_ID, Last_Name,
First_Name, M_I, DOB, Gender)
VALUES (Person_ID_SEQ.NEXTVAL, 'Marvelous',
'Marvin', NULL, '01-JAN-1951', 'M');
```

```
+ Oracle SQL*Plus                                            _ □ X
File  Edit  Search  Options  Help
SQL> INSERT INTO People (Person_ID, Last_Name,
  2  First_Name, M_I, DOB, Gender)
  3  VALUES (Person_ID_SEQ.NEXTVAL, 'Marvelous',
  4  'Marvin', NULL, '01-JAN-1951', 'M')
  5  ;
1 row created.

SQL> SELECT * FROM People
  2  WHERE Last_Name = 'Marvelous';

PERSON_ID LAST_NAME                 FIRST_NAME      M DOB        G EYE_COLOR
--------- ------------------------- --------------- - --------- - ----------
       22 Marvelous                 Marvin          H 01-JAN-51 M Brown
       25 Marvelous                 Marvin            01-JAN-51 M Brown

SQL>
```

Note that here I neglected to list the `Eye_Color` and it will default to `Brown`. I also set the middle initial to `NULL`, but that is allowed. Note also that we have two rows returned, as we have carried out two `INSERT`s in this section.

Multiple Row INSERT

The second flavor of the `INSERT` statement allows us to insert multiple rows, (possibly none, or even one). We do this by selecting from data that already exists in the database.

```
INSERT INTO <TableName1> [(<ColumnList1>)]
SELECT <ColumnList2> FROM <TableName2>
[WHERE <Condition>];
```

In this type of statement the rows will be inserted using the result of the `SELECT` statement that is embedded in it. `ColumnList1` and `ColumnList2` have to correspond exactly and their data-types have to agree. Again, omitting `ColumnList1` implies that all the columns (*) are used, in the exact order given by the table's description.

If all the information is already in the database why do we want to insert it again? Remember that we espouse only a single occurrence of atomic data. Well, it helps when doing reports and when we want to replicate data in data warehouses.

Here is a feasible scenario. Ms. Julia Caesar, our CEO, wants to know who joined the ranks of our employees last month. With just 7 active employees it would be easiest to just eyeball the roster, but let's do it anyway. We create a report table and tell Julia to do run the following query on her terminal:

```
SELECT * FROM LastMonthsRecruits;
```

We have already defined the table and it includes: `Last_Name`, `First_Name`, `Gender`, `Job_Code` and `Date_Started`.

In July 1999 Ziggy Freud, our operator, ran the following script:

```
DELETE FROM LastMonthsRecruits
INSERT INTO LastMonthRecruits
SELECT Last_Name, First_Name, Gender, Job_Code, Date_Started
FROM People, Employee, JobHistory
WHERE People.Person_ID = Employee.Person_ID
AND Employee.Employee_ID = JobHistory.Employee_ID
AND Date_Started
BETWEEN '01-JUN-1999' AND '30-JUN-1999'
Commit;
```

As the months are changing, we need to use a DELETE first to remove the old data before we see the new. This way the CEO only sees what she needs.

```
Oracle SQL*Plus
File  Edit  Search  Options  Help

SQL> INSERT INTO  LastMonthRecruits
  2  SELECT Last_Name, First_Name, Gender, Job_Code, Date_Started
  3  FROM People, Employee, JobHistory
  4  WHERE People.Person_ID = Employee.Person_ID
  5  AND Employee.Employee_ID = JobHistory.Employee_ID
  6  AND Date_Started
  7  BETWEEN '01-JUN-1999' AND '30_JUN-1999';

0 rows created.

SQL> Commit;

Commit complete.

SQL>
```

Running the Populate.sql Script

The Populate.sql script contains five groups of INSERT statements – one for each table. The order of insertion is important. You must have loaded all the People before you can load the Employees. You must load all the Employees before you can load Salary, and you must also load the JobDescription before you can load the JobHistory. The script is already in the proper order. The script cannot run without creating the sequences. Here is one line from each group:

```
INSERT INTO PEOPLE VALUES (PERSON_ID_SEQ.NEXTVAL, 'Steinzalts', 'Adin', 'R',
'01-JAN-1944', 'M', 'Green');

INSERT INTO JOBDESCRIPTION VALUES ('MRC', 'Mail Room Clerk', 6, 91, 18);

INSERT INTO EMPLOYEE VALUES (EMPLOYEE_ID_SEQ.NEXTVAL, 5);

INSERT INTO JOBHISTORY VALUES (HISTORY_ID_SEQ.NEXTVAL, 2, 'COO', '01-JAN-
1990', '31-DEC-1992');

INSERT INTO SALARY VALUES (SALARY_ID_SEQ.NEXTVAL, 2, 73500, '01-JAN-1990',
'31-DEC-1990');
```

The UPDATE Statement

Information is never stagnant. People change, move and even die, bills get paid, (eventually) and new services are rendered. In short we must be able to update our information constantly. In SQL we use the UPDATE command:

```
UPDATE <TableName>
SET <ColumnValueList>
[WHERE <Condition>];
```

ColumnValueList is a comma-delimited list of the following structure:

```
ColumnName = Value
```

The list must contain at least one such pair. Values may be any literal, Oracle function, or the result of a SubSelect that returns a single column from a single row (atomic SubSelect). Here are a few examples:

A Simple UPDATE Command

Here we modify the M_I and Eye_Color column values for Marvin Marvelous (if you have been executing the code you will have two people of this name in the People table (you know how to correct this):

```
UPDATE People SET M_I = 'H', Eye_Color = 'Gray'
WHERE Last_Name = 'Marvelous';
```

```
+ Oracle SQL*Plus                                                    _ □ ×
File  Edit  Search  Options  Help
SQL> UPDATE People SET M_I = 'H', Eye_Color = 'Gray'
  2  WHERE Last_Name = 'Marvelous'
  3  ;

2 rows updated.

SQL> SELECT * FROM People WHERE Last_Name = 'Marvelous';

PERSON_ID LAST_NAME                       FIRST_NAME       M DOB        G EYE_COLOR
--------- ------------------------------  ---------------- - ---------- - ----------
       22 Marvelous                       Marvin           H 01-JAN-51 M Gray
       25 Marvelous                       Marvin           H 01-JAN-51 M Gray

SQL>
```

While we're at it let us, once and for all, correct Mr. Menken's record:

```
UPDATE People SET Gender = 'M'
WHERE Last_Name = 'Menken';
```

```
+ Oracle SQL*Plus                                                    _ □ ×
File  Edit  Search  Options  Help
SQL> UPDATE People SET Gender = 'M'
  2  WHERE Last_Name = 'Menken'
  3  ;

1 row updated.

SQL> SELECT * FROM People WHERE Last_Name = 'Menken';

PERSON_ID LAST_NAME                       FIRST_NAME       M DOB        G EYE_COLOR
--------- ------------------------------  ---------------- - ---------- - ----------
       17 Menken                          Manus            M 04-JUL-76 M Red

SQL> |
```

Using Formulae in an UPDATE

```
UPDATE Salary
SET Income = Income * 1.1;
```

This will give everybody a raise of 10 percent. Every income in every row will be multiplied by 1.1. This is a bad idea. Our Salary table is in fact a history table. We don't really want to multiply past salaries by 1.1. If we do we lose valuable historical data. Again be careful what ye ask!

This request, in which we limit our change to current salaries, makes much more sense. This is because a record in which there is no end date is obviously current.

```
UPDATE Salary
SET Income = Income * 1.1
WHERE Date_Ended IS NULL;
```

Here is how it was before:

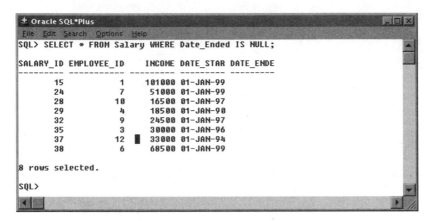

And here is the update and the results:

Summary

The SQL SELECT statement is a very powerful tool. In this chapter we've learned how to garner complex information in a variety of ways. Which way is best depends on the database design, and especially on how the tables are indexed.

We then went on to learn how to add new rows to a database table, how to get rid of superfluous rows and how to update existing rows. We have also covered transactions and how they work. Note that unlike the SELECT statement that allowed you to deal with one or many tables at once, the DML updates just one table at a time. When you've read Chapters 1, 3 and 4 as well, you are now in a position to completely build and maintain a database. Oracle, however, goes even further. It has a built in language for complex manipulation of data. This is PL/SQL and is dealt with in Chapter 13.

The key to writing efficient code is to avoid the superfluous and especially the meaningless. It is well worth the your time to put the material to use soon (and review it as needed) so as to cement the concepts that have been covered.

For now let's learn some more SQL - it's time for DDL!

3

Creating and Managing Database Tables

In most circumstances, we VB programmers arrive on the scene when a database has already been designed and a skeleton with test data has been put in place. Thus, in Chapter 2, we covered the fundamentals of database queries and data manipulation in some detail. Occasionally, however, we get the royal treatment and join the team from day one. That's when we wish to know how to do all these mysterious things that the database administrator (DBA) does in his or her sanctum sanctorum.

Some of these activities are outside our jurisdiction and will not be discussed in this book. They include:

❑ Creating and managing the database itself – for example, using the CREATE DATABASE and ALTER DATABASE commands to define the name of the database, log files, data files and other parameters. For further information I would refer you to the Oracle technet website (http://technet.oracle.com).

❑ Creating and managing **tablespaces** - a table space is a pre-assigned storage unit in an Oracle database. You may, for example, assign one tablespace for each set of user data (or for each application accessing the database).

❑ Creating Users, assigning user privileges and permissions.

Other activities better fit the role of a developer. These include creating and managing:

❑ Tables (including associated constraints and indexes)
❑ Sequences
❑ Views
❑ Stored procedures
❑ Triggers.

In this chapter we will investigate the creation and management of tables, sequences and views. Stored procedures and triggers will be dealt with in Chapter 13.

Of the three scripts introduced in Chapter 1, we have already executed the `CreateIt` script, which creates and alters the database objects that comprise the relational database of our HR application; and the `Populate` script, which loads the Human Resources database tables with sample data. I would like to start this chapter with a clean slate so open up SQL*PLUS and execute the `ClearIt` script. This will remove all of our tables, sequences and constraints but fear not, you still have the `CreateIt` script so you can recreate the tables at any time.

The SQL code in the `CreateIt` and `ClearIt` scripts forms part of the Data Definition Language, which is based around the CREATE, ALTER and DROP commands. By the end of this chapter you will understand the fundamentals of DDL, and thus the inner workings of both the `CreateIt` and the `ClearIt` scripts.

The HR Database Tables

In the introduction to this book we discussed the importance, and some of the features of, a well-designed relational database. Well, you'll be glad to hear that the design phase has been done for you! The following diagram (which follows the IDEF1X standard) shows all of the HR tables, the fields present in each one and the relationships that exist between each of the tables:

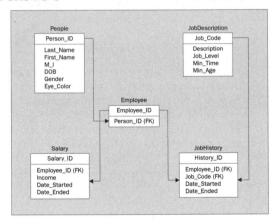

IDEF1X is the data element of the Integrated Definition Method (IDEF) standard. This standard was first developed for and by the US Air Force in 1979.

Occupying the upper compartment of each table in the diagram is the primary key (PK) column for that table. As you will recall from our discussion in the introduction to this book, in order to serve as PK, every value in this column must be unique (no two rows in the table can have the same value for that column). For every value there is at most one row (for some values there are none), for every row there is exactly one value. When a PK is designated, Oracle will automatically make an index using this column. The foreign key columns are denoted (FK). All of the relationships defined are of the one-to-many variety – marked in our diagram by a connector that ends with an arrowhead on the "many" side of the relationship.

Since the tables were designed for a simple HR application it is no surprise that we have the Employee table at the center. The PK of the Employee table (Employee_ID) references FKs in both the JobHistory and the Salary tables. The JobHistory table is also related to the JobDescription Table, where the job descriptions, and levels are maintained. Personal information (names, genders and dates of birth etc.) is stored in the People table. That's why the pivotal Employee table uses the Person_ID as a foreign key.

From our definitions of PKs and FKs, and from our rules of referential integrity, we know that any value entered into an FK column must already exist in the PK column that it references. In terms of the relationship between the People and Employee tables, this means that we cannot create an employee until his persona is in place. Conversely, and generally speaking, we cannot delete or modify a PK column value if it "points" to a corresponding value in the FK column. To do so would cause the production of orphaned records in the child table.

> *Oracle will actually allow us to delete PK column values, as long as we enable "cascade deletes" of related fields. This means that if a row is deleted from a primary table, all related records would also be removed in a cascade event. We will see how to do this shortly, in the Foreign Key Constraint section. Oracle does not have a cascade update option – we have to mimic this behavior using a stored procedure.*

For a column (or a concatenation of columns) to be an FK, it must first be a PK (or a UNIQUE key) of its own table. Can you tell me why? One reason is performance. To check that the value exists, it is best to have it accessed via an index. So why not just require that the foreign key be indexed on the foreign table? It must also be unique, as in a one-to-many relationship between the foreign table and the referencing table.

We are now ready to discuss the DDL commands that comprise our scripts. You may execute the commands from our Visual Basic View program, but you will receive the same "Object Closed" as described when modifying table data in Chapter 2 (the object *will* be created). However, it is more usual to execute such commands from the SQL*PLUS window, and this is the practice followed in this chapter.

We build database objects by issuing the appropriate CREATE command. We define our objects as we create them. The most complex creation is that of a table, which we will deal with first.

The CREATE TABLE Command

As intimated above, this command not only lets us create a table – it allows us to, for example, enforce various constraints, define default values and index columns. With all of this information folded into one CREATE TABLE command, it can look a bit overwhelming. For example, here is the full CREATE TABLE command for the People table:

```
CREATE TABLE People
(
PERSON_ID      NUMBER(10) CONSTRAINT PK_PEOPLE PRIMARY KEY,
LAST_NAME      VARCHAR2(25) NOT NULL,
FIRST_NAME     VARCHAR2(15) NOT NULL,
M_I            VARCHAR2(1),
DOB            DATE,
GENDER         VARCHAR2(1) NOT NULL,
EYE_COLOR      VARCHAR(10) DEFAULT 'Brown'
);
```

And here is the one for the `Employee` table:

```
CREATE TABLE Employee
(
EMPLOYEE_ID    NUMBER(10)
   CONSTRAINT PK_EMPLOYEE PRIMARY KEY,
PERSON_ID      NUMBER(10)
   CONSTRAINT PEOPLE_FK_EMPLOYEE REFERENCES People(PERSON_ID)
);
```

You can execute these commands from the SQL*PLUS window and the full tables will be created. We will now work through the creation of such commands in a step-by-step fashion.

We'll start with the most basic form of this command, which simply identifies the column names, their data types and, optionally, their size. The general syntax is:

```
CREATE TABLE TableName
(ColumnName DATA_TYPE[(a [,b])]);
```

The basic `CREATE TABLE` command for the `Salary` table, for example, would look as follows:

```
CREATE TABLE Salary
(
SALARY_ID      NUMBER(10),
EMPLOYEE_ID    NUMBER(10),
INCOME         NUMBER(8,2),
DATE_STARTED   DATE,
DATE_ENDED     DATE
);
```

The equivalent statement for the `People` table would be:

```
CREATE TABLE People
(
PERSON_ID      NUMBER(10),
LAST_NAME      VARCHAR2(25),
FIRST_NAME     VARCHAR2(15),
M_I            VARCHAR2(1),
DOB            DATE,
GENDER         VARCHAR2(1),
EYE_COLOR      VARCHAR2(10)
);
```

You will find that the syntax of the CREATE TABLE command varies considerably from one database provider to the next. One of the reasons for this is the different data types that each provider accepts. Another reason is that vendors tend to provide a unique mechanism for creating constraints and keys. Let's investigate the data types accepted by Oracle.

> *Oracle allows us to create **partitioned** tables, using the* partition by
> range <ColumnName> *syntax, as part of the* CREATE TABLE *command.*
> *See http://technet.Oracle.com for further details.*

Oracle Data Types

Oracle is rich with data types. Each such data type is identified by an integer (VB integer) code. Later, in Chapter 7, when we investigate the Fields collection of an OO4O dynaset, we'll encounter such codes again. Here are the various data types:

DATA_TYPE	Code	Description
CHAR(Size)	96	Fixed length character field. The size is in bytes and must be 1 to a maximum of 2000.
NCHAR(Size)	96	A fixed length national (that's what the N signifies) character field of up to 2000 bytes in size. The length of the character depends on the alphabet used. Minimum length is 1 character – however long that is. Some national character sets are fixed-width, with each character occupying a fixed number of bytes. Other sets are variable width. We're not going to discuss the National Language Sets (NLS) in this book.
VARCHAR(Size)	1	An archaic synonym to VARCHAR2. Use VARCHAR2 instead. In other databases VARCHAR may be the norm.
VARCHAR2(Size) (#)	1	A variable length character field. Oracle will only store what you use without trailing blanks, but limits the field to a maximum defined by the Size argument. The field cannot contain more than 4000 bytes. The number of characters depends on the alphabet or character set used.
NVARCHAR2(Size) (#)	1	Same as VARCHAR2 only using a national character set. Not used in this book.

DATA_TYPE	Code	Description
NUMBER [(p [,s])] (#) Also: DECIMAL (does not accept size or decimal digits as argument) INTEGER (does not accept decimal digit as argument) SMALLINT (as *NUMBER*)	2	Stores positive and negative numbers with a magnitude as little as 10** -130 to as large as 9.999…**125. The maximum precision (number of digits displayed) is 38 plus space for a decimal point and a sign. The optional arguments p and s stand for precision and scale. Precision is the number of digits displayed. Scale is the number of digits displayed after the decimal point. NUMBER(8,2) will display 8 digits with 2 decimal places. Just a penny short of a million. NUMBER without scale and precision is a floating-point number with a precision of 38. NUMBER(10) is equivalent to NUMBER(10,0) – no decimal point and ten digits displaying.
FLOAT[(b)]	2	FLOAT is the ANSI-equivalent of NUMBER without a precision and scale. It is supported for compatibility. In FLOAT(b), b is the number of binary digits in the floating point number We don't use FLOAT much in business processing (NUMBER will do just as well).
LONG (#) (*)	8	A long variable character field of up to 2 gigabytes. LONG is restricted in usage. A table cannot contain more than a single LONG column. LONG columns cannot be indexed (or used as primary keys). They cannot be used in the WHERE clause of SELECT or in a subquery, or function. We'll discuss LONG further with the GetChunk and AppendChunk methods of OO4O and ADO, in Chapters 8 and 12.
DATE	12	Any date and time from 1-JAN-4712 BC to 31-DEC-4712 AD.

DATA_TYPE	Code	Description
RAW(Size) (#)	23	Binary data up to 255 bytes long. Binary data is not converted by Oracle and is sent as is – the recipient does the interpretation of the data. The data is variable in length and Oracle only uses what it gets without any padding.
LONG RAW (#) (*)	24	Raw binary data up to 2 gigabytes long. Because of its length, it suffers from the same restrictions as LONG.
ROWID (#)	69	ROWID is a unique identifier of a row in the database – not just the table. There are no two rows in the database with the same ROWID. I hardly ever use it and then only as a pseudo column. Oracle cannot update a row without the ROWID. In a read-only dynaset there is no ROWID. See Chapter 8, on Oracle Objects for OLE.
MLSLABEL (#)	106	Used only for backwards compatibility.
CLOB (*)	112	A character large object containing single byte characters. Varying-width character sets are not supported. Maximum size is 4 gigabytes. See the GetChunk and AppendChunk methods of ADO and OO4O, Chapters 8 and 12.
NCLOB (*)	112	Same as CLOB, only using national character set. Again no variable-width character sets. See the GetChunk and AppendChunk methods of ADO and OO4O, Chapters 8 and 12.
BLOB (*)	113	A binary large object of up to 4 gigabytes. Why should we use LONG RAW with only 2 gigabytes when we have this behemoth? See the GetChunk and AppendChunk methods of ADO and OO4O, Chapters 8 and 12.
BFILE (#)	114	A locator for a binary operating system file that resides on the same server as the database. Such a file can be up to 4 gigabytes.

(*) You will have noticed various references to the ADO or OO4O `GetChunk` and `AppendChunk` methods. When using large columns or columns containing raw data, there is no easy way to read or write data. As VB programmers we have to resort to the aforementioned methods, which retrieve (or send) data in chunks – the process being repeated until all data is transferred. This forces us to use updatable recordsets (the data cannot be sent through a stored procedure). I prefer to store such large data in a file rather than in a database field. I generally put a path to a file where the object of desire is stored. Normally, I use a file on a file server rather than the database server.

(#) These data types are Oracle-specific.

Let us now move on and consider how to enforce constraints and apply column default values.

Constraints

Constraints are rules that we impose on the database and its tables and columns. We will mainly apply them to individual columns but will demonstrate the application of a table constraint when we use the `UNIQUE` keyword. Column constraints allow us to restrict the values that may be entered into a particular column. Thus, they represent a basic method of enforcing our business rules.

In two-tier systems, also known as Fat-Server systems (and not necessarily synonymous with Larry Ellison's favorite Thin-Client systems), we put all the business rules in the data layer of the system. In three-tier systems we are taught to put some of this into a middle tier. However, basic data constraints, such as the primary key and foreign key constrains that we are about to cover, are best performed by the database. If you need to enforce more complex business logic you can use middle-tier business objects and triggers. However, you should never, for example, invoke a trigger to do what fundamental database referential integrity can do quite easily.

Middle tier business objects deal with data but on a different level. The withdrawal cannot exceed the balance is a rule that may be put in the middle tier (though I can still put it in the database if somebody coerces me enough). The decision as to what goes where is an art and not yet a science. I have a good idea as to what makes for a faster application. Validity checks belong on the client. This saves us superfluous round trips on the network. Complex checks involving data and business logic belong in the business tier; but they may also go to the database. It depends on the complexity of the logic. The more complex, the more likely it is that I'll opt for the middle tier.

However, as discussed, the constraints that we use here are of the simplest form. They all deal with referential integrity. They all belong in the database.

The NOT NULL Constraint

This constraint specifies that a column cannot contain a null value. It is very easy to append this constraint to the `LAST_NAME`, `FIRST_NAME` and `GENDER` columns in our `People` table:

> If you are working through this chapter in a practical manner and
> actually executing the code, you will already have created the basic
> People table. You cannot create it twice! The simplest approach might
> be to execute the DROP TABLE command (which is covered later in the
> chapter): DROP TABLE People;, before proceeding.

```
CREATE TABLE People
(
PERSON_ID       NUMBER(10),
LAST_NAME       VARCHAR2(25) NOT NULL,
FIRST_NAME      VARCHAR2(15) NOT NULL,
M_I             VARCHAR2(1),
DOB             DATE,
GENDER          VARCHAR2(1) NOT NULL,
EYE_COLOR       VARCHAR2 (10)
);
```

If a column is defined as NOT NULL and a user attempts to load it with a NULL, then the
database will return an error. The example below shows you what happens when you
try to set the value of the GENDER column of a new row to NULL (refer to Chapter 2, if
you skipped the DML chapter and need a quick refresher on the INSERT command):

```
INSERT INTO People (Person_ID, Last_Name, First_Name, M_I, DOB, Gender)
VALUES (1, 'Marvelous', 'Marvin', NULL, '01-JAN-1951', NULL);
```

The error message is pretty descriptive – we have attempted to violate the NOT NULL
constraint on the Gender column of the People table in the SCOTT schema.

Note that, since our database was previously empty, I simply gave the
Person_ID column a value of 1. In practice, we will generate this value
using a sequence, to ensure its uniqueness (see later in the chapter).

The Primary Key Constraint

This constraint defines a column as the primary key. If a column is designated as primary key then each row must have a unique value in this column. There can be only one PK per table. When the PK constraint is applied, a column index is created automatically – we don't have to issue a CREATE INDEX command for this column. Actions performed by the database, without specific requests, are called implicit. Here, we define the PK for our People table:

```
CREATE TABLE People
(
PERSON_ID     NUMBER(10) CONSTRAINT PK_PEOPLE PRIMARY KEY,
LAST_NAME     VARCHAR2(25) NOT NULL,
FIRST_NAME    VARCHAR2(15) NOT NULL,
M_I           VARCHAR2(1),
DOB           DATE,
GENDER        VARCHAR2(1) NOT NULL,
EYE_COLOR     VARCHAR2 (10)
);
```

The CONSTRAINT keyword is followed by the name of the constraint (PK_PEOPLE) and the type of constraint.

The Foreign Key Constraint

This constraint defines a column as a foreign key. When a column is defined as an FK, Oracle won't let you add a new row to a table without it pointing to an existing row in the table it references by the FK. We have created a PK column (PERSON_ID) in the People table. Let's now look at how we establish this referential relationship between the Employee table and the People table:

```
CREATE TABLE Employee
(
EMPLOYEE_ID NUMBER(10) CONSTRAINT PK_EMPLOYEE PRIMARY KEY,
PERSON_ID NUMBER(10) CONSTRAINT PEOPLE_FK_EMPLOYEE REFERENCES
People(PERSON_ID)
);
```

Note that this column constraint could more accurately be called the REFERENCES constraint. We place a constraint on the Person_ID column of the Employee table (called PEOPLE_FK_EMPLOYEE) and, using the REFERENCES keyword, specify that any value in this column must also exist in the PK of a parent table – in this case the Person_ID field of the People table.

We do not actually need to use the CONSTRAINT keyword when creating PK and FK constraints – Oracle will create them implicitly. Thus we could declare a PK on the Person_ID column of the People table, as follows:

```
CREATE TABLE People
(
Person_ID     NUMBER(10) PRIMARY KEY,
LAST_NAME     VARCHAR2(25) NOT NULL,
FIRST_NAME    VARCHAR2(15) NOT NULL,
M_I           VARCHAR2(1),
DOB           DATE,
GENDER        VARCHAR2(1) NOT NULL,
EYE_COLOR     VARCHAR2 (10)
);
```

Similarly, we can declare the corresponding FK on the Employee table as follows:

```
CREATE TABLE Employee
(
EMPLOYEE_ID NUMBER(10) PRIMARY KEY,
PERSON_ID NUMBER(10) REFERENCES People(Person_ID)
);
```

When an implicit constraint is created, Oracle names it automatically. The name is of the form SYS_Cxxxxx (where xxxxx is a number), which is actually pretty meaningless. If a referential integrity problem arises, we get a cryptic error message that gives us a mumbo-jumbo constraint name. When we put in the constraints separately, we have the privilege of naming the constraint in a meaningful way, and this is the method I would recommend.

An Aside on Naming Conventions

It is healthy to implement a naming convention for database objects. As you've already noticed I have obvious conventions. I name tables and columns meaningfully. I name the primary key for a table PK_TableName. Foreign keys are named for the two tables they encompass, with the master table first – UpperTable_FK_LowerTable. You don't have to follow my conventions, but I strongly suggest that you follow a convention of some kind.

> **Most DBAs will have a convention in place. If you work on their database use their conventions.**

Oracle limits the names of objects to thirty characters. It is best to use full names, but in the case of foreign key constraints you may need to revert to shorthand. The "_FK_" is already four characters, and it is difficult to find table names such that two of them will not exceed 26 characters. My shorthand method is to remove all vowels first. Do whatever else is necessary if this is not enough. There is no accepted wisdom on that.

Enabling Cascade Delete

Databases such as Access and SQL Server allow us to enable CASCADE DELETE and CASCADE UPDATE quite easily. Oracle will not allow us to do it directly. We enable a CASCADE DELETE by adding ON DELETE CASCADE to foreign key constraints. For example:

```
CREATE TABLE Employee
(
EMPLOYEE_ID NUMBER(10) CONSTRAINT PK_EMPLOYEE PRIMARY KEY,
PERSON_ID NUMBER(10) CONSTRAINT PEOPLE_FK_EMPLOYEE REFERENCES
People(PERSON_ID) ON CASCADE DELETE
);
```

Now when we delete a person we'll also delete the employee. The cascading mechanism has to permeate all the levels before it works. This means that you'll have to do the same with the JOBHISTORY and SALARY (only cascading on the Employee_ID column). As discussed previously, Oracle does not have a CASCADE UPDATE option.

The CHECK Constraint

We do not actually implement this constraint on our HR tables but, in Chapter 2, I promised to show you how we could have avoided having an erroneous Gender value entered into the database:

```
CREATE TABLE People
(
PERSON_ID    NUMBER(10) CONSTRAINT PK_PEOPLE PRIMARY KEY,
LAST_NAME    VARCHAR2(25) NOT NULL,
FIRST_NAME   VARCHAR2(15) NOT NULL,
M_I          VARCHAR2(1),
DOB          DATE,
GENDER       VARCHAR2(1) NOT NULL
   CONSTRAINT CHK_GENDER CHECK (GENDER IN ('M', 'F')),
EYE_COLOR    VARCHAR2 (10)
);
```

We create a CHECK constraint (called CHK_GENDER) on the GENDER column, which uses the IN keyword to ensure that the column can contain one of only two possible values: 'M' or 'F' (this is case sensitive so the column will only accept the capitalized letters). If we now try to enter any other value, we will encounter an error message:

```
INSERT INTO People (Person_ID, Last_Name, First_Name, M_I, DOB, Gender)
VALUES (1, 'Marvelous', 'Marvin', NULL, '01-JAN-1951', 'm');
```

For the sake of completeness, we still have one more constraint to cover.

The UNIQUE Constraint

Again, this is not a feature that we use in our HR tables. It ensures that each value in a column is unique. If used, Oracle will automatically build an index on this column. The reason is that in order to check for uniqueness Oracle needs a fast search on its values, and that is what an index is built for. We can enforce the UNIQUE constraint on as many columns as we like, whereas there can be only one PK column. This constraint is applied in a very similar way as the PK constraint. For example:

```
PERSON_ID    NUMBER(10) CONSTRAINT UQ_PEOPLE UNIQUE
```

The UNIQUE constraint is most useful when we apply it to a combination of columns. Consider the following code:

```
CREATE TABLE People
(
PERSON_ID     NUMBER(10) CONSTRAINT PK_PEOPLE PRIMARY KEY,
LAST_NAME     VARCHAR2(25) NOT NULL,
FIRST_NAME    VARCHAR2(15) NOT NULL,
M_I           VARCHAR2(1),
DOB           DATE,
GENDER        VARCHAR2(1) NOT NULL
   CONSTRAINT CHK_GENDER CHECK (GENDER IN ('M', 'F')),
EYE_COLOR     VARCHAR2 (10),
CONSTRAINT UQ_FULLNAME UNIQUE(FIRST_NAME, LAST_NAME, M_I)
);
```

Here our UNIQUE constraint (UQ_FULLNAME) appears as a table constraint, at the end of the code, and ensures that the column values for FIRST_NAME, LAST_NAME and M_I, when considered together should be unique. Let's enter our faithful employee, Mr. Marvin Marvelous:

```
INSERT INTO People (Person_ID, Last_Name, First_Name, M_I, DOB, Gender)
VALUES (1, 'Marvelous', 'Marvin', NULL, '01-JAN-1951', 'M');
```

Now, say we enter our second employee and by some amazing coincidence his name is also Marvin Marvelous:

```
INSERT INTO People (Person_ID, Last_Name, First_Name, M_I, DOB, Gender)
VALUES (2, 'Marvelous', 'Marvin', NULL, '12-JAN-1945', 'M');
```

The second Marvin will not be entered:

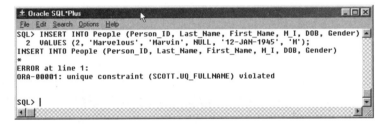

We would have to persuade at least one of them to divulge their middle initial!

Default Values

If we do not enter a value for a column the database normally fills it with a NULL:

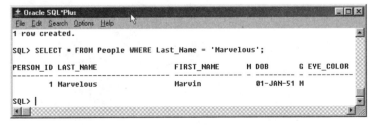

We use the DEFAULT keyword to tell the database that, in an absence of an assigned value, it should use the default value instead:

```
CREATE TABLE People
(
PERSON_ID      NUMBER(10) CONSTRAINT PK_PEOPLE PRIMARY KEY,
LAST_NAME      VARCHAR2(25) NOT NULL,
FIRST_NAME     VARCHAR2(15) NOT NULL,
M_I            VARCHAR2(1),
DOB            DATE,
GENDER         VARCHAR2(1) NOT NULL,
EYE_COLOR      VARCHAR2 (10) DEFAULT 'Brown'
);
```

Now, if you entered Marvin's details into the People table, as previously, and ran the SELECT command, the value 'Brown' would be entered in the Eye_Color column.

Default values are stored in the data dictionary as large objects (because they might be!). This can sometimes cause us problems when returning these values to VB. As noted in Chapter 1, if we are using the Oracle data control as our conduit (bound to the DataGrid control) our program is very prone to crashing. The ADO data control does not seem so prone to this difficulty. We will find out the correct way to deal with large objects in Chapters 8 and 12.

The DESC Command

When you come to a project after the initial design stage, you'll need to see what the database includes. One of your tools is the DESCRIBE (or DESC) command. The general syntax is:

```
DESC <TableName>;
```

Here we describe the People table:

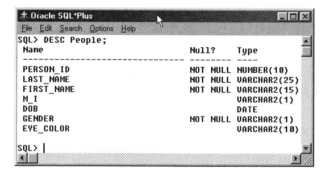

118

The ALTER TABLE Command

Once you have created your tables you may find that, at a later date, you will need to modify some aspect of their structure. We can use the ALTER TABLE command to add new columns, modify columns and add new parameters (constraints, keys etc.).

> **Altering the database is easily done while we design it. This is because we still own the database to do with it what we will. Once in production, the database is owned by the users, and altering it will be much more difficult.**

Those of you who have had a peek at the Createit script will know that I use the ALTER TABLE command quite extensively. I use the CREATE TABLE in a basic format, including only the NOT NULL constraint and, perhaps, any default values that are required:

```
CREATE TABLE PEOPLE
(
PERSON_ID    NUMBER(10),
LAST_NAME    VARCHAR2(25) NOT NULL,
FIRST_NAME   VARCHAR2(15) NOT NULL,
M_I          VARCHAR2(1),
DOB          DATE,
GENDER       VARCHAR2(1) NOT NULL,
EYE_COLOR    VARCHAR2(10) DEFAULT 'Brown'
);
```

I add in all other data integrity constraints using the ALTER TABLE command.

Adding Constraints using ALTER TABLE

There are a few reasons for this approach. One is that it is easier to remember. Another is that the code is easier to read when it is kept in a script file – which is where one should keep the code for these creations. The scripts should also become a part of a project's documentation. The need to repeat these actions frequently arises. Not putting complex constraints in the CREATE TABLE command also makes it easier to create interdependent tables in any order. For example, if we put all of the constraints in the CREATE TABLE command we cannot create the Employee table before the People table.

Adding a Primary Key

The general syntax is:

```
ALTER TABLE TableName
ADD CONSTRAINT ConstraintName
PRIMARY KEY (ColumnName);
```

The code needed to append a PK to our People table is very straightforward:

```
ALTER TABLE PEOPLE
ADD CONSTRAINT PK_PEOPLE
PRIMARY KEY (PERSON_ID);
```

Notice that we must now identify the PK to the appropriate column. The following will work just as well but, again, you will not have the luxury of a meaningfully named constraint:

```
ALTER TABLE PEOPLE
ADD PRIMARY KEY (PERSON_ID);
```

We can append UNIQUE and CHECK constraints in a very similar fashion.

Adding a Foreign Key

The general syntax is:

```
ALTER TABLE TableName
ADD CONSTRAINT ConstraintName
FOREIGN KEY (ColumnName) REFERENCES AnotherTable(ColumnName);
```

In a sense this syntax is much clearer, since we can now use the FOREIGN KEY keyword. The referenced column – AnotherTable(Column) – must be a PK column or a UNIQUE column of that table. Of course, AnotherTable(Column) must exist before we can reference it!

Thus, we start with the creation of the basic Employee table:

```
CREATE TABLE EMPLOYEE
(
EMPLOYEE_ID  NUMBER(10),
PERSON_ID    NUMBER(10)
);
```

We now modify this table twice: once to create a primary key and once to create a foreign key referencing the People table:

```
ALTER TABLE EMPLOYEE
ADD CONSTRAINT PK_EMPLOYEE
PRIMARY KEY (EMPLOYEE_ID);

ALTER TABLE EMPLOYEE
ADD CONSTRAINT PEOPLE_FK_EMPLOYEE
FOREIGN KEY (PERSON_ID) REFERENCES PEOPLE(PERSON_ID);
```

Adding a New Column using ALTER TABLE

The ALTER TABLE command may be used to add a new column to the table. The general syntax is:

```
ALTER TABLE <TableName>
ADD (<NewColumnName> DATA_TYPE [(a [,b])] [DEFAULT <DefaultValue> [NOT
NULL]]);
```

For example:

```
ALTER TABLE People
ADD (Shoe_Size Number(2) DEFAULT 8 NOT NULL);
```

Over a period of time, a company's business rules change, and database tables need to be adjusted to accommodate these new rules. Many DBA teams run major projects a few times per year when table changes are needed, and the changes are done all at once.

Modifying a Column using ALTER TABLE

We can use the ALTER TABLE command, in conjunction with the MODIFY keyword, in order to change the data type of a column:

```
ALTER TABLE <TableName>
MODIFY (<ColumnName> DATA_TYPE[(a [,b])]
[DEFAULT <DefaultValue> [NOT NULL]]);
```

For example:

```
ALTER TABLE People
MODIFY (Shoe_Size varchar2(10) DEFAULT 'large');
```

Modifying a database table that is loaded with data is a complex issue and it is beyond the scope of the book to discuss it in detail. Oracle will allow you to lengthen any VARCHAR2 column. Shortening it will be allowed only if all the current values are NULL. An error message will be issued otherwise.

Removing a NOT NULL constraint is always possible. Adding a NOT NULL constraint will only work if the column does not contain any nulls. If this needs to be done you must first do a global update converting all NULLS to say 0 or ' ' (a single space) and then alter the column.

We will now move on to discuss our final table manipulation command, DROP TABLE.

The DROP TABLE Command

The DDL command to remove tables is simply:

```
DROP TABLE <TableName>;
```

Remember, if we have defined foreign-key relationships between our tables, then this will dictate the order in which we can drop them. For example, if we have created the full People and Employee tables, then Oracle will not let us drop the People table:

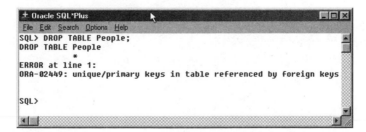

If we were allowed to drop the parent table then all of the records in the child table would become orphaned and the referential integrity of the database would be compromised. By the same argument, we cannot remove JOBDESCRIPTION before we have removed JOBHISTORY and we must remove both SALARY and JOBHISTORY before we may remove the EMPLOYEE table.

Thus we can drop the tables in the following order: SALARY, JOBHISTORY, JOBDESCRIPTION, EMPLOYEE, and finally PEOPLE.

A similar mechanism to that seen for CASCADE DELETEs on column values also works for dropping tables. The following code will allow you to drop a table even if it contains columns that are referenced by other tables:

```
DROP <TableName> CASCADE CONSTRAINTS;
```

Sequences

A sequence is a persistent counter that does not loose its count even when the computer is turned off. We normally use sequences to generate unique record numbers to be used whenever we INSERT a new row into a table. An Oracle sequence has a minimum value, a maximum value, a starting point (which must not be less than the min value, nor can it be above the max value) and it may even cycle.

Because a normal sequence simply generates running numbers (1 then 2 then 3, and so on) we may actually use one such sequence to generate unique keys for all the tables, rather than creating a sequence per table. This means that the keys for any given tables will not be consecutive, just increasing. Other databases, such as Access and SQL Server, generate a unique key column automatically upon execution of an INSERT command. Oracle for some reason does not. We have to ask for the next sequence number and insert it into the column. We may lighten our load somewhat, by relegating this duty to a trigger.

When a user gets a sequence number, it can be used as a unique key at any chosen time. This is because different users will never have the same sequence number from the same sequence generator (unless the CYCLE option is in use – see below).

The CREATE SEQUENCE Command

The general syntax of this command is as follows:

```
CREATE SEQUENCE <SequenceName>
Options;
```

Where the Options parameters are a space-delimited list of one or more of the following:

Option	Default	Description
INCREMENT BY x	1	The difference between two consecutive sequence numbers. The value of x may be positive or negative. If value of x is 3 and the sequence starts at 1 it will generate: 1, 4, 7, 10…
MINVALUE x	- (10**26)	The smallest number the sequence can generate.
NOMINVALUE	1 for ascending sequences (the INCREMENT BY is positive) and - (10**26) for descending.	This is the default for the minimum value of a sequence. If you don't use either MINVALUE or NOMINVALUE, NOMINVALUE is assumed.
MAXVALUE x	10**26	The largest number any sequence can produce.
NOMAXVALUE	-1 for descending, 10** 26 for ascending	This is the default for the maximum value of a sequence. If you don't use either MAXVALUE or NOMAXVALUE, NOMAXVALUE is assumed.
START WITH		The first value of the sequence. It must be no less than the MINVALUE and no more than the MAXVALUE.
CYCLE	NOCYCLE	If CYCLE is used, the sequence will go back to MINVALUE after it has reached MAXVALUE and continue from there. When you use MINVALUE 1 MAXVALUE 2, START WITH 1 and CYCLE, the sequence will go 1,2,1,2…
CACHE x	20	The system caches the next x sequence numbers for quicker performance. Caching sequence numbers may mean that you'll discard a few. This will make holes in the continuity of your key, but the uniqueness will always be preserved. If you have to restart the database, the cache will be lost.

Option	Default	Description
NOCACHE		No sequence number caching.
ORDER	NOORDER	Using ORDER guarantees that the sequence numbers will be issued in the order they were asked for. This is normally the case anyhow even if NOORDER was selected or defaulted to. ORDER simply guarantees it.

Here are a couple of examples (note that I use a separate line for each option to enhance readability):

```
CREATE SEQUENCE MODULO_7
START WITH 0
MAXVALUE 6
MINVALUE 0;
```

This sequence will generate cycles of 0,1,2,3,4,5,6,0,1,2... (which are the possible remainders of 7, hence the name). There is no practical reason that I can think of, to use such a scheme, but if you can think of one, you have the option.

The second example is one of the sequences we use with our HR tables:

```
CREATE SEQUENCE PERSON_ID_SEQ;
```

No options are used, so the sequence will start with 1 and go all the way to 10**26. We create our other sequences in a similar fashion:

```
CREATE SEQUENCE EMPLOYEE_ID_SEQ;
CREATE SEQUENCE HISTORY_ID_SEQ;
CREATE SEQUENCE SALARY_ID_SEQ;
```

Of course, we need to be able to access the next available sequence number. We do this using the NEXTVAL function:

```
<SequenceName>.NEXTVAL
```

Then, to find out what the current value of the sequence is we use the CURRVAL function:

```
<Sequencename>.CURRVAL
```

We use our PERSON_ID_SEQ sequence to generate the next Person_Id for the People table. Thus, we insert a new row as follows:

```
INSERT INTO People (Person_ID, Last_Name, First_Name, M_I, DOB, Gender)
VALUES (PERSON_ID_SEQ.NEXTVAL, 'Marvelous', 'Marvin', NULL, '01-JAN-1951',
'M');
```

Personally, I only use sequences in this simplest of forms. When I need fancy cycles I use VB where the code is easier to test and debug.

Pseudo Columns

As discussed above, you can determine the current or the next sequence number by asking for it. A sequence value is one of the so-called pseudo columns in the system. The pseudo columns are queried using the DUAL Table. Oracle created the DUAL table just for the purpose of pseudo column enquiries. I call DUAL the pseudo table.

This following code will increment the sequence to its next number and show it to you:

```
SELECT PERSON_ID_SEQ.NEXTVAL FROM DUAL;
```

Alternatively we can obtain the current sequence value, without incrementing it:

```
SELECT PERSON_ID_SEQ.CURRVAL FROM DUAL;
```

If, in a new session, you try to obtain the current value of the sequence before getting the next available number, you will receive the following error message:

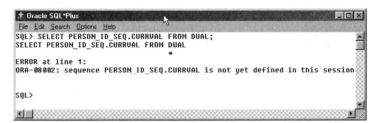

Modifying and Dropping Sequences

The DDL command to remove a sequence is simply:

```
DROP SEQUENCE <SequenceName>;
```

For example, to drop the PERSON_ID_SEQ sequence:

```
DROP SEQUENCE PERSON_ID_SEQ;
```

You do not have to remove the sequences in any particular order.

The DDL command to alter a sequence is of the form:

```
ALTER SEQUENCE <Sequencename>
NewOptions;
```

For example, we could change the maximum possible value of our PERSON_ID_SEQ sequence as follows:

```
ALTER SEQUENCE PERSON_ID_SEQ
MAXVALUE 100;
```

Next we need to discuss briefly the subject of indices (or, as the word is commonly misused, indexes).

Indexes

An index is a database object containing a sorted set of values and the ROWID associated with each of these values.

> **The ROWID is a pointer to the physical location of a row. Oracle lets us access the ROWID information, and hence the location of the data, using indexes.**

Oracle uses a data object called a B*-TREE to store indexes (a sorted object with a quick search routine). The index will contain an entry for every value in the indexed column (null values are not stored in an index), allowing us to home in on values quickly without having to search the entire table. If we place our indexes judiciously and construct our queries with them in mind, they can vastly improve the performance of our queries.

We have already seen that Oracle creates implicit indexes when we create PRIMARY KEY or UNIQUE columns. If we expect to search on any other columns frequently (and the table is large) then we should ask Oracle to build an index for it. Here is how we ask:

```
CREATE [UNIQUE] INDEX <IndexName> ON
<TableName> (ColumnList);
```

Where ColumnList is a comma-delimited list of column names all in the same table.. Usually you would use the UNIQUE keyword to specify that every value in the indexed column be unique, although it is not mandatory.

On the production database you would create a separate tablespace in which to store your indexes.

For example, we may create an index on the Last_Name field of our People table:

```
CREATE INDEX IDX_LASTNAME
ON People(Last_Name);
```

Now, if we invoke a search on an indexed column (for example, via the WHERE clause of a SELECT statement) then we should see an improvement in query performance (we won't notice any difference for tables of the size we have). Alternatively we can create a unique compound index. The columns comprising the index do not have to be contiguous (unlike in Access):

```
CREATE UNIQUE INDEX IDX_LASTNAME
ON People(Last_Name, First_Name, M_I);
```

Oracle also provides a useful mechanism by which we can keep track of our table indexes, using one of our data dictionary tables:

```
SELECT Index_Name, Table_Name FROM USER_INDEXES;
```

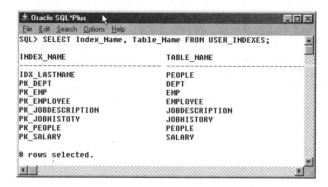

Note that we get a list of all of the implicitly created indexes, along with our manually created one.

Views

A view is an object – a "compiled" SQL query – that is stored on the database server. When a view is executed, we are provided with a *virtual* table, which allows us to retrieve and work with data in the underlying base tables.

> It is important to understand that data in the base database tables is *not* duplicated and stored in the virtual table. When the query is terminated the virtual table is destroyed. However the view remains on the server and can be called the next time a client wishes to view the data.

Some of the main benefits derived from the use of views are as follows:

❑ *They can be used for security purposes.* A view extracts and displays in a virtual table *only* the records and fields that are defined in the view. A user can be assigned permission to a view in the same way they can be assigned permission to a normal table. Thus, a user may be granted access only to a certain view and, in effect, denied access to other confidential data stored elsewhere in the database.

❑ They can be used to extract only the information that is relevant to the user's needs. Different groups of people within an organization require frequent access to different data from the database. Furthermore, large and complex SQL statements are often required in order to provide access to highly specific data, often drawn from multiple tables. This complex SQL statement can be defined as a view and a "special purpose" view can be created to suit each requirement. The clients that require data from the view may then execute a simple SQL statement to retrieve the same data, over and over.

127

Consider the following complex JOIN statement, that we used in Chapter 2 to provide us with a list of our current Computer operators:

```
SELECT JobHistory.Employee_ID, Employee.Person_ID, Last_Name
FROM JobHistory, Employee, People
WHERE Employee.Person_ID = People.Person_ID
AND JobHistory.Employee_ID = Employee.Employee_ID
AND Job_Code = 'CO' AND Date_Ended IS NULL;
```

If an employee needed regular access to this information, it would be a trial to have to enter this statement every time. The good news is that we can create a View called, say, vw_CO_INFO and define the characteristics of this view using the previous statement:

```
CREATE VIEW vw_CO_INFO AS
(SELECT JobHistory.Employee_ID, Employee.Person_ID, Last_Name
FROM JobHistory, Employee, People
WHERE Employee.Person_ID = People.Person_ID
AND JobHistory.Employee_ID = Employee.Employee_ID
AND Job_Code = 'CO' AND Date_Ended IS NULL);
```

Note the use of parentheses to distinguish the entire SELECT statement as part of the view. Now that the view has been created, all that we need do each time we want to see our data is to call it, as follows:

```
SELECT * FROM vw_CO_INFO;
```

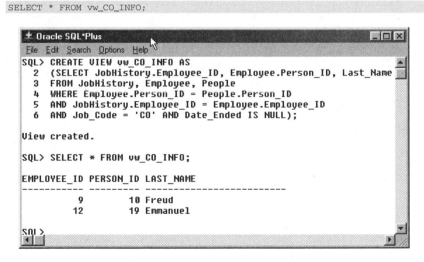

Since version 7.3 of Oracle we have been allowed to perform INSERT, UPDATE, and DELETE operations on views involving multi-table joins.

When the view has outlived its usefulness we can drop it in the usual fashion:

```
DROP VIEW vw_CO_INFO
```

Using Script Files

The SQL*PLUS window is very unforgiving so I always keep my CREATE, ALTER and DROP statements in scripts. Should I need to repeat them, they're there to be used again and again and serve as excellent documentation. Scripts, created and run on your Personal Oracle, can then be run on your server. This way you can develop the application in one place, and still deploy it in another. I also keep frequently used queries in a query text file. When necessary I just open a Notepad session where I edit the queries. I then cut and paste them into the SQL*PLUS window. If I made any error – which, considering my typing skills and dyslexia, is very likely – I correct the code in Notepad and re-paste it. For these purposes it helps to put comments in the code. There are three ways to put comments in Oracle SQL. My philosophy is to use the first two methods in regular queries and the third method in script files (although all variations work in all forms).

Method 1: Commenting SQL code using */<Comment> */

Put the comments anywhere enclosed in /* and */ as you would when coding in C. This allows line wrapped comments. For example:

```
/* Add A foreign key */
ALTER TABLE EMPLOYEE  /* Employee table */
ADD CONSTRAINT PEOPLE_FK_EMPLOYEE
FOREIGN KEY (PERSON_ID) REFERENCES PEOPLE(PERSON_ID);
```

Method 2: Commenting SQL code using --<Comment>

Put the comment at the end of a line after a dual dash --. Such a comment ends with a carriage return and is limited to just one line. For example:

```
ALTER TABLE EMPLOYEE --. Add a foreign key
ADD CONSTRAINT PEOPLE_FK_EMPLOYEE
FOREIGN KEY (PERSON_ID) REFERENCES PEOPLE(PERSON_ID);
```

Method 3: Commenting SQL code using REMARK<Comment>

This is the method I use for commenting scripts. You must put script comments in a separate line that starts with the word REMARK:

```
REMARK we're going to add a primary key
ALTER TABLE EMPLOYEE
ADD CONSTRAINT PK_EMPLOYEE
PRIMARY KEY (EMPLOYEE_ID);

REMARK and here we add a foreign key
ALTER TABLE EMPLOYEE
ADD CONSTRAINT PEOPLE_FK_EMPLOYEE
FOREIGN KEY (PERSON_ID) REFERENCES PEOPLE(PERSON_ID);
```

The following sections give a full listing of the CreateIt and ClearIt scripts. They are available to download for free from the Wrox website.

The CreateIt.sql Script

This script consists of the following lines and creates all of the tables (created in the correct order of course!), sequences and constraints for our HR tables:

```
REMARK Create the basic People table
CREATE TABLE PEOPLE
(PERSON_ID NUMBER(10),
 LAST_NAME VARCHAR2(25) NOT NULL,
 FIRST_NAME VARCHAR2(15) NOT NULL,
 M_I VARCHAR2(1),
 DOB DATE,
 GENDER VARCHAR2(1) NOT NULL,
 EYE_COLOR VARCHAR2(10) DEFAULT 'Brown');

REMARK we're going to add a primary key
ALTER TABLE PEOPLE
ADD CONSTRAINT PK_PEOPLE
PRIMARY KEY (PERSON_ID);

REMARK Create the basic Employee table
CREATE TABLE EMPLOYEE
(EMPLOYEE_ID NUMBER(10),
 PERSON_ID NUMBER(10));

REMARK we're going to add a primary key
ALTER TABLE EMPLOYEE
ADD CONSTRAINT PK_EMPLOYEE
PRIMARY KEY (EMPLOYEE_ID);

REMARK add a foreign key that references the People table
ALTER TABLE EMPLOYEE
ADD CONSTRAINT PEOPLE_FK_EMPLOYEE
FOREIGN KEY (PERSON_ID) REFERENCES PEOPLE(PERSON_ID);

REMARK Create the basic JobDescription table
CREATE TABLE JOBDESCRIPTION
(JOB_CODE VARCHAR2(5) NOT NULL,
 DESCRIPTION VARCHAR2(30) NOT NULL,
 JOB_LEVEL NUMBER(2),
 MIN_TIME NUMBER(4),
 MIN_AGE NUMBER(2));

REMARK add a primary key to the Jobdesription table
ALTER TABLE JOBDESCRIPTION
ADD CONSTRAINT PK_JOBDESCRIPTION
PRIMARY KEY (JOB_CODE);

REMARK Create the basic JobHistory table
CREATE TABLE JOBHISTORY
(HISTORY_ID NUMBER(10),
 EMPLOYEE_ID NUMBER(10),
 JOB_CODE VARCHAR2(5),
 DATE_STARTED DATE,
 DATE_ENDED DATE);
```

```
REMARK add a primary key to the JobHistory table
ALTER TABLE JOBHISTORY
ADD CONSTRAINT PK_JOBHISTORY
PRIMARY KEY (HISTORY_ID);


REMARK add a foreign key that references the JobDescription table
ALTER TABLE JOBHISTORY
ADD CONSTRAINT JOBDESCRIPTION_FK_JOBHISTORY
FOREIGN KEY (JOB_CODE) REFERENCES JOBDESCRIPTION(JOB_CODE);


REMARK and a foreign key that references the Employee table
ALTER TABLE JOBHISTORY
ADD CONSTRAINT EMPLOYEE_FK_JOBHISTORY
FOREIGN KEY (EMPLOYEE_ID) REFERENCES EMPLOYEE(EMPLOYEE_ID);


REMARK Create the basic Salary table
CREATE TABLE SALARY
(SALARY_ID NUMBER(10),
 EMPLOYEE_ID NUMBER(10),
 INCOME NUMBER(8,2),
 DATE_STARTED DATE,
 DATE_ENDED DATE);


REMARK add a primary key to the Salary table
ALTER TABLE SALARY
ADD CONSTRAINT PK_SALARY
PRIMARY KEY (SALARY_ID);


REMARK add a foreign key that references the Employee table
ALTER TABLE SALARY
ADD CONSTRAINT EMPLOYEE_FK_SALARY
FOREIGN KEY (EMPLOYEE_ID) REFERENCES EMPLOYEE(EMPLOYEE_ID);


REMARK create all of the sequences
CREATE SEQUENCE PERSON_ID_SEQ;
CREATE SEQUENCE EMPLOYEE_ID_SEQ;
CREATE SEQUENCE HISTORY_ID_SEQ;
CREATE SEQUENCE SALARY_ID_SEQ;
```

The ClearIt.sql Script

The ClearIt.sql script removes our database objects, when we want to make a fresh start (like when I went back to re-edit a chapter and the data was no longer as it was). This script consists of the following lines:

```
REMARK drop the tables in reverse order
DROP TABLE SALARY;
DROP TABLE JOBHISTORY;
DROP TABLE JOBDESCRIPTION;
DROP TABLE EMPLOYEE;
DROP TABLE PEOPLE;


REMARK Drop the sequences in any order
DROP SEQUENCE PERSON_ID_SEQ;
DROP SEQUENCE EMPLOYEE_ID_SEQ;
DROP SEQUENCE HISTORY_ID_SEQ;
DROP SEQUENCE SALARY_ID_SEQ;
```

The BookInit.sql Script

The Populate.sql script was described in Chapter 2. I also create a fourth script that is a combination of all three scripts and allows me to clear then recreate and populate, all in one fell swoop. There are two ways to create this script:

- ❏ Simply append the separate scripts, one after the other into one long file.
- ❏ Put a script inside a script.

In order to embed one script within another, you must remember that you run a script by typing the at sign @ followed by a path. If the path contains spaces, enclose it in double quotes. The final piece of the path is the file name and extension `File.Ext`. If you just put a file name without an extension SQL*PLUS will assume that the extension is `sql`. You can use the same technique inside the script. The following script does the trick!

```
REMARK We're running the drop script
REMARK the path is enclosed in quotes because it contains spaces
@"c:\My Documents\OracleBook\ClearIt.sql"

REMARK Now the Create it
@"c:\My Documents\OracleBook\CreateIt.sql"

REMARK and finally the INSERT statements
@"c:\My Documents\OracleBook\Populate.sql"
```

Summary

You are not a DBA yet, but the mystery has been penetrated. The Emperor may not be naked, but he is not remote and out-of-reach either. We've discussed how to:

- ❏ Create, alter and drop database objects.
- ❏ Add column constraints to tables, including a "cross-referencing" system in the form of Primary Key and Foreign Key constraints.
- ❏ Create indexes and views.
- ❏ Create the sequences that guarantee the unique IDs of table records.

You should have a very clear understanding of the inner workings of our scripts.

Unlike SQL Server and Access, there is no way in Oracle to view the relationships between tables. You must use a third party tool, (Erwin, Rational Rose, etc.) or link your tables to Access (see Appendix B) and use it to depict the relationships.

4

Object Oriented Programming, Data Classes and Data Access Technologies

The Trietsch law of Re-Usability: In order to be re-usable an object has to be usable. There is no point in writing useless objects.

This is a "concepts" chapter. We are going to cover three very important areas and we are going to have to do it quickly. They are:

❑   Object Oriented Programming – By breaking down an application into objects and developing those objects, we end up with a solution much closer to the real world problem we are developing for. The application is also neater and easier to understand, making maintenance and support easier.

❑   Visual Basic Data Classes – We will walk through a very simple application first to demonstrate some of the principles of OOP. We will then have a look at some code from our HR application that you were introduced to in Chapter 1.

❑   Data Access – It's all very well having a well-designed front end but we have to connect it to our Oracle database. In the world of data access technology acronyms abound: ADO, OO4O, OLE DB, ODBC, UDA and the list goes on. This section will present a brief introduction to each of these, show how they fit together and offer guidance on which you might consider using when connecting to an Oracle database.

An Introduction to Object Oriented Programming

Object Oriented Programming (OOP) is going strong (even though the concept is about 30 years old). Is it just a fad? In my book (literally) it is not, and I believe it is important for VB programming. Here is my view of what it is and why and how we use it.

In 50 years of modern programming we've constantly thrived to improve our code by reducing errors. We've also tried to be more productive. The demand for computer systems grows exponentially and despite better and better programming tools, the code backlog is forever growing.

One of the methods we've developed is code **reusability** and **portability**:

❑ Reusable code may be used again and again within the same project. A good example is that of a function or a subroutine. We call them again and again with different parameters.

❑ Portable code is reusable across different projects.

Through the years we've learned how to write modular code with local variables and insert it into different projects. Each programmer carried his or her own SDK – Software Development Kit – with the tricks of the trade invented or learned from others. Some companies even sold SDKs. The various pre-canned functions and subs that come with an operating system or a compiler are also considered SDKs. OOP is yet another step in the right direction. It gave portability another boost (hopefully not the last).

Portability is based around component-oriented design, whereby we break applications down into **components** that can be distributed in separate binary files – Dynamic Link Libraries (DLLs) or executables (EXEs). Thus a component can be thought of as a pre-compiled interacting piece of software that can act as a building block for creating applications. As a Visual Basic programmer you will be well aware of COM - the Microsoft standard that provides the mechanism for communication between such components.

> We will not actually be discussing COM components and objects until the final section of this book, where we will also take a brief look at the alternative standard, CORBA, which is actually implemented on most Oracle Application servers.

This portability and reusability, and thus the crux of good Object-Oriented design, is really all about **interfaces** – the mechanism by which the functionality of a object can be used by another object (it can be thought of as a list of the public methods and properties that an object supports).

Objects may be dynamically linked to a project even after they have been compiled – a feat made possible by the presence of standard interfaces. These objects expose themselves to the VB programmer by the IntelliSense feature and we don't even have to bother with the intricacies of the interface. Why OOP? Again, because it is the best portability (and reusability) tool so far.

What is an Object?

Objects are abstract data containers. That is, they are often **abstractions** of a real-world entity. An object has state, and identity. To the user, an object is a container with an instance of complex data. Each element in the data is named and may be read and sometimes changed using this name. We call these elements **properties**. An object's state is essentially the values of their properties.

Objects also perform actions – normally on their own encapsulated data. The methods we use to make the object perform a specific action are functions and subroutines. We may pass parameters to these methods. The object is abstract because, like the proverbial black box, the user does not know how the object performs its duties. All he needs to know is how to ask for them to be performed.

Apart from abstraction, we must consider a few other important object-related properties.

Encapsulation

This is essentially the "black-box" concept. We can ask our object to perform a certain task or action and expect a certain result, without having to know how it was implemented. We just need to know how to interact with the object via the interface that it exposes. Each object contains its own copy of the data (properties). Changing this data affects only this particular copy or instance. This feature enhances the safety of programs. There is no cross contamination.

Polymorphism

This is best explained with the well-worn car analogy: Pressing the accelerator increases your speed whether you are in a Honda or in a Chevrolet; the objects are different, but the interface is similar. We can use the same interface to perform an operation on an object, but the implementation may be somewhat different depending on the class of which the object is an instance.

This means that we are allowed to use the same names for properties and methods across different object classes. This is very convenient for three reasons:

- ❑ The English language, vast as it is, does not have enough meaningful words to accommodate different names
- ❑ Even if it had we could not coordinate the naming effort around the globe
- ❑ It is mighty convenient

Inheritance

For ease of programming we wanted to be able to reuse code. So we wanted one object type or class to inherit some (or all) of the properties of another. VB does not support true inheritance. We use **aggregation** and **delegation** instead. In the next chapter you'll see how we aggregate the `Connection` class inside each `Data` class. Aggregation means the inclusion of one object inside another. Delegation is the use of the aggregated (included) object's properties and methods in place of those of the outer object.

Classes and Objects

In VB we create a new type of an object in a **class**. We later use these classes as cookie-cutters for making objects. An object is an instance of its class. OOP programmers often use the term class where the proper term is object. I suffer from the same malady. The best way to know which is which is by context.

The following simple program explains the mechanics of Form and Class interaction. It only takes about half an hour to complete and it will give you a better understanding of the process of using classes.

Let us look at a simple class. The class will have two properties – the data variables that the class (shamelessly) exposes to the world; one internal variable, which will not be exposed, and one method – a callable function that performs an action inside the class. A method may be a function or a sub. The former returns a value to the caller and may even give the impression that it is a property. The latter returns no values to the caller. Our method is a function that semi-exposes the private class variable. To understand the class and object mechanism we'll also build a simple form that uses the class. By the way a form is a class too, but this book will not expound on it any further.

Start a new project in VB and proceed to build a class module. Do so by selecting the **New Project** tab and double clicking on the **Standard Exe** icon. Once in, click on the **Project** menu and select **Add Class Module**. Continue by selecting **New** and **Class Module**. You're now facing an empty class module.

 If the line **Option Explicit** does not yet appear in the code window, type it in. If that's the case I strongly suggest that you click on the **Tools** menu and select **Options**. Now go to the **Editor** tab and check the **Require Variable Declaration** tab. (While you are at it check every tab.) The **Require Variable Declaration** will insert the **Option Explicit** line in every one of your modules. This in turn will cause a compiler error every time it encounters undeclared variables and thus force you to declare all your variables, saving you tons of frustration in the future.

Now declare your variables by entering the following three lines:

```
Private msV1 As String
Private mlV2 As Long
Private miV3 As Integer
```

These are the class variables. They are declared `Private` and are thus local to the module. We continue by learning how to expose these variables to the world (using a raincoat and a flashlight). We'll allow `msV1` to be both seen and changed by other objects. We allow `mlV2` to be seen but not changed. The last variable – `miV3` – remains hidden from the world. Here is how it's done.

In the Tools menu select Add Procedure. Now type the name V1 in the text box and click on Property and then OK. The code window is now adorned with the empty structures for the Property Get and Property Let:

```
Public Property Cct V1() As Variant

End Property

Public Property Let V1(ByVal vNewValue As Variant)

End Property
```

Note that the system assumes that the variables are of the Variant type. This is somewhat inconvenient since msV1 is a String and m1V2 is Long. Change the As Variant clauses to As String. Also change vNewValue to sNewValue.

Next, insert a line in the Property Get that says V1 = msV1. Insert a line in the Property Let that says msV1 = sNewValue. The end result is:

```
Public Property Get V1() As String
    V1 = msV1
End Property

Public Property Let V1(ByVal sNewValue As String)
    msV1 = sNewValue
End Property
```

Note that, except for the naming, the routines look like normal functions and subs. Change the Property Let to Function, and End Property to End Function and you'll have:

```
Public Function V1() As String
    V1 = msV1
End Function
```

In short, a Property Let is a special case of a function. By the same token a Property Let, since it does not return a value, is a special case of a sub.

We've just exposed msV1 to be read (looked at) by Property Get and to be written into by Property Let.

Let's render m1V2 a read only variable. Again we add a procedure, name it V2 and click on Property and OK. This time we change the Variant to Long since m1V2 is Long. Because we don't want other objects to change m1V2, we now remove the Property Let lines from the code. We, of course enter the proper line in the Property Get. The end result is:

```
Public Property Get V2() As Long
    V2 = m1V2
End Property
```

We are not going to create any property for miV3. This way since it is private, foreign objects will not be able to see it at all.

Finally, let us add the promised method to the class:

Again select **Add Procedure** in the **Tools** menu. This time name it **V3** and make it a **Public Function**. The result is:

```
Public Function V3()

End Function
```

Type the words As Integer after the closing parenthesis and hit ENTER. Now enter the line:

```
V3 = 3 * miV3 + 1
```

The resulting function is:

```
Public Function V3() As Integer
    V3 = 3 * miV3 + 1
End Function
```

Because the function resides in a class module, rather than in a form or a standard module we call it a method. The same applies to subroutines that reside in the class – they are methods. The only difference is in the naming.

All we need to do now is to initialize the class variables, and incorporate an object cut from this class into a form where we can test it. There are two important routines that we may add to each class. These routines are Class_Initialize and Class_Terminate. One is automatically run when we initialize an object based on the class, the other when the object terminates. The Class_Initialize is the equivalent of the Form_Load routine that we all know and love. Click on the **Class** ComboBox in the code window (it says **(General)**) and click on **Class**. In the code window we see the Class_Initialize routine and even the cursor will be ready for action. Type in:

```
msV1 = "String"
mlV2 = 33001 'just a notch bigger than 32767 which is the biggest integer
miV3 = 1
```

The end result is:

```
Private Sub Class_Initialize ()
    msV1 = "String"
    mlV2 = 33001 'just a notch bigger than 32767 which is the biggest integer
    miV3 = 1
End Sub
```

When we start the project these will be the initial values of the class variables.

For good measure, let us create a `Class_Terminate` routine as well. This is the equivalent of a `Form_Unload` routine.

In the other combo – where it says **Initialize** -- select **Terminate**.

Make the routine look like:

```
Private Sub Class_Terminate ()
    MsgBox "I'm dying..."
End Sub
```

Now that we have a class module, let us build a form where it will be used:

Put three textBoxes on the form. Call them `txtV1`, `txtV2`, and `txtV3`. We use them, as their names imply, to view the `V1` and `V2` properties as well as the result of the `V3` method. TextBox `txtV1` will also be used to type in a new value for the `V1` property.

Put six command buttons on the form. Call them cmdShow1, cmdShow2, cmdRun3, cmdClear, cmdLoad1, and cmdExit. Put a meaningful caption in each of them -Show1, Show2, Run3, Clear, Load1 and Exit should do the trick. Here is how I painted my form:

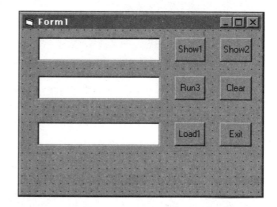

Type all the code below in the form's code window. These are the various subs that make the program run:

```
Option Explicit
Private cSimple As clsSimple 'declare a clsSimple type object

Private Sub cmdClear_Click()'Clears the form to demonstrate the Get and Let
    txtV1.Text = ""
    txtV2.Text = ""
    txtV3.Text = ""
End Sub

Private Sub cmdExit_Click()
    Set cSimple = Nothing 'Will run through the Class_Terminate
    End
End Sub

Private Sub cmdLoad1_Click()
    cSimple.V1 = txtV1.Text 'this is a call to the Property Let in the class
End Sub
```

```
Private Sub cmdRun3_Click()
    txtV3.Text = CStr(cSimple.V3) 'This calls the method V3 in the class
End Sub

Private Sub cmdShow1_Click()
    txtV1.Text = cSimple.V1 'This calls the Property Get V1 in the class
End Sub

Private Sub cmdShow2_Click()
    txtV2.Text = CStr(cSimple.V2) 'This calls the Property Get V2 in the
class
End Sub

Private Sub Form_Load()
    Set cSimple = New clsSimple 'Make a new instance of the object
End Sub
```

A note about naming forms and objects. When you run VB you see various windows on the screen. Three of these are particularly important: The Code window, the Project window, and the Properties window.

When you click on any object in the Project window, the Properties window shows its properties. Click on the **Name** property and change the name of the object to be more meaningful than just **Form1** or **Class1**. In this simple sample I called the class clsSimple and the form. I also renamed the project from **Project1** to **Simple**. Note that all names are in Hungarian notation. If everything in your directory is aptly named, it will be easier to find.

It is now time to test the simple program. Click on **Show1** then **Show2** and then **Run3**. Bring the cursor to the V1 TextBox and change its contents. Then click **Load1**. Click **Clear** and then on the **Show** and **Run** buttons. See any difference? Click **Exit** and watch the Class_Terminate routine in action. Put a breakpoint in the code and follow it while testing. Get a good feel for how objects behave.

In subsequent chapters, we'll apply the methodology to the Oracle data classes.

Guide to Data Access

There are many layers of hardware and software between a VB program running on your desk and the Oracle database that runs somewhere out there. Somewhere out there may be across the universe or right inside your own PC. The various software layers along the route are built so that the user or the programmer does not have to know where and how they are connected.

How can we achieve such wonders? Each software layer investigates its environment and makes intelligent selections about routing. The end result is that you and I can write a VB and Oracle application using Personal Oracle on our own PC, and deploy it on a client site where the users are in Philadelphia and the database runs on a Unix server in Duluth.

Some of this software is supplied by Oracle, other parts by Microsoft, and still others by third parties.

Here is a diagram that shows you how the database connection works. I conveniently removed staples such as your NT, NetWare, FTP or HTTP network:

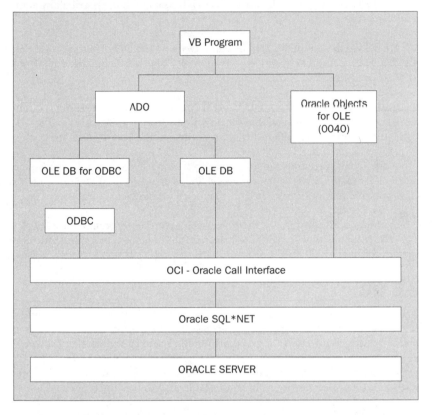

Here is a list of the objects and layers of the diagram above:

- ❑ **ODBC** - Open DataBase Connectivity
- ❑ **OLE DB** - Object Linking and Embedding for Databases
- ❑ **ADO** - ActiveX Data Objects
- ❑ **OO4O** - Oracle Objects For OLE
- ❑ **OCI** - Oracle Call Interface
- ❑ **Oracle SQL*NET**
- ❑ **Oracle Server**

In the next few pages, I'll explain each of them and give you an explanation of how they are used in this book.

ODBC

ODBC is the oldest middleware – or software that helps two processes communicate with each other. It is made up of scores of functions or APIs (Application Programming Interfaces) that translate the requests made by a data control or a program written in C, COBOL, VB, etc. into a language that a particular database server can understand.

With ODBC we use an ODBC Driver and a Driver Manager. There are several sources of ODBC drivers for Oracle, but the choice really boils down to two - one from Oracle and one from Microsoft.

The Oracle driver is packaged with several Oracle products, including the servers. The latest version will also be available for download from the Oracle site. The Microsoft ODBC driver comes with VB and is, in my opinion, the better of the two.

To this day ODBC provides the most comprehensive access to the greatest variety of relational databases. Unfortunately the ODBC is an additional layer of software, and to us it represents the route with the most layers. This slows performance.

In spite of this drawback, this is the route I took for the programs in this book that use ADO. The reason is that some of the features that I wanted to demonstrate could only be achieved through ODBC.

OLE DB

What ODBC does via APIs OLE DB does via a COM interface. The COM interface is Microsoft's way of exposing objects' methods and properties to the user. It is a much easier approach to programming and also much more transportable.

There are many OLE DB providers for Oracle. Oracle itself provides one. Ironically the Microsoft OLE DB for Oracle is far more stable and thus is the one I use.

Two techniques are available for developers. The first uses the ODBC data provider that interfaces with the existing ODBC drivers. The second is a native driver that bypasses ODBC and communicates directly with the OCI.

OCI

Oracle likes to be spoken to via its own set of APIs. This is a similar layer to the familiar ODBC, except that it is specific, not only to Oracle, but also to the programming language that it is called from. The OCI is a native interface to Oracle regardless of whether you use ODBC, OLE DB or OO4O. The ODBC for Oracle actually translates ODBC API to OCI API.

SQL*NET

Oracle talks to any outside network via its own protocol. SQL*NET translates this protocol to other protocols of various network providers.

ADO

ADO or ActiveX Data Objects is a way to get at any provider of tabular data. Tabular data may be a relational data base, Table Query/View; or it may be in the form of a spread sheet, XML or even a flat file. It is built as a relatively thin layer above OLE DB. This means that when we change the OLE DB provider we may still use an existing program, because it still talks to ADO and does not know how ADO is doing its job. The idea is ingenious. Microsoft has put ADO as the centerpiece of its still evolving UDA (Universal Data Access) strategy.

Interim Summary

The sum of all of this is that if we use ADO to talk to an Oracle database we go through the OLE DB layer, then through the OCI. If we use ODBC we still have a fourth layer of code to slow us down. This is not all bad.

ADO is an event source and is thus asynchronous. This means that it may run in parallel to other processes in our applications and thus is not really all that slow. In fact it is surprisingly fast for so many layers. But the greatest advantage of deploying through ADO is that you may indeed change the OLE DB provider later in the project's life, giving you a greater flexibility and greater choice in your DB provider. If you run a system with many database vendors it is your only choice.

Merant (formerly INTERSOLV) has an OLE DB provider for Oracle that can go directly from your program to the Oracle server. This software, I am told, is so fully featured that it surpasses even Oracle's own OO4O. It is also reported to be lightning fast because it uses fewer layers. However, unlike the others, this OLE DB provider doesn't come free.

Oracle Objects For OLE

Oracle Objects for OLE is a fully featured COM layer by which VB and C++ can converse with an Oracle database. We use it in place of ADO. Its greatest advantage is that it allows you to fully use every feature of the Oracle database. This includes REF CURSORS and PL/SQL Tables, which are in fact just arrays. Another advantage of OO4O is that it provides a direct link to the OCI, and thus uses fewer layers to talk to the database.

Its disadvantages include being synchronous (without events) and being proprietary. It will be harder to convert from OO4O than from ADO.

In Chapter 14 of this book you'll see that if you plan and program smartly, such conversions are not as daunting as you feared.

Comparing ADO and OO4O – A Bird's Eye View

When I sent a proposal to speak about Oracle and VB in a recent conference, the organizers wondered why I even suggested speaking about OO4O. One technical reviewer said that it was "sucky" (thanks for teaching me a new term!), slow, and unstable and that everybody uses ADO anyway. He added that I shouldn't waste my, and other people's time on it. The accepted "wisdom" is that the programming community has rallied behind ADO, and that OO4O is dead. I have used OO4O and ADO for quite a while and I definitely don't find either to be sucky.

There is no simple way to compare ADO to OO4O. To begin with, ADO may be connected to Oracle in two major ways: OLE DB and ODBC. Each of these offers at least two avenues. Each of the ADO options still cannot escape talking to Oracle via the OCI (Oracle Call Interface).

The table below compares all of ADO to OO4O. Each option is listed with relative strengths and weaknesses:

Technology	Strengths/Weaknesses
ADO In General	+ Known by many practitioners.
	+ Asynchronous
	+ fits MTS like a glove
	+ runs in a separate process space
	- Makes an extra layer above OCI.
	- Was built for SQL Server
	- Does not Bind Oracle Parameters
	- Requires updates in the command object
	- Problems with Oracle stored procedures especially with parameters.
OLE DB In General	- Less stable than ODBC
MSDAORA – the Microsoft OLE DB for Oracle	+ Faster in creating a connection.
	+ Runs without ODBC. Less Layers.
MSDASQL – The Microsoft OLE DB provider for ODBC	- Runs atop ODBC.

Technology	Strengths/Weaknesses
ODBC In General	+ More stable than OLEDB
	- Slower to connect than OLEDB.
	- Requires MSDASQL anyway.
ODBC Driver 2.573.3513.00	+ Quicker.
	- Less stable with older versions of Oracle (7.x)
ODBC Driver 2.00.00.6325	+ More stable
	- slower.
	- Fits older versions of Oracle (7.x)
Oracle OO4O	+ Direct through OCI. Least Layers.
	+ Binds Oracle variables
	+ Built for Oracle stored procedures
	+ Simpler updates that are done in the dynaset
	+ Multithread (apartment & free)
	- Runs in process (as a dll)
	- Synchronous
	- Requires a COM wrapper to work in MTS

ADO always uses an OLE DB provider. This means that connecting "directly" through ODBC actually isn't. The OLE DB provider for ODBC will be used implicitly.

There are additional known problems with ADO, most with OLE DB. The inability to handle server side cursors is a big one. Because of this cursors are not closed, and the database server slows down and may even stop altogether. This is a problem that seems to exist in older versions of Oracle (7.x). Regardless of the version, this will not happen with OO4O.

One problem I have with OO4O is that it must be run with early binding, or it's slow. This requires you to enwrap it in COM to work well with ASP. The way to do it is rather simple:

❑ Start an ActiveX DLL project and put all your classes, connection and data in it. Also include the modGeneral.

❑ Now compile the DLL and register it with MTS. Use the MTS context to create objects in your ASP page.

I also use the same technique for ADO, and enjoy the greater speed of early binding there as well. Another drawback to OO4O is that it is In-Process, and thus synchronous and without events. Finally, it lacks ADO's ability to work in a disconnected manner, but I've programmed around it, saving and reloading the disconnected dynaset using XML.

Most of my knowledge about ADO and OO4O comes from personal experience. A few of the problems have been brought to me as questions from practitioners who I meet in my consulting career. You can't get much on the web either. One site that has more than anybody else is:

`http://www.asplists.com/asplists/asporaclegurus.asp`

where you have to read between the lines to learn about ADO's problems. The site offers nothing, except questions, about OO4O. I did not even include Oracle's (as opposed to Microsoft's) OLE DB for Oracle in the comparison table. It is much worse then MSDAORA.

In the Philadelphia area, where I practice, I know of three businesses using OO4O. The rest of my clients are using ADO, and some are sticking with it in spite of problems that they encounter. If you try hard enough you'll find workarounds for almost every problem. Maybe one day, the programming community will have all the ADO-Oracle answers. Until then I recommend that you try both the ADO and OO4O projects presented in this book and form your own judgment.

Finally in this we will show you how to connect to Oracle using a System DSN.

Creating a System DSN

From the Windows Start menu select **Settings** and then **Control Panel**. Double Click the **ODBC Data Sources** icon. The **ODBC Data Source Administrator** appears. Click on the **System DSN** tab. You now see something like the following screen (the screenshot in the book already contains two entries that I've created).

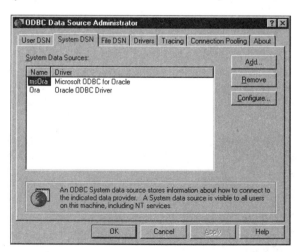

Now click on the Add button and select the Microsoft ODBC for Oracle driver:

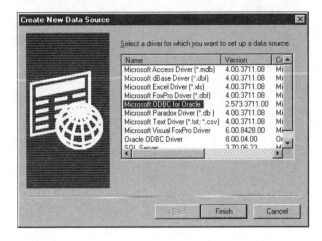

Click the Finish Button. The following screen appears. Fill it out as shown below. Note that we left the server name empty. This is because we connect to the default server on your own machine. If you connect to a 'real' server on your network, consult your DBA before you fill this form.

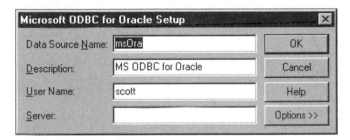

That's it. You now have a system DSN.

You have now reached the end of Section I and should now have a good understanding of

❑ Oracle database architecture

❑ SQL - the language we use to access and manipulate data in our database tables

❑ The object-oriented programming philosophy that we use throughout the book

❑ The Data Access technology that you can use to connect to your Oracle database

You are now ready to tackle the marrying of VB and Oracle using Oracle Objects for OLE.

Section II

Using OO4O and Oracle

An OO4O Application

Oracle Objects for OLE – also known as OO4O – is a set of lightweight loosely connected objects by which COM (OLE) capable applications can connect to and use Oracle databases. This includes languages such as VB, C++, FoxPro, and J++, among others, and OLE containers such as Word and Excel.

In this chapter we are going to use OO4O in its simplest form to write a simple program that is used to maintain a single database table. It should provide a good basic understanding of OO4O.

This is by no means a comprehensive discussion of OO4O. This section of the book aims to build your knowledge in this area with a series of practical chapters, culminating in a full reference in Chapter 8.

In this section you will encounter:

❑ The **OraSession** object. We will use the OpenDatabase method of this object to establish a connection to our Oracle database.

❑ The **OraDatabase** object. We will use the CreateDynaset method of this object to create OraDynaset objects to store our data.

❑ The **OraDynaset** object. We will define the dynaset using a simple SELECT statement and it will be updatable. We will use various methods of this object to navigate through and modify our data.

❑ The **OraFields** Collection. We will read and write data to the database via the OraField objects that belong to the OraDynaset object. We will use the Value property of the OraField object.

In addition you will see how, in practice, we retrieve sequence numbers to uniquely identify new rows. On the VB side, we will apply good OOP principles to the development of our VB data and connection classes.

Let's start by looking at a simplified version of the OO4O object model.

A Simplified OO4O Object Model

This model includes `OraSession`, `OraDatabase` and `OraDynaset` objects and the `OraFields` collection. The `OraSession` object "owns" the `OraDatabase` object and is where the connection to Oracle is maintained. The `OraDynaset` object also contains a collection of `OraField` objects. The objects in this model are related as shown in the diagram below. The full OO4O object model, as seen in Chapter 8, is more involved than the simplified version we use here. This, however, is the crux of it:

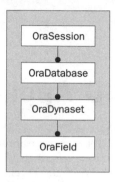

The OraSession Object

When a user "talks" to an Oracle database, the conversation takes place as a session. This is the real root of Objects for OLE. An active session implies that the user's computer is connected to the Oracle server.

The OraDatabase Object

The `OraDatabase` is where it all happens. It represents a single session with an Oracle database. The center of the `OraDatabase` object is the `OraDynaset` around which we build the various VB data classes. We may have many `OraDynasets` under the `OraDatabase`.

The OraDynaset Object

Those of you who are over thirty probably know what a dynaset is. For you youngsters, the modern `Recordset` was once named `Dynaset` (the DAO or Larva stage). As it aged its name was changed to `Resultset` (the RDO or Cocoon Stage), before its latest transition to the `Recordset` butterfly. I don't think this is the last name we'll have to memorize, but I digress. The OO4O object model bears a strong similarity to that of DAO and the dynaset terminology has been retained. When using the ORADC, however, we do refer to a `Recordset` (see Chapter 1), but it is in fact an OO4O dynaset. Here, again, Oracle is sinning in not being consistent. Why name an object a `Dynaset` in one place and a `Recordset` in another?

A dynaset is an object containing the result of a SELECT statement. The dynaset is updateable only if:

❑ The user has the proper privileges to modify data this way.

❑ The SELECT statement deals with a single table. If it uses table JOINs then the dynaset becomes read-only.

❑ This table is not locked by another process.

❑ The dynaset is not specifically defined as read-only.

❑ Oracle has ROWID references to the rows selected by the query.

In this chapter you'll deal with an updateable dynaset, as opposed to a read-only dynaset, and actually add, delete and update table rows using the appropriate methods provided by this dynaset.

The OraField Object

The OraFields collection consists of OraField objects – each one relating to a specific column in the dynaset – which have properties that allow us to see the structure of the table. We'll use one of the field's properties (the Value property) in this chapter.

I don't know a better way of guiding you into the mysteries of OO4O than building a program that uses it.

Maintaining a Database Table using OO4O

Again, let us start with a new standard exe VB project. Let us rename the project (I hate this auto naming that makes each project Project1) PeopleDynaset. Rename the form as frmPeople. Change the form's caption to Maintaining the PEOPLE table.

We need to incorporate OO4O into the project. To add this, click on the Project menu, select References and, in the dialog box that is displayed, check the line item that says OracleInProcServer 2.2 Type Library. The Oracle InProcess library is a DLL (InProcess means DLL) and is installed with Personal Oracle. It is also installed when the Oracle Client Software is installed on user machines.

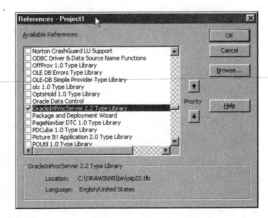

Versions 2.2 and later of OO4O support **early binding**, so when we have included the object library in your project we can take advantage of this. All of the programs in this book will use early binding.

We may bind objects early or late. In early binding we `Dim` (or `Private`, or `Public`) the object as its type. For example:

```
Dim txtMyName As TextBox
```

We immediately know what the object is and how it works. We even get the advantage of intellisense so when we type the object name and a period, we get a dropdown menu with all the properties and methods already named. When we choose a method, its parameters are immediately available for us to view. This is like an object browser at our fingertips. This is a bonus, but the real advantage is that our program is going to be compiled with all that wealth of information already wired in. This is why it will run faster.

In late binding we declare the object as a generic object:

```
Dim txtMyName As Object
```

We then `Set` it to be whatever we like. This defers the wiring to run-time, making for a slower application. This is not the only reason why it will be slower. The other has to do with object interfaces and this is not the place to get into it. Early binding gives you this level of efficiency at every level of the object (complex objects are made of sub-objects which, in turn are made of sub-objects, and so on). Late binding is inefficient in all the levels.

Those of you, and I am one, who use ASP, other scripts, or MTS, probably have a bone to pick with me because of this choice. Scripts, by definition, are interpreted rather than compiled and are therefore limited to late binding. My answer is that when using these modern technologies you are allowed to late-bind to your heart's delight, but you may opt for a middle-of-the-road solution. Build the OO4O items in a COM or DCOM object, where all the bindings are early and use this COM object in your project. I even go further and build a COM database server.

> **Building a COM object or even a COM server is a middle-of-the-road solution to the inefficiencies of late binding. All the internal sub-objects are resolved and the inefficiencies remain only on one level.**

Back to the project. Place seven labels, seven text boxes, and eight command buttons on the form, so that it looks something like this:

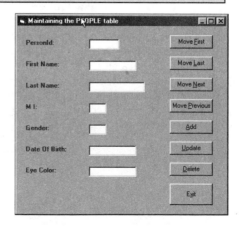

Name each object meaningfully. I suggest using the following:

From top to bottom name the labels lblPersonId, lblFirstName, lblLastName, lblMI, lblGender, lblDOB, lblEyeColor. Caption them as they are captioned on the screen. Naming a label is not really important, unless you change its caption at run time.

Name the text boxes according to the same pattern: txtPersonId, txtFirstName, txtLastName, txtMI, txtGender, txtDOB, txtEyeColor. Make the Property value of each text box blank.

From top to bottom name the command buttons: cmdMoveFirst, cmdMoveLast, cmdMoveNext, cmdMovePrevious, cmdAdd, cmdUpdate, cmdDelete, and cmdExit. Caption all the command buttons as they are seen in the illustration (Move&First, Move&Last, Move&Next, Move&Previous, &Add, &Update, &Delete, &Exit).

> **If you use different names, remember to change the code accordingly.**

We now have the framework in which to program. Obviously what I am shooting for is a program that allows us to traverse the People table, viewing the fields for each record in the table, by clicking on the appropriate "Move" buttons. The values of the columns of the current row will display in the proper text boxes, where we'll be able to modify them. Any changes made will not be saved to the database until we call the Update method of the dynaset, by clicking on the Update command button. We will also be able to add new values, by calling the AddNew method, and delete existing records by clicking the Delete button. Finally, clicking Exit will close the program down. The changes we made to the table will, of course, persist.

So far all we have is a code-less form. Let's get down to some serious coding.

Building the Class Modules

We are going to use two class modules in this program:

❑ **clsConnection**: this will be a generic, portable class which we will use to create OraSession and OraDatabase objects, and to connect to a database. This is the most primitive form this class will take. In the next chapter, when we discuss OO4O in more detail, we'll add transaction control to its duties.

❑ **clsPeople**: this data class will contain two OraDynaset objects. The first, mdynPeople, will be used to maintain the People table. We'll rebuild all the methods of the dynaset as clsPeople methods in order to simplify their use. The dynaset methods and properties that we use in this program will be explained as we go along.

> **Comprehensive coverage of all methods and properties available to our OO4O objects can be found in Chapter 8.**

The second dynaset, `mdynLastRec`, is for the `PERSON_ID_SEQ`. When the class is initialized, the next available sequence number will be retrieved and stored in this dynaset. We'll use this number to guarantee the uniqueness of values entered into the `Person_ID` column (our PK field).

> *Creating an `Oradynaset` object just to store a single value is rather inefficient. In later chapters, when we discuss the PL/SQL language and how to use it to build stored procedures and triggers, we'll learn how to write a better and faster program that does not need to use the second dynaset to produce the sequence.*

Let's start by investigating the `clsConnection` class.

The clsConnection Class

As stated previously, this is a portable class that we use to establish our connection to Oracle. Let's have a look at the code and then we will discuss it in more detail:

```
Option Explicit

'   This class contains the session and database objects that serve all the
'   dynasets in a program.

Private mOraSession As OraSession      'Declare the OraSession object

Private mOraDatabase As OraDatabase    'Declare the OraDatabase object

Public Sub OpenDB(sUser As String, sPW As String, sDBName As String)

'   The parameters are passed in from the Form_Load routine

'   Declare and define our connection string, which is the username and
password values
'   separated by a forward slash

Dim sConnect As String
sConnect = Trim$(sUser) & "/" & Trim$(sPW)

'   Create our OraSession object and a Oradatabase object within it

Set mOraSession = CreateObject("OracleInProcServer.XOraSession")
Set mOraDatabase = mOraSession.OpenDatabase(sDBName, sConnect, 1&)
End Sub

'   Allow other objects such as forms and other classes get a pointer to
'   the database.

Public Property Get Database() As OraDatabase
   Set Database = mOraDatabase
End Property
```

We create a reference to a new `OraSession` object using the VB `CreateObject` method, which we then assign to our `mOraSession` variable.

The method by which we establish a connection to the Oracle database, within the session, is worthy of further discussion. We use the `OpenDatabase` method of the `OraSession` object:

```
Set mOraDatabase = mOraSession.OpenDatabase(sDBName, sConnect, 1&)
```

We pass in three parameters:

❑ `Database_Name` – in our case `sDBName`, which is an empty string.

❑ `Connection_String` – this defines the username and password for the connection. In our case it is `sConnect` (scott/tiger).

❑ `Options` – We use the value 1, which represents the constant `ORABDB_ORAMODE`. This option tells Oracle to use default column values when a value in a newly inserted row is missing. We will discuss the options parameter in full in Chapter 8.

The `OpenDB` routine is called from the `Form_Load` event. When the call is made we pass in the parameters that define our connection:

```
cConnection.OpenDB "scott", "tiger", ""
```

In order to keep the programs in this book as simple as possible, we do not deal with logon screens. Usernames and passwords really belong in invisible text boxes and not in the code. This is a general principle regardless of the database used (or even if a database is used at all).

Finally, a `Property Get` routine allows other objects to get a reference (or "pointer") to the database (so we don't have to create new session and database objects for every object that needs to connect to the database).

The class will serve the form as well as the data class. This class is so general that you may use it in every project in which you use OO4O. There is no need to change even a single line. This kind of portability is why we use Object Oriented Programming in the first place.

The clsPeople 0040 Data Class

In its most primitive form a data class is simply a dynaset, but here we are going to encapsulate two of them into a single class. A well-written class will also allow us to program faster. We build every future data class on the same principles and use the same methods. This creates a methodology, which will speed future projects even further. As you've already noticed, I like to build software in a continuous improvement process. I build a feature and test it, then I add another and test them together. This process continues until all the features are in. People constantly have ideas about how to do new things and how to improve on the old. Whenever I have such an idea, I implement it. If I have two or more, I implement them one by one – never two at once. Doing many changes together complicates testing. The same concept also applies to learning. We are going to introduce better ways to program the data classes as we progress through the book. This, however, is not our main purpose. Our real purpose is to marry Oracle and VB. A full treatment of writing better data classes will come in my next book.

Before we start a full discussion of the `clsPeople` code we need to have a quick word about notation.

I use `dyn` to denote a dynaset, and `fld` to denote a field object. It is common to use scope prefixes in Hungarian Notation and I adhere to this. Thus:

❑   `dynPeople` would be a local, procedure level variable of the dynaset type.

❑   `mfldGender` would be a module (or class module) level field object.

❑   `gdynPeople` would be a global level variable of the dynaset type (we will not encounter global variables in this book).

OK, let's start with the General Declaration code of our `clsPeople` class. It will give you a feel for what is coming.

General Declaration Code

Let's break this code down into bite-size chunks. The first section is fairly self-explanatory:

About the first thing we need to do is to create an instance of `clsConnection`. This is needed because we want to use its methods. We also include a private copy of the `oraDatabase` object. This will be opened inside the private copy of the connection class. We also declare our dynaset variables. Thus in the General Declarations section, we have:

```
Option Explicit

'   Create a private instance of of our clsConnection class so that we may
'   use its methods
Private mcConnection As clsConnection

'   A private copy of the OraDatabase object to be opened inside
'   omcConnection
Private mOraDatabase As OraDatabase
```

```
'     Declare our dynaset objects
Private mdynLastRec As OraDynaset          ' to hold the next available
                                           ' Sequence number
Private mdynPeople As OraDynaset           ' to maintain the People table


'     Declare the Strings that will hold the SELECT statements that define
'     our dynasets

Private msSelect As String                 'to define mdynPeople
Private msFindLastKey As String            'to define mdynLastRec
```

We also need to define dynaset `OraField` objects. An `OraField` object represents a single column in the `OraDynaset` object. In other words, each `OraField` object will map to one column in a row in the result set defined by our query. Each `OraField` object is stored in the `OraFields` collection within the `OraDynaset`.

The `OraDynaset` works faster if its field references are direct and for that purpose we build an `OraField` object for every column defined in the SELECT statements that define our dynasets:

```
'     Field objects for each column in our mdynPeople dynaset
Private mfldPersonId As OraField
Private mfldLastName As OraField
Private mfldFirstName As OraField
Private mfldMI As OraField
Private mfldDob As OraField
Private mfldGender As OraField
Private mfldEyeColor As OraField

'     and one field for the sequence
Private mfldVeryLast As OraField
```

Each of the class properties reports and updates a Private class variable to the "world". To speed and simplify the communications between the form and the object, we will expose simple class variables rather than the `Oradynaset` field values. Here they are:

```
'     Class variables
Private mlPersonId As Double          'Get and Let
Private msLastName As String          'Get and Let
Private msFirstName As String         'Get and Let
Private msMI As String                'Get and Let
Private mdDob As Date                  'Get and Let
Private msGender As String            'Get and Let
Private msEyeColor As String          'Get and Let

'     Make a place for LastRec Variable that will hold our Sequence number
Private mlLastPersonId As Double      'Save Last Value
```

The ConnectX Method

In this method, we get a reference to our connection, instantiate our dynaset objects and use the `OraFields` collection of our `mrsPeople` dynaset to assign the appropriate column values to our `OraField` objects.

My real-life data classes connect to other objects as well. Thus, I also have other Connect methods. I use ConnectX as the method that connects to the database, ConnectP as the method that connects to a parent class, etc.

Let's look at the code then discuss:

```
Public Sub ConnectX(ByVal NewValue As clsConnection) 'Required for connection
                                                      'to clsConnection
Set mcConnection = NewValue

'   We're calling the database method defined in clsConnection
'   to get a reference to the connection

Set mOraDatabase = mcConnection.Database

'   Create our dynasets
'   mdynPeople will allow Oracle to assign coulmun default values
'   when adding or updating records
'   This eliminates unnecessary OIP 4119 errors

Set mdynPeople = mOraDatabase.CreateDynaset(msSelect, 16) 'ORADYN_ORAMODE

'    mdynLastRec will be Read-only
'ORADYN_READONLY
Set mdynLastRec = mOraDatabase.CreateDynaset(msFindLastKey, 4)

'   Set the OraFields to the columns
  With mdynPeople
      Set mfldPersonId = .Fields!PERSON_ID
      Set mfldLastName = .Fields!LAST_NAME
      Set mfldFirstName = .Fields!FIRST_NAME
      Set mfldMI = .Fields!M_I
      Set mfldDob = .Fields!Dob
      Set mfldGender = .Fields!Gender
      Set mfldEyeColor = .Fields!EYE_COLOR
  End With
  Set mfldVeryLast = mdynLastRec!VERY_LAST      'VERY_LAST is the alias we
                                                'gave the next
                                                'availabe sequence number
SetProperties
End Sub
```

Creating the Dynasets

Within the `ConnectX` method we create our dynasets using the `CreateDynaset` method of the `OraDatabase` object. The general syntax is:

```
Set mOraDynaset = mOradatabase.CreateDynaset (SQL, Options)
```

The `SQL` argument is a string that represents the data source for the `OraDynaset`, in our case a SQL SELECT statement. The strings `msSelect` and `msFindLastKey` define the dynasets `mdynPeople` and `mdynLastRec` respectively.

The `Options` argument sets characteristics of the dynaset. I use Option 16 (`ORADYN_ORAMODE`) for the `mdynPeople` dynaset, since it is both read and write and I want missing values to be entered as their default values rather than as nulls.

When we discuss OO4O in full detail, in Chapter 8, you'll see why I prefer this option.

I used option 4 (ORADYN_READONLY) for the mdynLastRec dynaset. Option 4 simply makes the dynaset read-only. We don't need to update the sequence (nor can we in any other way than simply using it).

Assigning Field Values

The OraField objects in the dynaset form a collection (each one mapping to a single column in the result set). We may refer to a specific OraField object by name or by index (we use name in our code). Here is how we reference the Person_ID field:

```
mdynPeople.Fields("Person_ID")
mdynPeople.OraFields!Person_ID
mdynPeople.Fields(0)
```

The two first are references by name shown in two ways. The bang syntax, which I still use (force of habit), is a remnant of VB's earlier versions.

Note that the Value property is the default for the OraField object. If we were being more explicit we would write:

```
mdynPeople.Fields("Person_ID").Value
```

We use these field objects again and again and I prefer not to resolve the references every time I call a field. Therefore, once I have defined a field object, I point it to the dynaset object within the ConnectX method. When this is done the references are resolved and remain fixed from then on. This yields a 6 to 1 performance increase.

We call the ConnectX method from the Form_Load event and pass in cConnection, as you will see later when we discuss the form code.

Let's move on to the Class_Initialize sub where, among other things, we actually define our dynasets using SQL SELECT statements.

The Class_Initialize Routine

Every time a new object is created from its class, it goes through the Class_Initialize routine. This is where we create the SQL statements that define our dynasets ands set the class variables to default values, by calling the SetDefaults subroutine (described later in the chapter):

```
Private Sub Class_Initialize()

'   Set the class varaibles to initial default values
SetDefaults

'   Create the mdynPeople SQL, to retrieve data from te People table

msSelect = "Select "
msSelect = msSelect & "PERSON_ID, "
```

```
msSelect = msSelect & "LAST_NAME, "
msSelect = msSelect & "FIRST_NAME, "
msSelect = msSelect & "M_I, "
msSelect = msSelect & "DOB, "
msSelect = msSelect & "GENDER, "
msSelect = msSelect & "EYE_COLOR"
msSelect = msSelect & " FROM PEOPLE"

'    Create the FindLastKey SQL to retrieve the next available sequence number
msFindLastKey = "Select PERSON_ID_SEQ.NEXTVAL As VERY_LAST from dual"

End Sub
```

We use the SQL SELECT statement to read information stored in the database. Let's consider the SELECT statement that defines mdynPeople:

```
SELECT Person_ID, First_Name, Last_Name, M_I, Gender, DOB, Eye_Color
FROM People
```

This SELECT statement is without a WHERE clause and will thus return the complete table. The dynaset will have a column for each column selected and a row for each row returned. Our initial People table contains twenty-one rows, so our dynaset will also have twenty-one rows. If we select every column, the dynaset will have seven fields in each row.

> *The SELECT statement you use to define an updateable dynaset is automatically modified to include a ROWID psuedocolumn (a unique database-wide identifier). You cannot update a row in Oracle without a ROWID.*

Why don't we use the following statement instead – after all it is shorter:

```
SELECT * from people
```

Well, in the first place, I get the fields in the order I like to get them. Using * would return them in the order in which they were created. Secondly, if we use * and the DBA adds fields to the table we're lost. We no longer even know every field name and end up having to rewrite pieces of the code. Thirdly, it is generally faster across all SQL servers to only get the rows that we need. We're better off putting in a little extra effort up front and saving much frustration later.

> *You may, under some circumstances opt to use * in order not to bind your embedded SQL to a particular schema. You can determine the names of the columns returned from a * by looking at the Dynaset.fields(index).name. This makes for a very dynamic environment, but will certainly not always be appropriate.*

The approach I adopt is akin to the unwritten agreement governing objects and components. When the author writes a new version of a component, he is bound to continue to expose all the old properties and methods exactly as they were. He may add new methods (in which case he must define a secondary interface), but he cannot even renumber the old ones, or change the number, types, or order of their parameters. This way all the programs that have been written based on the old interface continue to work, unchanged, with the new component. We improve the chances of such continuity when we use specificity in our SELECT statement. As long as the DBA does not remove or rename columns, we're fine.

We use the following query to retrieve the last sequence for the mdynLastRec dynaset:

```
Select PERSON_ID_SEQ.NEXTVAL As VERY_LAST from dual
```

Class Property Get/Let Routines

We need to be able to read and assign new values to our class variables. We do this via a set of Property Get and Let routines:

```
Public Property Get PersonId() As Double
    PersonId = mlPersonId
End Property

Public Property Let PersonId(ByVal NewValue As Double)
    mlPersonId = NewValue
End Property

Public Property Get LastName() As String
    LastName = msLastName
End Property

Public Property Let LastName(ByVal NewValue As String)
    msLastName = NewValue
End Property

Public Property Get FirstName() As String
    FirstName = msFirstName
End Property

Public Property Let FirstName(ByVal NewValue As String)
    msFirstName = NewValue
End Property

Public Property Get MI() As String
    MI = msMI
End Property

Public Property Let MI(ByVal NewValue As String)
    msMI = NewValue
End Property

Public Property Get Dob() As Date
    Dob = mdDob
End Property
```

```
Public Property Let Dob(ByVal NewValue As Date)
   mdDob = NewValue
End Property

Public Property Get Gender() As String
   Gender = msGender
End Property

Public Property Let Gender(ByVal NewValue As String)
   msGender = NewValue
End Property

Public Property Get EyeColor() As String
   EyeColor = msEyeColor
End Property

Public Property Let EyeColor(ByVal NewValue As String)
   msEyeColor = NewValue
End Property
```

There are three other `Property Get` routines that are related to navigating through the records in the `OraDynaset` object:

```
Public Property Get EOF() As Boolean
   EOF = mdynPeople.EOF
End Property

Public Property Get BOF() As Boolean
   BOF = mdynPeople.BOF
End Property

Public Property Get IsEmpty() As Boolean
   IsEmpty = mdynPeople.EOF And mdynPeople.BOF
End Property
```

We make use of two important properties of the `OraDynaset` object:

❑   EOF – which returns whether the current dynaset position is after the last record (returns `True`, if an attempt is made to move beyond the last record).

❑   BOF – which returns whether the current dynaset position is before the first record (`True`, if an attempt is made to move before the first record).

If the dynaset is empty then both `BOF` and `EOF` are `True`.

Dynaset Move Methods

As stated previously, we expect our dynaset to contain twenty-one rows. This number will change as we add and delete rows. When the dynaset is initialized it is positioned at the first row. To move from row to row, we use the dynaset 'Move' methods. They are:

❑   **Dynaset.MoveFirst** – which brings us to the first row in the dynaset

❑   **Dynaset.MoveLast** – which moves to the last row in the dynaset

❑   **Dynaset.MoveNext** – which makes the next row in the dynaset

❑   **DynasetMovePrevious** – which moves to the previous row in the dynaset

The row where the dynaset is positioned is the current row. MoveNext works differently when positioned in the last row. If we attempt to perform a MoveNext from the last record in the dynaset, we get an empty record and the End Of File (EOF) condition will be set to True. If we attempt a MoveNext again, an error will be raised. A similar thing happens to MovePrevious.

If the SELECT statement returns no rows at all, both EOF and BOF are true. Any move below BOF raises an error, as does an attempt to move above EOF. Both BOF and EOF are Boolean and are properties of the dynaset.

Following is the code for all of the 'Move' methods:

```
Public Sub MoveFirst()
    If Not mdynPeople.BOF Then
        mdynPeople.MoveFirst
        SetProperties
    End If
End Sub

Public Sub MoveLast()
    If Not mdynPeople.EOF Then
        mdynPeople.MoveLast
        SetProperties
    End If
End Sub

Public Sub MoveNext()
    If Not mdynPeople.EOF Then
        mdynPeople.MoveNext
        If mdynPeople.EOF Then mdynPeople.MoveLast
        SetProperties
    End If
End Sub

Public Sub MovePrevious()
    If Not mdynPeople.BOF Then
        mdynPeople.MovePrevious
        If mdynPeople.BOF Then mdynPeople.MoveFirst
        SetProperties
    End If
End Sub
```

You can see that circumventing the overflow error adds a little complexity to the MoveFirst and MoveLast methods, but prevents any mishaps. When we have just moved to the last record, EOF is not yet set. We want to stay at the last record when EOF is raised, so we ask if the EOF condition was just raised, and if so position the dynaset at the last record again, using a MoveLast. This will also set EOF to False.

The `MovePrevious` and `MoveNext` methods are more devious. How so? OO4O has a bug in the `MovePrevious` method that requires this extra code. Your humble servant discovered this bug in both versions 2.2 and 2.3 of OO4O and came up with a fix (most of my clients are still using 2.2). In fact, Personal Oracle 8.0.4, which is what you're asked to install, and on which this program runs (it is the highest version available, as of this writing, for Windows 95/98), still has the error. Be that what it may, my routine works without a hitch in all the versions so far. It ensures that if the user deletes the first record, they will actually remain at the first row (in Chapter 14 I'll make the routine even more sophisticated). I added the line to the `MoveNext` to get the same kind of behavior.

You will have noticed that in every Move routine, we call the `SetProperties` routine. This private sub assigns a field value to the appropriate class variable and deals with the problem that would arise from assigning Null values to a String (say) in VB. We will discuss this a little later.

We want our data class to be able to do all the 'Moves', we also want to know if we're at `EOF`, `BOF` or both. It would be nice to be able to 'AddNew' rows 'Edit' and then 'Update' old rows and 'Delete' old rows. We also want easy access to each and every field in the current row. We are going to build properties and methods for each of these requirements. The end result is a working data class. Except for the field names and the properties thereof, data classes that maintain any other table will be identical in function. In OOP parlance, that means that they are polymorphic.

Let's move on now and discuss the 'modify' methods of the dynaset.

Dynaset Modify Methods

The four dynaset methods we use to modify database data are (they are discussed in fuller detail in Chapter 8):

❑ **AddNew** – effectively calling a SQL INSERT command. It begins a record insertion operation into the specified dynaset and associated database. The values of our fields are modified through our `OraField` objects. They are not committed to the database until `Update` is called. Because of the way we created the mdynPeople dynaset, Field values that have not been explicitly assigned will be given Oracle default values.

❑ **Edit** – prepares for a data modification by locking the corresponding row in the database.

❑ **Update** – commits changes made to the database.

❑ **Delete** – deletes the current row of the dynaset (and corresponding database row is removed automatically).

In all the routines below we are using predefined and early bound `OraField` objects.

```
Public Sub AddNew()

FindLastKey

'    Load the latest sequence number into the class variable
mlPersonId = mlLastPersonId

'    Call the AddNew method
mdynPeople.AddNew

'    Assign the class variable to the Value property of the Field object
mfldPersonId.Value = mlPersonId
mfldLastName.Value = msLastName
mfldFirstName.Value = msFirstName
mfldMI.Value = msMI
mfldDob.Value = mdDob
mfldGender.Value = msGender
mfldEyeColor.Value = msEyeColor

'    Commit the new record to the database
mdynPeople.Update
End Sub

Public Sub Update()

'    Go into edit mode
mdynPeople.Edit

'    Insert all the values into the fields (except the key)
mfldLastName.Value = msLastName
mfldFirstName.Value = msFirstName
mfldMI.Value = msMI
If mdDob = #1/1/1800# Then
    mfldDob.Value = Null
Else
    mfldDob.Value = mdDob
End If
mfldGender.Value = msGender
mfldEyeColor.Value = msEyeColor

'    Commit the changes
mdynPeople.Update
End Sub

Public Sub Delete()
    mdynPeople.Delete
End Sub
```

Note the line:

```
If mdob = #1/1/1800# Then...
```

All will become clear when we discuss the SetDefaults routine! First we must deal with the FindLastKey routine, which is called at the start of out AddNew sub.

The FindLastKey Routine

FindLastKey is used to generate the next number in the sequence. This number will be inserted into the new row. This routine introduces another dynaset method – Refresh, which tells the database to run the query again and reload the rows of the dynaset.

```
Private Sub FindLastKey()
   mdynLastRec.Refresh
   mlLastPersonId = mfldVeryLast.Value
End Sub
```

The SetProperties Routine

You will have noticed that after calling any particular Move method of the dynaset we call the SetProperties routine to check for any possible attempt to assign a null value from the database to our VB textboxes, before doing the assignment. SetProperties is a private sub and thus not a method of the class.

> *Some people call any sub or function that resides in a class a 'method'. So, to them, this is a private method.*

This is an interesting routine. The way it is written is a reflection on VB 6.0, which has an idiosyncratic behavior that VB5 (and before) spared us. If you try to assign a Null value to a MsgBox or TextBox or Label or a string you get the following error message:

```
'run time error 94 - invalid use of Null'
```

If you don't believe me, start a new standard project in VB and put the following code in the Form_Load event routine:

```
Dim x
x = Null
MsgBox x
```

Now run the program and see what happens.

To circumvent a misuse of nulls in VB5, I used to do the following correction:

```
X = "" & Null
```

This no longer works. Even x = CStr(Something) does not work when Something is a null. The null is not converted to a null string even when we try this trick and the same error as that shown above will be produced. So what's a programmer to do?

When you do the assignment x = Something and Something might be a Null, write:

```
If IsNull(Something) then
    X = ""
Else
    X = Something
End If
```

Here is an interesting question. Is the above code better or worse than:

```
If Not IsNull(Something) then
    X = Something
Else
    X = ""
End If
```

What do you think? Actually, it depends on the probability of Something having a null value. If the probability is higher than 50% the first solution is better, if it is lower than 50% then the second option is preferred. At 50/50 it's a toss up. Why is that? With the If statement, once the antecedent is found to be True, the proper code is run without continuing into the Else part. Thus it is best to write the more probable occurrences first. In the case of the database, null values are usually the rare exception and the second form is better. The same general rule applies to compound If statements with nested ElseIf statements. The checks will run fastest (on average) if they are done in descending order of probability. The same again is true in a Select Case structure. Back to SetProperties:

```
Private Sub SetProperties()

If mdynPeople.EOF Then Exit Sub
    SetDefaults

If Not IsNull(mfldPersonId.Value) Then
    mlPersonId = mfldPersonId.Value
End If

If Not IsNull(mfldLastName.Value) Then
    msLastName = mfldLastName.Value
End If

If Not IsNull(mfldFirstName.Value) Then
    msFirstName = mfldFirstName.Value
End If

If Not IsNull(mfldMI.Value) Then
    msMI = mfldMI.Value
End If

If Not IsNull(mfldDob.Value) Then
    mdDob = mfldDob.Value
End If

If Not IsNull(mfldGender.Value) Then
    msGender = mfldGender.Value
End If
```

```
If Not IsNull(mfldEyeColor.Value) Then
   msEyeColor = mfldEyeColor.Value
End If

End Sub
```

Why do I use the `SetProperties` routine at all? Why don't I get the value of the current row from the dynaset fields? This is a matter of probability. I may want to get to the values more than once. That being the case, it is much faster to go to a variable than to go to a field object. `SetProperties` saves the value of each field in a simple VB variable so that it may be used again and again. This also leads to persistent objects, which is a subject that belongs in another book.

The SetDefaults Routine

Let's now have a look at the `SetDefaults` routine, which is called from our `SetProperties` routine, `Class_Initialize` routine and, as you have seen, affects the way we code our Update routine:

```
Private Sub SetDefaults()
   mlPersonId = 0
   msLastName = ""
   msFirstName = ""
   msMI = ""
   mdDob = #1/1/1800#
   msGender = ""
   msEyeColor = ""
End Sub
```

We have to perform a similar trick to the one we saw in the previous section, to deal with the possibility of a null date. I convert them to an impossible date #1/1/1800# and check for that value. This, by the way, is not a VB error, but a Null takes us to #1/1/1900#, a date on which many of our cohabitants of earth were already born.

That is all of the code that belongs in our `clsPeople` data class. We are now going to deal with the date formatting functions.

Standard Module Code

I handle the #1/1/1800# date problem in the `ConvertDate` routine. I format dates for display in the `FormatDate` function below.

```
Public Function FormatDate(dDate As Date, sFormat As String) As String
   If dDate = #1/1/1800# Then
      FormatDate = ""
   Else
      FormatDate = Format$(dDate, sFormat)
   End If
End Function
```

```
Public Function ConvertDate(sDate As String) As Date
   If Trim$(RemoveDashes(sDate, "/")) = "" Then
      ConvertDate = #1/1/1800#
   Else
      ConvertDate = CDate(sDate)
   End If
End Function
```

These two functions and the RemoveDashes function that is called from within ConvertDate are used repeatedly. We are much better off putting all three in a regular module. All the data classes that a project may contain may then use them.

Removedashes is a function that removes a delimiter from a string. For example, if we have a string:

S = 'abracadabra'

then RemoveDashes(S, 'bra') will return acada. In our case it converts / / to a null string. This is useful if you use a preformatted text box.

```
Public Function RemoveDashes(ByVal sIn As String, ByVal sDash As String) As
String

'   Remove all hyphens from a string (SSN) or slashes from a Date
    Dim lPos As Long, sTemp As String, lLenDash As Long
    lLenDash = Len(sDash)
    sTemp = sIn
    lPos = 99
    Do Until lPos = 0
        lPos = InStr(1, sTemp, sDash)
        If lPos <> 0 Then
            sTemp = Left$(sTemp, lPos - 1) & Mid$(sTemp, lPos + lLenDash)
        End If
    Loop
    RemoveDashes = sTemp
End Function
```

To create a new standard module in the program, go to the project menu and select **Add module**. Name it modGeneral and type the three functions in it.

That's it! We have built a data class. Complete code for this and other samples may be downloaded from the WROX site.

Let's recap:

❑ We built all the class variables at the top and class field objects.

❑ We then built the ConnectX subroutine and the Class_Initialize routine. In the ConnectX routine, the data class finds a connection, creates the dynasets and binds the field objects the dynasets. In the Class_initialize routine our dynasets are defined by SQL statements.

❑ We built the various Move and AddNew, Update, Delete and Refresh routines that will be used by the main program to navigate the database and update it.

❑ We put the FormatDate, ConvertDate and RemoveDashes functions in a .bas module and named it modGeneral.

We are ready to tie it all together in the form.

Form Code

There is very little that we need to do. A good class and module design has already taken care of most of the work. First, define two objects, one for the connection class, and the other for the data class. Do this in the General section of the form, just below the 'Option Explicit' statement:

```
Option Explicit
Private cConnection As clsConnection
Private cPeople As clsPeople
```

In the form load routine, center the form and establish the connection by calling OpenDB and telling cPeople that it should connect through cConnection.

```
Private Sub Form_Load()
Me.Left = (Screen.Width - Me.Width) / 2
Me.Top = (Screen.Height - Me.Height) / 2

Set cConnection = New clsConnection
Set cPeople = New clsPeople

cConnection.OpenDB "scott", "tiger", ""
cPeople.ConnectX cConnection
Display
End Sub
```

In each of the Move commands, call the proper Move sub of cPeople and call the Display routine to put the results on the form:

```
Private Sub cmdMoveFirst_Click()
   cPeople.MoveFirst
   Display
End Sub

Private Sub cmdMoveLast_Click()
   cPeople.MoveLast
   Display
End Sub

Private Sub cmdMoveNext_Click()
   cPeople.MoveNext
   Display
End Sub

Private Sub cmdMovePrevious_Click()
   cPeople.MovePrevious
   Display
End Sub
```

When we update the database either by AddNew or by Update we use the Store sub, which moves content from the form to the class.

```
Private Sub cmdAdd_Click()
   Store
   cPeople.AddNew
End Sub
```

```
Private Sub cmdUpdate_Click()
   Store
   cPeople.Update
End Sub

Private Sub cmdDelete_Click()
   cPeople.Delete
   cmdMoveNext_Click
End Sub
```

Next we write the `cmdExit_Click` sub in which we set the two objects to `Nothing` and end the program.

```
Private Sub cmdExit_Click()
   Set cPeople = Nothing
   Set cConnection = Nothing
   Unload Me
End Sub
```

We call the `cmdExit_Click` sub also if the program terminates for any other reason (the user clicks the "X" for instance)

```
Private Sub Form_QueryUnload(Cancel As Integer, UnloadMode As Integer)
   cmdExit_Click
End Sub
```

Lastly we add the `Display` and `Store` subs:

```
Private Sub Display()

'   Read data from class variables into our textboxes (in correct format)
'   via class Propery Get

   txtPersonId = Format$(cPeople.PersonId, "##########0")
   txtLastName = cPeople.LastName
   txtFirstName = cPeople.FirstName
   txtMI = cPeople.MI
   txtDOB = FormatDate(cPeople.Dob, "mm/dd/yyyy")
   txtGender = cPeople.Gender
   txtEyeColor = cPeople.EyeColor
End Sub

Private Sub Store()
'   Assign textbox values to our class variables (via class Property Let)

   cPeople.LastName = txtLastName
   cPeople.FirstName = txtFirstName
   cPeople.MI = txtMI
   cPeople.Dob = ConvertDate(txtDOB.Text)
   cPeople.Gender = txtGender
   cPeople.EyeColor = txtEyeColor
End Sub
```

The complete code sits in the Chapter 5 section in the WROX site. These are 5 files:

```
OO4OPeopleDynaset.vbp
frmPeople.frm
modGeneral.bas
OO4OclsConnection.cls
OO4OclsPeople.cls
```

Save your work in the **Chapter5** subdirectory of VBOraBook.

Summary

In this Chapter you have built a simple program that maintains a database table, using OO4O.

We covered the basics of how to create an `Oradynaset` object within an `OraSession` object. We defined our dynasets using SQL `SELECT` statements. One dynaset was used to maintain the `People` table and the other to retrieve Sequence numbers from the database to ensure the uniqueness of the `Person_ID` field. We used the Move methods of the dynaset to navigate through the records.

Our dynasets were defined by data from a single table, so they were updatable. We called the Modify methods of the dynaset to modify data in the dynaset, and thus the database. The read/write process was accomplished using the `OraFields` collection of the `OraDynaset` object.

We encapsulated our mdynPeople and mdynLastRec dynasets in a VB class. We also created a second class. These classes (along with the form) contained a private copy of a second class (clsConnection), which maintained our connection to the database. All classes were built on sound OOP principles. We invoked all of this encapsulated functionality from our user interface.

> *Conspicuously missing from this chapter (and others) is error handling. The aim here was to stick to the mechanics of how VB talks to Oracle.*

Build the program and play with it. Put breakpoints in strategic places in the code and follow the progress line by line. Get a gut feeling for how it all works. The process is easy. You've probably done the exact thing before using DAO and the Jet engine. If you want to see how we build exactly the same program using ADO, go to Chapter 9 now. If you are intent on continuing to build your OO4O knowledge, proceed directly to the next chapter. We are going to investigate passing parameters via OO4O, which will introduce the `oraParameters` collection, along with the concept of transactions.

6

Using Parameters with OO4O

This chapter will deal with the use of parameters with OO4O. We're all familiar with using parameters (arguments) in subs and functions. They are invaluable expeditors of the programming process. ADO and OO4O, each in its own fashion, allow us to pass parameters to SQL statements and stored procedures. The use of parameters makes for better, faster, and more general data classes.

We are going to modify our basic OO4O application so that we can use parameters with our SQL statement. Again, we are going to do a single table manipulation. This does not require stored procedures. In fact stored procedures do not offer any advantage in such cases.

> *In our final application (Chapter 14) we will perform a two-table manipulation and use parameters to provide input and output to **stored procedures**. This will also introduce the **OraSQLStmt** object that allows us to define a SQL statement that Oracle will parse only once and then can use many times, thus improving performance.*

Thus we will:

❑ Modify the SELECT statement that defines our mdynPeople dynaset to accept a bind variable (parameter).

❑ Add a parameter to the OraParameters collection of the OraDatabase object, using the Add method.

❑ Dynamically bind our parameter to the SQL statement by calling the Refresh method of the mdynPeople dynaset.

With OO4O this really is a very simple process. Our dynaset is still updatable so we will only have to make minor alterations to our basic OO4O application.

The OraParameter Object

In the diagram below you will see the full OO4O object model:

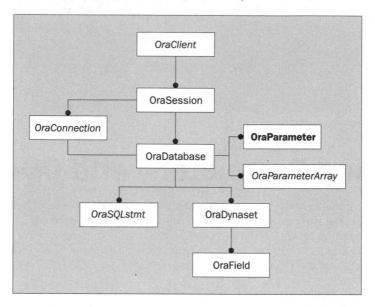

The main focus of our attention in this chapter will be the OraParameters collection, which maintains a list of all of our OraParameter objects. An OraParameter object represents a scalar type variable that we can bind to our SQL SELECT statement.

An OraParameterArray object represents an array-type bind variable

As you can see from the diagram, OraParameters are the property of the OraDatabase object. OraParameters are bound (parsed, or compiled to p-code) in the Oracle database, as are the SQL statements using them. Binding makes the SQL perform much faster because the bound statement is already parsed after the first time it was run, making subsequent executions much more efficient.

> **Binding or compiling a statement also allows the server to figure the best way to conduct the query. This means deciding which part of a join (left or right) to do first, which index to do first, and so on. The result is an optimized code.**

A parameterized SQL statement in OO4O always binds both parameter and statement after first use (when we start using stored procedures in Chapter 14, we will use the OraSQLStmt object that will also bind a non-parameterized statement).

We handle parameters very differently with ADO, as you will see in Chapter 10. The problem with ADO and Oracle (thus far) was that the ? parameters were not bound in the database except in the case of stored procedures. The exception is because it is the stored procedure that binds its parameters - not ADO. In case of standard SQL, ADO simply replaces the ? placeholder with the `Parameter.Value` so there is no binding on the server side.

Before we can use our parameter with a SQL statement we must define it and, in the process, add it to the `OraParameters` collection. We do this using the `Add` method of the `OraParameters` collection. This is discussed in full detail in Chapter 8, but the general syntax is:

```
OraDatabase.Parameters.Add ParamName, ParamValue, ParamType
```

Where:

- ❏   `ParamName` is the name of the parameter
- ❏   `ParamValue` is the initial value we assign to it
- ❏   `ParamType` describes the mode of operation of the parameter (either input, output or both)

The parameter type is defined a constant or a value, from the following:

- ❏   `ORAPARAM_INPUT` or 1,
- ❏   `ORAPARAM_OUTPUT` or 2
- ❏   `ORAPARAM_BOTH` or 3.

OK, let's modify our OO40 application so that we can use parameters.

Parameters and OO40

We are going to create a parameter and dynamically bind it to our SQL statement. When the dynaset is refreshed, it will be populated according to the value we specify for the parameter. We are going to use this functionality to institute gender discrimination. In order to implement this non-politically-correct atrocity by using the `Gender` as a parameter that is passed into the `WHERE` clause of the `SELECT` statement, the user will simply enter the required gender value in the proper text box, click the `Find` button and then all the rows for the specified gender will be returned to the `mdynPeople` dynaset.

To achieve all of this we need to make just a few simple alterations to the code of our code.

Before we start, create a **Chapter6** subdirectory in your **VBOraBook**. Make a true copy of the following files from our previous program into our new directory (right-click on the icon, drag to the folder, release the mouse button and select **Copy Here**):

- ❑ frmPeople.frm
- ❑ modGeneral.bas
- ❑ clsConnectionOO4O.cls
- ❑ clsPeopleOO4O.cls
- ❑ OO4OPeople.vbp

Now open the OO4OPeople project. You may want to immediately save and rename the project. I chose the following names: frmPeoplePrm.frm, clsPeopleOO4OPrm.cls and OO4OPeoplePrm.vbp. The clsConnectionOO4O class and modGeneral.bas remain untouched from our previous program.

We've been talking about a user entering the gender value in the appropriate textbox and clicking a "Find" button to retrieve gender-specific result set. Let us then, start with modifications to the user interface and the form code that will allow us to "call" this functionality.

Modifying the Form

Add a command button to your form. Name it cmdFind and change the caption to &Find. You may also want to change the from caption to Maintaining the PEOPLE table, using OO4O:

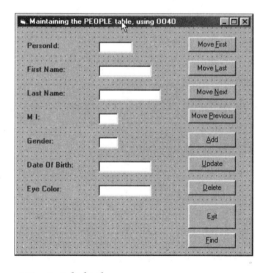

Here is how the cmdFind code looks:

```
Private Sub cmdFind_Click()
    cPeople.Gender = UCase(txtGender.Text)
    cPeople.Refresh     'Read again
    cmdMoveFirst_Click  'Position the form at the first row
End Sub
```

When a user enters a `Gender` value and clicks `Find`, the text entered is converted to upper case and stored in our `msGender` class variable (via `Gender Property Let` routine). We then call the `Refresh` routine (which you will see in the `clsPeople` code), where the variable value is assigned to our parameter. Finally we move the record pointer to the first row.

That's the form taken care of. Let's move behind the scenes and consider the modifications that need to be made to our `clsPeople` class. The first thing we need to do is modify the `SELECT` statement that defines our `mdynPeople` dynaset, so that it will accept a parameter.

Modifying the Class_Initialize Routine

We must modify our `msSelect` string in the `Class_Initialize` routine of the `clsPeople` class so that it will accept a parameter. We do this by adding a single line of code:

```
Private Sub Class_Initialize()
'** Initialize Class Variables
    SetDefaults

'Make a parameter SQL for the reading the dynaset
    msSelect = "Select "
    msSelect = msSelect & "PERSON_ID, "
    msSelect = msSelect & "LAST_NAME, "
    msSelect = msSelect & "FIRST_NAME, "
    msSelect = msSelect & "M_I, "
    msSelect = msSelect & "DOB, "
    msSelect = msSelect & "GENDER, "
    msSelect = msSelect & "EYE_COLOR"
    msSelect = msSelect & " FROM PEOPLE"
    msSelect = msSelect & " Where (GENDER = :pGender)"

'** Create the FindLastKey SQL
    msFindLastKey = "Select PERSON_ID_SEQ.NEXTVAL As VERY_LAST from DUAL"
End Sub
```

The code above is the complete `Class_Initialize` sub from the `clsPeople` data class. The last line of the `SELECT` statement is highlighted. As you can see, include the parameter reference in the `WHERE` clause:

```
msSelect = msSelect & " Where (GENDER = :pGender)"
```

The parameter name, `pGender`, acts as a placeholder in the SQL statement. It is identified as a parameter by placing a colon in front of the name. This implies that the parameters are named inside the statements in which they are used. This is a very convenient feature that enhances the readability of the program.

Before we can use our parameter in the `SELECT` statement we must add it to the `OraParameters` collection and, in the process, define it. We do this in the `ConnectX` method of `clsPeople`.

Modifying the ConnectX Method

Following is the full ConnectX code, with the modifications highlighted:

```
Public Sub ConnectX(ByVal NewValue As clsConnection) 'Required for connection
to clsConnection
Set mcConnection = NewValue
    'our class relies on an already open database.
    Set mOraDatabase = mcConnection.Database
    'Parameters are added with: Name;  Value; and type where 1 is Input
    '                                              and  2 is output.
    mOraDatabase.Parameters.Add "pGender", "F", 1
    'we now create an empty dynaset option 16 -- or ORA_DEFAULT
    'this way we refresh new and updated records, and
    'eliminates unnecessary OIP 4119 errors
    Set mdynPeople = mOraDatabase.CreateDynaset(msSelect, 16&)
    'Option 4 is for a Read Only dynaset
    Set mdynLastRec = mOraDatabase.CreateDynaset(msFindLastKey, 4&)
    'Set the OraFields to the columns
    Set mfldPersonId = mdynPeople.Fields!PERSON_ID
    Set mfldLastName = mdynPeople.Fields!LAST_NAME
    Set mfldFirstName = mdynPeople.Fields!FIRST_NAME
    Set mfldMI = mdynPeople.Fields!M_I
    Set mfldDob = mdynPeople.Fields!Dob
    Set mfldGender = mdynPeople.Fields!Gender
    Set mfldEyeColor = mdynPeople.Fields!EYE_COLOR
    Set mfldVeryLast = mdynLastRec!VERY_LAST
SetProperties
End Sub
```

Our pGender parameter is an input parameter of type VARCHAR2 and its initial value is set to "F".

> *Be warned that trying to add the same parameter again will cause an error.*

Even though the parameters are database objects I prefer to declare them in the data class rather than in the connection class. The connection class normally serves many data classes, but I use the parameters in the SQL statements of the data classes. Keeping declarations close to where they are used helps readability and maintainability.

This convenience may cause a problem though. As stated above, you can only declare a parameter once. Certain columns appear in multiple tables. The Employee_ID column, for example, is used in the Salary, Employee, and JobHistory tables and may be needed as an EmpID parameter (say) in all of the corresponding data classes. However, we know that the parameter is a property of the database – once it is declared, that is where it is stored. If we declare the parameter in all 3 classes we'll actually try to create an object that already exists.

For the time being our sample programs deal with just one table at a time so this problem will not occur. The general solution, however, is to trap the error and ignore it. The database will not create a parameter it already has, and the parameter is available throughout the session. Even if a parameter is declared for the use in one table, it may be used without any problems in another.

The final addition to the `clsPeople` class is a `Refresh` routine. When the user selects a gender, we need to reload the dynaset with the appropriate records by calling the `Refresh` method of mdynPeople. Here is how we do it:

```
Public Sub Refresh()
'** Set parameters and re-read
    mOraDatabase.Parameters("pGender").Value = msGender
    mdynPeople.Refresh
    If mdynPeople.EOF And mdynPeople.BOF Then
        SetDefaults
    End If
End Sub
```

We assign the value of our msGender class variable to the `Value` property of our pGender parameter. We then reload the dynaset with the appropriate data by calling its Refresh method. If no records are selected then we call the `SetDefaults` method to set the default values of our class variables.

That's all the changes we need to make! The `clsConnection`, a truly universal class, is unchanged (but we are going to improve it in the next chapter). The `clsPeople` class is identical except, as you have already seen, in the `SELECT` statements with the parameterized `WHERE` clause, the added parameter in the `ConnectX` method, and the new `Refresh` routine.

All you need to do now is run the program and test it. We set the initial value of the parameter to 'F' so you should see displayed the first woman in our `People` table:

Navigate through the records in the dynaset and you will only see F in the Gender textbox. Change this to an M and call a move method… and you will still see only the female employees! However, change the value in the Gender textbox to M and press Find and the dynaset will be loaded with men only.

Summary

The way we program with OO4O does not change much when parameters are added. We still use the same approach and can build on what we've learned before. This is OO4O's greatest strength. It stems from the designers' desire to build an interface that allows for easy database updates. Those of you who have worked with the VB 3.0 data controls to maintain a database can see what the OO4O designers tried to achieve (and have).

Of course, modifying data in this way in modern relational databases has very serious data integrity issues. In certain environments updatable dynasets will simply not be an option. If you want any real measure of control over the process the modifications should be performed using DML or, even better, stored procedures.

As you will see in Chapter 10, when we tackle the self-same program, ADO makes life slightly more difficult for us but, in a sense, forces us to do things the right way. In ADO we use parameters in the Command object and when we execute the command we end up with a read-only recordset. This means that we have to perform our modifications using INSERT, UPDATE and DELETE statements, each with its own parameters.

A short chapter then, reflecting the ease with which OO4O utilizes parameters in relatively simple scenarios such as this one.

7

Optimizing the OO4O Connection and Data Classes

In Chapter 5 we discussed how to build a VB program that connects to and manipulates an Oracle database using OO4O. In Chapter 6 we refined the program so that we could pass parameters. We are now going to carry out some modifications that will improve the program's performance. We will:

❑   Add **transaction control** to our `OO4OclsConnection` class. Our transaction-level object in OO4O is the `OraSession` object. Thus we progress our understanding of OO4O still further.

❑   Modify the `OO4OclsPeoplePrm` class so that we `Let` and `Get` all of the class properties together by passing a variant array whose elements are the individual properties (rather than getting or letting each property by itself).

❑   Dispense with the `mdynLastRec` dynaset and, instead, retrieve the next sequence number from an Oracle database **trigger**.

These changes are relatively simple to implement. Our underlying methodology remains unaltered. Our dynaset is still updatable so we can still use its 'Modify' and 'Move' methods. We still use our `OraField` objects to map to the columns in the `mdynPeople` dynaset.

Every improvement that we make in this chapter relates to a data class or the connection class. The connection class is universal and the change is done just once. In our final application (Chapter 14) there will be five data classes, so whatever we do to our `clsPeople` class in this chapter should also be done to all the others. We simply use `clsPeople` as an example to a general rule.

When we are finished we are going to have a method for producing programs to help the user maintain an Oracle database using OO4O. This methodology is built upon the following:

❑ A connection object that is portable without change to all our future VB and Oracle projects.

❑ A polymorphic data class building method to be used in all our future VB and Oracle projects.

❑ A polymorphic form building method to be used in future VB and Oracle projects.

We are going to write a program for ADO with exactly the same functionality, following the same methodology, in Chapter 11.

Note that we are improving the program slowly. We make one improvement at a time. All our past efforts have already been tested and we only need to verify the new code. Testing becomes much easier, and so does the development process as a whole.

Enough with the evangelism. Let's add transaction control to our `clsConnection` class.

Adding Transactions to the Connection Class

Real life applications are not made of a simple form and a single database table. They involve multiple tables carefully related to each other. A single business transaction often involves multiple rows in multiple tables. These complex operations might fail midway, leaving us with bad data. We use two mechanisms to guarantee our data against such half-baked operations. One is stored procedures, the other is transaction control. We'll need both in the next chapter, where the application involves our complete sample database. Here we prepare the ground by enabling safe transaction control.

We need transaction control when we effect more than a single row in one logical operation. This allows us to retract when any part of update process fails. Transactions are controlled (at least in my programs) in the connection class. This is a logical choice. OO4O has the transaction control methods in the OO4O `OraSession` object, which we encompass in the `clsConnection` class:

Function	OraSession Method
Start a transaction	`BeginTrans`
Accept	`CommitTrans`
Reject	`RollBack`

Since many objects share the same connection (through cConnection) and because committing or rolling back effects all the rows that went through DML changes, a commit issued by one user might commit a half-baked transaction of another user prematurely. Or worse – roll a good and almost complete transaction of another user back. To prevent such calamities from happening I have added a safety feature to the transaction mechanism: only one user or object will be allowed to perform a transaction at any one time. We do this by passing a unique token to the object that started the transaction. Once the token is passed, no other object can start a transaction or end it by acceptance or rejection. Only the object that passes back the correct token can end it. Once ended, the cConnection may start a new transaction at the request of the next calling object.

> *You may remember the Token Ring networks of old, and they did the same thing with the permission to send data across the network. Only the chief holding the pipe can smoke it, and he passes it to the others at his leisure.*

This transaction control mechanism will be used in our final project.

Before you continue make the obligatory **Chapter7** directory and make a true-copy of the material from **Chapter6** to it. Open the OO4OPeoplePrm project and immediately save the various pieces as follows:

- ❑ frmOO4OPeoplePrmTrans
- ❑ OO4OclsPeoplePrmTrans.cls
- ❑ OO4OclsConnectionTrans.cls
- ❑ OO4OPeoplePrmTrans.vbp
- ❑ ModGeneralTrans.bas

For the first time we are going to have to make a small change to our trusty modGeneral. We make no more design alterations to the form but, later in the chapter, we will add some new code.

Let's start by declaring two new variables in the declaration section of our connection class. One is to tell us if we're in the middle of a transaction, the other to serve as the transaction's token:

```
Private mbBeginTrans As Boolean    'have we begun a trans?
Private mlTransactorId As Long     'identity of object that begun the trans
                                   'only this object can Commit it
                                   'or Roll it Back.
```

We are now going to add a Class_initialize routine to our class, in which we Randomize. This process creates a new seed in the random number generator. We want the tokens to be different for every transaction started and without the new seed it will always repeat, allowing a smart hacker to note the repeating order of tokens and use it to wreak havoc. Our transaction token (mlTransactorId) is a random number between 1 and 1,000,000. This makes the probability of disturbing the process by random stabbing just one in a million:

```
Private Sub Class_Initialize()
    Randomize   'To protect the programmer from inadvertently unregistering
End Sub
```

We add a new read-only property to the class. This is the `InTransaction` property. It tells the caller if the class is now in transaction.

```
Public Property Get InTransaction() As Boolean
'should anybody want to know if we've begun a trans
    InTransaction = mbBeginTrans
End Property
```

Finally we add three new methods: one to begin a transaction, one to commit it, and the third to roll it back. Here they are:

```
Public Function BeginTrans() As Long

' BeginTrans, CommitTrans and RollBack are methods in the OraSession
' object and should be used with care.  They are thus methods of
' the connection class.

    If Not mbBeginTrans Then
        mlTransactorId = Int(1000000 * Rnd) + 1 'returns a random number
                                        'from 1'to one million
        mOraSession.BeginTrans
        mbBeginTrans = True
        BeginTrans = mlTransactorId
    Else
        BeginTrans = 0
    End If
End Function

Public Function CommitTrans(lCallerId As Long) As Boolean

    CommitTrans = False
    If mbBeginTrans Then
        If lCallerId = mlTransactorId Then
            mOraSession.CommitTrans
            mbBeginTrans = False
            CommitTrans = True
        End If
    End If
End Function

Public Function RollBack(lCallerId As Long) As Boolean
    RollBack = False
    If mbBeginTrans Then
        If lCallerId = mlTransactorId Then
            mOraSession.RollBack
            mbBeginTrans = False
            RollBack = True
        End If
    End If
End Function
```

We now have a transaction ready OO4O-connection-class. We are not yet going to use the transactability of the connection class, but we are fully prepared for its use in our final OO4O application (Chapter 14).

Enhancing the OO4O Data Class

As intimated in the introduction to this chapter, we are going to make two improvements here. Firstly we will change the way in which we pass our class properties and, secondly, we will drop our `mdynLastRec` dynaset and instead retrieve the next sequence number using a trigger on the Oracle database.

Passing Class Properties in an Array

We improve the programs' performance by eliminating unnecessary communications between the form and the data class. Rather than getting or letting each property by itself, we'll let and get them all together by passing a variant array whose elements are the individual properties. This will increase the speed of communication between the data classes and the calling procedures (in other words, forms).

The simplest way to pass all the class properties at once is to put them in a variant array and pass this array. Doing that will pass all the class properties, which are in fact the fields of a single database row, to and from the form in one round trip. This does not make a measurable difference in a setup such as ours, where all the pieces work in a single PC, but makes quite a difference when the data class is in a server of its own. This is where the combination of 1) round trips across the network and 2) the data marshalling that happens with each call across different program spaces will slow us down. In this situation a single trip is measurably faster than seven are.

To enjoy this benefit we add the following to the declaration section of the class:

```
'** for less round trips keep all the properties in a variant array
Private mvAll As Variant 'Get and Let
```

We `ReDim` this variant to an array of seven elements in the `Class_Initialize` routine:

```
Private Sub Class_Initialize()
ReDim mvAll(0 To 6) 'we have 7 properties rolled into the array
SetDefaults
```

We now add a new read/write property to the class:

```
Public Property Get All () As Variant

    mvAll(0) = mlPersonId
    mvAll(1) = msLastName
    mvAll(2) = msFirstName
    mvAll(3) = msMI
    mvAll(4) = mdDob
    mvAll(5) = msGender
    mvAll(6) = msEyeColor
    All = mvAll
End Property

Public Property Let All(ByVal vNewValue As Variant)
```

```
    mvAll = vNewValue
    mlPersonId = mvAll(0)
    msLastName = mvAll(1)
    msFirstName = mvAll(2)
    msMI = mvAll(3)
    mdDob = mvAll(4)
    msGender = mvAll(5)
    msEyeColor = mvAll(6)
End Property
```

That's it! The data class is ready for faster communication.

Form Code

All these changes have to be reflected in the form. We are going to make immediate use of the new Property All to make fewer roundtrips. This requires us to change the way we store and display our data. We also have to add a new variable in the declaration section of the form:

```
Private vAll As Variant
```

This variable is going to be used in the Display and Store subs as follows (just delete the old ones and replace them with these):

```
Private Sub Display()

    vAll = cPeople.All 'get all the properties in one trip
    txtPersonId = Format$(vAll(0), "##########0")
    txtLastName = vAll(1)
    txtFirstName = vAll(2)
    txtMI = vAll(3)
    txtDOB = FormatDate(vAll(4), "mm/dd/yyyy")
    txtGender = vAll(5)
    txtEyeColor = vAll(6)
End Sub

Private Sub Store()

    vAll(1) = txtLastName
    vAll(2) = txtFirstName
    vAll(3) = txtMI
    vAll(4) = ConvertDate(txtDOB.Text)
    vAll(5) = txtGender
    vAll(6) = txtEyeColor
    cPeople.All = vAll
End Sub
```

When you try to run the program now, it won't. This is because we have to change the way we call one of the subs in the general module.

Modifying the General Module

Function and Sub parameters may be called by value (`ByVal`) or by reference (`ByRef`), the latter being the default. Passing a parameter by reference simply passes a pointer to its memory location. The function or sub will change this *in-situ* (Latin for in place) and thus the original value will change. Passing by value passes a copy of the variable. If this copy is changed by the sub or function the original value remains intact. For the `vAll(4)` to be understood as a date in the `FormatDate` sub it has to be passed by value. You might think that we are passing `vAll(4)` by value in order to protect it. This is not the case. The `ConvertDate` function does not change the parameter; it merely uses it to compute the result and leaves it intact. The true reason is that we have a reference problem. VB can only handle a simple variable pointer whereas `vAll (4)` is a variable within a variable and had to be passed by value.

Let us then go to `modGeneralTrans.bas` and make this small change:

```
Public Function FormatDate(ByVal dDate As Date, sFormat As String) As String
```

Just add the `ByVal` in front of the `dDate` parameter declaration.

Implementing a Trigger

We have to retrieve the next available sequence number in order to ensure the uniqueness of our `Person_ID` column when we insert a new row into the dynaset, and hence to the Oracle database. Our existing method (retrieving the number into `mdynLastRec`) works well enough but it is simply not very efficient to create a dynaset object and other related variables and `OraField` objects just to retrieve a single number when we insert a new row. Instead we will create a trigger on Oracle to do this job for us.

Triggers are discussed in full detail in Chapter 13. They are compiled (p-code) objects stored on the Oracle database. They are not called directly from VB. Instead they are associated with a specific database table and are automatically invoked whenever a user attempts to modify data (in our case `INSERT` a new row) on the table that is protected by the trigger. A trigger cannot be circumvented.

In order to create a trigger for our People table, open up Oracle Navigator and drill down to the People table (by clicking on the + signs).

> *This process is described in detail in Chapter 13, where you can also find out how to create triggers in SQL*PLUS. If you feel you need more information now, I would refer you to there.*

Click on the + besides the People table icon and you should see two more icons: **Index** and **Trigger**. Right-click on **Trigger** and select **New**. Fill in the New Trigger Properties dialog according to the following screenshot:

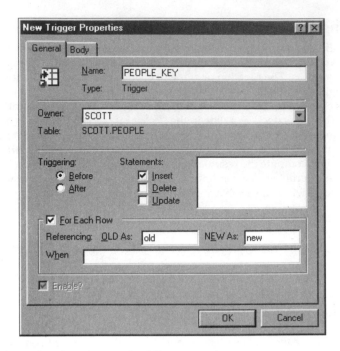

Click on the Body tab and enter the following code to create our PEOPLE_KEY trigger (just delete the BEGIN...END; that is already there) and click OK:

```
DECLARE X NUMBER;
BEGIN
  IF :new.PERSON_ID = 0 THEN
     SELECT PERSON_ID_SEQ.NEXTVAL INTO X FROM DUAL;
     :new.PERSON_ID := X;
  END IF;
END;
```

The code is fairly simple. You will recognize the SELECT statement as the msFindLastKey string from the Class_Initialize routine of our previous project. It changes the PERSON_ID to the next value of the sequence if the input was set to 0. Otherwise it uses what it was given. What is the reason for this "crazy" arrangement? If the programmer wants to handle the sequence in the class and then use it, he can. If he does not, he only has top set the PERSON_ID to 0, and the trigger will do the job. I did it because it gave me a choice. This choice will be used inside the stored procedure in the final application.

Our database trigger is invoked every time we try to insert a new row into the People table and provides us automatically with the next available sequence number.

Now that we have a trigger to guarantee that an incoming record has a unique key we no longer need the mdynLastRec dynaset or the FindLastKey routine.

Thus we can *remove* the `FindLastKey` routine:

```
Private Sub FindLastKey()
    mdynLastRec.Refresh
    mlLastPersonId = mfldVeryLast.Value
End Sub
```

Remove the first two lines from the `AddNew` method and set the `Value` property of the `mfldPersonId` OraField object to zero. The new routine will look like this:

```
Public Sub AddNew()
    mdynPeople.AddNew
        ' Insert all the values into the fields
        mfldPersonId.Value = 0
        mfldLastName.Value = msLastName
        mfldFirstName.Value = msFirstName
        mfldMI.Value = msMI
        mfldDob.Value = mdDob
        mfldGender.Value = msGender
        mfldEyeColor.Value = msEyeColor
    mdynPeople.Update
End Sub
```

Remove the next following lines from the declaration section:

```
Private mdynLastRec As OraDynaset '    Last rec

Private msFindLastKey As String    'to define mdynLastRec

'and one field for the sequence
Private mfldVeryLast As OraField

'** Make a place for LastRec Variable
Private mlLastPersonId As Double   'Save Last Value
```

Remove the following lines from the `ConnectX` method:

```
'Option 4 is for a Read Only dynaset
    Set mdynLastRec = mOraDatabase.CreateDynaset(msFindLastKey, 4)

Set mfldVeryLast = mdynLastRec!VERY_LAST
```

Now remove these lines from the `Class_Initialize`:

```
'** Create the FindLastKey SQL
    msFindLastKey = "Select PERSON_ID_SEQ.NEXTVAL As VERY_LAST from dual"
```

That's it. We have a smaller and faster class, without the baggage and extra roundtrip of maintaining the unique key. This also allows the database to do its job to maintain the integrity of the primary key. This is much better handled in the database especially with Oracle, Sybase, and SQL Server.

Save all your work. Test it to your heart's delight. Put breakpoints at strategic places in the code and step through it until you have a deeper understanding of what makes it tick.

Summary

We now have the core of the technique by which we can build great applications. Our connection object is portable and may be re-used without change. It also handles transactions safely. Our data class allows the main program to imitate the dynasets of old. They also let the program address each data column by itself or, to save roundtrips, all of them at once.

We have also developed a form mechanism that, except for the textboxes (and thus the `Display` and `Store` procedures), is identical for any data (we now use the `All` property to get all the individual data pieces and only break it down in these two subs). We are going to capitalize on this when we build our final application in Chapter 14.

8

Oracle Objects For OLE Reference

The standard approach taken by "VB Database How To" books is to deal mainly with Access and SQL Server. The preceding practical chapters have introduced you to many of the important objects of the OO4O object model, along with a few of their methods and properties. Hopefully, it has given you a good feel for how OO4O works, and the advantages it offers for Oracle to VB connectivity.

Now we move on to the full object model, where you will become conversant with all of the OO4O objects, how they work together, and all of the methods and properties available to each. You will take this knowledge forward to the PL/SQL Chapter, where we will discuss how OO4O handles stored procedures and triggers.

> *A good source of information on OO4O is the Oracleo.hlp file that is available on the Oracle web site (www.oracle.com). The help file is also available where the Oracle Client is installed on a PC. This is normally in the following directory:*
>
> *c:\orawin95\MSHELP\ in a Windows95 or Windows98 system, and in*
>
> *c:\orant\MSHELP\ on an NT System.*

Let's pause for a moment and recap some of the features of OO4O:

❑ OO4O offers the quickest, most direct access to Oracle since it talks directly to the native OCI.

❑ It is a mature and stable product, making the widest possible range of Oracle functionality available to the VB programmer.

❑   OO4O is a lightweight and simple set of objects; very similar to the old DAO and RDO object models. However, the VB programmer can handle OO4O in one third of the number of lines required for RDO and a half of those required for ADO.

❑   It has much fewer properties, methods, and collections to be memorized (compared to ADO) and is therefore much, much easier to master. Of course, this also implies that it is less versatile.

❑   OO4O strongly supports access to and modification of data using updatable dynasets.

❑   The OO4O Parameters collection supports SQL bind variables.

On the down side, OO4O ties you to Oracle databases so is not the best choice if you have multiple databases installed, or, if you plan to change database systems anytime soon.

Most (better than 50% in my non-scientific survey of the NY and Philadelphia markets) of the Oracle databases in use are still at release 7.3. This will soon become the minority (though still a hefty one), as many companies are converting to version 8.0.x, which some are already using. All these versions use OO4O versions 2.1, 2.2 and 2.3. Oracle has lately released its Internet version of the database. This is Oracle 8i and its version is 8.1.5. Hardly anybody uses it in his or her businesses; I actually know of none. In this latest edition, Oracle deals with web-centric applications and addresses connections and databases in pools (collections to the VB speaker). It also deals with transaction servers such as MTS. OO4O has been upgraded to accommodate all these changes.

OK, let's get to the object model. The relative simplicity of the model means that we can cover it pretty comprehensively in less than thirty pages (to cover ADO in the same depth and detail requires a whole book).

The Full OO4O Object Model

In the object hierarchy below, I have highlighted 7 of the 9 objects. These are the objects we'll discuss at length.

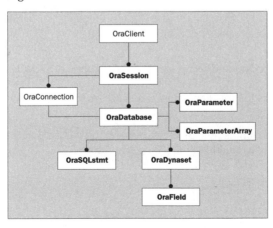

Let's dispense with the less important objects first, and then continue with the important ones.

The OraClient Object

OraClient is just figurehead. Its purpose is merely to contain the OraSession. In Microsoft's terminology, Oraclient is a "House of Bricks" implementation of a container class. It has no properties or methods that are exposed to the programmer. This means that there is nothing we can do to change its behavior. OraClient represents the OracleInProcessServer, which is introduced at the project level. In your project menu click on the references and select the OracleInProcessServer by clicking on its checkbox. That's it! Your project now includes an Oraclient.

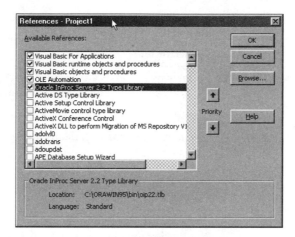

The OraConnection Object

OraConnection is automatically created when we make an OraSession object, and serves no other unique purpose. The only property of OraConnection is a reference to the session that spawned it – OraConnection.OraSession.

The OraSession Object

When a user "talks" to an Oracle database, the conversation takes place as a session. This is the real root of Objects for OLE. A session implies that the user's computer is connected to the Oracle server. We only need two lines of code to create a session. The lines below were copied from clsConnection – a class we have encountered in all of our VB and Oracle Projects – and which will be discussed at length a little later. From our standpoint, OraSession is the actual connection object.

```
Private mOraSession As OraSession
Set mOraSession = CreateObject("OracleInProcServer.XOraSession")
```

The essential importance of OraSession arises because it contains the OraDatabase object. However, some of the OraSession methods are very important too. Here they are:

Method	Description
BeginTrans	Begins a Transaction – see below.
CommitTrans	Commits the Transaction.
OpenDatabase	Uses a DatabaseName, ConnectString and Options to open a Database.
ResetTrans	Don't even think about using this one! It indiscriminately cancels all open transactions.
Rollback	Cancels a transaction.

Other methods include:

Method	Description
ConnectSession	Allows us to connect to a specifically named OraSession. The named session must already exist. X = OraSession.ConnectSession("Name")
CreateNamedSession	We may create many sessions under one client. Using this method names a session. X = OraSession.CreateNamedSession("Name")
LastServerErrReset	Sets the LastServerErr property (the last non-zero error code generated by an Oracle database function for the Session object) to a zero value and sets LastServerErrText property to NULL. Also in the OraDatabase object., which is where I use it. See full description in there.

The OpenDataBase Method

The most important OraSession method is the imperative OpenDatabase. We need to open a database in order to be able to work with it. We pass the OpenDatabase method three parameters: A string with the name of the database, a connect string consisting of user name followed by a slash and a password, for example "JohnQPublic/abracadabra", and finally a constant that describes the method by which we wish to open the database. Here is an example:

```
msConnect = msUser & "/" & msPassWord
Set mOraDatabase = mOraSession.OpenDatabase(msDatabaseName, _
msConnect, ORADB_ORAMODE)
```

Let's discuss in more detail the last parameter in the OpenDatabase method – the Options parameter. Each constant used in OO4O has been given a descriptive name. These names are included in the Oraconst.txt file that comes with the Oracle OO4O installation disk. I include them in a standard VB module as constants.

The code in such classes as clsConnection is written once and used forever, and I hate long lines of code, so I prefer to put these options as numbers rather than descriptive constants. You may opt to go the other way.

Whatever way you decide to go, here are the values, the constants they represent and a description of how they work:

Value	Constant	Description
0	ORADB_DEFAULT	VB mode (the default). Field (column) values not explicitly provided are set to NULL when using the AddNew or Edit methods. The NULL values override any server column default constraints. The option of choice if you **don't** plan to use updatable dynasets.
1	ORADB_ORAMODE	Oracle Mode. Lets the Oracle database set the default field (column) values when using AddNew or Edit. The Oracle default column values are refetched from database immediately after the insert or update. This mode allows the program to do successive edits without encountering error 4119 (see your Oraconst.txt file).
2	ORADB_NOWAIT	Turns off waiting on rowlocks. When you use Edit to update a row that is locked by another user or process, Lock No Wait mode results in the immediate return of an error code (ORA-00054).
4	ORADB_NO_REFETCH	Like ORAMODE, but data is not re-fetched to the local cache, thus boosting performance. I'm against it! It is designed to work with programs that only AddNew rows to a table, but most systems read data often and only occasionally write it out. It is better to use parameter arrays in OraSQLStmt for 'Add Only' programs.
8	ORADB_NONBLK	Only for 16 bit systems (Win 3.1)

These may be added like any other set of VB constants. I generally use option 1 with my databases, but may opt to react to a record lock by notifying the user of delays and then retrying. In this case I use option 3, which is 1 OR 2. Here is where using descriptive constants gets to my nerves; 3 would be written as:

```
ORADB_ORAMODE OR ORADB_NOWAIT
```

I find this a bit too much but many would argue in favor of this method due to ease of understanding. You will see in Chapter 7 that the ORADB_ORAMODE option allows us to use a trigger to assign sequence values in our updatable dynasets.

We will now investigate the OraSession transaction methods.

The Transaction Methods

A transaction is a very important concept. Think about what happens when you transfer money from your savings account to your checking account. First the balance in your savings is reduced, and then your checking balance is increased. This, by the way, is the order in which the bank prefers to do the transfer. Should the process fail midway, you end up short. But I digress. It would be much better if we could guarantee that the transfer is performed in its entirety, or not at all. This is where transactions come in. Our `OraSession` object supports transaction methods, starting a transaction with `BeginTrans` and ending a transaction with a `CommitTrans` or a `Rollback`. We commit the transaction if all went well (no errors were encountered) or roll it back if we encounter an error. The `Rollback` of an unfinished transaction will happen even when thing go awry, as in the case of power failure.

Here is how these transaction methods are coded in Oracle:

```
mOraSession.BeginTrans

mOraSession.CommitTrans

mOraSession.ResetTrans 'Please don't do it!!!

mOraSession.RollBack
```

Using transactions is mandatory whenever you update more than a single row at a time – even if the rows are in the same table.

Whenever you use OO4O you must use a session that includes a database. This will happen in project after project. It makes sense, therefore, to encapsulate these two objects in a class and include the class in every one of our VB projects.

> **The fact that the transaction methods occur at the "connection" level means that we can perform transactions that span several VB forms within an application.**

This class, in its simplest form should include properties containing user name, password and database name. It should also have methods corresponding to four of the session methods – we're not going to use `ResetTrans`. The class is named `clsConnection`. A more appropriate name in projects that use OO4O would have been `clsSession`, but I use a similar class in ADO where `clsConnection` is a better name. We have already seen this class in action in previous chapters. The enhanced class that handles transactions safely is explained in detail in Chapter 14.

The OraDatabase Object

The `OraDatabase` object is where it all happens. This is where we store data and where we retrieve it. It represents a single session with an oracle database. It is the raison d'être of this book. The center of the `OraDatabase` object is the `OraDynaset` around which we build the various data classes. The creation of dynasets is the most important method in OO4O, but also the most elaborate. I save it for last.

OraDatabase Properties

Here are the OraDatabase properties. Most are superfluous, one should be avoided, and three are useful:

Property Name	Description
Connect	Returns the username of the connection string. This is a very dangerous property. The only use I have for it is breach of security. The availability of such dangerous items is one of the reasons I encapsulate the database as a Private object in the clsConnection. Connection_String = mOraDatabase.Connect
DatabaseName	Ditto! As if the programmer does not already know the Database name. Not really very useful, but at least not dangerous. Database_Name = mOradatabase.DatabaseName
Connection	Returns the oracle Connection object – actually a pointer thereof – associated with the database object. Another harmless property that you probably won't use too often! Set Oraconnection = Oradatabase.Connection
RDBMSVersion	Returns the DB version i.e. 8.0.4 (hot stuff!)
Options	Returns the options you've just set with the OpenDatabase method of the OraSession. How could I survive without it?!
LastServerErr	Contains the last non-zero error number returned from the database. Use this, and the next two properties, to check for errors.
LastServerErrPos	Contains the position (character number) of the error in your SQL statement.
LastServerErrText	Contains the description of the last server error.
Parameters	Returns the OraParameters collection of the database. Parameters are the equivalent of SQL statement variables. We create them in a database method.

The LastServerErr, LastServerErrPos and LastServerErrText properties deserve to go hand-in-hand with the LastServerErrReset method of the OraDatabase. For example:

```
Dim lErr As Long
Dim sErr As String
LErr = OraDatabase.LastServerErr
If lErr <> 0 Then
sErr = OraDatabase.LastServerErrText
MsgBox "Database Error: " & CStr(lErr) & " " & sErr
OraDatabase.LastServerErrReset
End If
```

OraDatabase Methods

Method Name	Description
Close	The OraDatabase object always closes the database when the application terminates. The Close method was included solely for VB compatibility. Skip it!
CreateDynaset	This and the next three methods are the mother lode. We create dynasets in which we perform database maintenance.
CreateCustomDynaset	My preferred method of creating dynasets. You can fine-tune performance and memory requirements.
CreatePLSQLDynaset	Creates a dynaset around a PL/SQL cursor. See Chapter 13.
CreatePLSQLCustomDynaset	Ditto, only fine–tunable.
CreateSQL	Creates the OraSqlStmt object. Equivalent to ADO Command object.
ExecuteSQL	Executes a SQL statement upon request. It is more efficient to execute a statement inside an OraSQLstmt object. The number of rows affected by the statement is returned. The result is automatically committed. If you want to be non-committal, use BeginTrans. RowCount = OraDatabase.ExecuteSQL(sql_statement) Where sql_statement is a valid SQL Command, including anonymous PL/SQL blocks (see Chapter 13). The statement must not be a SELECT statement.

Method Name	Description
LastServerErrReset	After you've read and acted upon server errors, use this method to clear them. This is important because the server does not send us an OK, or error 0 message. The error you get (unless you reset) may be from yesteryear.

The CreateDynaset Method

A SELECT statement produces results in a tabular form. These have rows and columns and are, therefore, virtual tables. The early Microsoft name for such a table was a snapshot. You could look at it to your heart's delight, but you couldn't change it. An updatable dynaset allows you to change its contents. It is a picture with a photo editor. Better still, while a photo editor allows you to change the photo, the dynaset allows you to change the landscape itself. Any change you introduce to the updatable dynaset is immediately reflected in the underlying database. This is true if the following criteria are met (assuming the user has permission to write to the database in the first place!):

❑ The SELECT statement that defines the dynaset is based on a single table.

❑ The dynaset is not specifically designated as Read-only by applying the ORADYN_READONLY constant to the Options argument when the dynaset is created (see the the following table).

❑ Oracle allows ROWID references to the rows selected by the query (A ROWID is a database wide unique identifier. No two rows in the whole database have the same ROWID. Oracle does not let you do an Update or Delete of a row for which you don't have a ROWID. The underlying reason is that the database is one big hash of data and that the search mechanism is based on hashing algorithms).

You can retrieve the results of more complex searches, such as joins, into a dynaset, but the results will not be updatable.

The OraDynaset object holds the results of our queries. Dynasets are the Oracle equivalent of RDO and ADO recordsets. An OraDynaset object automatically maintains a local cache of data retrieved from the database server (so it is important to restrict queries to the data required).

Here is how we create a dynaset in OO4O, using the CreateDynaset method:

```
Set mOraDynaset = mOraDatabase.CreateDynaset (SQL, Options)
```

The method has two arguments (or parameters):

❑   SQL – A string that represents the source of the data – typically a SQL SELECT statement. This statement, unlike standard SQL statements, must not end with a semicolon. OO4O inserts the semicolon.

❑   Options – A long integer that assumes any combination (Boolean logical OR) of the following:

Value	Constant	Description
0	ORADYN_DEFAULT	Much like the ORADB_DEFAULT, the values not explicitly set in an Edit or AddNew method are inserted as Nulls. This may cause problems because of subsequent 4119 errors. I always use option 16 (ORADYN_ORAMODE).
1	ORADYN_NO_AUTOBIND	Use only if your SQL has no parameters (it prevents the binding of parameters to the query). Mine almost always do, so 1 in not an option for me.
2	ORADYN_NO_BLANKSTRIP	The dynaset normally strips trailing blanks from character fields. This option leaves the trailing blanks in.
4	ORADYN_READONLY	Many times you use dynasets just as hinges to other dynasets. If you don't intend to update the records at all (or you intend to do it via stored procedures), open the dynaset for read only. It will run much faster. This is also great for reports.

Value	Constant	Description
8	ORADYN_NOCACHE	With this option, only one record is held in memory (Oracle creates an anonymous procedure and fetches the records one by one on a cursor). In this case you can do only forward movement (you get a forward-only cursor – MoveNext, but no MovePrevious) but you get faster results. I don't use the option much and skip it in this book.
16	ORADYN_ORAMODE	Column values not specifically provided in an Edit or AddNew are set to the database default column value and the dynaset is refreshed with the actual database values after such updates. This means that I achieve my goals with fewer 4119 headaches. I still get 4119 errors if another user changed data while I contemplated my change, which is the way it should be.
32	ORADYN_NO_REFETCH	Same as 16, but without refreshing updated values. I avoid it.
64	ORADYN_NO_MOVEFIRST	The dynaset is unpopulated. EOF and BOF are both True. Useful when you only intend to insert new rows. If used in conjunction with parameter arrays (see later), it can produce a fast database loader and is a good choice for a batch operation such as importing data from another company or a call-center.

Table Continued on Following Page

Value	Constant	Description
128	ORADYN_DIRTY_WRITE	I advise against using it! It was invented to avoid error 4119 in very busy databases, but actually allows you to rewrite over previously updated information with impunity. Dangerous to the health of your data!

As you surmised from the way I described the options, I only use option 4 or option 16. The two are obviously mutually exclusive. When I only need to read data I use 4, otherwise I use option 16.

As stated previously, the CreateDynaset method builds a default cache, where the fetched records are held in memory. The ORADYN_NOCACHE constant – option 8 – eliminates this cache at the cost of having a forward-only dynaset. The default cache parameters are set in the Registry of Win32 and therefore any set of records, large or small, will occupy the same space. The default cache size that you get upon installation is 80KB (which, by default breaks down to 256*16*20, as explained in the next section). The default field size – or the slicesize property in Oracle parlance – is 256 and is rather large for day-to-day databases. To fine-tune the cache we have another method for creating dynasets – CreateCustomDynaset. This is the method that I prefer.

The CreateCustomDynaset Method

Here is how we create a custom dynaset in OO4O:

```
Set mOraDynaset = mOraDatabase.CreateCustomDynaset (SQL, Options, sliceSize,
PerBlock, Blocks, FetchLimit, Fetchsize)
```

The Oracle default value for SliceSize is 256, for PerBlock it is 16, and for Blocks it is 20. These values are set in the registry when you install the database.

The SQL and Options parameters are identical to those in the CreateDynaset method. The other arguments allow you to fine-tune the cache for performance and memory. In order to understand this better, let's take a look at a dynaset created to handle the following SELECT statement.

```
Select DEMO_ID, FIELD_1, FIELD_2 from DEMO
```

Where:

❑   DEMO is the name of the table.

❑   DEMO_ID is a ten-digit unique ID number.

❑   FIELD_1 is of data type VARCHAR2(11), which is a variable-length string of at most 11 characters.

❑   FIELD_2 is of the same description as FIELD_1.

There will be a maximum of 11 characters in any column so we can actually limit the `Slicesize` to 11 (remember, the default is 256 which is rather wasteful in this case). There are 3 fields in the statement so we do not need 16 slices (fields) per block – 3 will do!

That makes a block a maximum of only 33 characters long and we can try to get as many of them as we can into memory. The maximum number of blocks allowed in OO4O is 127 (I wish it were bigger), yielding a total of 4,191 characters.

A valid command might be as follows:

```
Set mOraDynaset = mOraDatabase.CreateCustomDynaset (msSelect, ORADYN_ORAMODE,
11, 3, 127, 127, 4096)
```

Note the last number, which stands for the `FetchSize` argument of the method. FetchSize is used to fetch `LONG` and `LONG RAW` columns. These are the equivalent of `Memo` fields and `BLOB`s (Binary Large Object). We set the number to 4K just for compatibility with the method's structure. We did all the fine-tuning we could in the other 4 arguments. Note that the value `127` appears twice. A block is made of slices. The `PerBlock` parameter determines how many slices we get back with every Fetch. We have already set each slice to be a field, so the blocks are now blocks of fields. If we equate a block (in other words, set the `PerBlock`), as we should, to the number of columns in the SELECT statement, we actually equate blocks to rows, thus the number of blocks is identical to the `FetchLimit`.

Optimizing in this manner allows us to fetch 127 rows in slightly over 4K, instead of the default of only 20 rows in 80K. In many cases we add a `WHERE` clause to the `SELECT` statement which limits the number of records to just 1. It is better, in such cases, to set both the Blocks and the `FetchLimit` to 1.

The OraDynaset Object

As you know by now, the OraDynaset object is where we cache the data we retrieve from the database during our queries.

Most of the dynaset properties and methods are hardly ever used. You have already seen those that I favor in the sample programs. Here are all:

The OraDynaset Properties

Property	Description
BOF	`True` or `False`. `True` if you have moved to before the first record in the set. It is also `True` if the set is empty. If that's the case `EOF` is also `True`. It may also be `True` if you used option 64 (ORADYN_NO_MOVEFIRST), when creating the dynaset.

Table Continued on Following Page

Property	Description
BookMark	A string that uniquely identifies a particular row in the Dynaset.
BookMarkable	Indicates whether the dynaset can support bookmarks.
EditMode	Returns the editing status of the current row in the dynaset. Possible values are: 0 (no editing in progress), 1 (editing on existing row) or 2 (a new record is being added).
EOF	True or False. True if you have moved to past the last record in the set. It is also True if the set is empty. If that's the case BOF is also True.

Fields	The default property. Returns the Fields collection (the collection of OraField objects) for the current dynaset row. For example:
	
	`Set mOraFields = mOraDynaset.Fields`
	
	The OraFields collection has one important property of its own – Count. Fields may be accessed by name or by their index (0 to Count – 1).
	
	`mOraFields("Last_Name").Value`

LastModified	A bookmark of the row that was last modified by an AddNew or Edit method.
NoMatch	Boolean. True if the last Find method did not find a matching record. See the Find methods in the "Oradynaset Methods" section for further details.
RecordCount	Returns the number of records in the dynaset. The entire result set is automatically returned in order to perform the count. Unlike RDO and DAO, you don't need to MoveLast before you count (unless this is a dynaset that was created with the ORADYN_NOCACHE option – in which case the MoveLast will be done implicitly and the current record will become the last record).
RowPosition	Each row in an Oracle table has a rownum (the relative position of a row in its table and unique within that table). RowPosition is the rownum of the current dynaset record. This is similar to the AbsolutePosition in ADO.
SQL	Returns the SELECT statement that defined the dynaset.
Transactions	Boolean. A dummy property that indicates if you can use transactions – it always returns True and has been implemented for compatibility. Don't Use!

Property	Description
Updatable	Boolean. Only single table dynasets can be updatable, and only if opened for read-write (not Read-Only). Even then, the dynaset may not be updatable because the user lacks write privileges.

The OraDynaset also supports the following properties, the usage of which I hope is obvious from our discussion of the OraDatabase methods and properties: CacheBlocks, CacheChanged, CacheSliceSize, CacheSlicesPerBlock, Connection, Database, FetchLimit, FetchSize, Options and Session. The following sections demonstrate the usage of some of the more interesting methods.

The BOF and EOF Properties

An empty dynaset – when there are no records matching the query – returns both EOF and BOF as true:

```
If mDynaset.BOF and mDynaset.EOF Then
MsgBox "The Dynaset is empty!"
End If
```

Remember that in most cases, opening a dynaset will automatically invoke a MoveFirst, so you can safely test for EOF only.

BookMark

We save a bookmark in a string variable. After traversing the dynaset and going to and fro, we can use the bookmark to go back to the marked row.

```
Dim sBM As String
sBM = mDynaset.Bookmark      'save the current row's bookmark
mDynaset.MoveLast            'wander around in the dynaset
mDynaset.Bookmark = sBM      'return to the original record
```

LastModified

LastModified is a bookmark that marks the record (row) last added or changed. If you perform successive updates then only the last one will be bookmarked in LastModified.

```
mDynaset.AddNew   'add a new record.

'Here we set the dynaset fields with values
mDynaset.Fields(0).Value = something

mDynaset.Update   'Sets the LastModified bookmark

'After many other operations (not addnew or update) return
mDynaset.Bookmark = mDynaset.LastModified   'return to the record
```

Updatable

It is best to warn your users if a dynaset is not updatable:

```
If mDynaset.Updatable = False Then
MsgBox "Warning, This Dynaset is read only!!
End If
```

The OraDynaset Methods

Many of the methods described below result in updating the database. Earlier we used DML for the same purpose and you were asked to commit as frequently and as early as possible. In the OraDynaset, the actions are automatically committed. This is true unless you performed a BeginTrans in the session. Records added and updated in a transaction are not committed until you perform an OraSession.CommitTrans. We will now investigate the various methods in some detail. In the code snippets we're using the DEMO table described in conjunction with the CreateCustomDynaset method.

The Move Methods

The following methods move the cursor to the specified row in the dynaset:

Method	Description
MoveFirst	Moves to the first record in the set, unless the set is empty.
MoveLast	Moves to the last record in the set, if any. It is possible to build up the local cache incrementally, by performing a MoveFirst, followed by MoveNext. However, MoveLast forces the dynaset to complete the query and store all of the data defined by the query.
MoveNext	Moves to the next record. Executing this method when the last record is current sets EOF to True. Executing a MoveNext from the EOF causes an error.
MovePrevious	Moves to the Previous record. Executing a MovePrevious from the BOF causes an error.
MoveNextn	Allows you to move more than a single position forward. For example: `mDynaset.Movenextn 3` If the move brings you beyond the last record, the dynaset will be positioned on the last record and EOF will be True. Allows only a positive parameter. I hardly ever use it.

Method	Description
MovePreviousn	Allows you to move more than a single position backward. If the move brings you beyond the first record, the dynaset will be positioned on the first record and BOF will be True. Allows only a positive parameter. I hardly ever use it.
MoveRel	Allows positive (forwards) and negative (backwards) movement from the current position. Sets EOF and BOF as needed. For example `mDynaset.MoveRel -2` Would move the cursor backwards (or "up" the table) two spaces relative to the current record.
MoveTo	Moves to the row number specified. MoveTo 1 will go to the first record. MoveTo 5 to the fifth. Check the RecordCount property before you use it. I hardly ever use this method.

These methods are similar to the ADO, DAO and RDO methods. You must check for EOF and BOF before moving. For example:

```
Public Sub MoveRel(lRows As Long)
    If lRows <> 0 Then
        mdynPeople.MoveRel lRows
        SetProperties
End If
End Sub

Not mDynaset.EOF Then
mDynaset.MoveLast
End If

If Not mDynaset.EOF Then
mDynaset.MoveNext
End If
```

A MoveNext issued when the current record is last will result in EOF property being set to True and the current record will be empty. Trying to do another MoveNext will result in an error, but the record will still be empty and the EOF property will still be True. The same logic applies to MovePrevious. If the current record is the first, BOF will be raised and the current record will be empty. Issuing MovePrevious again, will result in an error, but the record and BOF condition will remain empty and True respectively. See code sample in the "OraField" section.

> When a dynaset is attached to a data control, these methods first notify the data control's Validate event that record motion is about to occur – see the section on the Oracle Data Control at the end of this section.

The Find Methods

The following four methods are unique to OO4O. They exist in DAO but have been dropped from RDO, and ADO. OO4O can do a cache search for conditions you preset in a FindClause (a string used to search the dynaset). The condition can include any syntax that would be valid in the WHERE clause of a SELECT statement, but without the use of the term WHERE itself – just use X = Y instead of WHERE X = Y. If a matching record cannot be found then the NoMatch property of the OraDynaset is set to True and you will remain at the record that was current before the call was made. As with the Move methods, you should check for EOF and BOF before executing a Find method.

The processing associated with a Find method is performed locally on the cached recordset and does not involve the server, unless you do not have the whole dynaset cached.

Method	Description
FindFirst	Finds the first occurrence, if any, of the FindClause in the dynaset.
FindNext	Finds the next occurrence, if any, of the FindClause after the current record.
FindLast	Finds the last occurrence, if any, of the FindClause.
FindPrevious	Finds the Previous occurrence, if any, of the FindClause.

Here are some examples utilizing various types of FindClause:

```
mOraDynaset.FindFirst "Last_Name LIKE 'St%'"

mOraDynaset.FindLast "Income < 50000"
```

We can also use subqueries in the FindClause. Remember that this is OO4O so you can use Oracle functions in the condition. In the following code snippets, note the use of the Oracle UPPER function (see Chapter 6). This cannot be done in ADO.

```
mOraDynaset.FindFirst "UPPER(FIELD_1) = 'MMMM'" 'note, there is no WHERE
If mOraDynaset.NoMatch Then
MsgBox "None Found"
End If

mOraDynaset.FindNext "UPPER(FIELD_1) = 'MMMM'"
If mOraDynaset.NoMatch Then
MsgBox "No More MMMMs"
End If
```

Modifying Data using Oradynaset Methods

Following is a table of the "modify" methods. I have included the Refresh method in amongst them – occasionally we must reload our dynaset to check for alterations made by other users.

Method	Description
AddNew	Adds a new record to the dynaset. The record will not be added to the actual database until the Update method is called. If, for example, a Move method is called after AddNew then the new row will not be added. Behind the scenes the record will be added using the SQL INSERT statement.
Delete	Deletes the database table row corresponding to the current dynaset record.
Edit	Prepares the database to accept changes that were made in the dynaset. Actual database update will happen only upon using the Update method. Edit locks the record in the database using a SELECT...FOR UPDATE command. The correct way to release an Edit is by calling an Update.
Refresh	Runs the SELECT statement again and reloads the dynaset. Use it sparingly and mercifully.
Update	Edit and AddNew only change the array of records in the dynaset. Update cements the content in the database. It releases the lock that started with the Edit.

If you call an Edit, AddNew, or Delete method, any outstanding Edit or AddNew calls will be cancelled, before proceeding (in other words, any previous changes that were not committed to the database by calling Update will be lost). A move away from a record while in edit mode will cause the edit to be lost, if in OO4O direcly, but will force them through if the move was peformed on a control (such as a grid) bound to the ORADC. OO4O is different than ADO. In ADO both kinds of move will force an update.

The AddNew method

When AddNew is called, the field values in the dynaset are maintained in a buffer, and are committed to the database only upon calling Update. Field values are modified through the OraField object. If you do not explicitly assign a value to a field the value may be set to NULL or to a column default value (see the Options parameter of the CreateDynaset method):

```
mDynaset.AddNew
mDynaset.Fields("DEMO_ID").Value = 2
mDynaset.Fields("FIELD_1").Value = "Erwin"
mDynaset.Fields("FIELD_2").Value = "Zapper"
mDynaset.Update
```

The Delete Method

The current record in the dynaset will be deleted from the database. The record will still be the current record, but it cannot be deleted again. The next time you perform a Move method the new record will become current and you'll not be able to return to the deleted record. This requires you to be extra cautious if you deleted a bookmarked record and try to move to it. If you delete the record that has the LastModified bookmark and try to return to it the same error will ensue.

> You cannot retract a `Delete` (or an `Update`) unless it was executed within a transaction – the selected rows will remain locked until `CommitTrans` or `Rollback`.

In that respect the `Delete` is not like an `Edit`. In an edit you can re-edit to the old values and still maintain the same `rownum` and `ROWID`. If you reinsert a deleted record it will have a different `rownum` and `ROWID`.

```
mDynaset.Delete
```

The Edit Method

An `Edit` creates a lock in the database. Note that we release the lock using `Update`.

```
mDynaset.Edit        'Lock the database row
mDynaset.Fields("FIELD_1").Value = "Erwin"
mDynaset.Fields("FIELD_2").Value = "Zapper"
mDynaset.Update      'Update and unlock
```

The Refresh Method

The SQL statement initially used to define the dynaset is stored in a buffer. The contents of this buffer are executed whenever the `Refresh` method is called and the first row of the resulting dynaset becomes current. The Refresh method cancels all Edit and `AddNew` operations.

During a `Refresh`, the `OraDynaset` object automatically binds all new input parameters to the specified SQL statement, using the parameter names as placeholders. Thus we can build queries dynamically, modifying the SQL statement without having to create a new dynaset each time (see also the `OraSQLStmt` object).

For example we can define an input parameter for the Parameters collection of the OraDatabase Object (see the section on the `OraParameters` Collection, later in this chapter):

```
mOraDatabase.Parameters.Add "PID", 8, 1
```

We could set up a dynaset, defined by a SELECT statement that accepts "PID" as an input parameter:

```
Set mOraDynaset = mOraDatabase.CreateDynaset _
("SELECT * from People WHERE Person_ID = :PID", 0&)
```

This will return the record that has a value of 8 in the Person_ID column. We may then change the value of the parameter to 10:

```
mOraDatabase.Parameters("PID").Value = 10
```

However, before we can view the corresponding record, we must refresh the dynaset:

```
mOraDynaset.Refresh
```

The OraField Object

The OraDynaset has a built-in OraFields collection, which maintains a list of OraField objects. Essentially, an OraField object represents one column of a dynaset row (defined by the underlying SELECT statement). The OraField objects are referenced rather frequently in the VB code. There are two methods for referencing a field:

1) We can assign a field property to a variable in one of the following ways (the third way works because Fields is the default property of the Oradynaset object):

```
xyz = mdynTestDemo!FIELD_1.Property

xyz = mdynTestDemo.Fields("FIELD_1").Property

xyz = OraDynaset("FIELD_1").Property
```

The second (or third) way is preferred.

2) The second and preferred method is to reference the field by its position in the collection. This index is 0 to Count -1:

```
xyz = mdynTestDemo.Fields(iX).Property
```

The OraField Properties

Property	Description
OraIDataType	The internal Oracle data type, for the specified field, is returned as a VB Long. The available values are:

ORAITYPE_VARCHAR2	1	VARCHAR2
ORAITYPE_NUMBER	2	NUMBER
ORAITYPE_LONG	8	LONG
ORAITYPE_ROWID	11	ROWID
ORAITYPE_DATE	12	DATE
ORAITYPE_RAW	23	RAW
ORAITYPE_LONGRAW	24	LONG RAW
ORAITYPE_CHAR	96	CHAR
ORAITYPE_MLSLABEL	106	MLSLABEL

These values can be found in the file ORACONST.TXT. See Chapter 2 for descriptions of the types.

Table Continued on Following Page

Property	Description
OraMaxDSize	A VB Long. The number of characters needed to display the value.
OraMaxSize	A VB Long. The maximum length of the column in the database. Date is always 7, Number always 22. In the case of an Oracle function this variable returns the MaxDSize. Returns zero for LONG and LONG RAW fields. Use the FieldSize method (see later in the chapter).
OraNullOK	Boolean. Is a null value allowed for the column?
OraPrecision	VB Long. The total number of digits displayed.
OraScale	VB Long. The number of digits after the decimal point.
Name	Returns the name of the field object (in other words, the column name in the SELECT statement, or the alias, if used).
Size	The returned value of the field is a variant. This is the length, in bytes, of this variant. Returns 0 for LONG and LONG RAW fields. Use the FieldSize method.
Truncated	Boolean. In case of LONG and LONG RAW fields, the data is most likely returned in pieces (see the methods dealing with these fields). If that's the case, Truncated will be set to True.
Type	VB Integer. Returns the variant type of the OraField.Value. This is a standard VB variant type.
Value	Returns or sets the value of the variant containing the field value. This is the default property of the field object.

Value is the most important of these properties, and the only one that is both 'read' and 'write' (Let and Get). We'll discuss it separately. All the other properties are read only. They are useful when one wants to investigate the structure of the database.

The Value Property

Here are the various ways we can find the value of a field object (returned as a Variant data type) and assign it to a VB variable:

```
xyz = mdynTestDemo.Fields("FIELD_1").Value

xyz = mdynTestDemo.Fields(iX).Property
```

Conversely, we can assign a value to the Value property as follows (this is the only property to which a value may be assigned):

```
mdynTestDemo.Fields("FIELD_1").Value ="xyz"

mdynTestDemo.Fields(iX).Value ="xyz"
```

Let us, then, investigate the database structure. We will assume that all the variables are declared and of the proper type, and that we have already created a read-only OraDynaset with SELECT * FROM TableName as its SQL. We count the number of field objects in the collection, subtract 1 (because the index is zero-based) and assign the value to our variable, iCount. We then loop through the field collection, assigning property values appropriately:

```
iCount = mDynStructure.Fields.Count - 1
For iX = 0 To iCount
    sName(iX)  = mDynStructure.Fields(iX).Name
    lType(iX)   = mDynStructure.Fields(iX).OraDataType
    lSize(iX)   = mDynStructure.Fields(iX).OraMaxSize
    lPrecision(iX)  = mDynStructure.Fields(iX).OraPrecision
    lScale(iX)  = mDynStructure.Fields(iX).OraScale
Next iX
```

Alternatively, all of this can also be achieved using the Value property alone. We build a read-only dynaset using the Oracle data dictionary table USER_TAB_COLUMNS. This also provides a good example of handling the EOF condition when traversing the dynaset.

```
SELECT COLUMN_NAME, DATA_TYPE, DATA_LENGTH, DATA_PRECISION, DATA_SCALE FROM
USER_TAB_COLUMNS WHERE TABLE_NAME = TableName

iX = 0
mDynStructure.MoveFirst
    Do Until mDynStructure.EOF
        sName(iX) = mDynStructure.Fields("COLUMN_NAME").Value
        sType(iX) = mDynStructure.Fields("DATA_TYPE").Value
        lSize(iX) = mDynStructure.Fields("DATA_LENGTH").Value
        lPrecision(iX) = mDynStructure.Fields("DATA_PRECISION").Value
        lScale(iX) = mDynStructure.Fields("DATA_SCALE").Value
        mDynStructure.MoveNext
    iX = iX + 1
Loop
```

Thus we could do without the other properties, but Value is a must!

Dealing with Nulls

As you remember from Chapter 5, VB6 has an idiosyncratic behavior when assigning a null value to a string. This is not very convenient. After all, passing the OraField.Value to a text box is quite common and Fields do contain null values (sometimes they are quite prevalent!). When a field in a row was not entered and NULL is allowed, its value will be a NULL. It is also very common to expect a VARCHAR2 field to translate to a VB string variable and to be displayed in a textbox, label and the like.

There are two ways to handle this NULL idiosyncrasy: One is the VB way of using the IsNull() function to determine whether the returned value is a NULL. The other is the Oracle way, whereby we circumvent the error is by using the NVL function that, as you may recall from Chapter 2, allows us to assign our own value to a null value.

> Remember you're in OO4O now and using Oracle functions in the SQL is not going to render your dynaset 'read-only'.

We create a different SELECT statement for the OraDynaclass as follows:

```
SELECT DEMO_ID, FIELD_1, NVL(FIELD_2, ' ') AS FLD_2
```

The NVL function will return a single space if FIELD_2 is NULL, or FIELD_2 otherwise. Now you can safely use:

```
sX = mDynTestDemo.Fields("FLD_2").Value
```

Conversely (and you may be surprised by this!), there are no problems in assigning a NULL to the Value property:

```
mdynTestDemo.Fields("FIELD_2").Value = NULL
```

The common wisdom is that in VB you cannot do an assignment of the sort:

```
X.Value = NULL
```

While it is true most of the time, this is totally dependent on the type of object X is. If it is an OO4O object, then the assignment is valid.

Early Binding

If we need frequent access to a field (for example, if there are many records to scan through) then our code will be more efficient if we create a separate field object for that field (remember, these objects will come with some overhead). We set a reference to the field:

```
Set mfldField1 = mdynTestDemo.Fields("FIELD_1")
```

Then, every time we need access to FIELD_1, we simply refer to the field object:

```
mfldField1 = xyz

xyz = mFldField1
```

There is another issue we have to consider here, though. How did we declare our field object? Each time we call a property or method of OO4O, VB has to determine what arguments are required for that call. If we declare our OraField object generically:

```
Private mfldField1 As Object
```

Then, at run time, VB must refer to the Type library to find out what the object type is and what arguments are required. This is known as **late binding**. We may find ourselves needing to assign an OraField property value to a variable (and vice versa) whenever we retrieve a record, add a new record, or edit an existing record. We have resolved our field reference but if VB has to find the proper object before it can do the assignment of the value every time then we will still have inefficient code.

The answer to this is to use **early binding**, whereby we declare our objects as the correct type so that VB can look it up during compile:

```
Private mfldField1 As OraField
Set mfldField1 = mdynTestDemo.Fields("FIELD_1")
```

This speeds performance noticeably.

OraField Methods

Method	Description
AppendChunk	Allows us to write fields larger than 64K by appending chunks (strings) to the copy buffer.
FieldSize	Returns a VB Long with the length (in bytes) of LONG or LONG RAW fields. This function is unreliable. If the field length is greater than 64K, the function returns –1.
GetChunk	Allows us to read a chunk of data from a LONG or LONG RAW field. We specify the offset and length.
GetChunkByte	Another method to get chunks of data from LONG or LONG RAW fields.

The examples below assume that we have a file with binary data (a pdf file, or a jpg picture for instance) that we want to save in an Oracle table and then read and use. We assume that the dynaset (representing our table) only includes one field of type LONG RAW and the name of FLD. The file name is test.pdf and it resides in the current directory.

The AppendChunk Method

The following code demonstrates how to transfer the file content to a LONG RAW column in a database table:

```
Dim nChunks As Integer, nChunkSize As Integer
Dim lTotalSize As Long, sChunk As String
Dim iX As Integer, FNum As Integer, nChunkLast As Integer

nChunkSize = 8192                    'Set the size of each chunk.

mDynDemo.AddNew                      'Begin an add operation

mDynDemo.Fields("FLD").Value = ""    'Clear the field

FNum = FreeFile                      'Get a free file number

Open "test.pdf" For Binary As #FNum  'Open the file

TotalSize = LOF(FNum)                'Get the total size
                                     'of the file

nChunks = lTotalSize \ nChunkSize    'Division resulting in an
                                     'integer number of chunks

nChunkLast = lTotalSize Mod nChunkSize 'Set number of remaining
                                       'bytes

For iX = 0 To nChunks                'Loop through the file.
   If iX = NumChunks Then
      nChunkSize = nChunkLast
   End If
```

```
    sChunk = String$(nChunkSize, 32)        'or Space(nChunkSize)

    Get #FNum, , CurChunk                    'Read a chunk

'Append chunk to LONGRAW field.
    MDynDemo.Fields("FLD").AppendChunk (sChunk)
Next iX

'Update the dynaset
MDynDemo.Update

'Close the file.
Close Fnum
```

The GetChunk Method

The following code demonstrates how to transfer the database LONG RAW to a file:

```
Dim nChunks As Integer, nChunkSize As Integer
 Dim lTotalSize As Long, sChunk As String
 Dim iX As Integer, FNum As Integer, nChunkLast As Integer

nChunkSize = 8192
FNum = FreeFile
Open "test.pdf" For Binary As #FNum

 iX = 0
'Loop through all of the chunks because Oracle does not return
'the size of columns > 64KB, we should loop until the length of
'our block is less than what we asked for (8192)
Do
'The GetChunk function gets a chunk starting at the offset
'position (in our case this offset is iX * nChunkSize) and
'in the length requested(in our case nChunkSize)

    sChunk = mDynDemo.Fields("FLD").GetChunk(iX * nChunkSize, _
                                             nChunkSize)

'Get the length of the current chunk.
    nChunkLast = Len(sChunk)

'Write chunk to file.
    Put #FNum, , sChunk
    iX = iX + 1
Loop Until nChunkLast < nChunkSize
Close FNum
```

The OraSQLStmt Object

At times we need to execute SQL statements from the OraDatabase object. The simple way is to use the ExecuteSQL method of this object. I did not bother to discuss this method in detail because, for SQL statements that are executed more than once, there is a better vehicle. This is the OraSQLStmt object.

An OraSQLStmt object is defined by a single SQL statement, which is compiled in the database the first time it is used. The term "compiled" is used loosely when SQL is concerned. In reality it merely creates Oracle pseudo-code (p-code), and requires a run file. Nonetheless, compiling makes statements run faster because we save the time it takes to interpret (parse) them again and again. The compiled statements are our Static SQL, as opposed to the constantly interpreted Dynamic SQL.

The SQL statement may be a stored procedure and may include parameters. The statement is not limited to SELECT and is used most of the time for action queries (UPDATE, INSERT, DELETE). To execute the statement from within the OraSQLStmt object, we invoke the Refresh method (which binds all relevant parameters to the SQL statement).

Executing SQL statements directly or in the OraSQLStmt causes an automatic Commit. This can cause problems if complex transactions are executed in the background. For that reason we must use the OraSession.BeginTrans method before running any SQL. This not only improves safety, but also boosts performance.

We create an OraSQLStmt using the CreateSQL method of OraDatabase:

```
Private mMyQuery As OraSQLStmt
Set mMyQuery = OraDatabase.CreateSQL(SQL, Options)
```

Where:

❏ SQL – is an argument that defines any valid SQL statement, including stored procedures enclosed in a Begin – End structure.

❏ Options – are one or more of the following:

Constant	Value	Description
ORASQL_DEFAULT	&H0&	Default Behavior.
ORASQL_NO_AUTOBIND	&H1&	Stop automatic binding of parameters.
ORASQL_FAILEXEC	&H2&	Raise an error if the SQL statement is invalid (OraSQLStmt object will not be created).

Option 2 is the one I regularly use. I haven't yet used a SQL without parameters in an OraSQLStmt object. I also have yet to use a parameter-less stored procedure.

The only interesting property of the OraSQLStmt object is RecordCount, which returns the number of records affected in an action query. The only significant method is Refresh, which we covered for the OraDynaset object.

The OraParameters Collection

Each OraDatabase object contains a single OraParameters collection, which maintains a list of OraParameter objects. The OraParameters collection has a Count property (returns the number of objects in the collection) and the following methods:

- ❑ Add – adds a parameter to the OraParameters collection.
- ❑ AddTable – adds a **parameter array** to the collection.
- ❑ Remove – Removes a parameter from the collection.

We create a parameter by adding it to the OraDatabase as follows:

```
OraDatabase.Parameters.Add ParamName, ParamValue, ParamType
```

Where:

- ❑ ParamName – a string that defines a unique name for the parameter.
- ❑ ParamValue – the initial value of the parameter – a number or date or string, as the case may be.
- ❑ ParamType – which specifies the Parameter type:

Constant	Value	Direction
ORAPARM_INPUT	1	IN
ORAPARM_OUTPUT	2	OUT
ORAPARM_BOTH	3	IN/OUT

Here is an example that defines an input parameter called Param1, which is a fifty spaces string:

```
OraDatabase.Parameters.Add "Param1", Space(50), 1
```

And here is one that defines an output parameter called Param2, which is a number of value 0:

```
OraDatabase.Parameters.Add "Param2", 0, 2
```

Once we have created a parameter, we can use it as a bind variable in a SQL statement. The parameter name serves as a placeholder inside a SQL statement.

> **Remember that parameters belong to the database and not to any particular dynaset so they are available to any SQL statement or PL/SQL block executed within the database.**

In the following SQL statement `IdField` is a parameter:

```
Select FirstName, LastName from Users where UserId = :IdField;
```

You know it is a parameter because it is preceded by a colon (:). This is the equivalent of ADO's "?":

```
Select FirstName, LastName from Users where UserId = ?;
```

The advantage of using parameters is that we do not have to re-issue a SQL statement with every change in the `UserId`. We may simply assign a new value to `IdField` and rerun the existing statement, which is done by issuing the `Refresh` command to the dynaset. Using parameters increases performance and also eases our programming effort.

The OraParameter Object

This is a good opportunity to deal with the `OraParameter` object in more detail. As discussed previously, `OraParameters` are `OraDatabase` objects and serve as bind variables (arguments) to the precompiled SQL.

The `AutoBindDisable` and `AutoBindEnable` methods are worthy of mention. With `AutoBindEnable` enabled, then before a SQL statement or PL/SQL block is executed Oracle will attempt to bind all parameters of the associated `OraDatabase` object (whether or not they are applicable to a particular SQL statement). This may degrade performance. You can prevent this occurrence by temporarily disabling a parameter, using `AutoBindDisable`.

One property of this object that it is important to set is the `ServerType` – the external data type. Remember that the SQL is parsed on the database and Oracle needs to match the data type of the placeholder. Oracle usually knows what variable type to assign to a parameter, but good programming habits require that we don't leave it to chance. After adding a parameter you may assign it a type. Most of the various types were listed previously in the `OraDataType` property of the `OraField` object (a full list can be found in the `ORACONST.TXT` file. If we want to do it for `Param1`, here is how it looks:

```
OraDatabase.Parameters.Add "Param1", Space(50), 1
OraDatabase.Parameters("Param1").ServerType = ORATYPE_VARCHAR2
```

And for `Param2`:

```
OraDatabase.Parameters.Add "Param2", 0, 2
OraDatabase.Parameters("Param2").ServerType = ORATYPE_NUMBER
```

Let's assume that the statement has a single parameter – `Param1`. We can change the value of the parameter as follows:

```
OraDatabase.Parameters("Param1").Value = NewValue
mMyQuery.Refresh
```

After the parameter has outlived its usefulness it may be removed:

```
OraDatabse.Parameters.Remove ParramName
```

Using Parameters with the OraSQLStmt Object and Stored Procedures

Once we have created our parameters, we can use them in our `OraSQLStmt`. The most common use of parameters is with stored procedures and the `OraSQLStmt` object. Stored procedures are precompiled PL/SQL subprograms. They are discussed fully in Chapter 13. They are invoked by the same syntax that is used in most programming languages:

```
ProcedureName(:Parameter1, :Parameter2, ...,:LastParameter)
```

Note that a colon precedes each parameter name. So what allows us to use stored procedures in the OraSQLStmt? The SQL statement itself:

```
Dim StoredProcSQL as String
StoredProcSQL = "Begin ProcedureName(:Param1    ,:LastParam); End;"
Set mMyQuery = OraDatabase.CreateSQL(StoredProcSQL, Options)
```

The `StoredProcSQL` is a stored procedure call enclosed in a Begin-End structure and followed by a semicolon. For some reason the designers make us put a semicolon after the statement, yet they do not allow it in the dynaset or in a regular SQL statement in the `OraSQLStmt`.

The OraParamArray Object

The OraParamArray object is the smart manner by which OO4O passes multiple parameters to the server. This is useful when updating multiple records because it allows you to pass the requirements in a single roundtrip – saving network activity as well as object overhead – rather than by a loop in which you send the requests one by one.

We add a **Parameter Array** to the collection using the `AddTable` method of the `OraDatabase`. The best way to explain how it's done is by example. The example uses the DEMO table we used as in the `CreateCustomDynaset` example. For brevity I only declare the "pertinent" variables. Assume that all variables are declared correctly:

```
Dim OraStmt As OraSqlStmt
Dim DemoIdArray As OraParamArray
Dim Field1Array As OraParamArray
Dim Field2Array As OraParamArray
sSQL = "Insert into DEMO (demo_id, Field1, field2) "
sSQL =  sSQL & "VALUES(:DemoId, :Field1, :Field2)"
```

We now prepare the ground for the parameter arrays:

```
OraDatabase.Parameters.AddTable "DemoId", ORAPARM_INPUT,
ORATYPE_NUMBER, 10, 22

OraDatabase.Parameters.AddTable "Field1", ORAPARM_INPUT,
ORATYPE_CHAR, 10, 11

OraDatabase.Parameters.AddTable "Field2", ORAPARM_INPUT,
ORATYPE_CHAR, 10, 11
```

The AddTable Method has five arguments:

- ❑ ParameterName As String.

- ❑ ParameterType As Integer where 1 is for Input, 2 for Output, 3 for Both.

- ❑ ServerType As Integer – the data type of the array to be bound to the database object (constants are to be found in ORACONST.txt).

- ❑ ArraySize As Integer (in our case 10).

- ❑ DataLength as Integer. Numbers are always of length 22.

Next we use what we've just created to define the arrays:

```
Set DemoIdArray = OraDatabase.Parameters("DemoId")
Set Field1Array = OraDatabase.Parameters("Field1")
Set Field2Array = OraDatabase.Parameters("Field2")
```

And now the ground is ready to insert 10 lines into the DEMO table:

```
For iX = 0 To 9
   DemoIdArray(iX) = 1 + iX
   Field1Array(iX) = "BLAH" & CStr(iX)
   Field2Array(iX) = "BLUE" & CStr(iX)
Next iX

Set OraSqlStmt = OraDatabase.CreateSql(sSQL, ORASQL_FAILEXEC)
```

The Oracle Data Control (ORADC)

I did not originally intend to write a section on this subject but felt compelled to do so as a result of the confusion I felt when reading the OracleO.hlp help file!

Most of us have some experience using Data Controls. They have been around in one form or another since version two of VB. Were it not for political correctness, I would say that all data controls look the same to me. The Oracle data control is not much different from the others either.

A data control is actually a combination of an OraDynaset (recordset), an OraDatabase, and an OraSession encapsulated in an ActiveX control. To confuse the unsuspecting programmer, Oracle refers to the encapsulated dynaset as a recordset rather than as a dynaset, forgetting that consistent object naming is the heart of polymorphism. The ORADC is often referred to as a "wrapper" around OO4O.

Data controls are indispensable when we want to write quick and dirty programs for small work groups, prototyping or proof of concept. They are not of much use outside of this purpose. They are easy to bind to other controls such as drop down combos, list boxes, text boxes and especially data grids.

Before we can use the ORADC, we must first add it to our toolbox. To do this, navigate
Project I Components from the menu and select it:

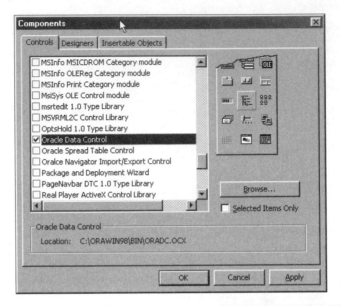

The control will be included among the
others in the left-hand side of your screen.
Now you can use it like any other control.
Here is how the control looks to the user:

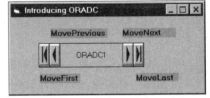

I've added four labels to the screen. They explain the action taken when the user clicks
on any of the four areas on the control, directly above or below the first letter of the
appropriate label. As you can see, the data control buttons map to the Move methods
of the OraDynaset object.

ORADC Properties

The table below lists only the properties that are unique to the ORADC. There is no
point in discussing the `Caption`, `Font`, `Left`, `Width` and similar properties that are
common to all the controls rather than ORADC specific. Many of the properties pertain
to the ORADC underlying Recordset (`Recordset` itself is a property of ORADC)
which is the OraDynaset associated with the control. It means that we're using the
ORADC to control the OraDynaset. I prefer to use the ORADC for quick and dirty
assignments, leaving the detailed and sophisticated tasks to OO4O. In the tables below,
(*) next to a property name means that the property change does not take effect
immediately, and will affect the ORADC behavior only following the next Refresh.

When displaying a form, if the information is not already in the properties of the
control, these should be set in the form initialize event (such as `Database` and
`RecordSource`).

Property Name	Description
AllowMoveLast (*)	Boolean. With True as the default. When False the MoveLast button is grayed. This is true only until successive clicking on MoveNext bring us to the last record. Then the button activates and remains active. The same applies when the underlying Oradynaset reaches the last record. Setting the property to False may be useful when the selected view is very large and MoveLast takes a very long time.
AutoBinding (*)	Boolean. With True as the default. Allows or disallows binding the OraParameters of the OraDatabase to the ORADC RecordSource. It only takes effect when you change the RecordSource. I don't see why you'd want to set it to False. Leave It Alone!
CacheBlocks, CacheSliceSize, CacheSlicesPerBlock	Pertain to the Oradynaset. See CreateCustomDynaset method in OO4O.
Connect (*)	String. Here this property returns the username and password needed to connect the control to the database. Read Only. Set at design time.

Database	An OraDatabase object. This property returns the OraDatabase object that was created with the control. You may use this object pointer for your OO4O programming as follows:
	
	 `Dim MyDB as OraDatabase`
	
	 `Set MyDB = ORADC1.Database`

DirtyWrite	Boolean. With False as the default. It allows dirty write to the data base. It is the equivalent of the ORADYN_DIRTY_WRITE in the CreateDynaset method of OO4O.
EditMode	Not really important (used in asynchronous operations). Integer taking the values: 0 – No Editing in Progress 1 – Editing an existing row 2 – Now adding a record.

Table Continued on Following Page

Property Name	Description
FetchLimit, FetchSize	Pertain to the OraDynaset. See CreateCustomDynaset in OO4O.
NoRefetch (*)	Boolean. With False as the default, which is the way I like it. See OpenDatabase options in OO4O.
Options (*)	See OpenDatabase options in OO4O.
OracleMode (*)	Boolean. With True as the default. Equivalent to selecting the option ORADB_ORAMODE in the OpenDatabase method. See OpenDatabase options in OO4O.
ReadOnly (*)	Boolean. With False as the default. See CreateDynaset in OO4O.

Recordset	An OraDynaset Object. We may assign this to an OO4O dynaset, or, inversely, create a dynaset in OO4O and let the data control handle it:
	
	`Dim MyDS As OraDynaset`
	
	`Set MyDS = ORADC1.Recordset`
	
	`Set ORADC1.Recordset = MyDS`
	
	Again, I rarely use such tricks. For example, if you want to move between records without the user clicking on the ORADC buttons, you may associate a dynaset with the Recordset and do the move operations on it:
	
	`MyDS.MoveNext`

RecordSource (*)	String. The SQL statement defining the underlying recordset. It must be a SELECT statement.

Session	An OraSession object. If you have an ORADC running and don't want to open another session with the CreateObject method you may use the ORADC Session:
	
	`Dim MySession As OraSession`
	
	`Set MySession = ORADC1.Session`
	
	See OraSession in OO4O.

Property Name	Description
TrailingBlanks (*)	Boolean. With False as the default. False means that if a character field in the dynaset contains trailing blanks they'll be stripped. True means they'll stay.
Visible	Boolean. Is the data control itself visible on the form? I generally use an ORADC to get an easy binding to a Grid. When that's the case I use the Grid to traverse the data and do not need to click on the control. Making it invisible eliminates confusion.

ORADC Methods

Again, I am listing only the ORADC specific methods. Here they are:

Method	Description
Refresh	Re-creates the OraDatabase and OraDynaset objects referenced within the data control and reestablishes a dynaset using the SQL statement from the RecordSource property and the connection information from the Connect and DatabaseName properties. OO4O refresh is simpler and faster because it deals only with the dynaset.
UpdateControls	This method belongs to the Recordset property rather than to the ORADC. This is an anachronism that is still with us since the days of VB3. Usage is: `ORADC1.Recordset.UpdateControls` This is useful for persistence. E.g. If the user wants to disregard changes made to the data on the form, and clicks the Cancel button, we use UpdateControls. The data as it is in the dynaset current record is displayed in the bound controls.
UpdateRecord	Allows you to save the current value of bound controls during a Validate event without generating another Validate event, thus forcing the change. It has the effect of executing the Edit method, changing a field, and executing the Update method, except that no events occur.

Table Continued on Following Page

Method	Description
Edit	This is a recordset method. Usage:
	ORADC1.Recordset.Edit
	See OO4O section.
Update	This is a recordset method. Usage:
	ORADC1.Recordset.Update
	See OO4O section.

The Validate event is called before many operations take place. For example, when an attempt is made to move to a new record position, to delete a record or to add a new record.

Summary

In this preceding series of chapters we built up our practical knowledge of OO4O, and how to use it in conjunction with VB, in incremental steps. We have now capped this with a full reference. You should now feel pretty confident of your ability to harness the power of OO4O in your applications. In Chapter 13 we will investigate PL/SQL, and find out how to utilize stored procedures with OO4O. You will then be in a position to write truly powerful applications, such as that found in Chapter 14.

Section III

Using ADO and Oracle

An ADO Application

The aim of this chapter is to introduce you to ADO, not to describe it in full detail. This is a practical chapter that will teach us enough about ADO to get a simple application up and running. We continue to introduce more of its capabilities in the next chapter, and will provide a complete reference to ADO in Chapter 12.

The application we'll build is a replica of the OO4O introductory program. In here we will use ADO and the simplest form of the SQL SELECT statement to build a program that maintains the People table of our database.

This will introduce us to:

❑ A simplified version of the ADO object model - featuring the Connection object, Recordset object, Field object, and Command object

❑ Connecting to Oracle via ODBC and OLE DB

❑ Using the ADO Recordset object to store the results

❑ Using the Move methods of the Recordset object to navigate through the data

❑ Using methods of the Recordset object to modify database data

❑ Using the Command object to return the next available sequence value

❑ Using the Value property of the Field object

ActiveX Data Objects – a.k.a. **ADO** – is a set of lightweight loosely connected objects by which COM (OLE) capable applications can connect to and use a great variety of data sources. It is a descendant of a long succession of Microsoft Data Access 'inventions' that spans DAO, ODBC, OLE DB, RDO and, by now, four versions of ADO. Its model constructs was derived from DAO, and connectivity functionality from RDO. ADO, however, has flattened the object hierarchy and some of the "lower" objects can exist in your code in their own right. This means that a programmer can use the object most suitable to a particular task, without having to create objects that are not really required by the code. In fact, there is no hierarchy between the three main objects (Connection, Command and Recordset) – each may exist independently in your code.

Among the data sources that ADO can deal with are: Relational Database Systems (RDS or RDBMS) of various sources, flat files, and even user created data sources.

> *This is not a Programmer's Reference for ADO. We'll only handle the marriage of ADO and Oracle. For a complete discussion of ADO read David Sussman's* ADO 2.1 Programmer's Reference *available from WROX. I'll discuss the object model in greater detail later in the book, but not to the full extent that David did.*

For now I only want to recreate the OO4O program to work on an Oracle database using ADO in place of OO4O, and this will be done best by imitation and by stressing the similar.

When you finish the reading and the exercises in this chapter you'll have a warm and fuzzy understanding of ADO and how it works with Oracle.

A Simplified ADO Object Model

Again, for the time being let us look at a simplified object model of ADO. It includes a **Connection** object, a **Command** object, a **Recordset** object and **Fields** collection. As stated previously, there is no ownership relationship between the objects except that the `Recordset` object owns its collection of `Fields`. Both the `Command` object and the `Recordset` object require an open Connection if they are to exist in a database context (and will create it given a connect string). A `Recordset` object may be detached from its database and even updated and persisted in this state, but this is outside the scope of this section and will be discussed in Chapter 14 (with a short example). For us an ADO `Recordset` is just a way to handle the data in an online Oracle database.

The objects are related as shown in the diagram below:

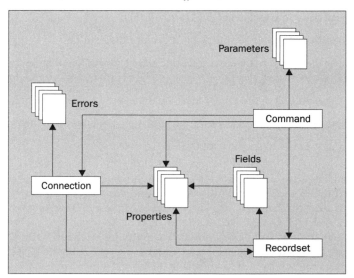

Connection Object

A connection is the hinge of ADO. Command objects and Recordset objects need it to talk to the database. Unlike OO4O, you don't need to create a Connection (Session is the OO4O parlance) before you create a Recordset (OO4O's Dynaset). The connection may be created implicitly for a Recordset when the latter is created, and the same applies to the Command object. We are not going to make use of this shortcut. In our programs (and hopefully yours) all the connections will be created explicitly. A connection is an expensive resource that should not be wasted. An explicitly-built connection may be shared by many Command and Recordset objects (for all interaction with a particular database) whereas the implicit ones belong to just one such object and we would use a different connection every time.

Recordset Object

A Recordset object receives the result sets returned from queries to the Oracle database and allows you to manipulate them in a manner similar to the OO4O Dynaset object, but is more powerful. This is because ADO supports events, so it may be used asynchronously. It may run in a different process space or even a different server. OO4O is eventless and thus is synchronous and must be run in process. Another advantage is the ability to persist a recordset off-line and even to update it off-line. For our present purposes of minimizing the upheaval we'll use it in an almost equivalent way. A Recordset object represents the result set of a SQL SELECT query. It is essentially a client-side scrollable, and possibly updatable table, that allows for browsing the set of rows generated by the query it executes.

A Recordset connected to an Oracle database is updateable only if:

❑ The user has the proper privileges

❑ The SELECT statement deals with a single table

❑ This table is not locked by another process

❑ It has been created with the proper keywords

❑ The table rows are accessible via a UNIQUE or PRIMARY key

Again, in this chapter you'll deal with an updateable Recordset and actually add, delete and update table rows by using this Recordset. Of course, you should be wary of this in a multi-user environment. The cursor will not inform your application of changes made by other users, until you call the Refresh method. Thus you may find yourself trying to modify data that has been deleted!

The Recordset object gives us access to most of the same methods as the OO4O Dynaset object. The main methods – MoveFirst, MoveNext, MovePrevious, MoveLast, AddNew and Update behave identically to those of OO4O. The Edit method does not exist in ADO – you'll soon find that you can live without it.

Field Object

A Field object represents a single column in the `Recordset` object. Each field will map to one column in a row in the query result set. This Field has properties and is therefore an object. Each Field is held in a `Fields` collection within each Recordset. We'll use one of the `Field` object's properties (the `Value` property) in this chapter. `Value` is the default property of the `Field` object.

Command Object

The `Command` object allows us to pass commands into the database; among them all the forms of SQL statements – including `SELECT`, `INSERT`, `UPDATE`, and `DELETE`. This allows for the maintenance and storage of queries and `Parameters` collection, and the execution of stored procedures with input and output parameters. The `Command` object is a very powerful weapon in our arsenal. ADO was not created for Oracle and does not handle Oracle bound parameters and special functions too well. Using the `Command` object is the way in which we circumvent these shortcomings, and we'll end up using it a lot. The `Command` object may have an associated Recordset, which is a feature we're going to use in this chapter. OO4O has an equivalent object that we have not discussed yet, called `OraSQLStmt`.

Again, the ADO object model is more involved than the simplified version we use here. This, however, is the crux of it.

Connecting to Oracle

Again, let us start with a new standard exe VB project and rename the project `ADOPeople`.

We need to incorporate ADO into the project. We do this by selecting the **Microsoft ActiveX Data Objects 2.x Library**. In the **Project** menu, click on **References** and then check the proper ADO library. You may use ADO 2.0, 2.1, or 2.5. For this sample program, the version you use makes no difference, but it is always best to work with the latest.

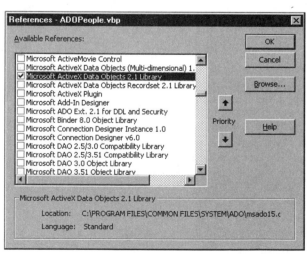

As you know from Chapter 4, there are several ways in which we can connect our VB program to Oracle. We are connecting to Oracle using a system DSN (this is using ODBC), but I will point out the minor alterations that will allow the application to connect via the Microsoft OLE DB provider (MSDAORA).

In order to be able to connect via ODBC you'll need to create a system DSN, in this case called **msOra** (if you name it differently you will have to correct the code accordingly). If you have forgotten how to do this please refer back to Chapter 4.

We will use this DSN in the `Connection` object we use to connect to Oracle, inside the `clsConnection` class, as you will see below.

Maintaining the People Table using ADO

This book is all about giving you a thorough overview of the ways in which we can marry VB and Oracle. The program in this chapter will provide exactly the same functionality as that in Chapter 5, where we used OO4O. It would be well worth your while to look through this chapter and get a good feel for the OO4O way of doing things. For this basic application the similarities between the two camps outweigh the differences. As we start to pass parameters, use transactions and employ stored procedures you will find that the approaches we adopt start to differ markedly..

As you know, I am a strong proponent of code reuse. In fact, if you have already worked through Chapter 5 you can save time and effort by creating a `Chapter9` subdirectory in your `VBOraBook` directory and making a copy of your `Chapter5` `frmPeople.frm` and `modGeneral.bas` in the new directory.

> *Be careful to make a real copy, not just move the files between directories. In Chapter5 highlight the two files, then while holding down the* right *mouse button, drag them to the new directory. When you release the button, a dropdown menu will appear. Choose the* **Copy Here** *option. This is going to be referred to as* `True_Copy` *in the rest of the book.*

The module will be used "as is" and the form code will require only a small alteration. If you have jumped straight in to the ADO chapters, I would refer you to these chapters for this code. Of course, all of the code for this chapter can be downloaded form the Wrox website.

Include the newly copied form in your VB project and remove the automatically generated **Form1**. Don't forget to change your **Startup Object** (from **Project I Properties**) to be the new form. Include the `modGeneral.bas` in your project as well.

We are going to give this program the very same functionality that we've already seen in Chapter 5. We are going to build a new `clsConnection` class – using the same name and the very same method names as before. We will also build a new `clsPeople` class - again using the very same name and methods to achieve the same behavior. I obviously value polymorphism very highly.

The clsConnection class:
In here we'll connect to the database the ADO way. This connection, as before, will be used by clsPeople.

The clsPeople Class:
This will contain the mrsPeople (rs is my Hungarian prefix to a Recordset, m is to designate that the scope of the recordset is this class module) Recordset, which we'll use to maintain the People table. You'll note that not much needs to be changed significantly in this class from the OO4O version, with one notable exception: we cannot create the mrsLastrec dynaset – the equivalent of mdynLastRec – directly. We must use the Command object to create it.

> The "SELECT Sequence.NextVal" query is not a plain-vanilla SQL – it is Oracle-specific. We have to cheat the system and use a Command object. More about this later.

Let's start with the clsConnection class.

The clsConnection Class

This is a generic, portable class that will maintain our connection to Oracle. You may recall from Chapter 5 that with OO4O we use the CreateObject method to create an OraSession object. Then we created an OraDatabase object within the OraSession object. The flatter hierarchy of the ADO object model simplifies things considerably. We simply declare our Connection object, instantiate it then pass in our connection string as a parameter in the Open method of the object. The connection class also contains a Property Get routine so that our other classes can get a "pointer" to the connection. The code looks like this:

```
Option Explicit

Private mADOConnection As ADODB.Connection    'Declare the Connection object

Public Sub OpenDB(sDSN As String, sUser As String, sPW As String)

'sDSN in this case is the name of the System DSN (msORA).
'The username and password are scott and tiger
'These arguments are passed in from the Form_load event.

Dim sConnect As String    'Declare our connection string

sConnect = "Data Source=" & sDSN & ";" & _
           "User ID=" & sUser & ";" & _
           "Password=" & sPW & ";"

Set mADOConnection = New ADODB.Connection    'Let's instantiate the object!

'Utilizing the ADO Connection object,we set the object parameters
'and open the Connection.

With mADOConnection
```

```
    .ConnectionString = sConnect
    .ConnectionTimeout = 10    'stop the process if failed to connect in 10
secs
    .CursorLocation = adUseClient 'the cursor can be client side or server
side
    .Open
End With
End Sub

Public Property Get ADOConnection() As ADODB.Connection
    Set ADOConnection = mADOConnection
End Property

Private Sub Class_Terminate()
    Set mADOConnection = Nothing 'Good behaviour requires that we clean up.
End Sub
```

We use the `CursorLocation` property of the `Connection` object to set the location of the cursor engine. We will discuss the various options in full in Chapter 12.

If you wish to connect through MSDAORA, the first change we have to make is to pass the connection string (`sConnect`) in as a parameter to the `Open` method, rather than applying it to the `Connection` object's `ConnectionString` property. We also use the `Provider` property of the `Connection` object to specify MSDAORA:

```
With mADOConnection
    .ConnectionTimeout = 10    'stop the process if failed to connect in 10
secs
    .CursorLocation = adUseClient 'the cursor can be client side or server
side
    .Provider = "MSDAORA"
    .Open sConnect
End With
```

The `OpenDB` method is called from the form in the `Form_Load` event routine. This is the only place in the form where it requires a change from the OO4O form code. With OO4O we used:

```
cConnection.OpenDB "scott", "tiger", ""
```

With ADO (using our DSN) the call is:

```
cConnection.OpenDB "MSORA", "scott", "tiger"
```

If you wish to connect via MSDAORA, the call is:

```
cConnection.OpenDB "", "scott", "tiger"
```

> Note: In order to keep the programs in this book as simple as possible, we do not deal with Logon screens. User name and Password really belong in invisible text boxes and not in the code. This is a general principle regardless of the database used (or even if a database is used at all).

Another minor change from the OO4O code is seen in the `Property Get` function. Here it is called `ADOConnection`. In OO4O it was called `Database`. The difference is reflected only in `clsPeople`, it does not affect the form code.

The clsPeople ADO Data Class

There is very little difference between the ADO data class and the OO4O data class of Chapter 5. When I sat down to convert the program from OO4O to ADO I actually made a copy of the class in the new directory and edited it, here and there, as needed. As such there are certain subs that we will not discuss in detail again in this section:

❑ **Private Sub Class_Initialize** – where we assign default values to our class variables, describe the msSelect variable that defines our mrsPeople Recordset and the msFindLastKey string that holds the SQL that retrieves the next available sequence number.

❑ **Private Sub SetDefaults()** – see above.

❑ **Private Sub SetProperties()** – which assigns the field values to the appropriate class variables and deals with the problem that would arise from assigning a Null value to a VB string.

❑ **Property Get and Property Let routines.**

For the sake of completeness, the full `clsPeople` code will be listed at the end of the chapter and any relevant differences between this and the OO4O code will be highlighted there.

General Declaration Code

Let's start with the General Declaration code, which is all pretty self-explanatory but is well commented:

```
Option Explicit

'    A private instance of clsConnection so that we can use its methods
Private mcConnection As clsConnection

'    A private copy of our connection object to be opened inside mcConnection
Private mADOConnection As ADODB.Connection

'    Declare our objects
Private mrsPeople As ADODB.RecordSet
Private mrsLastRec As ADODB.RecordSet
Private mFindLastCmd As ADODB.Command

'    Declare the variables to hold the SELECT statements that define our
'    Recordsets
Private msSelect As String
Private msFindLastKey As String

'    Declare an array to store the sequence number from mrsLastRec
Private mvResults As Variant
```

```
'   Class variables
Private mlPersonId As Double        'Get and Let
Private msLastName As String        'Get and Let
Private msFirstName As String       'Get and Let
Private msMI As String              'Get and Let
Private mdDob As Date               'Get and Let
Private msGender As String          'Get and Let
Private msEyeColor As String        'Get and Let

'   Make a place for LastRec Variable that will hold our Sequence number
Private mlLastPersonId As Double    'Save Last Value

' Field objects for each column in our mrsPeople Recordset object
Private mfldPersonId As ADODB.Field
Private mfldLastName As ADODB.Field
Private mfldFirstName As ADODB.Field
Private mfldMI As ADODB.Field
Private mfldDob As ADODB.Field
Private mfldGender As ADODB.Field
Private mfldEyeColor As ADODB.Field
```

There are some obviously some differences in syntax from that we saw in the realm of OO4O:

❑ The Hungarian prefix `mdyn` of OO4O became `mrs`. This difference also applies to the rest of the class.

❑ We've declared a `ADODB.Recordset` rather than an OraDynaset.

❑ The fields are declared as `ADODB.Field` (instead of `OraField`).

The more interesting differences are as follows:

❑ We have added a variant called `mvResults` in which we'll keep the Last Key. This will introduce you to one of ADO's finest features – The `GetRows` method which is a Recordset method that allows us to return multiple rows to an array (more later).

❑ We've declared an `ADODB.Command`.

❑ We have not declared a field object for our sequence number.

The last two arise because we cannot create the `mrsLastRec` Recordset without a `Command` object. This is because ADO and Oracle were not really meant for each other in the beginning, and since the `"SELECT PERSON_ID_SEQ.NEXTVAL FROM dual"` uses Oracle-specific SQL (not plain vanilla), the recordset cannot be created directly.

The `Recordset` created via the `Command` object is not preserved. Every time the Command is executed, the Recordset is recreated. This explains the way the `ConnectX` method and the `FindLastKey` sub are coded.

The ConnectX Method

Let's split the code into two halves. First let's deal with the code that sets a reference to our connection, instantiates the `Recordset` object and then use the `Fields` collection of the `Recordset` to assign to appropriate column values to our `Field` objects:

```
Public Sub ConnectX(ByVal NewValue As clsConnection) 'Required for connection
                                                     'to clsConnection

Set mcConnection = NewValue

'   our class relies on an already open ADOConnection.

Set mADOConnection = mcConnection.ADOConnection

'   we now create the RecordSet and assign values to the Field objects

Set mrsPeople = New ADODB.RecordSet
    mrsPeople.Open msSelect, mADOConnection, adOpenDynamic, adLockOptimistic
    With mrsPeople.Fields
        Set mfldPersonId =!PERSON_ID
        Set mfldLastName = !LAST_NAME
        Set mfldFirstName = !FIRST_NAME
        Set mfldMI = !M_I
        Set mfldDob = !Dob
        Set mfldGender = !Gender
        Set mfldEyeColor = !EYE_COLOR
    End With
```

Note that the `Value` property of the `Field` object is the default. In the above code we are using it implicitly (we are assigning the column value to the `Value` property of the `Field` object).

The `Open` method of the `Recordset` object deserves further discussion:

```
mrsPeople.Open msSelect, mADOConnection, adOpenDynamic, adLockOptimistic
```

We pass in the following parameters:

- ❑ Source – in our case the `msSelect` string that contains our SELECT statement.

- ❑ `ActiveConnection` – a valid connection object (or connection string) that identifies the connection to be used. In our case the `mADOConnection` object.

- ❑ `CursorType` – the type of cursor used in the `Recordset` object. In our case `adOpenDynamic` that makes the `Recordset` updatable (discussed further in Chapter 10).

- ❑ `LockType` – the type of lock placed on records during editing. In our case `adLockOptimistic`. An optimistic lock locks the database record just before the actual update. A pessimistic lock starts when the record is fetched. In OO4O we used the `Edit` method of the `OraDynaset` (which has no ADO equivalent) to start the locking process at the very last instance.

This sub is totally different from its OO4O counterpart. If you try to set the Recordset normally (in the Open method) using the following statement:

```
SELECT PERSON_ID_SEQ.NEXTVAL FROM dual
```

it will not work – the Recordset will not be created and you'll find out that this is so only when you try to use the Field object. Hence, we are forced to take a different route, using the Command object:

```
Set mFindLastCmd = New ADODB.Command
   With mFindLastCmd
      .ActiveConnection = mADOConnection
      .CommandType = adCmdText
      .CommandText = msFindLastKey
   End With
SetProperties
End Sub
```

After we have instantiated our Command we issue three instructions:

❑   Use the already open connection.

❑   Execute a text command – in our case the pseudo column Nextval of the sequence.

❑   The command text is to be found in the string msFindLastKey.

Now we need to get the Sequence value into a Recordset and then into a multidimensional array.

The FindLastkey Routine

The actual handling of the Sequence happens in the FindLastKey sub of the class. Note that we still use the same name for the sub because it actually performs the very same function – it returns the next available key. We execute our SQL command using the Execute method of the Command object. The command was instructed in the ConnectX method to use a text command and to find it in msFindLastKey. When it is executed, it fetches the next key into the newly created mrsLastRec Recordset. The Recordset that could not be created directly using the Recordset.Open method was easily created using the Command.Execute method:

```
Private Sub FindLastKey()
   Set mrsLastRec = mFindLastCmd.Execute
   mvResults = mrsLastRec.GetRows
   mlLastPersonId = mvResults(0, 0)
End Sub
```

The last line of code retrieves the result into our variant array using the GetRows method of the Recordset. We can actually get mlLastPersonId in one of two ways. One is to use mrsLastRec.Fields(0), the other is to use the GetRows method of the Recordset. I elected the following method simply in order to introduce it. I used GetRows in its default form, without parameters or arguments. By so doing, we make it possible to return all the rows of the Recordset into the named two-dimensional variant array. In this case we know that the query returns just one number. That being the case, we obviously find it in the first column of the first row – or the (0, 0) position. GetRows is a very powerful and very useful method and we are going to discuss it at length in Chapters 10 and 11.

Modifying Data

In this application we can update, delete or insert data simply by calling various methods (Update, Delete, AddNew) of the Recordset. These are as described for the OraDynaset in Chapter 5 with one exception. In OO4O we used the Edit method to lock the database row before it is updated. We then assigned new values to the fields and executed the Update method. In ADO we skip the Edit method. It simply does not exist in the ADO Recordset object. Thus, in the Update routine, the Edit line is commented out.

All the rest of the methods, properties, and subs of the ADO version of the class are identical except for the mrs versus the mdyn prefix of the Recordset object.

> **Conclusion: If you stick to the basics, it is not all that difficult to convert OO4O to ADO and vice versa.**

In Chapter 11 we'll return for a few short minutes to this project and learn how to avoid using the mrsLastRec altogether (we'll do the same for our OO4O equivalent, mdynLastRec). We'll achieve this by using a trigger in the database. A trigger is a database procedure that is fired when certain events occur. In this case the trigger will be fired when a new record is inserted. This will allow us to get rid of the Command object and really minimize the differences between the ADO and the OO4O approach.

To complete the discussion, here is the complete code for the clsPeople.cls (with differences from the OO4O program highlighted):

```
Option Explicit
Private mcConnection As clsConnection
Private mADOConnection As ADODB.Connection 'Required for connection to
                                           'clsConnection
Private mrsPeople As ADODB.RecordSet
Private mrsLastRec As ADODB.RecordSet
Private mFindLastCmd As ADODB.Command

'** The select statement
Private msSelect As String
Private msFindLastKey As String
Private mvResults As Variant

'** Class variables
Private mlPersonId As Double   'Get and Let
Private msLastName As String   'Get and Let
Private msFirstName As String  'Get and Let
Private msMI As String  'Get and Let
Private mdDob As Date  'Get and Let
Private msGender As String  'Get and Let
Private msEyeColor As String  'Get and Let

'** Make a place for LastRec Variable
Private mlLastPersonId As Double    'Save Last Value

Private mfldPersonId As ADODB.Field
Private mfldLastName As ADODB.Field
```

```
Private mfldFirstName As ADODB.Field
Private mfldMI As ADODB.Field
Private mfldDob As ADODB.Field
Private mfldGender As ADODB.Field
Private mfldEyeColor As ADODB.Field

Private Sub Class_Initialize()
'** Initialize Class Variables
    SetDefaults

'Make a parameter SQL for the reading the RecordSet
msSelect = "Select "
msSelect = msSelect & "PERSON_ID, "
msSelect = msSelect & "LAST_NAME, "
msSelect = msSelect & "FIRST_NAME, "
msSelect = msSelect & "M_I, "
msSelect = msSelect & "DOB, "
msSelect = msSelect & "GENDER, "
msSelect = msSelect & "EYE_COLOR"
msSelect = msSelect & " FROM PEOPLE"

'** Create the FindLastKey SQL

msFindLastKey = "Select PERSON_ID_SEQ.NEXTVAL from dual"

End Sub

Public Sub ConnectX(ByVal NewValue As clsConnection) 'Required for connection
to clsConnection
    Set mcConnection = NewValue

'our class relies on an already open ADOConnection.

Set mADOConnection = mcConnection.ADOConnection

'we now create the RecordSet

Set mrsPeople = New ADODB.RecordSet
mrsPeople.Open msSelect, mADOConnection, adOpenDynamic, adLockOptimistic

Set mfldPersonId = mrsPeople.Fields!PERSON_ID
Set mfldLastName = mrsPeople.Fields!LAST_NAME
Set mfldFirstName = mrsPeople.Fields!FIRST_NAME
Set mfldMI = mrsPeople.Fields!M_I
Set mfldDob = mrsPeople.Fields!Dob
Set mfldGender = mrsPeople.Fields!Gender
Set mfldEyeColor = mrsPeople.Fields!EYE_COLOR
Set mFindLastCmd = New ADODB.Command

With mFindLastCmd
    .ActiveConnection = mADOConnection
    .CommandType = adCmdText
    .CommandText = msFindLastKey
End With
SetProperties
End Sub

Public Property Get EOF() As Boolean
    EOF = mrsPeople.EOF
End Property
```

```vb
Public Property Get BOF() As Boolean
    BOF = mrsPeople.BOF
End Property

Public Property Get IsEmpty() As Boolean
    IsEmpty = mrsPeople.EOF And mrsPeople.BOF
End Property

Public Property Get PersonId() As Double
    PersonId = mlPersonId
End Property

Public Property Let PersonId(ByVal NewValue As Double)
    mlPersonId = NewValue
End Property

Public Property Get LastName() As String
    LastName = msLastName
End Property

Public Property Let LastName(ByVal NewValue As String)
    msLastName = NewValue
Ed Property

Public Property Get FirstName() As String
    FirstName = msFirstName
End Property

Public Property Let FirstName(ByVal NewValue As String)
    msFirstName = NewValue
End Property

Public Property Get MI() As String
    MI = msMI
End Property

Public Property Let MI(ByVal NewValue As String)
    msMI = NewValue
End Property

Public Property Get Dob() As Date
    Dob = mdDob
End Property

Public Property Let Dob(ByVal NewValue As Date)
    mdDob = NewValue
End Property

Public Property Get Gender() As String
    Gender = msGender
End Property

Public Property Let Gender(ByVal NewValue As String)
    msGender = NewValue
End Property

Public Property Get EyeColor() As String
    EyeColor = msEyeColor
End Property
```

```
Public Property Let EyeColor(ByVal NewValue As String)
    msEyeColor = NewValue
End Property

Public Sub MoveFirst()
    If Not mrsPeople.BOF Then
        mrsPeople.MoveFirst
        SetProperties
    End If
End Sub

Public Sub MoveLast()
    If Not mrsPeople.EOF Then
        mrsPeople.MoveLast
      SetProperties
    End If
End Sub

Public Sub MoveNext()
    If Not mrsPeople.EOF Then
      mrsPeople.MoveNext
        If mrsPeople.EOF Then mrsPeople.MoveLast
        SetProperties
    End If
End Sub

Public Sub MovePrevious()
    If Not mrsPeople.BOF Then
        mrsPeople.MovePrevious
    If mrsPeople.BOF Then mrsPeople.MoveFirst
        SetProperties
    End If
End Sub

Private Sub SetDefaults()
    mlPersonId = 0
    msLastName = ""
    msFirstName = ""
    msMI = ""
    mdDob = #1/1/1800#
    msGender = ""
    msEyeColor = ""
End Sub

Private Sub SetProperties()
    If mrsPeople.EOF Then Exit Sub
        SetDefaults
    If Not IsNull(mfldPersonId.Value) Then
        mlPersonId = mfldPersonId.Value
    End If
    If Not IsNull(mfldLastName.Value) Then
        msLastName = mfldLastName.Value
    End If
     If Not IsNull(mfldFirstName.Value) Then
        msFirstName = mfldFirstName.Value
    End If
     If Not IsNull(mfldMI.Value) Then
        msMI = mfldMI.Value
    End If
    If Not IsNull(mfldDob.Value) Then
```

```
            mdDob = mfldDob.Value
        End If
        If Not IsNull(mfldGender.Value) Then
            msGender = mfldGender.Value
        End If
         If Not IsNull(mfldEyeColor.Value) Then
            msEyeColor = mfldEyeColor.Value
        End If
End Sub

Private Sub FindLastKey()
    Set mrsLastRec = mFindLastCmd.Execute
    mvResults = mrsLastRec.GetRows
    mlLastPersonId = mvResults(0, 0)
End Sub

Public Sub AddNew()
    FindLastKey
    mlPersonId = mlLastPersonId 'assigns our sequence number to class property
    mrsPeople.AddNew

' Insert all the values into the fields
    mfldPersonId.Value = mlPersonId
    mfldLastName.Value = msLastName
    mfldFirstName.Value = msFirstName
    mfldMI.Value = msMI
    mfldDob.Value = mdDob
    mfldGender.Value = msGender
    mfldEyeColor.Value = msEyeColor
    mrsPeople.Update
End Sub

Public Sub Update()
    'mrsPeople.Edit

'Insert all the values into the fields (except the key)
    mfldLastName.Value = msLastName
    mfldFirstName.Value = msFirstName
    mfldMI.Value = msMI
    If mdDob = #1/1/1800# Then
        mfldDob.Value = Null
    Else
        mfldDob.Value = mdDob
    End If
    mfldGender.Value = msGender
    mfldEyeColor.Value = msEyeColor
    mrsPeople.Update
End Sub

Public Sub Delete()
    mrsPeople.Delete
End Sub
```

That is it. We have built our ADO data class!

The complete code sits in the Chapter 9 section in the WROX site. These are the five files:

- ❑ ADOPeople.vbp
- ❑ frmPeople.frm
- ❑ modGeneral.bas
- ❑ ADOclsConnection.cls
- ❑ ADOclsPeople.cls

Save your own work in the Chapter9 subdirectory of VBOraBook.

Summary

In this chapter you have learned how to use ADO and the simplest form of the SQL SELECT statement to build a program that maintains a database table. We've done this by making a minute change to the form, leaving modGeneral.bas alone, and making changes to the clsConnection.cls and clsPeople.cls. None of these changes is major. Because the SELECT Sequence.NextVal query is not a plain-vanilla SQL we had to cheat the system and use a Command object to get the desired result. All the other changes are relatively small. Almost all the methods we've used in OO4O even have the same names in ADO. Build the program and play with it like you did in Chapter 5. Put breakpoints in strategic places in the code and follow the progress line by line. Get a gut feeling for how it all works.

10

Using Parameters with ADO

This chapter will deal with using parameters with ADO. If you have read Chapter 6, you may have been pleasantly surprised by the ease with which we were able to incorporate parameters into our OO4O application. We were able to add versatility to our data class with relatively little effort.

In ADO we can also pass parameters to SQL statements and stored procedures but I'm afraid things aren't quite as easy for us. In fact, when using ADO in conjunction with Oracle, our program works very differently:

❑   In ADO, it is best to work with parameters in the Command object. When you execute a parameterized query from the Command object, the recordset cursor provided is read-only. This means that we can no longer modify our database data by simply calling methods of the Recordset object. We must do all of our record manipulations as SQL action queries (INSERT, UPDATE, and DELETE) in the Command object. Fortunately, you should have obtained a sound grasp of DML from Chapter 2.

❑   We cannot traverse our Recordset by calling the 'Move' methods. Instead we must extract the data into a two-dimensional variant array using the GetRows method of the Recordset, and traverse that instead.

It is also worth of note that ADO also does not bind (compile to p-code) parameterized statements in Oracle, though it may in other database engines. More accurately, the parameters are not bound except in the case of stored procedures. In this instance it is the stored procedure itself that binds the parameters and not ADO. In the case of normal SQL, ADO replaces the placeholder with the Parameter.Value, so there is no binding on the server side.

In this chapter we are once again performing a single table manipulation, so stored procedures do not offer us any advantages. However, as described above, ADO is forcing us to do our updates etc. using DML – a process by which we can have much greater control over the modification process.

On the surface, the program that we create in this chapter will be identical to the one we saw in Chapter 6. The user will enter a certain Gender value into the appropriate textbox, click the Find button and the `Recordset` will be loaded gender-specifically. However, what is going on behind the scenes will be significantly different. In particular we will:

❑ Create `Command` objects to handle our INSERT, UPDATE, DELETE and SELECT commands, all of which are parameterized.

❑ Create a `Parameters` collection for each Command object. Each `Parameter` object in the collection will correspond to a column in our `Recordset`.

As we discuss how we handle parameters in ADO, so we will gain a more in-depth understanding of ADO in general.

> *A complete reference to ADO may be found in David Sussman's "ADO 2.1 – Programmers reference" from WROX press.*

OK, let's start by having another look at the ADO object model, and the `Command` and `Parameter` objects in particular.

Parameters and ADO

Here is a somewhat more detailed, though still incomplete, picture of the ADO object relationships (it is missing the `Property` and `Error` objects which, in order to maintain a strong focus and the chapter's core issues, we will dispense with for the time being:

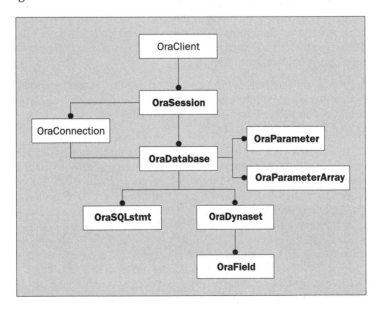

You'll notice that a `Parameter` object, which is a part of the `Parameters` collection (not shown in the diagram), is associated with the `Command` object. That means that if we want to do a parameterized query, it must be done in the `Command` object. The parameter object contains details of a single parameter. In our program we are going to use sixteen of them. Let's start, however, with the `Command` object.

The Command Object

As we saw in the previous chapter, the `Command` object allows us to pass parameters into stored procedures and stored queries. We create a new `Parameter` object using the `Command` object's `CreateParameter` method (discussed in full in Chapter 12). The general syntax is:

```
Set Parameter = Command.CreateParameter ([ParamName],[DataType], _
[Direction], [Size], [Value])
```

The `CreateParameter` method has five positional and optional arguments. Positional means that the order in which they are entered is important, and when skipped, the comma still remains, except for trailing arguments. You should omit the trailing comma(s):

❑   `ParamName` is the name of the parameter

❑   `DataType` is...its data type!

❑   `Direction` defines the mode of operation of the parameter (input, output, both or return value, for example)

❑   `Size` is the maxiumum length of the parameter value in characters or bytes

❑   `Value` is the value of the parameter

We can actually pass parameters using the `Command` object's `Execute` method. We pass them in as a variant array into the second argument of this method (see Chapter 12). However, there is a much better way to do it, and that is to use the `Parameters` collection. It gives you complete control over the individual parameters passed to a procedure or query. Also, it is the only way to use stored procedures that have output parameters.

The Parameter Object

A `Parameter` object contains all of the information regarding a single parameter to be used in our SQL query (or stored procedure). It is only really used in conjunction with the `Command` object and its associated `Parameters` collection.

The `CreateParameter` method discussed in the previous section works hand-in-hand with the `Append` method of the `Parameters` collection. After we have created and defined our `Parameter` object, we add it to the `Parameters` collection:

```
Command.Parameters.Append Parameter
```

We create one `Parameter` object for every parameter to be passed (including one for any output parameter or return value.

OK, let's get down to business.

Modifying the ADO Program to use Parameters

As stated previously, using ADO parameters in an SQL query to an Oracle database produces a static, read-only `Recordset` (or, more accurately the `Recordset` is provided with a static, read-only cursor). This is perhaps the biggest difference between the program that we created in the last chapter and the one I am going to guide you through now. In Chapter 9 our `Recordset` was updateable and the program was very similar to its OO4O sibling. We simply called the 'Modify' methods of the `Recordset` and everything we did was reflected in local memory and the database itself.

With a read-only `Recordset`, we are going to update our database using DML command, each with its own parameter, in the ADO `Command` object. For example, we will have an "Insert" `Command` object. The associated `Parameters` collection will have seven `Parameter` objects, each one describing a parameter for use with a column in the `People` table. This is not really an inconvenience. Using the `Command` object to update is the preferred method with ADO, regardless of the database engine used. The Oracle-ADO combination forces us to do the right thing.

The cursor we have is static – all of the values are cached and fixed in local memory. This means that our `Recordset` has no idea what is going in the database. Other users may have changed values or deleted rows and we will not be aware of it. This means that, every now-and-then (or very frequently, depending on how often you expect the database data to be modified) we must "reload" our `Recordset` to bring it up to date. Even that is not so bad because in a multi-user system we have to refresh (requery) every now and then to see what other users have done to the data. In the ADO model we only do it more frequently.

> Even if we are able to declare a dynamic cursor (`adOpenDynamic`), we still have to requery to see changes when using Ado and Oracle.

This is not the last difference between our OO4O and ADO parameter applications. As we proceed, another problem will rise. As discussed in the introduction to this chapter, we cannot traverse that `Recordset` as we did before, by calling the 'Move' methods of the `Recordset`. This means that we have to load our data into a two-dimensional array. We will discuss this in more detail later in the chapter.

We did the same thing out of choice for our `mrslastRec` recordset in the previous chapter. Here, ADO is, again, forcing us to do the right thing.

To produce our ADO parameter application we are going to modify the program from the previous chapter. Therefore, make a true copy (right-click on the file, drag it to its destination, release the mouse button, and select **Copy Here**) of the classes, forms and module from the Chapter 9 directory into a new Chapter 10 directory.

Open the `ADOPeople` project and immediately save the project, form and classes as follows:

❑ `ADOPeoplePrm.vbp`

❑ `ADOfrmPeoplePrm.frm`

❑ `modGeneral.bas`

❑ `ADOclsConnection.cls`

❑ `ADOclsPeoplePrm.cls`

Note that the module and the connection class are named as before. The `modGeneral` is not altered in any way. You may also use the connection class as is. If you download the code from the Wrox website you will see that this program uses the Microsoft OLEDB driver (`MSDAORA`) rather than ODBC. The choice is yours. Connection details for either approach were given in the previous chapter.

We need to allow a user to enter a gender and then "call" a male or female-oriented result set, by clicking a Find button. Let's start with the minor changes to our form. If you have read Chapter 6 this will be a refresher.

Modifying the Form

The simplest changes are going to take place in the form. We are going to add a Find button and the associated code. You should also change the form's caption to Maintaining the PEOPLE table, using ADO. Not surprisingly, the code for the Find button is identical to the code in the OO4O program. As before, we do our best to preserve our work.

Add a new command button (`cmdFind`) and change its caption to Find. Here is how the new form looks:

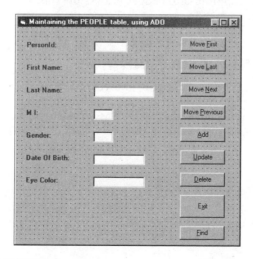

And here is the code Find button routine:

```
Private Sub cmdFind_Click()
    cPeople.Gender = UCase(txtGender.Text)
    cPeople.Refresh     'Read again
    cmdMoveFirst_Click  'Position the form at the first row
End Sub
```

When a user enters a Gender value and clicks Find, the text entered is converted to upper case and stored in our msGender class variable (via Gender Property Let routine). We then call the Refresh routine (which you will see in the clsPeople code), where the variable value is assigned to our parameter. Finally we move the record pointer to the first row.

Voila! That is the only change we need to make to the form. As before, there is no need at all to touch the clsConnection. It remains intact (unless you wish to switch to MSDAORA).

The big work is in the clsPeople. Here we have to build new SQL statements and deal with Command objects and their associated Parameter objects.

Coding the clsPeople Data Class.

The first thing we need to do, as before, is to modify the SELECT statement that defines our mrsPeople recordset so that it will accept a parameter. However, this is not all we have to do. In the previous program we relied on the Update, Insert and Delete methods of our updatable Recordset to modify the database data. With ADO and its read-only Recordset we must write the INSERT, DELETE and UPDATE statements ourselves. These statements should be no mystery to you after reading Chapter 2.

> I am assuming that you are modifying Chapter 9 code. As such, I have
> highlighted the appropriate changes, unless the code has changed so
> much that I recommend a straight replacement.

The Class_Initialize Routine

Since we have so much SQL code to add, I moved it all to a separate sub called BuildSQL. This means that our Class_Initialize routine has changed drastically. Apart from setting the default values to our class variables, it merely calls the BuildSQL routine. I suggest you delete the old Class_Initialize code and replace it with this:

```
Private Sub Class_Initialize()
' Initialize Class Variables
    SetDefaults
' Make a parameter SQL for the reading and Updating
    BuildSQL
End Sub
```

The BuildSQL Routine

Let's break this code block into four sections and discuss each in turn. We'll start with the modification to our `msSelect` string, which defines our `mrsPeople Recordset` object:

```
Private Sub BuildSQL()
'Make a parameter SQL for the reading the RecordSet
    msSelect = "SELECT "
    msSelect = msSelect & "PERSON_ID, "
    msSelect = msSelect & "LAST_NAME, "
    msSelect = msSelect & "FIRST_NAME, "
    msSelect = msSelect & "M_I, "
    msSelect = msSelect & "DOB, "
    msSelect = msSelect & "GENDER, "
    msSelect = msSelect & "EYE_COLOR"
    msSelect = msSelect & " FROM PEOPLE"
    msSelect = msSelect & " Where GENDER = ?"
```

In ADO, the question mark is the placeholder for an ADO parameter. The parameter will allow us to dynamically change the definition of our `mrsPeople` recordset.

We cannot call the `AddNew` method of the `Recordset`, so instead we must write our own `INSERT INTO` statement to be able to add new records to the database:

```
'Make a parameter SQL for Inserting into the RecordSet
    msInsert = "INSERT INTO "
    msInsert = msInsert & " PEOPLE ("
    msInsert = msInsert & "PERSON_ID, "
    msInsert = msInsert & "LAST_NAME, "
    msInsert = msInsert & "FIRST_NAME, "
    msInsert = msInsert & "M_I, "
    msInsert = msInsert & "DOB, "
    msInsert = msInsert & "GENDER, "
    msInsert = msInsert & "EYE_COLOR) "
    msInsert = msInsert & "VALUES ("
    msInsert = msInsert & "?, "
    msInsert = msInsert & "?, "
    msInsert = msInsert & "?, "
    msInsert = msInsert & "?, "
    msInsert = msInsert & "?, "
    msInsert = msInsert & "?, "
    msInsert = msInsert & "?)"
```

Also note that the `INSERT INTO` statement has seven such placeholders – one for each column in the `People` table. These parameters have to be created in the exact order in which they appear in the corresponding statements. The `Command` object assigns the first parameter to the first placeholder (?), the second to the second, and so on.

We must do a similar trick in order to update database records:

```
'Make a parameter SQL for Updating the RecordSet
    msUpdate = "UPDATE "
    msUpdate = msUpdate & " PEOPLE SET"
    msUpdate = msUpdate & " LAST_NAME = ?,"
```

```
   msUpdate = msUpdate & " FIRST_NAME = ?,"
   msUpdate = msUpdate & " M_I = ?,"
   msUpdate = msUpdate & " DOB = ?,"
   msUpdate = msUpdate & " GENDER = ?,"
   msUpdate = msUpdate & " EYE_COLOR = ?"
   msUpdate = msUpdate & " WHERE PERSON_ID = ?"
```

Finally, we need to code our own DELETE statement, which requires one further parameter:

```
'Make a parameter SQL for the "deleting from the RecordSet
   msDelete = "DELETE "
   msDelete = msDelete & " FROM PEOPLE "
   msDelete = msDelete & " WHERE PERSON_ID = ?"

'** Create the FindLastKey SQL
   msFindLastKey = "Select PERSON_ID_SEQ.NEXTVAL from DUAL"
End Sub
```

That makes sixteen parameters in all. Notice, by the way, that our SQL to retrieve the next Sequence number remains unchanged.

Now let's define our Parameter objects and add them to the Parameters collection. We do this in the ConnectX method.

The ConnectX Routine

As you should recall, we create our parameters in the Command object using the CreateParameter method. This is a task in which accuracy and adherence to detail is mandatory. Not only do parameters have to be entered in the exact order of their corresponding SQL statement, but also each parameter has to be defined to exactly match the field type and length.

After a parameter has been created, we append it to the command object using the Append method. For example:

```
With mUpdateCmd

Set mUpdatePrmEyeColor = .CreateParameter("pEyeColor", _
   adVarChar, adParamInput, 10, "Brown")

.Parameters.Append mUpdatePrmEyeColor
```

The EyeColor parameter is of type adVarChar – it is, after all, a VARCHAR type field. Its direction is input (adParamInput) and its length is 10. I also gave it the value of Brown to match its default. The length is very important with adVarChar parameters. They have to match the length of the corresponding column. This is the only time when specifying the correct size is important. The length of other types of parameters is implied.

Following is the complete ConnectX method, with all the parameters. Again, this method has changes so radically that it is just easy to delete the old ConnectX method and replace it with this:

```
Public Sub ConnectX(ByVal NewValue As clsConnection)

    Set mcConnection = NewValue

'** Our class relies on an already open ADOConnection.
    Set mADOConnection = mcConnection.ADOConnection

'** Instantiate the "SELECT" Command object and set its properties

    Set mSelectCmd = New ADODB.Command
        With mSelectCmd
            .ActiveConnection = mADOConnection
            .CommandType = adCmdText
            .CommandText = msSelect

'** Create and define our Parameter object in mSelectCmd
'** and appeand it to the parameters collection
    Set mSelectPrmGender = .CreateParameter("pGender", adVarChar, _
            adParamInput, 1, "F")
        .Parameters.Append mSelectPrmGender
        End With

'** execute the command and reutrn to result set to the mrsPeople
'** recordset

    Set mrsPeople = mSelectCmd.Execute
        mvRows = mrsPeople.GetRows
        mlRows = UBound(mvRows, 2) + 1 'The 2nd dimension is the rows
        SetProperties (0)     ' needs a parameter.
                             'this is the equivalent of MoveFirst

'** Instantiate the "DELETE" Command object and set its properties

    Set mDeleteCmd = New ADODB.Command
    With mDeleteCmd
        .ActiveConnection = mADOConnection
        .CommandType = adCmdText
        .CommandText = msDelete

'** Create and define our Parameter object in mDeleteCmd
'** and appeand it to the parameters collection

    Set mDeletePrmPersonId = .CreateParameter("pPersonId", adDouble, _
            adParamInput)
        .Parameters.Append mDeletePrmPersonId
        End With

'** Instantiate the "Update" Command object and set its properties

    Set mUpdateCmd = New ADODB.Command
        With mUpdateCmd
            .ActiveConnection = mADOConnection
            .CommandType = adCmdText
            .CommandText = msUpdate

'**Create, define, append "last_name" Parameter object

        Set mUpdatePrmLastName = .CreateParameter("pLastName", adVarChar, _
            adParamInput, 25, "")
        .Parameters.Append mUpdatePrmLastName
```

```
'**Create, define, append "first_name" Parameter object

    Set mUpdatePrmFirstName = .CreateParameter("pFirstName", adVarChar, _
        adParamInput, 15, "")
    .Parameters.Append mUpdatePrmFirstName

'**Create, define, append "M_I" Parameter object

    Set mUpdatePrmMI = .CreateParameter("pMI", adVarChar, _
        adParamInput, 1, "")
    .Parameters.Append mUpdatePrmMI

'**Create, define, append "DOB" Parameter object

    Set mUpdatePrmDob = .CreateParameter("pDob", adDBTimeStamp, _
        adParamInput)
    .Parameters.Append mUpdatePrmDob

'**Create, define, append "Gender" Parameter object

    Set mUpdatePrmGender = .CreateParameter("pGender", adVarChar, _
        adParamInput, 1, "F")
    .Parameters.Append mUpdatePrmGender

'**Create, define, append "Eye_Color" Parameter object

    Set mUpdatePrmEyeColor = .CreateParameter("pEyeColor", adVarChar, _
        adParamInput, 10, "Brown")
    .Parameters.Append mUpdatePrmEyeColor

'**Create, define, append "Person_ID" Parameter object

    Set mUpdatePrmPersonId = .CreateParameter("pPersonId", adDouble, _
        adParamInput)
    .Parameters.Append mUpdatePrmPersonId
    End With

'** Instantiate the "INSERT" Command object and set its properties

    Set mInsertCmd = New ADODB.Command
    With mInsertCmd
      .ActiveConnection = mADOConnection
      .CommandType = adCmdText
      .CommandText = msInsert

'**Create, define, append "Person_ID" Parameter object

    Set mInsertPrmPersonId = .CreateParameter("pPersonId", adDouble, _
        adParamInput)
    .Parameters.Append mInsertPrmPersonId

'**Create, define, append "Last_Name" Parameter object

    Set mInsertPrmLastName = .CreateParameter("pLastName", adVarChar, _
        adParamInput, 25, "")
    .Parameters.Append mInsertPrmLastName

'**Create, define, append "First_Name" Parameter object
```

```
        Set mInsertPrmFirstName = .CreateParameter("pFirstName", adVarChar, _
            adParamInput, 15, "")
        .Parameters.Append mInsertPrmFirstName

'**Create, define, append "M_I" Parameter object

        Set mInsertPrmMI = .CreateParameter("pMI", adVarChar, adParamInput, _
            1, "")
        .Parameters.Append mInsertPrmMI

'**Create, define, append "DOB" Parameter object

        Set mInsertPrmDob = .CreateParameter("pDob", adDBTimeStamp, _
            adParamInput)
        .Parameters.Append mInsertPrmDob

'**Create, define, append "Gender" Parameter object

        Set mInsertPrmGender = .CreateParameter("pGender", adVarChar, _
            adParamInput, 1, "F")
        .Parameters.Append mInsertPrmGender

'**Create, define, append "Eye_Color" Parameter object

        Set mInsertPrmEyeColor = .CreateParameter("pEyeColor", adVarChar, _
            adParamInput, 10, "Brown")
        .Parameters.Append mInsertPrmEyeColor
    End With

'**Create the Command object for our last sequence, as before
    Set mFindLastCmd = New ADODB.Command
    With mFindLastCmd
        .ActiveConnection = mADOConnection
        .CommandType = adCmdText
        .CommandText = msFindLastKey
    End With
    Set mrsLastRec = New ADODB.Recordset
    Set mrsLastRec = mFindLastCmd.Execute
End Sub
```

The last section of the ConnectX method, by which we advance the sequence that generates the People table unique keys, remains unchanged.

You may have noted the lines:

```
        mvRows = mrsPeople.GetRows
        mlRows = UBound(mvRows, 2) + 1 'The 2nd dimension is the rows
```

after we execute the mSelectCmd Command object. All will become clear when we discuss the GetRows method later in this chapter.

We have declared all of these objects (and a few more) in the declaration section of the class.

The General Declaration Code

As usual, I use early binding. All of the `Parameter` and `Command` objects are declared as class variables in the declaration section of the class. For ease of reading, they are declared in the order in which they are used in their respective `Command` objects. The first parameter corresponds to the first question mark, the second to the second, and so on. Here I have indicated where the code has changed from last time.

```
Option Explicit
'    A private instance of clsConnection so that we can use its methods
Private mcConnection As clsConnection

'    A private copy of our connection object to be opened inside mcConnection
Private mADOConnection As ADODB.Connection

'* Recordsets
Private mrsPeople As ADODB.Recordset
Private mrsLastRec As ADODB.Recordset

'* Command Objects
Private mFindLastCmd As ADODB.Command
Private mSelectCmd As ADODB.Command
Private mUpdateCmd As ADODB.Command
Private mInsertCmd As ADODB.Command
Private mDeleteCmd As ADODB.Command

'* Parameters
'* Select
Private mSelectPrmGender As ADODB.Parameter

'* Insert - in order of the select statement
Private mInsertPrmPersonId As ADODB.Parameter
Private mInsertPrmLastName As ADODB.Parameter
Private mInsertPrmFirstName As ADODB.Parameter
Private mInsertPrmMI As ADODB.Parameter
Private mInsertPrmDob As ADODB.Parameter
Private mInsertPrmGender As ADODB.Parameter
Private mInsertPrmEyeColor As ADODB.Parameter

'* Update - in the order of the update statement
Private mUpdatePrmLastName As ADODB.Parameter
Private mUpdatePrmFirstName As ADODB.Parameter
Private mUpdatePrmMI As ADODB.Parameter
Private mUpdatePrmDob As ADODB.Parameter
Private mUpdatePrmGender As ADODB.Parameter
Private mUpdatePrmEyeColor As ADODB.Parameter
Private mUpdatePrmPersonId As ADODB.Parameter

'* Delete
Private mDeletePrmPersonId As ADODB.Parameter

'** The SQL statements
Private msSelect As String
Private msUpdate As String
Private msDelete As String
Private msInsert As String
Private msFindLastKey As String
Private mvResults As Variant
```

```
'** Class variables
Private mlPersonId As Double      'Get and Let
Private msLastName As String      'Get and Let
Private msFirstName As String     'Get and Let
Private msMI As String            'Get and Let
Private msEyeColor As String      'Get and Let
Private mdDob As Date             'Get and Let
Private msGender As String        'Get and Let

'** Make a place for LastRec Variable
Private mlLastPersonId As Double    'Save Last Value
```

```
'    Declare an array to store the rows from mrsLastRec
Private mvRows As Variant

'* the size of the recordset (how many rows)
Private mlRows As Long

'* the index of the current row
Private mlX As Long
```

Note that we no longer use the `Field` objects to access the column values so all mention of them has been removed from the code – make sure you do the same.

The very end of the declaration section contains the declarations of the `mvRows` variant array. We are going to load this array with the rows from the `mrsPeople Recordset` using the recordset's `GetRows` method.

`GetRows` returns all the rows in the `Recordset` into a two dimensional variant array that is made of columns (the first dimension) and rows. Our program will keep the number of rows in `mlRows`, and we'll use the `mlX` variable as an index for the rows.

Why on earth do we need to use these variables? Here is the surprising answer: It is rather hard, in fact impossible, to traverse the `Recordset` using the standard methods of `MoveFirst, MoveNext, MovePrevious,` and `MoveLast`. I say surprising because I was expecting a forward only cursor, which would at least allow us to use `MoveFirst, MoveNext` etc. If you try to execute a `MoveFirst` you'll get a mysterious error message:

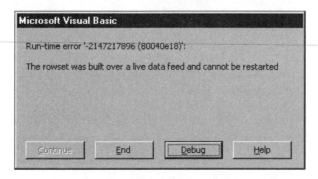

I actually leave a place in the code for you to test this in the `MoveFirst` method of the class. This is in the commented line:

```
mrsPeople.MoveFirst
```

If you activate the line and run the code, the message will appear.

What, then, can we do to traverse the Recordset without changing the calling routines? We use the GetRows method and traverse the mvRows variant array by changing the index. This calls for a deeper understanding of the GetRows method and of the array that it generates.

The GetRows Method

The general syntax of the Recordset.GetRows method is:

```
Variant = Recordset.GetRows([Rows],[Start],[Fields])
```

Rows is a long. It tells the method how many rows to retrieve. It defaults to adGetRowsRest, which will fetch all the rows from the current row to the end of the Recordset. When the expected Recordset is large, we may want to fetch the rows in smaller chunks. This is when we use the Rows argument, rather than let it default to all.

Start is a variant holding the bookmark for the starting row. This will be the first row fetched. It defaults to the current row. When we have just read the recordset for the first time, this current row is the first row.

Fields is a list of columns to be fetched. It defaults to all.

We use the GetRows method in the Refresh routine. Add this code to clsPeople:

```
Public Sub Refresh()
    mSelectPrmGender.Value = msGender
    Set mrsPeople = mSelectCmd.Execute
    If mrsPeople.BOF And mrsPeople.EOF Then
        SetDefaults
        mlRows = 0
    Else
        mvRows = mrsPeople.GetRows
        mlRows = UBound(mvRows, 2) + 1    'The variants second dimension is
                                          'the rows
    End If
End Sub
```

We assign our msGender class variable to the Value property of the mSelectGender Parameter object (setting the ? in our SELECT statement to F or M). We then execute the Command object and load the data into our mrsPeople Recordset. We extract the data into our array using the GetRows method (because we use all the defaults, we get all the rows and all the columns)

We then need to find out how many rows have been fetched so that we can use this number in the various 'Move' routines. Our variant is a two dimensional array. The first dimension is used for the columns, the second for the rows. Both columns and rows start with the index of 0 and go to the actual number of rows (columns) minus 1. Thus mvRows(0,0) will return the Person_Id of the first row, mvRows(1,0) yields the Last_Name of the first row, and mvRows(6,0) the Eye_Color of the first row. The order depends on the order of columns in the SELECT statement. In our case we have exactly 7 columns, numbered 0 to 6. But how many rows do we have? We have exactly Ubound(mvRows, 2) + 1 rows. This is because the Ubound function returns the last index, which is one less than the number of rows. How many items do we have in the set {0,1,2,3}? I say 4. What is it Ubound? In VB it is 3. Thus, to get a count we add 1 to the Ubound.

Once we got all the rows into mvRows we use it to traverse the Recordset.

The 'Move' Methods

A different way of coding the 'Move' methods will allow us to preserve the way the form uses the class. Again, the MoveFirst method includes the erroneous (and commented) "mrsPeople.MoveFirst" line which is left here so that you may test out the mysterious error message.

The general trick is to use the row index (mlX) to get to a given row. Advancing it by one is akin to MoveNext. Of course we have to be careful not to let mlX go beyond mlRows − 1. Setting it to 0 is the same as our old MoveFirst. Setting it to mlRows − 1 is the same as MoveLast. Diminishing it by one, but not below 0, is our new MovePrevious method. Here they are (delete the old ones and replace them with these):

```
Public Sub MoveFirst()
    'mrsPeople.MoveFirst
    mlX = 0
    SetProperties (mlX)
End Sub

Public Sub MoveLast()
    mlX = mlRows - 1
    SetProperties (mlX)
End Sub

Public Sub MoveNext()
    If mlX < mlRows - 1 Then
        mlX = mlX + 1
    Else
        mlX = mlRows - 1
    End If
    SetProperties (mlX)
End Sub

Public Sub MovePrevious()
    If mlX > 0 Then
        mlX = mlX - 1
    Else
        mlX = 0
```

```
      End If
      SetProperties (mlX)
End Sub
```

The SetProperties Routine

We also need a new way of coding the SetProperties routine. Note that it is called using the row number. Also note how the columns are numbered from 0 to 6. Delete the old routine and replace it with this one:

```
Private Sub SetProperties(lRow As Long)

   SetDefaults

   If Not IsNull(mvRows(0, lRow)) Then
      mlPersonId = mvRows(0, lRow)
   End If

   If Not IsNull(mvRows(1, lRow)) Then
      msLastName = mvRows(1, lRow)
   End If
   If Not IsNull(mvRows(2, lRow)) Then
      msFirstName = mvRows(2, lRow)
   End If

   If Not IsNull(mvRows(3, lRow)) Then
      msMI = mvRows(3, lRow)
   End If

   If Not IsNull(mvRows(4, lRow)) Then
      mdDob = mvRows(4, lRow)
   End If

   If Not IsNull(mvRows(5, lRow)) Then
      msGender = mvRows(5, lRow)
   End If

   If Not IsNull(mvRows(6, lRow)) Then
      msEyeColor = mvRows(6, lRow)
   End If

End Sub
```

We still have to handle 'Modify' methods. They use the Command object and are thus are rather different than the ones we have seen before.

The 'Modify' Methods

The AddNew, Delete, and Update methods now set the Command object parameters before the Command object is executed. Here they are (again delete the old ones and replace with these):

```
Public Sub AddNew()
   FindLastKey    'retrieve the next sequence number
```

```
    mlPersonId = mlLastPersonId     'sets the class property

' Insert all the values into the parameters

    mInsertPrmPersonId.Value = mlPersonId
    mInsertPrmLastName.Value = msLastName
    mInsertPrmFirstName.Value = msFirstName
    mInsertPrmMI.Value = msMI
    mInsertPrmEyeColor.Value = msEyeColor
    mInsertPrmDob.Value = mdDob
    mInsertPrmGender.Value = msGender
    mInsertCmd.Execute
Refresh
End Sub

Public Sub Update()

'Insert all the values into the Parameters

    mUpdatePrmLastName.Value = msLastName
    mUpdatePrmFirstName.Value = msFirstName
    mUpdatePrmMI.Value = msMI
    If mdDob = #1/1/1800# Then
        mUpdatePrmDob.Value = Null
    Else
        mUpdatePrmDob.Value = mdDob
    End If

    mUpdatePrmGender.Value = msGender
    mUpdatePrmEyeColor.Value = msEyeColor
    mUpdatePrmPersonId.Value = mlPersonId
    mUpdateCmd.Execute
Refresh
End Sub

Public Sub Delete()

    mDeletePrmPersonId.Value = mlPersonId
    mDeleteCmd.Execute
Refresh
End Sub
```

The following line from the `Update` sub is not a mistake!

```
    mUpdatePrmDob.Value = Null
```

The generally accepted wisdom is that in VB you may not assign a Null to a `Value` property. This is a truism, but it is not true! The ability to assign a value to the `Value` property (pun intended) depends on the object. Most objects may not allow for the assignment of Null to their `Value` property, but an ADO `Parameter` object is one of many exceptions. In fact the same applies to OO4O, where a field's value, as well as a parameter's value may be assigned Nulls. This is just another example of the fallacy of generalization.

A sigh of relief is now called for. We're done at last! Here is the first screen that the program produces:

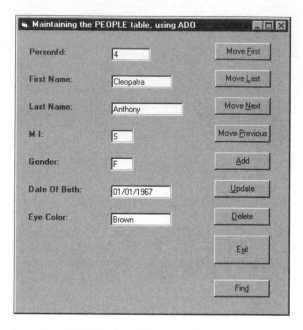

As before, we can change the gender value, click **Find** and the records for the men in the People table will be returned. The program looks the same as our OO4O equivalent and provides the same functionality – but what a difference beneath the hood!

Summary

To use parameters with ADO we had to make numerous changes to our basic application. The key issues are:

❑ When we execute a parameterized query form the `Command` object you end up with a read-only `Recordset`. We have to do all of our data modifications using DML.

❑ We cannot navigate through the records by calling the various 'Move' methods of the `Recordset`.

Using the `GetRows` method to traverse the `Recordset` is actually a better way of using ADO even when the database is SQL Server. Again, the idiosyncrasy of using Oracle forced our hand in the right direction, but the ADO program is really much more convoluted than perhaps it ought to be. The OO4O approach is much simpler.

Optimizing the ADO Connection and Data Classes

In Chapter 9 we built a simple VB program that allowed us to connect to and manipulate an Oracle database using ADO. It mirrored the functionality of its OO4O counterpart in Chapter 5 and had a very similar structure. When we moved on to modify this program to pass parameters, the differences between this program and its OO4O partner vastly outweighed the similarities.

We are now going to modify our ADO parameters program to improve its performance and to add transaction control to our ADO Connection class. We will:

❑ Add **transaction control** to out `ADOclsConnection` class. Our transaction-level object in ADO is the `Connection` object.

❑ Modify the `ADOclsPeoplePrm` class so that we `Let` and `Get` all of the class properties together by passing a variant array whose elements are the individual properties (rather than getting or letting each property by itself)

❑ Dispense with the `mrsLastRec` `Recordset` and, instead, retrieve the next sequence number from an Oracle database **trigger**.

If you have already worked through Chapter 7, where we did the same for OO4O, you will find that the alterations only really differ with regard to the transactions. In terms of the last two points, I repeat some information from Chapter 7 in order that those of you who have dived straight in to ADO will not have to continually refer back.

Again, when we create the version of our final application using ADO (Chapter 14) there will be five data classes, so whatever we do to our `clsPeople` class in this chapter should also be done to all the others in that chapter.

Transaction Methods of the Connection Object

Using transactions, we group potential changes to the database data together and they will succeed or fail as a group. If one change fails in some way then every one of the changes in the transaction will also fail. If all the changes succeed then they are all committed to the database in one go. This is known as **atomicity**, and is an essential property of the transaction.

> **Microsoft Transaction Server provides an excellent framework on which to host transaction-enabled components. We will discuss this in more detail in Chapter 17.**

The transaction-level object in ADO is the `Connection` object, and we will briefly consider each of the transaction-related methods:

Function	`Connection` object method
Start a transaction	BeginTrans
Accept	CommitTrans
Reject	RollBackTrans

The methods are identical to those supported by the `OraSession` object in OO4O, with the exception that we have `RollBackTrans` whereas OO4O has simply `RollBack`.

In the name of polymorphism I used the same method names in both approaches. Since we built the OO4O classes first, I used its properties and method names in ADO as well. This common naming and usage allows other modules to use both OO4O and ADO. They don't really care. They always use `cConnection.BeginTrans, cConnection.CommitTrans, and cConnection.RollBack.`

The BeginTrans Method

The general syntax is:

```
ADOConnection.BeginTrans
```

Once a transaction has been started, any changes to a Recordset attached to the `Connection` object are cached until the transaction is either completed or abandoned. At that stage, all of the changes will be either written to the database (if the transaction is committed) or discarded (if the transaction is aborted).

The CommitTrans Method

The general syntax is:

```
ADOConnection.CommitTrans
```

All changes made since the previous `BeginTrans` will be written to Oracle. Affects only the most recently-opened transaction.

The RollBackTrans Method

The general syntax is:

```
ADOConnection.RollBackTrans
```

All changes made since the previous `BeginTrans` will be cancelled. Applies only to the most recent transaction.

Adding Transactions to the ADO Connection Class

A single business transaction often involves multiple rows in multiple tables. These complex operations might fail midway, leaving us with bad data. In order to safeguard against such mishaps we use stored procedures and transaction control. Here we are going to enable safe transaction control. In the final application we will use stored procedures as well.

Many "users" may share `cConnection`. As with our OO4O project, we are going to make sure that our transactions do not interfere with one another, thereby, for example, committing an unfinished transaction or rolling back a good transaction. We will pass the calling object a token (`TransactorID`) when it starts a transaction. No other object is allowed to start a transaction until the first object returns the correct token. Then `cConnection` may start a new transaction at the request of the next calling object.

> This transaction control mechanism will be used in our final project.

Again, we are going to control our transactions in the Connection class. ADO built the mechanism into the ADO `Connection` object, which lies at the heart of our ADO version of `clsConnection`.

Before you continue make a **Chapter11** directory and make a true-copy of the material from **Chapter10** to it. Open the `ADOPeoplePrm` project and immediately save the various pieces as follows:

- ❑ `frmADOPeoplePrmTrans`
- ❑ `ADOclsPeoplePrmTrans.cls`
- ❑ `ADOclsConnectionTrans.cls`
- ❑ `ADOPeoplePrmTrans.vbp`
- ❑ `ModGeneralTrans.bas`

Open up `ADOclsConnectionTrans.cls` and make the following modifications. The first thing we need to do is declare our transaction token and a second variable that can be passed to identify whether or not a transaction is currently underway:

```
Private mbBeginTrans As Boolean   'have we begun a trans?
Private mlTransactorId As Long    'identity of object that begun the trans
                                  'only this object can Commit it
                                  'or Roll it Back.
```

The full code for the declarations section looks like this:

```
Option Explicit

' For connection purposes we need the database name e.g "MyDB"
' and the connect string e.g. "scott/tiger"

Private msDSN As String
Private msConnect As String
Private msUser As String
Private msPW As String
Private msRole As String    'for setting DB role (permissions)
Private msErrMsg As String 'This is where the class announces an ERROR!!
Private mADOConnection As ADODB.Connection
Private mbBeginTrans As Boolean 'are we in the middle of a transaction?
Private mlTransactorId As Long   'identity of object that begun the trans
                                 'Only he can Commit it or Roll it Back.
```

We initialize the random seed using the `Randomize` method in the `Class_Initialize` routine (ensuring that the token identifiers follow no set pattern):

```
Private Sub Class_Initialize()
    Randomize  'To protect the programmer from inadvertently unregistering
End Sub
```

Here are the three public functions that allow transaction control in the connection class:

```
Public Function BeginTrans() As Long

    If Not mbBeginTrans Then
        mlTransactorId = Int(1000000 * Rnd) + 1 'returns a random 1 to 1M
        mADOConnection.BeginTrans
        mbBeginTrans = True
        BeginTrans = mlTransactorId
    Else
        BeginTrans = 0
    End If
End Function

Public Function CommitTrans(lCallerId As Long) As Boolean

    CommitTrans = False
    If mbBeginTrans Then
        If lCallerId = mlTransactorId Then
            mADOConnection.CommitTrans
            mbBeginTrans = False
```

```
            CommitTrans = True
        End If
    End If
End Function

Public Function RollBack(lCallerId As Long) As Boolean

    RollBack = False
    If mbBeginTrans Then
        If lCallerId = mlTransactorId Then
            mADOConnection.RollbackTrans
            mbBeginTrans = False
            RollBack = True
        End If
    End If
End Function
```

Our `OpenDB` method now looks as follows. It is probably worth simply deleting the old method and replacing it with this:

```
Public Sub OpenDB(sDSN As String, sUser As String, sPW As String, _
        Optional sRole As String = "")

    Dim sConnect As String

'Now make the Session and Database objects

    msErrMsg = ""
    On Error GoTo OpenConnectionErr

'open the ADO connection

msConnect = "Data Source=" & sDSN & ";" & _
            "User ID=" & sUser & ";" & _
            "Password=" & sPW & ";"

    Set mADOConnection = New ADODB.Connection     'Let's instantiate the
                                                  'object!

'   Utilizing the ADO Connection object
'   Set the object paramaters and open the Connection.

    With mADOConnection
        .ConnectionString = msConnect
        .ConnectionTimeout = 10
        .CursorLocation = adUseNone
        .Open
    End With

' Check the Connection State to see if the Connection was opened
' successfully. Set the return value accordingly!

    If mADOConnection.State = 1 Then
        msErrMsg = ""
    Else
        msErrMsg = "Failed to open Database Connection!"
    End If
    Exit Sub
```

```
OpenConnectionErr:
    msErrMsg = "clsConnection.OpenConnection: Error #: " & _
        CStr(Err.Number) & vbCrLf & Err.Description
End Sub
```

We add a new read-only `InTransaction` property, which tells the caller if the class is now in transaction:

```
Public Property Get InTransaction() As Boolean

'should anybody want to know if we've begun a trans
    InTransaction = mbBeginTrans
End Property
```

The rest of the class is as before:

```
Public Property Get ADOConnection() As ADODB.Connection
    Set ADOConnection = mADOConnection
End Property

Private Sub Class_Terminate()
    Set mADOConnection = Nothing
End Sub
```

Let's now move on to the refinements we need to make to our `ADOclsPeoplePrmTrans` data class.

Enhancing the ADO Data Class

First we will improve the programs' performance by eliminating unnecessary communications between the form and the data class.

Passing Class Properties in an Array

The programs that we have built in this book run on a single machine. If we host VB components on a separate server from the presentation layer then it is important that we minimize network traffic as far as possible, as frequent, and often unnecessary, trips across the network to retrieve data will slow your applications considerably. To this end we are going to improve our programs' potential performance by passing all of the class properties together in a variant array whose elements are the individual properties.

The method we employ here is exactly that used for the OO4O version (Chapter 7). We don't need to do any deep changes, just add a few lines of code to enhance the behavior of the class. This is possible because our methodology is well thought out and field-tested. A well thought out process is one in which you may literally add enhancements rather than change existing code to achieve them. One hour of planning saves you ten hours, maybe even a hundred, of rebuilding.

We declare our variant array in the declaration section of the data class:

```
'** for less round trips keep all the properties in a variant array
Private mvAll As Variant 'Get and Let
```

We `ReDim` this variant to an array of seven elements in the `Class_Initialize` routine:

```
Private Sub Class_Initialize()
ReDim mvAll(0 To 6) 'we have 7 properties rolled into the array
SetDefaults
BuildSQL
End Sub
```

We now add two new properties – Get and Let – to the class, allowing us to read or write all of the properties in one go:

```
Public Property Get All() As Variant
    mvAll(0) = mlPersonId
    mvAll(1) = msLastName
    mvAll(2) = msFirstName
    mvAll(3) = msMI
    mvAll(4) = mdDob
    mvAll(5) = msGender
    mvAll(6) = msEyeColor
    All = mvAll
End Property

Public Property Let All(ByVal vNewValue As Variant)
    mvAll = vNewValue
    mlPersonId = mvAll(0)
    msLastName = mvAll(1)
    msFirstName = mvAll(2)
    msMI = mvAll(3)
    mdDob = mvAll(4)
    msGender = mvAll(5)
    msEyeColor = mvAll(6)
End Property
```

That's it! The data class is ready for faster communication. All these changes have to be reflected in the form. Again, we also have to add a new variable at the declaration section of the form.

```
Private vAll As Variant
```

This variable is going to be used in the Display and Store subs as follows (replace the old subs with these):

```
Private Sub Display()
    vAll = cPeople.All    'get all the properties in one trip
    txtPersonId = Format$(vAll(0), "##########0")
    txtLastName = vAll(1)
    txtFirstName = vAll(2)
    txtMI = vAll(3)
    txtDOB = FormatDate(vAll(4), "mm/dd/yyyy")
    txtGender = vAll(5)
    txtEyeColor = vAll(6)
End Sub
Private Sub Store()
    vAll(1) = txtLastName
    vAll(2) = txtFirstName
    vAll(3) = txtMI
    vAll(4) = ConvertDate(txtDOB.Text)
    vAll(5) = txtGender
    vAll(6) = txtEyeColor
    cPeople.All = vAll
End Sub
```

And once again we have to make a small change to `modGeneral.bas` in order to pass vAll(4) `ByVal`, rather than `ByRef` – which is the default.

> **VB can only handle a simple variable pointer whereas vAll (4) is a variable within a variable and had to be passed by value.**

Make the following small change:

```
Public Function FormatDate(ByVal dDate As Date, sFormat As String) As String
```

Implementing a Trigger

If you have worked through Chapter 7, then you will already have your trigger in place. If you have not, I would refer you to the section called "Implementing a Trigger" in this chapter for details of how to build a trigger on our `People` table using Oracle navigator.

> *Alternatively you can refer forward to the full discussion of triggers in Chapter 13.*

Our trigger is invoked whenever we try to `INSERT` a new row into the `People` table and will automatically supply us with the next sequence number, if we supply an input value of zero. This allows us to dispense with the inefficiency associated with creating a `Recordset` object and a `Command` object just for the purpose of retrieving this number.

Thus we can remove from our data class all that deals with the last key. We start at the top and work our way down. In the declaration section remove:

```
Private mrsLastRec As ADODB.Recordset

Private mFindLastCmd As ADODB.Command

Private msFindLastKey As String

'** Make a place for LastRec Variable
Private mlLastPersonId As Double    'Save Last Value
```

In the `ConnectX` method remove the last 8 lines:

```
Set mFindLastCmd = New ADODB.Command
    With mFindLastCmd
        .ActiveConnection = mADOConnection
        .CommandType = adCmdText
        .CommandText = msFindLastKey
    End With
    Set mrsLastRec = New ADODB.Recordset
    Set mrsLastRec = mFindLastCmd.Execute
```

In the `BuildSQL` routine, remove the last 2 lines:

```
'** Create the FindLastKey SQL
   msFindLastKey = "Select PERSON_ID_SEQ.NEXTVAL from dual"
```

Now remove the whole sub below:

```
Private Sub FindLastKey()
   Dim mvResults As Variant
   Set mrsLastRec = mFindLastCmd.Execute
   mvResults = mrsLastRec.GetRows
   mlLastPersonId = mvResults(0, 0)
End Sub
```

Last but not least, change the `AddNew` method to look like this:

```
Public Sub AddNew()
' Insert all the values into the parameters
   mlPersonId = 0
   mInsertPrmPersonId.Value = mlPersonId
   mInsertPrmLastName.Value = msLastName
   mInsertPrmFirstName.Value = msFirstName
   mInsertPrmMI.Value = msMI
   mInsertPrmEyeColor.Value = msEyeColor
   mInsertPrmDob.Value = mdDob
   mInsertPrmGender.Value = msGender
   mInsertCmd.Execute
Refresh
End Sub
```

Save all your work and test it thoroughly.

Summary

We now have an application that:

❑   Can handle transactions safely

❑   Has speedier communication between the data class and other objects, such as forms – all of the class properties can be passed in one go rather than making several trips across the network.

❑   Has improved efficiency, by letting the database handle what it does best – in this case maintaining the integrity of our primary key column (`Person_ID`) by way of a trigger.

This series of chapters have hopefully given you a firm practical grasp of how to marry VB and Oracle using OO4O. The next chapter will cement this knowledge with a thorough ADO reference (skewed towards what we can do with ADO and Oracle, of course).

From there you will move on to PL/SQL, stored procedures and triggers. With this knowledge, you will be in a position to appreciate Chapter 14, where most of these concepts are brought together in our final HR application.

12

An ADO Reference

ADO is almost the object king; the one-for-all "simple" yet full-featured data access tool. It definitely comes close! Who knows, maybe when ADO 3.0 comes along (why is it that the real breakthrough in Microsoft software is version 3?) it really will. This book discusses version 2.1; version 2.5 is imminent, but is not covered in detail here.

The trouble is that Microsoft and Oracle are not really cooperating, and ADO loses much of its punch when connected to Oracle. ADO is nonetheless a viable conduit to Oracle, and we are going to cover it to the extent that Oracle allows. Even that little is quite a lot. For a complete ADO reference, I suggest trying David Sussman's excellent, 600-page opus magnum – *ADO 2.1 Programmer's Reference* – also from the house of WROX (pun intended).

To those of you who already use some of ADO's more esoteric features – Shapes and ADOX – it will be nice to know that we can't use them with Oracle.

So why do we use ADO with Oracle? We may have a smattering of database engines in our enterprise and we want to use but one tool, or we may like some of ADO's features enough to warrant the extra work involved. Three of these features are tempting reasons indeed:

- ❏ The `GetString` method - `GetString` returns a recordset as a string. This particular method of the `Recordset` object is useful to create HTML tables in ASP code.

- ❏ The `GetRows` method - This method of the Recordset allows the retrieval of multiple records into an array.

- ❏ The `Save` method - Allows the saving of a recordset to a file. This method is useful in the way that you can store the recordset as an XML data file or as a HTML file method.

I know of four different providers for Oracle and ADO and we have tested three of them with ADO 2.1. They are:

❑ **The Microsoft OLE DB Provider for Oracle**. This is by and large a good conduit but not as complete as the Microsoft ODBC provider. We could not get PL/SQL tables to work through it.

❑ **The Microsoft ODBC Provider for Oracle**. This is the most complete provider that I've tested. It is slower than the Microsoft OLE DB provider is, but more stable and more complete.

❑ **The Oracle OLE DB Provider**. Because I found it unstable, I did not even test it to the tilt. Too many mishaps.

The fourth provider is:

❑ **The Merant (INTERSOLV) OLE DB Provider for Oracle**. It is complete – more complete than the ODBC, faster and completely stable. One serious drawback – it is very expensive ($15,000 per server).

Oracle is now conducting Beta tests on its new OLE DB provider.

Last but not least there is ADO 2.5. Merant is also coming with a 2.5 version of its OLE DB driver.

The ADO Object Model

The ADO object model is simple if seen from a lunar satellite and gets more and more complex the closer you get to earth. Here is the simple model:

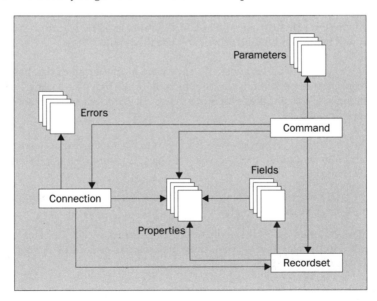

ADO is made of three independent main objects: Connection, Command, and Recordset. Each may be created by itself (although if you create a Command or Recordset object by themselves, they implicitly open their own Connection), and all three cooperate beautifully. The main objects also own other objects, which are kept in **collections**. They are:

❑   Parameters – a collection of individual Parameter objects, owned by the Command object, and used to pass arguments to stored procedures and SQL statements.

❑   Fields – a collection of individual Field objects, owned by the Recordset. Each Field will map to one column in a row in the result set.

❑   Errors – a collection made of Error after Error, by our own sweat and blood, owned by the Connection object.

❑   Properties, which every object seems to have. There are Field properties, Connection properties, Recordset properties, Command properties, and even Properties of properties, to the nth generation.

You have already seen plenty of examples of how ADO is used with Oracle, from the simple example of Chapter 9, through the more complex example of Chapter 10, and finally the examples you'll see in the code of Chapter 14. In here, we are going to recap all of this in tabular form and with short code snippets. We are also going to supplement the information with features that we have not used in the live examples.

The Connection Object

In order for anything to really work there must be an open connection to a real database. Even if we have only defined a Recordset object, it has an ActiveConnection property, which is actually a Connection object that was created implicitly. The same applies to a Command object. I don't like things implicitly. I therefore see to it that I open a Connection willfully. Here is how this is done with Oracle.

Using an OLE DB Provider

The best OLE DB provider for Oracle is the one provided by Microsoft (makes sense, doesn't it?). Here is how our user scott is going to connect. He must first declare the object:

```
Private mADOConnection As ADODB.Connection
Private sConnect As String
sConnect = "Provider=MSDAORA.1;Password=tiger;User ID=scott; " & _
"Data Source=;Persist Security Info=True"
Set mADOConnection = New ADODB.Connection       'Let's instantiate the object!
With mADOConnection
        .ConnectionString = sConnect
        .ConnectionTimeout = 10
        .CursorLocation = adUseNone
        .Open
End With
```

ConnectionString, ConnectionTimeOut, and CursorLocation are
Connection properties; Open is a Connection method.

Here is how scott connects using a system DSN (ODBC):

```
Private sDSN As String
Private sUser As String
Private sPW As String
Private mADOConnection As ADODB.Connection
Private sConnect As String
sDSN = "msORA"
sUser = "scott"
sPW = "tiger"
sConnect = "Data Source=" & sDSN & ";" & _
"User ID=" & sUser & ";" & _
"Password=" & sPW & ";"
Set mADOConnection = New ADODB.Connection    'Let's instantiate the object!
With mADOConnection
        .ConnectionString = sConnect
        .ConnectionTimeout = 10
        .CursorLocation = adUseNone
        .Open
End With
```

We can also use a DSNless ODBC connection. The only difference, again, is in the
structure of the ConnectionString:

```
SConnect = "SERVER=" & sServer & "DRIVER={Microsoft ODBC for Oracle}" & _
";UID=" & sUser & ";PWD=" & sPW & ";"
```

In our case, because we run on an 'empty' (or default) server name, skip the
"SERVER=" & sServer piece of the ConnectionString. Instead use:

```
"DRIVER={Microsoft ODBC for Oracle};UID=" & sUser & ";PWD=" & sPW & ";"
```

> **ADO uses connection pooling. This means that when you close a
> connection, ADO actually keeps it open. To really close a connection you
> have to set it to Nothing. Because of security considerations, ADO can
> only reuse such a 'closed' connection if a user request a connection that
> uses exactly the same ConnectionString (same user and password). If
> no such request is made for say 10 minutes (the default), the connection
> will be set to Nothing. This is done because opening a connection is
> very time consuming (30 seconds is not entirely uncommon).**

Unlike OO4O, which is an eventless InProcess DLL, ADO generates events and may
therefore be used asynchronously. Objects that can generate events may be used
asynchronously. We don't have to wait for them before we perform other operations.
We know they are done when the proper event is trapped, and we can react to it when
it is.

Even though I have not used ADO's asynchronicity in this book (this is a subject worthy of another book) it may be used to greatly speed up applications by way of distributing them on the network (even and especially the web). Let's say that we need information that resides on two databases in two countries. We send two requests and wait for them to return. In a synchronous world we would have to twiddle our proverbial thumbs while waiting until all the info is in, wasting computing resources in the process. With an asynchronous system we may start to process whatever information comes first, while waiting for the other pieces. The user will get his response faster!

Connection Events

Event	Description
`BeginTransComplete`	The database has actually begun the transaction that you asked for. Usage may be to trigger other operations which are dependant upon the transaction that has been started.
`CommitTransComplete`	The transaction has been committed. This event can be used to create a final entry in an transaction logging / audit trail system to indicate the end of transaction
`ConnectComplete`	Self explanatory.
`Disconnect` (not `DisconnectComplete!`)	You asked to be disconnected? You got it!
`ExecuteComplete`	The Command Execute method has completed.
`RollbackTransComplete`	You have successfully rolled back your erroneous transaction.
`WillConnect`	Why do I need to bother with an event that fires before an attempt to connect? Only if I want to time the connection.
`WillExecute`	Another smart will do event - triggered before the execution of a query on this connection. Can be used to time the execution.

I haven't used any of these events in the samples in this book. This is because we did everything in parallel with OO4O. So here is how one of them may be used:

Declare:

```
Private WithEvents mADOConnection as ADODB.Connection
Set mADOConnection = New ADODB.Connection
```

Connect as you have connected before.

Add an event trapper for the `CommitTransComplete` event:

```
Private Sub mADOConnection_CommitTransComplete(ByVal pError As ADODB.Error,
adStatus As ADODB.EventStatusEnum, ByVal pConnection As ADODB.Connection)
    'If there's an  error let's see it!
    If adStatus = adStatusOK Then
        MsgBox "Hurray!!"
    Else
        MsgBox "Not Again! " & pError.Description
    End If
End Sub
```

Note that we have used the `Error` object.

Now some less eventful `Connection` properties and methods.

Connection Properties

Property	Description
Attributes	The way the server handles transactions. Defines whether a `CommitTrans` or `Rollback` starts a new transaction.
CommandTimeOut	The length of time before the command is timed out in seconds (default is 30 seconds).
ConnectionString	A dangerous property that returns the connection string including `user name` and `Password`. Avoid in the name of security.
ConnectionTimeOut	How long do we wait before we stop trying to connect? In seconds (default is 15 seconds).
CursorLocation	This property uses `adUseClient` to specify client-based cursors and `adUseServer` for cursors on the server or the provider. For Oracle, you should use `adUseClient`. `adUseNone=1`, `adUseClient=3`, `adUseServer=2`. See the `SAVE recordset` example below.
DefaultDatabase	Shows the default database when the provider can use more than one database per connection.
IsolationLevel	Deals with the way we handle nested transactions. Oracle allows but one transaction at a time so it is always 4096 = `adXactCursorStability`.

Property	Description
Mode	How do this and other processes use this connection? AdModeUnknown=0 is default, adModeRead = 1 is read only, adModeWrite = 2, adModeReadWrite = 3, adModeShareDenyRead=4 (deny other users the privilege of reading), adModeShareDenyWrite=8, adModeShareDenyNone=16 (others cannot open a connection at all).
Provider	The OLE DB driver used.
State	Describes whether the connection is open or closed: adStateClosed=0, adStateOpen=1
Version	Now 2.1, soon to be 2.5

Connection Methods

Method	Description
BeginTrans	Sends a BeginTrans command to the server.
Cancel	Cancels the execution of an asynchronous Execute or Open command before it is done. See more in the Command object section.
Close	Closes the connection. The connection may be reopened later. To get rid of a connection set it to Nothing.
CommitTrans	Commit the transaction
Execute	Execute an SQL statement (query or command). See Command Object.
Open	Opens a connection. See example above.
OpenSchema	The method is used to get a Recordset describing the database - its tables, columns, primary keys, foreign keys, indexes (indices) etc. There are close to 40 options to be used. The approach is too complex for my taste. I prefer to use the Oracle USER_OBJECTS tables. See Appendix D.
RollBackTrans	Roll back - returns the database to as it was before the transaction started. See Chapters 11 and 14 where we use it in an application.

The RecordSet Object

In Chapter 9 we used a simple Recordset to do our data manipulation. We could only use a simple SELECT statement with columns of one table. Otherwise we could not update the recordset. Ironically the most comprehensive recordset had to be built on the simplest form of a SELECT statement – we could not even use a parameter in the WHERE clause. This is a serious limitation that we had to overcome by using the Command object. For now, let us summarize the Recordset object.

The recordset is created in three ways. Firstly – with an existing ADO Connection object (using Connection.Execute), secondly with a connection string that creates the necessary Connection object implicitly, and finally by the Execute method of a Command object.

We assume that we open the People table here and that:

```
MsSelect = "SELECT Person_ID, Last_Name, First_Name, M_I , DOB," & _
" Gender, Eye_Color FROM People"

Private mrsPeople As ADODB.Recordset
Set mrsPeople = New ADODB.Recordset
mrsPeople.Open msSelect, mADOConnection, adOpenDynamic, adLockOptimistic
```

The general form is:

```
Recordset.Open Source, ActiveConnection, CursorType, LockType, Options
```

Because we have not discussed the Options parameter before, let us start with it:

Option	Description
adCmdText	This is the default option. The Source string contains a SQL command, such as a SELECT statement.
adCmdTable	We use a table name. ADO creates the SELECT * FROM table statement for you. This is less attractive than naming the columns, so it is better to use adCmdText.
adCmdStoredProc	The Source string contains the name of a stored procedure. Not applicable to Oracle (promised in 2.5). See Command object for further discussion.
adCmdUnknown	The type of command in the Source string is not known - ADO will parse the source string and decide what it is. Not recommended, as it is inefficient.
adCmdFile	The Source is a detached recordset saved in a file.

Option	Description
adExecuteAsync	The Source string is created asynchronously.
AdFetchAsync	ADO should read the number of records in Cache-Size first and fill the rest asynchronously. Can only be used if the recordset is created with events. Use the FetchComplete event to know when the fetch is done.

The Connection parameter is either a pointer to an ADO Connection object or a ConnectString.

The CursorType is one of:

Cursor-type	Description
adOpenForwardOnly	This is the default. Forward-only cursor. There is no MovePrevious.
adOpenDynamic	Dynamic cursor. Allows read and write.
adOpenKeySet	Keyset-driven cursor. Cannot be used with Oracle.
adOpenStatic	Static cursor. Read-only.

The LockType parameter of the Open method deals we the way we lock records when we update. It can be one of the following:

Lock-type	Description
adLockOptimistic	Optimistic concurrency using row values. Only lock before the update.
AdLockBatchOptimistic	Defers any updates until you use the **UpdateBatch** method. See the **SAVE** recordset example below.
adLockPessimistic	Pessimistic concurrency. Lock when you read. Assumes that you read to do an update.
adLockReadOnly	The default. Does not allow updates (read-only cursor). In fact this means no lock at all.

We still need to see how to connect with an implicit connection:

```
mrsPeople.Open msSelect, msConnect, adOpenDynamic, adLockOptimistic
```

msConnect will take one of the forms of the ADO Connection ConnectString:

```
mSConnect = "SERVER=" & sServer & "DRIVER={Microsoft ODBC for Oracle}" & _
";UID=" & sUser & ";PWD=" & sPW & ";"
```

In our case, because we run on an 'empty' (or default) server name, skip the
`"SERVER="` & `sServer` piece of the `ConnectString`. Instead use:

```
"DRIVER={Microsoft ODBC for Oracle};UID=" & sUser & ";PWD=" & sPW & ";"
```

This is not the way I open a recordset. I always create a connection first. If you connect implicitly, you will create a connection even if one existed before. Instead of using the same connection for two recordsets you'll have a separate connection for each. This is a waste. Creating a connection may take a very long time and we may run out of connections. Some licenses have a limited number of connections. For instance, your Personal Oracle is limited to 15.

Finally it may be created as a returned result from the `Execute` method of a `Command` object:

```
Rs = cmdCMD.Execute
```

BTW, I used the ODBC driver even though it is somewhat slower because it is the most fully featured option for working with Oracle.

Recordset Properties

A complete discussion of the ADO `Recordset` properties is in the David Sussman book, where every property (and the list is a mile long), no matter how esoteric is described in full.

Property	Description
AbsolutePage	Specifies in which page the current record resides. adPosUnknown=-1, adPosBOF=-2, adPosEOF=-3.
AbsolutePosition	Specifies the ordinal position of a Recordset's current cursor position. adPosUnknown=-1, adPosBOF=-2, adPosEOF=-3.
ActiveCommand	The Command object that created the Recordset. Null if not created from a Command object.
ActiveConnection	Another dangerous property. The Connection object the specified Recordset belongs to. The connection string is returned as the default property of the Connection, complete with Name and PW.
BOF	True if in the BOF position, for example before the first record in the Recordset. See the MoveFirst, MovePrevious methods below.
CacheSize	How many rows are kept in memory. You cannot set this with Oracle.
CursorLocation	Sets/returns the location of the cursor engine. adUseClient=1, adUseServer=2.

Property	Description
CursorType	Indicates the type of cursor used. AdOpenForwardOnly=0, adOpenUnspecified=-1, adOpenStatic=3 (read only), adOpenDynamic=2 (read and write). Oracle does not support keyset cursors with ADO.
DataMember	The data member in the bound control, if any.
DataSource	The bound control, if any.
EditMode	The editing status of the current record. AdEditNonc=0, adEditInProgress=1, adEditAdd=2, adEditDelete=4
EOF	True if in the EOF position, for example after the last record in the Recordset. See the MoveLast, MoveNext methods below.
Fields	The Fields collection, each with name, value, length, precision, scale, etc.
LockType	The types of locks placed on records during editing: adLockOptimistic=3 (lock just before an update). adLockBatchOptimistic = 4. This is the default of a disconnected set, and is used when we want to minimize the locking effects of an UpdateBatch. See the SAVE recordset example below. adLockPessimistic=2 (lock immediately assuming you are going to update sometime in the future). adLockReadOnly=1, adLockUnspecified=-1 (very helpful indeed!).
MarshalOptions	adMarshalAll=0, adMarshalModifiedOnly=1. What to send back to the server.
MaxRecords	How many records to return as the result of a query, if=0 (default) then all are returned.
PageCount	How many pages in the recordset. 1 + RecordCount/PageSize. Not supported by Oracle. Therefore = -1.
PageSize	How many records per page. Not supported by Oracle and therefore = -1.

Table Continued on Following Page

Property	Description
RecordCount	Not supported by Oracle. Returns –1 even after MoveLast in ODBC or MSDAORA. Use a SELECT (*) instead.

Properties	74 in all, properties extended by the provider. To see a list of names and values run this little loop.
	
	`For Each Property in Recordset.Properties`
	
	`    Print "Name " & Property.Name & " Value " &`
	`Property.Value`
	
	`Next`

Sort	If the Recordset SQL source (see below) had an Order By clause, the sort string will be returned by this property.
Source	The SQL SELECT statement that defined the recordset.
State	It indicates if the recordset is open, closed, or if it is executing an asynchronous query: adStateClosed=0, adStateOpen=1, adStateConnecting=2, adStateExecuting=4, adStateFetching=8.
Status	The status of the current record in the last bulk update operation. adRecOK = 0, others are less welcome!

A word (or two) about locking. When a record is locked only its current reader can use it. This is much like a book in the library. One reader borrows it and the others have to wait until it is returned. Why do we do such foolish things. Most of the time we don't. If all a user wants is to read the record, we allow other users to view it as well. It is only when a user intends to update it, that we lock the others from using it. This is done to gurantee a smooth updating without contentions. We may be pessimistic and say that every time a user reads a record it is for the purpose of updating it. That means that we lock the record immediately as it is read. This is a pessimistic lock.

Optimists, think that the world is already perfect, and that the record will never need to be changed. They will never lock a record. Realists who have optimistic tendencies will lock it when the user tries to update it. This is an optimistic lock. The system does a SELECT FOR UPDATE (read with lock) just before the update. Because the update is already in the pipeline, the record remains locked for a minimal period of time.

Recordset Methods

Because of ADO's asynchronicity, some methods have to be handled with care. In our sample programs, we run everything synchronously and cannot do a method before that program line becomes the current line (lines are done in order, one after the other until finished). That means that we don't have any synchronicity problems, and they are ignored in this discussion.

Most of the methods described in here have a counterpart in OO4O. Three deserve special attention. They are marked with * in the table below and will be expanded upon.

Method	Description
AddNew	Add a new record to the cached recordset. It is followed by inserting values into the fields and the Update Method. Example:

	``
	mrsPeople.AddNew
	
	    ' Insert all the values into the fields
	
	        mfldPersonId.Value = mlPersonId
	
	        mfldLastName.Value = msLastName
	
	        mfldFirstName.Value = msFirstName
	
	        mfldMI.Value = msMI
	
	        mfldDob.Value = mdDob
	
	        mfldGender.Value = msGender
	
	        mfldEyeColor.Value = msEyeColor
	
	    mrsPeople.Update
	``

Close	Close the recordset. If asynchronous, Close will abort any transaction, fetch, add or update.
Delete	Deletes the current record. Example: ``` mrsPeople.Delete ``` May also be used with a parameter. MrsPeople.Delete (9) will delete nine consecutive records starting with the current. Please use only in the first form.
GetRows(*)	Gets the rows of the recordset into a variant array.
GetString(*)	Gets each row of the recordset into a string.
The 'Move' methods	When moving to another row in the middle of an AddNew or Update, the Update will be done implicitly.
Move	The equivalent of OO4O MoveRel. Moves n records from the current record. n may be negative (backwards) or positive. If moving beyond the 1st or last row BOF or EOF will be set to True and the recordset will be positioned after (before) the Last (First) record. For example, after MoveFirst we did: ``` mrspeople.Move 10 ?mrsPeople.Fields(1) 'print the last_name Karabelle ```

Table Continued on Following Page

Method	Description

MoveFirst	Move to the first row (make it current). Example:
	
	`mrspeople.MoveFirst`
	
	`?mrsPeople.Fields(1)`
	
	   `Steinzalts`

MoveLast	Move to the last row. Example:
	
	`mrspeople.MoveLast`
	
	`?mrsPeople.Fields(1)`
	
	   `McManus`

MoveNext	Move to the next row. If already on the last Row `EOF` will occur. If already `EOF` an error will occur but `EOF` will remain true.
	
	`mrsPeople.MoveFirst`
	
	`mrsPeople.MoveLast`
	
	`?mrsPeople.EOF`
	
	`False`
	
	`mrsPeople.MoveNext`
	
	`?mrsPeople.EOF`
	
	`True`
	
	`mrsPeople.MoveNext`
	
	`'runtime error 3021 ensued`
	
	`?mrsPeople.EOF`
	
	   `True`

MovePrevious	Move to the previous row. If already on first `BOF` will be set to `True`. If already `BOF` an error will be raised but `BOF` will still be `True`.
Open	Open the Recordset. Already discussed at length earlier.

Requery	Refresh in OO4O parlance. Run the SQL on the server once more. Sets the current record to the first one.
	
	`mrsPeople.Requery`
	
	`?mrsPeople.Fields(1)`
	
	   `Steinzalts`

Save(*)	Save the recordset to a file.

Method	Description

Supports	Check if the Recordset can do various actions. Are these actions supported? Example, check if we can use bookmarks (With Oracle we can't – which lost us the `Find` method).
	
	`?mrsPeople.Supports(adBookmark)`
	
	`False 'not bookmarkable`
	
	`?mrsPeople.Supports(adResync)`
	
	`False 'not resyncable`
	
	`?mrsPeople.Supports(adUpdate)`
	
	`    True 'updateable`

Update	Used to cement changes made to the values of the fields in the current row, or after an add.
	
	`mfldLastName.Value = msLastName`
	
	`    mfldFirstName.Value = msFirstName`
	
	`    mfldMI.Value = msMI`
	
	`    mfldGender.Value = msGender`
	
	`    mfldEyeColor.Value = msEyeColor`
	
	`    mrsPeople.Update`

UpdateBatch(*)	Sends the complete Recordset to be updated in the server. Useful after working in detached mode. See below.

The starred methods of the table above are very special indeed. They deserve a longer discussion.

GetRows

`GetRows` returns all the rows into a two dimensional variant array. The syntax of the `GetRows` method is:

```
Variant = Recordset.GetRows([Rows],[Start],[Fields])
```

`Rows` is a `long`. It tells the method how many rows to retrieve. It defaults to `adGetRowsRest`, which will fetch all the rows from the current row to the end of the Recordset.

`Start` is a `variant` holding the bookmark for the starting row. This will be the first row fetched. It defaults to the current row. Because bookmarks are not supported for Oracle, we'll always start with the current row.

`Fields` is a `variant` listing the columns to be fetched. It defaults to all.

The first dimension of the array is used for the columns, the second for the rows. Both columns and rows start with the index of 0 and go to the actual number of rows (columns) minus 1. If we use our favorite Chapter 10 mrsPeople again and get the rows into mvRows, then mvRows(0,0) will return the Person_ID of the first row, mvRows(1,0) yields the Last_Name of the first row, and mvRows(6,0) the Eye_Color of the first row. The order depends on the order of columns in the SELECT statement. In our case we have exactly 7 columns, numbered 0 to 6. But how many rows do we have? We have exactly Ubound(mvRows, 2) + 1 rows. This is because the Ubound function (due to zero-based indexing) returns the last index, which is one less than the number of rows.

Chapter 10 and Chapter 14 use the GetRows method and the resulting variant Array extensively.

GetString

GetString returns the complete recordset as set of user-defined strings, one per row in the Recordset. The syntax of the GetString method is:

```
String = Recordset.GetString([StringFormat], [NumRows], [ColumnDelimiter],
[NullExpr])
```

The method has five parameters:

❑ StringFormat As StringFormatEnum = adClipString. The format in which the recordset should be returned. This is the default and also the only option. Can be skipped (a comma put in its place).

❑ NumRows As Long. Number of rows to be returned - defaults to –1, which is all, skip by placing a comma.

❑ ColumnDelimiter As String. The delimiter to use between columns - defaults to a tab, I usually enter a space " ".

❑ RowDelimiter As String. The delimiter to use between rows - I use vbCrLf (carriage-return Line-feed).

❑ NullExpr As String. Expression to replace a NULL value with. Defaults to a space.

Below is a debug print of our mrsPeople:

```
?mrsPeople.GetString(,,,vbCrLf)
1   Steinzalts Adin    R   1/1/44 M   Green
2   Perlman Ytzhak V   1/1/45 M   Brown
3   Abrams William J   1/1/76 M   Brown
4   Anthony Cleopatra  S       F   Brown
5   Caesar Julia  M    1/1/55 F   Blue
6   Cornwell   Joy     1/1/45 M   Blue
7   Cromwell   Olivierre  B   7/13/30 F   Hazel
8   Strange Bizarre Q   3/15/77 M   Yellow
9   Blenheim   Otto    R   4/13/48 M   Dark
```

10 Freud Ziggy J 5/13/66 F Light
11 Karabelle Larry M 5/15/51 M Brown
12 Stroh Ale B 5/19/77 F Gold
13 Feather Heather P 1/1/69 F Magenta
14 Winter Storm C 4/13/90 M Mist
15 Summer Haze H 1/1/87 F Ochre
16 Janice Jansen J 1/1/91 F Brown
17 Menken Manus M 7/4/76 m Red
18 Emmanuel Emmanuelle E 6/6/66 F Green
19 Emmanuel Emmanuel E 6/6/66 M Green
20 McManus Manny M 1/1/87 F Blue
21 McManus Erwin K 1/1/87 M Blue

Save

One of ADO's most alluring features is the ability to save a recordset to a local or network disk (even a diskette, if the set is small enough), disconnecting and working on it in its disconnected state, and at a later time reconnecting it and actually updating the database. This is very attractive if a salesman is the only one handling his customers, and can take his recordset – which nobody else would have updated – on the road with him. He then comes back to the office and reconnects and saves on the server. One of my clients (using Access though) has all their salemen work like that. This is also very attractive for web applications. The user can actually disconnect (connections being the dearest resources), do his updates off line and then reconnect and update. Here is how this is done:

```
Recordset.Save (Filename, [PersistFormat])
```

Where, `FileName` is the path to the file where the result set is to be saved and `PersistFormat` is one of:

❑ `adPersistADTG`: currently the default of binary file

❑ `adPersistXML`: which saves the recordset in XML format

So we save the recordset, but first we make sure that the cursor location is the client. This is because when we open it in its disconnected state we manipulate it in the client:

```
mrsPeople.CursorLocation = adUseClient
mrsPeople.Save "c:\temp\mrsPeople.dat"
```

We then disconnect and close:

```
Set mrsPeople.ActiveConnection = Nothing
mrsPeople.Close
mADOConnection.Close
```

Now we reopen the set – may be next week, may be immediately:

```
mrsPeople.Open "c:\temp\mrsPeople.dat"
```

Work on it until we are too tired to continue and reconnect. This can be done either by pointing the recordset to an open connection (the preferred way) or by giving it a connection string as an Open parameter.

Once connected we BatchUpdate the database on the server. Here we use the AdLockBatchOptimistic. This will only lock the records in the batch one by one, rather than all together, while updating. This way we have less active locks and each lock has a shorter life, and each record is available to other users sooner.

```
mrsPeople.LockType = AdLockBatchOptimisticmrsPeople.BatchUpdate
```

That's all folks!

The Command Object

The Command object is the main reason to use ADO. It allows us to do everything we need to do. It even returns a Recordset when the action we do involves a SELECT statement or a PL/SQL Table. We also use the Command object and its parameters to call stored procedures.

Command Properties

Property	Description
ActiveConnection	Returns or sets the connection.
CommandText	The text of the command.
CommandTimeOut	In seconds, the time after which we anounce failure (default is 30).
CommandType	What type of command the CommandText property represents. adCmdText=1 complete text of the statement, adCmdStoredProc=4, adCmdTable=2 Table Name (ADO will compose the SQL as SELECT * FROM Table), adCmdFile=256 command resides in a file, text contains path.
Parameters	The Command collection of parameters. More later.
Prepared	If set to prepared, a temporary stored procedure will be created for the duration of the object. Not applicable to Oracle (Always False).
State	Indicates the state of the Command object. adStateClosed=0, adStateOpen=1, adStateExecuting=4, adStateFetching=8.

Command Methods

Method	Description
Cancel	Cancel the execution of a statement before it is over. This may be used only if the command that you try to cancel is executing asynchronously.
CreateParameter	Create a `Parameter` object. This goes hand in hand with the `Parameters.Append` method of the parameters collection. See full discussion of parameters below.
Execute	It executes the query, SQL or stored procedure mentioned in `CommandText` property. It is discussed in full below.

The Execute Method

Let's cut to the chase. Here is the general syntax of this most important method:

```
[Set Recordset = ]Command.Execute ([RecordsAffected] [, Parameters] [,
Options])
```

RecordsAffected is an optional long into which the server returned the number of records that were affected by the command.

Parameters. Use them carefully. Better yet, use them scarcely or not at all. They override any parameters in the Parameters collection. Also output parameters won't work correctly here. Parameters are passed in the form of a variant array of values, for example Array ("George", 1, "Tall")

Options are telling the server what the CommandText is. As usual they may be one of:

❑ adCmdText: if you use an SQL statement

❑ adCmdTable: if you pass a table name

❑ adCmdStoredProc: if you call a stored procedure

❑ adCmdUnknown

The last one is not highly recommended.

The Command object may return a Recordset of all the rows selected. This is a very convenient way of working with ADO. See Chapters 10, 11 and 14.

It is best to use the Execute method without any of the optional arguments, and set the parameters and options in the Command object. One exception is the adExecuteNoRecords = 128 option. It tells the Command not to return a Recordset. You may use it only when the statement or the stored procedure returns no records (in short not in a SELECT statement). This speeds up the execution.

The Parameters Collection

`Parameters` are to Commands, as they are to functions and subs - a way to pass variable information without recoding time and again. The `CommandText` has place holders marked by question marks. Because all the parameter place holders are so marked, the order in which parameters are added (appended) is important. The command: `INSERT INTO xyx VALUES (?, ?, ?)` has three place holders for the 3 columns of table `xyz`. Their order is important. The first place holder goes with `Parameter(0)`, the second with `Parameter(1)`, and the third with `Parameter(2)`. Parameters may be named, a quality that I like and use. Named or unnamed, the order in which they are created is important. I can't say this enough – create in the order of the place holders!

Enough said, here is how parameters are created:

```
Set Parameter = Command.CreateParameter ([Name], [DataType], [Direction],
[Size], [Value])
```

All arguments (calling them parameters is a little confusing) to the method are optional.

❑   `Name` is a string. I like to name my parameters for the sake of readability.

❑   `DataType` is one of many, including `adVarChar=200`, `adInteger=3` (which is actually equivalent to a VB `long`), `adDBTimeStamp=135` (by which I pass date and time to Oracle), `adSingle=4`, and `adDouble=5`. I hardly ever use any others. The full list is longer than a pickpocket's arm.

❑   `Direction` tells which way the parameter works. I use `adParamInput=1`, `adParamOutput=2`, and `adParamInputOutput=3`.

❑   `Size` is only important when we pass a `VarChar` (`adVarChar`) and must be exactly the maximal length allowed. For instance, in the `People` table we have declared the last_name to be `VARCHAR2 (25)`. If we want to pass or receive a name via a parameter its size must be 25.

❑   `Value` is the actual data we pass or receive.

After we have created a parameter we append it to the `Parameters` collection. It is the order in which we append, that counts. For readability purposes I prefer to declare the parameters, then create them, and then append them in the order in which they are used:

```
Command.Parameters.Append Parameter
```

Is the general syntax of the `Append` method.

Chapter 10 is replete with examples of creating parameters. Here are two of them.

```
Private mInsertPrmPersonId As ADODB.Parameter
Private mInsertPrmLastName As ADODB.Parameter
With mInsertCmd
```

```
            Set mInsertPrmPersonId = .CreateParameter("pPersonId", adDouble,
    adParamInput)
            .Parameters.Append mInsertPrmPersonId
            Set mInsertPrmLastName = .CreateParameter("pLastName", adVarChar,
    adParamInput, 25, "")
            .Parameters.Append mInsertPrmLastName
    End With
```

Note that I did not use the `Size` in the first parameter whose type is `adDouble`, but did for the `pLastName` whose type is `adVarChar`.

Before we execute the Command we assign values to the parameters:

```
        ' Insert all the values into the parameters and execute
    mInsertPrmPersonId.Value = mlPersonId
    mInsertPrmLastName.Value = msLastName
    mInsertCmd.Execute
```

Using Stored Procedures

In Chapter 13 we will learn how to write stored procedures and packages and see them in action. We will also learn how to get PL/SQL tables from a stored procedure. Note that a PL/SQL table is not a database table but a stupid name for an array. Most stored procedures are used without PL/SQL tables and therefore the calling mechanism is much simpler.

Let us look at a simple example. Call a simple stored procedure that accepts a `Person_ID` as input and produces the corresponding `Last_Name` as output. The stored procedure name is `get_last_name`.

Here is what we do. First we create a `Command` object with `adCmdStoredProc` as its `CommandType`. Then we create and append two parameters, one as input, the other as output. Finally, we set the value of the input parameter and execute the Command. The resulting `Last_Name` is the new value of the output parameter.

Declarations:

```
Private mStoredProcCmd As ADODB.Command
Private mStoredProcPrmPersonId As ADODB.Parameter
Private mStoredProcPrmLastName As ADODB.Parameter
```

Creation:

```
Set mStoredProcCmd = New ADODB.Command
With mStoredProcCmd
    .ActiveConnection = mADOConnection
    .CommandType = adCmdStoredProc
    .CommandText = "get_last_name"   'the procedure name goes here.
    .Set mStoredProcPrmPersonId = & _
    CreateParameter("pPersonId", adDouble, adParamInput)
    .Parameters.Append mStoredProcPrmPersonId
    Set mStoredProcPrmLastName = & _
```

```
   .  CreateParameter("pLastName", adVarChar, adParamOutput, 25)
       .Parameters.Append mStoredProcPrmLastName
End With
```

And execution.

```
mStoredProcPrmPersonId.Value = mlPersonId   'set the input value
mStoredProcCmd.Execute      'execute
MsgBox "Last Name Is: " & mStoredProcPrmLastName.Value   'show the output
value
```

Chapter 14 has an example of using a stored procedure to gurantee data integrity involving three tables. There you can see the procedure itself and how it is used in VB.

Dealing with Large Objects

The `Field` object of the Recordset and the `Parameter` object of the Command are programmed to handle large objects. Each has a `GetChunk` method and an `AppendChunk` method. You'll find their counterparts in OO4O as well and they behave in a very similar manner (apparently all object designers copy from each other).

We may either use the `Parameter.AppendChunk` mechanism or the `Field.AppendChunk` mechanism to store large objects (Chunks) on the server. Similarly we use `Chunk = Field.GetChunk` or `Chunk = Parameter.GetChunk` to retrieve large objects. The parameter approach works well with stored procedures or with parameterized `SELECT` statements that gave us the read-only nonscrollable recordsets when running on Oracle (see Chapter 10).

When the large objects are really big, we encounter a limitation that Oracle imposes. It won't return anything larger than 64K in one trip. The standard `AppendChunk` routine takes or gives the whole chunk at once. With Oracle we have to do it in pieces. I use 8K as the size of the piece in this example.

The example below is a repeat from OO4O in Chapter 8. To show how we work in both `Parameter` object and `Field` object, I read the chunk from a Field and write the chunk using a Parameter.

Transferring the database LONG RAW to the file

I assume that we already have a Recordset that was filled by the `Command` object, and returned a single row from a parameterized `SELECT` statement executed in the `Command` object. This recordset is `mrsDemo` and the large field is `FLD`.

```
Dim nChunks As Long
 Dim lTotalSize As Long, vChunk As Variant
 Dim FNum As Integer, nChunkSize As Long, iX as Integer

nChunkSize = 8192
FNum = FreeFile
Open "test.pdf" For Binary As #Fnum
vChunk = mrsDemo.Fields("FLD").GetChunk(nChunkSize)
```

```
'Loop through all of the chunks because Oracle does not return
'the size of columns > 64KB, we should loop until the we get a NULL
While Not IsNull(vChunk)
'The GetChunk function gets a chunk as large as we ask it to
'(in our case nChunkSize) and returns a NULL when there is no more data
 Put #FNum, , vChunk    'Write chunk to file.
 vChunk = mrsDemo.Fields("FLD").GetChunk(nChunkSize)
Wend
Close FNum
```

Transferring the File to the database LONG RAW

I assume that all the other variables are defined as before and that we have a Command object by which we insert the BLOB. The file reads 8K at a time into the container and it is appended to the Parameter, then we execute the Command.

```
With mCmdInsert
Set mInsertPrmFLD = .CreateParameter("FLD", adVarBinary, adParamInput,
2000000)
     'an arbitrary long number. Here two million
 .Parameters.Append mUpdatePrmFLD
 End With

 Dim bChunk (8192) as Byte
 FNum = FreeFile
 Open "test.pdf" For Binary As #FNum
'Loop through the file.
 While Not EOF(FNUM)
    Get #FNum, , bChunk 'Read the file
    mCmdInsertPrmFLD.AppendChunk (bChunk)
 Wend
 mCmdInsert.Execute
 Close Fnum'Close the file.
```

Error Handling

ADO provides us with a collection that handles errors. This collection contains invaluable information (sometimes, when it doesn't simply say **Errors Occurred!!**) that is not available in the VB error object, and is therefore very useful in analyzing server side errors.

Errors is a collection that belongs to the Connection (explicit or implicit) object. The general reference is:

```
Connection.Errors(Index).Property
```

For instance:

```
Connection.Errors(0).Description
```

returns the Description property of the first error in the collection.

An Error object has no methods. Its properties are what we are really after.

Error Object Properties

All the error properties are read-only:

Property	Description
Description	A sentence (or a part thereof) explaining the error.
HelpContext	The help file Context ID of the error number – because it is provider supplied, it is normally 0.
HelpFile	The full name of the help file where the above Context ID is found. Normally an empty string.
NativeError	The provider's error number (data source error number).
Number	A unique error number provided by ADO. I still have to find a real use for it.
Source	The name of the app that generated the error. For example "Microsoft OLE DB Provider for Oracle".
SQLState	A five character ANSI standard error number.

Obviously it is the error Description that interests me the most. Of secondary importance is the SQLState, because I can actually look it up.

The Errors Collection Methods

Method	Description
Clear	Clears the collection so that all the old errors no longer clog issues.
Refresh	Asks the provider to send the latest errors, if any and fills the collection with them.

The Errors Collection Properties

Property	Description
Count	How many Error objects does the collection contain?
Item	The default property. Actually the index of the property in the collection. It can be from 0 to Count – 1.
	The following will give identical results:
	`Connection.Errors(0).Description`
	`Connection.Errors.Item(0).Description`

Usage

The sub below displays a message box with all the error descriptions separated by colons. Then `Clears` the collection:

```
Sub DBUpdate(sGender as String)
    'The Command object and its Connection and parameters are alredy declared
as module
    'variables.
    Dim oErr As ADODB.Error
    Dim sMsg as String
    OnError GoTo TrapIt
    mUpdatePrmGender.Value = sGender
    mUpdateCmd.Execute
    Exit Sub
TrapIt:
    For Each oErr In mADOConnection.Errors
        sMsg = sMsg & ": " & oErr.Description
    Next
    MsgBox sMsg
    mADOCOnnection.Errors.Clear
End Sub
```

Summary

In this seemingly short chapter we have covered quite a bit of the ADO set of objects. Enough to be able to do whatever our hearts desire with an Oracle database. This is by no means a complete reference to ADO. ADO is far too big for anything less than 200 pages. But it is enough to set you going. From now on you'll be able to program VB and Oracle using ADO without a problem. Should you need to drill very deeply into methods and properties, go to David Sussman's *ADO 2.1 Programmers Reference* from WROX.

Section IV

PL/SQL,
Stored Procedures
and Transactions

13

PL/SQL, Stored Procedures and Triggers

In the "classical" era of Mainframes, and even in the "romantic" age of two-tiered Client/Server, we performed our data processing in a central computer (server), while interacting with the client who might even have been using a dumb terminal. It is actually funny, because even in the COBOL-DB2 programs of old, we had a Client/Server model. The COBOL program was the Client, and the DB2 database, the Server. Only we didn't know that this is what we were doing. This is much like Moliere's "*Monsieur Jourdan, Le Bourgeois gentilhomme*", who in order to gain nobility, takes speech lessons. He is then amazed to find that he has been talking "prose" all his life – only he didn't know it! Doing complex processing in the database – in the form of stored procedures was a preferred approach even in the "good old days", but again, most of us didn't know it!

Stored procedures are particularly beneficial when they involve an activity that goes beyond the capacity of a single SQL statement. Here is an example:

When a client comes to the bank to transfer funds from his saving account to his checking account, the bank needs to perform many activities:

- ❏ It must verify that the savings account exists
- ❏ It must verify that the checking account exists
- ❏ It must verify that the saving account has sufficient funds
- ❏ It has to reduce the savings balance by the amount transferred
- ❏ It has to increase the checking balance by the same amount

If we do all these operations in our application program, we will need at least 4 round trips on the network (once we have found the savings account we don't need to read it again to verify the amount). This is a bit much. We can achieve it with one trip if we let the Server do the jobs all at once. Writing a stored procedure will do this.

A **stored procedure** is a precompiled procedure written in some Procedural Language that the database engine understands. Because most database purveyors run on multiple platforms, they compile to p-code rather than native code, much like VB (in VB, though, we may compile to Native Code). This p-code is then executed in the local run file. The precompiled p-code still runs significantly faster than dynamic SQL, which needs to be parsed before its resulting p-code, is run.

A **trigger** looks and feels like a stored procedure, only it is not invoked on request but by an event, such as a request to INSERT, DELETE or UPDATE rows in the database. Because it is invoked this way, it cannot have any parameters.

A **PL/SQL function** is another kind of procedure that may be precompiled and performed on the database. A function is a piece of precompiled code, with parameters, which is used repeatedly (we hope, or else why separate it?) by other functions, stored procedures, and triggers.

In Oracle, all of these come under the term **subprogram**, and are all written in **Procedural Language SQL** or **PL/SQL**.

In this chapter, we'll unfold the mysteries of writing PL/SQL. VB programmers are hereby warned to use this newly acquired knowledge with care. In some places it is safer not to admit this knowledge for fear of persecution. In others, such an admission will load your already overloaded plate, causing you to fall behind. But I digress. Let us dive into it!

A Simple PL/SQL Program

Many years ago, when I first learned to program in C, I used the famous "Kernighan and Ricthie" book. They started the book with the 'Hello World' program, and even though my feet are too small to follow in their footsteps, I am compelled to do the same with PL/SQL.

I am going to ask you to follow my example blindly. Go to SQL*PLUS and start typing as I wish you to. The code is actually self-explanatory, but I promise to explain it in the end.

The first thing we want to do is to type this mysterious line:

```
SET SERVEROUTPUT ON
```

There is no semicolon at the end (as it is a Session command), but you may hit return. This command enables the SQL*PLUS session as an output device. From now on, you'll be able to 'print' on the session's terminal.

It is best to write the rest of the code in a line editor (Notepad, Writepad, even Brief). When it is done, cut and paste all the lines into the SQL*PLUS window. Correcting typing errors is much simpler in the line editor. Oracle has an environment, not available on your Personal Oracle, called SQL Worksheet, where it is much easier to compose and correct code. Because of the Personal Oracle limitation, it is not covered in this book.

Type these lines:

```
BEGIN
    DBMS_OUTPUT.ENABLE;
    DBMS_OUTPUT.PUT_LINE('Hello World');
END;
/
```

By the way, DBMS_OUTPUT is an in-built package that produces output to a buffer. You'll learn what a package is, a bit later.

Now cut and paste them into SQL*PLUS and hit ENTER:

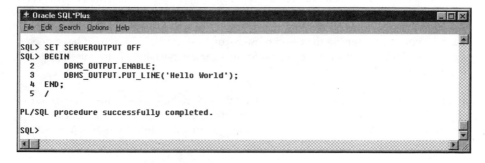

Now type:

```
SET SERVEROUTPUT OFF
```

And paste the same code again and run it. The slash is the PL/SQL run command, much like the semicolon is the SQL run command. Turning the SERVEROUTPUT option off will not allow the PL/SQL procedure to display the result:

The little piece of code that we've written and run is a very simple PL/SQL procedure. Like every language PL/SQL lives by rules. Here are a few:

❏   It is conveniently nested in a BEGIN . . . END block

❏   The BEGIN statement has no semicolon

❏   The END statement does have a semicolon

❏   All the statements in between end with a semicolon

A Slightly More Interesting Hello

Here is a little improvement on this old and tired example:

```
DECLARE
YOUR_NAME VARCHAR2(20) := &YOUR_NAME;
BEGIN
     DBMS_OUTPUT.PUT_LINE('Hello ' || YOUR_NAME || '!!!');
END;
/
```

We have added a Declaration section to the code, which is where we must declare all of our variable and data types. Here we declared a variable of type VARCHAR2. A declaration section starts with the word DECLARE without a semicolon and each successive line ends with a semicolon.

Each line resembles the column definitions of the CREATE TABLE we used in DDL, only each such declaration ends with a semicolon, including the last one. The declarations end when we encounter the BEGIN of the code block.

Our declaration has a kink. It is a declaration with an immediate assignment of value. The assignment of a value to a declared variable sets its initial value.

PL/SQL has its humble (nothing Larry Ellison did was ever humble) beginnings in ADA – and, thus, the colon equal (:=) combination is used for assignment.

> ADA is a software language developed by the U.S. Department of Defense in 1979, named in honor of Ada Lovelace who was Lord Byron's daughter and Charles Babbage's companion and student.

The same applies to Pascal and, for the real old-timers among us, ALGOL. This form of assignment was selected in order to use the equal sign as a comparison operator. This is a bit stupid, because we assign more than we compare and should have reversed the usage. Even worse, typing the colon requires us to shift. PL/SQL would have been improved if it went through a colondectomy. C and especially VB are much better in this respect. But I digress again.

In our case the assignment is even kinkier. We assign the variable the value of our own input. The ampersand (&) in front of the variable name on the right side of the assignment (:=) is a prompt command. The system will prompt the user to enter his name.

Declarations with an initial value assignment are called declarations with DEFAULT in Oracle parlance. In fact, you may use the word DEFAULT in place of the assignment (:=). Both of the following assignments are valid and yield the same result:

```
HOURLY_WAGE NUMBER := 5.15; -- until congress changes it
HOURLY_WAGE NUMBER DEFAULT 5.15;
```

The double hyphen (--) at the end of the first line signifies that the rest of the line, all the way to the carriage-return, is a comment.

You may also declare a variable as NOT NULL; in which case you must assign it an initial value.

```
HOURLY_WAGE NUMBER NOT NULL := 5.15;
```

If you do not assign it a value you'll get an error message. Try it!

Let us try to run the new code, but first set your SERVEROUTPUT to on again. When the system prompted me to enter the name, I answered **Johnny**. To my dismay (not really, because I knew it was going to happen) here is what I got:

```
± Oracle SQL*Plus                                                    _ □ x
File  Edit  Search  Options  Help
SQL> DECLARE
  2    YOUR_NAME VARCHAR2(20) := &YOUR_NAME;
  3  BEGIN
  4      DBMS_OUTPUT.PUT_LINE('Hello ' || YOUR_NAME || '!!!');
  5  END;
  6  /
Enter value for your_name: Johnny
old    2: YOUR_NAME VARCHAR2(20) := &YOUR_NAME;
new    2: YOUR_NAME VARCHAR2(20) := Johnny;
YOUR_NAME VARCHAR2(20) := Johnny;
                        *
ERROR at line 2:
ORA-06550: line 2, column 27:
PLS-00201: identifier 'JOHNNY' must be declared
ORA-06550: line 2, column 11:
PL/SQL: Item ignored
ORA-06550: line 4, column 38:
PLS-00320: the declaration of the type of this expression is incomplete or malformed
ORA-06550: line 4, column 5:
PL/SQL: Statement ignored

SQL>
```

Among a bunch of cryptic error messages I am told that 'JOHNNY' must be declared. There is a simple explanation for this. We needed to enter it enclosed in single quotes. Without the quotes, PL/SQL assumes that it is a variable. Here is a correct run:

```
± Oracle SQL*Plus                                                    _ □ x
File  Edit  Search  Options  Help
SQL> DECLARE
  2    YOUR_NAME VARCHAR2(20) := &YOUR_NAME;
  3  BEGIN
  4      DBMS_OUTPUT.PUT_LINE('Hello ' || YOUR_NAME || '!!!');
  5  END;
  6  /
Enter value for your_name: 'Johnny'
old    2: YOUR_NAME VARCHAR2(20) := &YOUR_NAME;
new    2: YOUR_NAME VARCHAR2(20) := 'Johnny';
Hello Johnny!!!

PL/SQL procedure successfully completed.

SQL>
```

You don't have such problems with numeric input. The opposite is true. If you are prompted for a numeric value and reply with a 'quoted' number, you'll err.

More about Assignments

The assignment statement is the meat of programming. PL/SQL assignments allow us to do complex computations, involving variables, operators, constants, literals, and functions.

Variables

We are all programmers, so I don't feel the need to tell you about mixing mangos and papayas. Variables come in three basic kinds: Numeric, String, and Boolean. Numeric variables come as `Integers` and `Floating Points` also known as REAL. The term NUMBER is general and includes all. If you mix and match, the results will always be of the more complex form (not the complex that is made of imaginary and real). So a computation involving `Integer` and REAL, will result in REAL. There is no limit to mixing and matching numeric variables.

Operators

Operator	Description
Numeric operators	+, -, *, /, and ** (for raising to the power of).
	This last operator does not exist in plain SQL, where you must use the POWER(m,n) function (see Chapter 2).
	Their order of precedence is:
	- (The unary minus - which simply makes a number a negative), **, * and /, + and -.
The one **string** operator	The concatenation operator ||.
Logical operators	(In order of precedence) NOT, AND, and OR.

All the functions of Chapter 2 are available for use in PL/SQL assignments.

Literals

Like variables, literals come in many forms, but here two will do. The logical or Boolean TRUE and FALSE; and NULL may be considered a third kind of literal - but only if you insist, and I don't!

> *In the CREATE_TABLE you cannot declare a Boolean column. We use VARCHAR2(1) and assign it values like Y and N instead.*

However, we are in PL/SQL land now and Booleans are welcome. In regular programming we use Boolean or Binary Logic, which means (Binary - of two values) that every statement or condition may be either TRUE or FALSE. No third option is available. In VB the Boolean is stored as an Integer. If this integer is made of 32 bits all of which are 0, it is FALSE. All else is TRUE. This is not so in PL/SQL.

In PL/SQL: 0 means FALSE, 1 means TRUE, but there is a third option -- NULL. This makes for a strange logic in which we have to check for the third option. I'll expand on this anomaly with a discussion of IF Blocks.

As stated, PL/SQL Boolean variables may assume three values: TRUE, FALSE, and NULL. I find it disturbing that this IF block below does not really cover all the possibilities:

```
DECLARE B BOOLEAN;
IF B  = FALSE THEN
    Statement1;
ELSE
    Statement2;
END IF;
```

It will do Statement2 if B is TRUE, but also when B is uninitialized. This is not what we intended.

The code below encompasses it all, but I don't think anybody really likes to program that way:

```
DECLARE B BOOLEAN;
IF B  = FALSE THEN
    Statement1;
ELSEIF B = TRUE
    Statement2;
ELSE DBMS_OUTPUT.PUT_LINE('Did you forget to set B?');
END IF;
```

My solution to this YES-NO-MAYBE logic is to declare all logical variables NOT NULL and assign them the initial value of FALSE.

Numeric literals

These can be floating point (REAL) or Integer. If you put a decimal point in your literal the number will be REAL. The same applies to literals entered in the engineering notation. Here are a few examples:

- ❑ 1234 – Integer
- ❑ 1234. -- REAL
- ❑ 123.4 – REAL
- ❑ .1234E2 – REAL
- ❑ 0.123 is the same as .123 and both are REAL
- ❑ NULL is also a numeric literal

The result of any arithmetic operation when one of the terms is NULL, is a NULL.

Anything enclosed in single quotes is a string (CHAR) literal. Double quotes are allowed to reside inside a literal, as are single quotes, but the latter have to be doubled. It is difficult to see the difference between a double quote and two adjacent single quotes, but I'll try.

'abc'
'a"bc' – double quote inside the literal
'a''bc' – two single quotes

Scalar Data Types

You may also use the scalar data types defined in Chapter 2 in your declarations. One important difference is that the RAW types – RAW and LONG RAW-- which can go up to 2GB in SQL, can only be up to 32KB long in PL/SQL.

There are two additional types of variables that are commonly used in PL/SQL.

%TYPE and %ROWTYPE

These are used to declare variables with a type that is like the type of an existing database column or table. The variable type of YOUR_NAME could be forced to be of the same type as People.First_Name. Here is how:

```
YOUR_NAME People.First_Name%TYPE := &YOUR_NAME;
```

This means that the new variable will assume the same characteristics. In this case it will be a VARCHAR2(15). Note that we do not have to declare an initial value here.

The advantage of this kind of declaration is that if we use the prompted input variable to update the People table, and, subsequently, we decide to change the precision of the First_Name, the code in the procedure will not have to be changed.

The %ROWTYPE is used with composite variables that resemble a row. These are akin to VB's UDTs. The code below was taken from a cursor declaration that returns a row. We also declared a row variable of the same type:

```
DECLARE
    -- display first name of women of all ages in the People table
    CURSOR Get_Women IS
        SELECT First_Name FROM People WHERE Gender = 'F';
    Name_Rec Get_Women%ROWTYPE;
```

Name_Rec has been declared to contain one row of the cursor above it.

Constants

If you add the keyword CONSTANT to your declaration, you create a constant. This constant must have an initial (DEFAULT) value and cannot be changed in the rest of the code.

It is a common programming practice to use constants in place of literals. This is especially convenient when the literals are in code (1 for read-only) and the constant may convey the meaning better e.g.

```
Opt_Read_Only CONSTANT NUMBER := 1
```

Branching

A programming language is not going to be any good without branching statements or constructs to control decision flow. We need our IFs, THENs and ELSEs.

The general structure of a PL/SQL IF statement is:

```
IF condition THEN
    Do one thing;
ELSEIF another condition THEN
    Do another thing;
ELSE
    Do yet another thing;
END IF;
```

Note the placement of the semicolons. PL/SQL does not have the equivalent of our beloved SELECT CASE, but you're allowed to use as many ELSEIF pieces as you need. You may put multiple lines in any of your choices:

```
IF condition THEN
        Statement1;
        Statement2;
        .

        .
        Last Statement;
END IF;
```

PL/SQL even has a GOTO statement for unconditional branching, but I feel that I have slaughtered many a sacred cow in this book already, and won't bother to go into this quagmire. Suffice it to know that it exists.

Loops and Arrays

It is hard to conceive of a programming language without **loops** and **arrays**. Most allow us multi-dimensional arrays. PL/SQL is a little more primitive than that. It only allows arrays of one dimension (vectors). These are called tables in PL/SQL and we are going to deal with them later on in this chapter.

PL/SQL seems a bit of a baffling name for a language, which, as you'll soon see, encompasses SQL and where a table is something entirely different!

PL/SQL loops come in a few flavors:

The LOOP...END LOOP

The Endless Loop

This is the simplest form of a loop and obviously the one to avoid.

```
LOOP
    Do Something;
END LOOP;
```

It is a good way to start because it illustrates the basic syntax. A loop starts with LOOP entered in its own line and without a semicolon. A line, or lines, of other valid PL/SQL instructions follow it. These include nested loops and code blocks. It ends with the line END LOOP - a semicolon is a must.

Using the EXIT Statement

A simple command – EXIT – solves the endlessness of the prior loop. It is usually enclosed in an IF...END IF block (or else it will be an empty loop).

```
LOOP
    Do Something;
    IF condition THEN
        EXIT;
    END IF;
END LOOP
```

Here is an example:

```
DECLARE i INTEGER;
... i := 0;
LOOP
    Do Something;
    i := i + 1;
    IF i > 10 THEN
        EXIT;
    END IF;
END LOOP;
```

Using the EXIT...WHEN Statement

This is a similar kind of loop that requires two less lines of code:

```
LOOP
    Do Something;
    i := i + 1;
EXIT WHEN i > 10;
END LOOP;
```

The WHILE...LOOP

Consider this example:

```
WHILE condition LOOP
    Do something;
END LOOP;
```

Careful! If the something that you do in the loop does not change the condition, you'll have an endless loop:

```
WHILE i  < 11 LOOP
    Do Something;
    i := i + 1; -- make sure to change the condition
END LOOP;
```

The FOR...LOOP

An example:

```
FOR i IN 1...10 LOOP
    Do something;
END LOOP;
```

The `FOR` loop has an interesting twist. It can go `IN REVERSE`:

```
FOR i IN REVERSE 1...10 LOOP -- countdown
    Do something;
END LOOP; -- countdown
```

The counting will start at ten and go down to one. They probably use this kind of loop for the countdown at Cape Canaveral.

Commenting your Code

It is a good programming practice to put in line comments at the beginnings and ends of loops. This is especially true if the loops are nested within each other, or if they are very long. Anything in a PL/SQL line, that follows a double hyphen (--) is a **comment**. These comments end at the end of the line. A CR terminates them.

Before we continue into cursors let us discuss the scope of PL/SQL variables.

Scope of Variables

The general rule is that the **scope** of a variable is the block in which it was declared, including other blocks within it. Variables declared before all the blocks are **global**.

Time to monkey around with variables and scopes. Let us investigate the scope by trial and error:

```
DECLARE B NUMBER := 16;
BEGIN
    DECLARE A NUMBER;
    BEGIN
        A := 1;
        BEGIN
            DECLARE B NUMBER;
            BEGIN
                B := 2;
            END;
        END;
    END;
    A := A + B;
END;
```

Here is what happens when you run it:

```
+ Oracle SQL*Plus                                              _ □ X
File  Edit  Search  Options  Help

SQL> DECLARE B NUMBER := 16;
  2    BEGIN
  3       DECLARE A NUMBER;
  4       BEGIN
  5          A := 1;
  6          BEGIN
  7             DECLARE B NUMBER;
  8             BEGIN
  9                B := 2;
 10             END;
 11          END;
 12       END;
 13       A := A + B;
 14    END;
 15    /
      A := A + B;
      *
ERROR at line 13:
ORA-06550: line 13, column 5:
PLS-00201: identifier 'A' must be declared
ORA-06550: line 13, column 5:
PL/SQL: Statement ignored

SQL>
```

A is out of scope!

We can easily remedy this error by moving line 13 one line up, just in front of the END;
statement. I also added a PUT_LINE statement, so that we may view the result.

> **This is useful for debugging code in PL/SQL. You use a procedure,
> DBMS_OUTPUT, and within this procedure, the PUT_LINE statement:**
>
> **DBMS_OUTPUT.PUT_LINE (message);**
>
> **This is the equivalent of Debug.Print in VB.**

Don't forget to type SET SERVEROUTPUT ON first, if you haven't already, to make sure you can view the results! Here is what we get now:

```
± Oracle SQL*Plus                                                    _□×
File  Edit  Search  Options  Help
SQL> DECLARE B NUMBER := 16;
  2  BEGIN
  3      DECLARE A NUMBER;
  4      BEGIN
  5          A := 1;
  6          BEGIN
  7              DECLARE B NUMBER;
  8              BEGIN
  9                  B := 2;
 10              END;
 11          END;
 12          A := A + B;
 13          DBMS_OUTPUT.PUT_LINE('The sum is: ' || TO_CHAR(A));
 14      END;
 15  END;
 16  /
The sum is: 17

PL/SQL procedure successfully completed.

SQL> |
```

Oops! You probably expected the sum to be 3. Why isn't it? The scope of B := 2 ended in its block, just above the line summing the numbers. The scope of the B variable declared at the top and initialized to 16 is still good. Thus the sum is seventeen.

Here we print the sum based on each scope of B:

```
± Oracle SQL*Plus                                                    _□×
File  Edit  Search  Options  Help
SQL> DECLARE B NUMBER := 16;
  2  BEGIN
  3      DECLARE A NUMBER;
  4      BEGIN
  5          A := 1;
  6          BEGIN
  7              DECLARE
  8                  B NUMBER;
  9                  C NUMBER := 1;
 10              BEGIN
 11                  B := 2;
 12                  C := C + B;
 13                  DBMS_OUTPUT.PUT_LINE('The sum is: ' || TO_CHAR(C));
 14              END;
 15          END;
 16          A := A + B;
 17          DBMS_OUTPUT.PUT_LINE('The sum is: ' || TO_CHAR(A));
 18      END;
 19  END;
 20  /
The sum is: 3
The sum is: 17

PL/SQL procedure successfully completed.

SQL> |
```

The first is the inner scope, the second is the outer. QED! I rest my case. And let's hope that the defense (Clarence Darrow) won!

Remember your scopes. Some purists even suggest that you name your variables by scope i.e.:

```
DECLARE INNER_B NUMBER := 1;
```

With scope out of the way it is time to deal with one of the main purposes of PL/SQL – handling cursors.

PL/SQL Cursors

What the heck are **cursors**? Are they creatures who cuss a lot? No! They provide the looping mechanism for SQL statements that are embedded in PL/SQL. When we select a table from the database and loop on its rows, the cursor is the pointer to the current row.

Cursors were invented to give old style data processing programs the ability to work with RDBs. The typical approach of the programs of the past was to run a sorted transaction file side by side with a sorted master file and apply each transaction to the master record of the matching key. Transactions were key punched by data-entry operators and the process was run nightly, or weekly, or monthly, as required.

In the first days of RDBs, we still ran our programs in batch mode and needed to be able to span the master file in the same way. The statement SELECT * FROM MASTER ORDER BY KEY gave us the sorted master file in one big table. We still needed to get to the records (rows) one by one. This was done by a cursor. Every time we did a FETCH on the cursor, we received the same kind of a record that was previously delivered by a READ command.

In short, a cursor is to mechanism by which the current row is delivered to the requestor. In modern lingo this is known as the pointer to the current row. Like historical COBOL sequential files, cursors are DECLAREd, OPENed, traversed by successive FETCHes, and finally CLOSEd.

How about fetching all the persons of the female persuasion and displaying the first name of each?

First we DECLARE the cursor:

```
DECLARE
    -- display first name of women of all ages in the People table
    CURSOR Get_Women IS
        SELECT First_Name FROM People WHERE Gender = 'F';
```

Then we OPEN it, FETCH it until the EOF, and CLOSE it. These last three operations are done implicitly by the FOR LOOP below:

```
BEGIN
    FOR Get_Women_cur IN Get_Women LOOP
        DBMS_OUTPUT.PUT_LINE(Get_Women_cur.First_Name);
    END LOOP;
END;
/
```

and here is the expected result:

```
+ Oracle SQL*Plus                                                      _ □ ×
File  Edit  Search  Options  Help

SQL> DECLARE
  2      -- display first name of women of all ages in the PEOPLE table
  3      CURSOR Get_Women IS
  4          SELECT first_name from PEOPLE WHERE Gender = 'F';
  5  BEGIN
  6      FOR Get_Women_cur IN Get_Women LOOP
  7          DBMS_OUTPUT.PUT_LINE(Get_Women_cur.first_name);
  8      END LOOP;
  9  END;
 10  /
Cleopatra
Julia
Olivierre
Ziggy
Ale
Heather
Haze
Jansen
Emmanuelle
Manny

PL/SQL procedure successfully completed.

SQL>
```

Like the i in the FOR i in 1...10, which was implicitly declared with a scope limited to the loop, so the Get_Women_cur is implicitly declared and scoped in the FOR... LOOP above. Note that I have sneaked a SQL statement into PL/SQL for the first time.

The example is the simplest cursor handling procedure. A bit more complexity is needed if we want to really control the cursor. We did not OPEN, FETCH, or CLOSE the cursor directly. In the FOR... LOOP it was done for us implicitly. Here we'll do it directly.

❑   OPEN is the command that actually brings the result of the query into the memory.

❑   FETCH is the command that advances the pointer by one row and thus effectively gives us the row.

❑   CLOSE allows us to free the memory for another operation. The memory itself is still filled with the data, but it will be overwritten as soon as another SELECT statement is performed.

In order to be able to control the loop we need information about the status of the cursor. Here are four built in indicators, which may be used after a FETCH.

❏ ISOPEN: Boolean - is the cursor open or closed?

❏ FOUND: Boolean - did the cursor retrieve a row?

❏ NOTFOUND: Boolean - The reverse of FOUND. TRUE when a row could not be retrieved.

❏ ROWCOUNT: NUMBER, which row is it? 1st, 2nd, etc. This is not the equivalent of a RecordCount in the Dynaset or Recordset. This is actually the current record number.

Using these indicators, we can control the loop:

```
DECLARE
-- display first name of women of all ages in the PEOPLE table
    CURSOR Get_Women IS
        SELECT First_Name FROM People WHERE Gender = 'F';
    Name_Rec Get_Women%ROWTYPE;
BEGIN
    OPEN Get_Women;
    LOOP
        FETCH Get_Women INTO Name_Rec;
        EXIT WHEN Get_Women%NOTFOUND;
        DBMS_OUTPUT.PUT_LINE(Name_Rec.First_Name);
    END LOOP;
    CLOSE Get_Women;
END;
/
```

Note the use of the % in front of the NOTFOUND indicator.

The FETCH command must have a variable into which the row will be fetched. It cannot exist without the INTO part – there is no FETCH without an INTO. The variable that holds the result of the FETCH must be of the same structure as the row that has been fetched; thus we use the %ROWTYPE to declare this compound variable.

We also displayed the resulting field from this row. Here is what it produces:

```
± Oracle SQL*Plus                                                    _ □ >
File  Edit  Search  Options  Help

SQL> DECLARE
  2     -- display first name of women of all ages in the PEOPLE table
  3     CURSOR Get_Women IS
  4        SELECT first_name from PEOPLE WHERE Gender = 'F';
  5     Name_Rec Get_Women%ROWTYPE;
  6  BEGIN
  7     OPEN Get_Women;
  8     LOOP
  9        FETCH Get_Women INTO Name_Rec;
 10        EXIT WHEN Get_Women%NOTFOUND;
 11        DBMS_OUTPUT.PUT_LINE(Name_Rec.first_name);
 12     END LOOP;
 13     CLOSE Get_Women;
 14  END;
 15  /
Cleopatra
Julia
Olivierre
Ziggy
Ale
Heather
Haze
Jansen
Emmanuelle
Manny

PL/SQL procedure successfully completed.

SQL> |
```

Stored Procedures and Functions

So far we had to reinsert the complete procedure block into SQL*PLUS whenever we wanted to run it. This is not the most convenient manner of running repetitive tasks. We need to be able to store the procedure and reuse it at will. This will be achieved by using **stored procedures**. The stored procedures may also be called from VB, using the OO4O or ADO interfaces.

What is different between the code we've written so far, and function or procedure code? Two things: one is that a functions or stored procedures are named blocks (what we have done so far were anonymous blocks), the other is that they use parameters.

Stored procedures are normally stored in **packages**. A package may contain multiple stored procedures and functions with a common theme. When any of the package's stored procedures is called, the complete package will be loaded into the server memory. Any subsequent call to the same procedure or any other in the same package will run faster because the package has already been loaded. It benefits us to collect procedures that are likely to run together into the same package. Procedures and functions ought to be grouped in packages of common content.

PL/SQL arrays, or as they are misnamed – tables, have to be declared in packages. A table cannot exist outside a package. Because using tables is one of the better ways to get the results of cursors into VB, we are going to use packages rather frequently.

Here is a procedure that will get the first names of the women:

```
PROCEDURE Get_Women_names IS
-- display first name of women of all ages in the People table
CURSOR Get_Women IS
             SELECT First_Name FROM People WHERE Gender = 'F';
    BEGIN
       FOR Get_Women_cur IN Get_Women LOOP
          DBMS_OUTPUT.PUT_LINE(Get_Women_cur.First_Name);
       END LOOP;
    END;
/
```

This procedure has to be created. If we are just repairing a procedure that has already been created we are going to REPLACE it. A common way to achieve both without hassle is to do a CREATE OR REPLACE on a stored procedure.

Here is creating the procedure and running it:

```
Oracle SQL*Plus
File  Edit  Search  Options  Help
SQL> SET SERVEROUTPUT ON
SQL> CREATE OR REPLACE
  2    PROCEDURE Get_Women_names  IS
  3    -- display first name of women of all ages in the PEOPLE table
  4        CURSOR Get_Women IS
  5                 SELECT first_name from PEOPLE WHERE Gender = 'F';
  6        BEGIN
  7            FOR Get_Women_cur IN Get_Women LOOP
  8                DBMS_OUTPUT.PUT_LINE(Get_Women_cur.first_name);
  9            END LOOP;
 10        END;
 11    /

Procedure created.

SQL>  exec get_women_names;
Cleopatra
Julia
Olivierre
Ziggy
Ale
Heather
Haze
Jansen
Emmanuelle
Manny

PL/SQL procedure successfully completed.

SQL>
```

It would be even better if we could decide which gender we would like use. Here is a stored procedure where this is made possible by the use of parameters.

Stored Procedure Parameters

Parameters come in three flavors: IN, OUT and IN OUT. They are PL/SQL variables and thus require a type. We may use types exactly as we have done so far.

Parameters are placed inside parentheses following the procedure name and form a comma-delimited list.

Here is our equal opportunity first name list:

```
PROCEDURE Get_first_names (p_gender IN People.Gender%TYPE) IS
-- display first name of men or women of all ages in the People table
CURSOR Get_people IS
                SELECT First_Name FROM People WHERE Gender = p_gender;
        Gender_prefix VARCHAR2(14);
    BEGIN
        IF p_gender = 'M' THEN
            Gender_prefix := 'The Men Are:';
        ELSE
            Gender_prefix := 'The Women Are:';
        END IF;
        DBMS_OUTPUT.PUT_LINE(gender_prefix);
        FOR Get_people_cur IN Get_people LOOP
            DBMS_OUTPUT.PUT_LINE(Get_people_cur.First_Name);
        END LOOP;
    END;
/
```

After you have successfully created this procedure it is time to test it. For that purpose you need to declare a variable named p_gender in your session. Here is a screen shot of how this is done, and tests of the procedure – one per gender:

```
Oracle SQL*Plus
File  Edit  Search  Options  Help

SQL> VARIABLE p_gender VARCHAR2 (1);
SQL> exec get_first_names('F');
The Women Are:
Cleopatra
Julia
Olivierre
Ziggy
Ale
Heather
Haze
Jansen
Emmanuelle
Manny

PL/SQL procedure successfully completed.

SQL> exec get_first_names('M');
The Men Are:
Adin
Ytzhak
William
Joy
Bizarre
Otto
Larry
Storm
Emmanuel
Erwin
Dog

PL/SQL procedure successfully completed.

SQL> |
```

The SQL*PLUS environment is very unforgiving. Remember to write your code in a line editor and paste it to SQL*PLUS. This may not be enough when working with stored procedures and triggers. If you introduce an error into your procedure and it does not compile cleanly, this is all you'll get to tell you about it. Note that I did name the procedure differently in order not to destroy a good procedure just for demonstrating an error:

```
± Oracle SQL*Plus                                                    _□×
File  Edit  Search  Options  Help
SQL> CREATE OR REPLACE
  2  PROCEDURE first_names  (p_gender IN people.gender%TYPE) IS
  3  -- display first name of men and of all ages in the PEOPLE table
  4  BEGIN
  5      DECLARE
  6          CURSOR Get_people IS
  7              SELECT first_name from PEOPLE WHERE Gender = p_gander;
  8          Gender_prefix VARCHAR2(14);
  9      BEGIN
 10          IF p_gender = 'M' THEN
 11              Gender_prefix := 'The Men Are:';
 12          ELSE
 13              Gender_prefix := 'The Women Are:';
 14          END IF;
 15          DBMS_OUTPUT.PUT_LINE(gender_prefix);
 16          FOR Get_people_cur IN Get_people LOOP
 17              DBMS_OUTPUT.PUT_LINE(Get_people_cur.first_name);
 18          END LOOP;
 19      END;
 20  END;
 21  /

Warning: Procedure created with compilation errors.

SQL> |
```

The little error that I introduced is in line 7. I mistyped p_gender as p_gander. It will take a person who committed this typo by mistake a year of Sundays to discover it. Even under the best of conditions. Oracle does not compare to VB as a development environment, but using the Navigator to write the procedures is an improvement over naked SQL*PLUS.

Using Navigator for Development

The Navigator or its Enterprise Edition counterpart 'Procedure Builder' is not a bed of roses either. Its biggest problem is that it the coding window is not resizable and is too small for my taste. You'll soon see for yourself.

1. Start the Navigator:

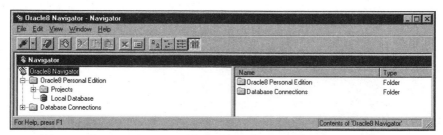

2. Click on the + next to **Oracle8 Personal Edition** in the left panel.

3. Click on **Local Database** (the blue icon).

4. When the database is up, click on the + next to it (all in the left panel). Now click on **Stored Program Unit**:

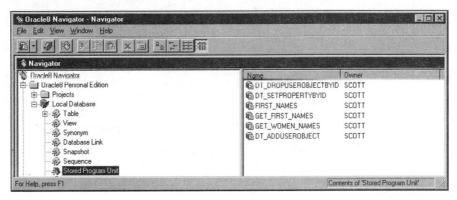

This is what you should see. (You may see fewer procedures in the right panel). Now right-click the **FIRST_NAMES** procedure. This is the one we've just created with the error, and choose **Properties**.

The procedure with its code window will appear. The code in the window is already selected and ready to be copied and pasted into you line editor. You may also do your editing in the window itself, but you have already noted how little of the code is visible.

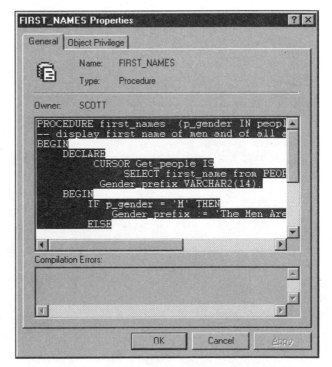

Click the Cancel button, then right-click the procedure again and select Compile:

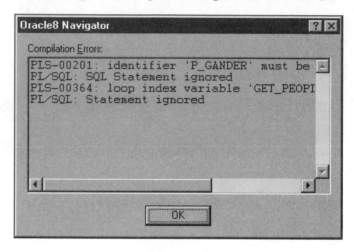

This time you get an error message, which you may correct. But let's not do it yet. I will get back to this routine after discussing the concept of a package and building a package for it to sit in. The procedure will also include a declaration for the other kind of table – the PL/SQL array that is called table.

Packages and Tables

One way of handling cursors in VB is using the PL/SQL table. We fill the table with the results of moving the cursor from the beginning to the end of the result set of the SELECT statement, and pass the table back to VB either as an ADO Recordset, or as an OO4O Parameter array. Here is how:

We are going to create a small package that includes an improved First_Names stored procedure, and a PL/SQL table (not a DB table) that houses the result set of the stored procedure. We are also going to show you how to work the procedure from VB.

It is best to start all this in the line editor. The typist that I am, I have yet to write one that compiles cleanly the first time!

We need an array (table) to hold the first names. To declare a table, we have to first define a user type:

```
TYPE table_name IS TABLE OF variable_type
   INDEX BY BINARY_INTEGER;
```

Here is the first names table:

```
TYPE tbl_fnames IS TABLE OF people.first_name%TYPE
   INDEX BY BINARY INTEGER;
```

The table is declared in the specification section of the package.

A package consists of the *specification* section, where we declare variables, tables and procedures, followed by a package *body*, where we actually build the procedures. In our example we'll only have one such procedure, but as we said before, we try to put birds of a feather in one cage, and procedures of the same ilk in the same package.

In the code below I use the term AS. This is the ADA equivalent of IS. You may use either in PL/SQL. They are the same:

```
PACKAGE  Human_Resources AS
-- we tell the package that we use a table and which procedure to expect.
TYPE tbl_fnames IS TABLE OF people.first_name%TYPE
    INDEX BY BINARY_INTEGER;
PROCEDURE first_names  (p_gender IN people.gender%TYPE, fname
                        OUT tbl_fnames);
END Human_Resources; -- it is nice to know what we have ended
```

In SQL*PLUS we create or replace the package by doing a CREATE OR REPLACE, and following it by pasting the code. We then type a slash (/) and press ENTER.

```
± Oracle SQL*Plus                                                      _□×
File  Edit  Search  Options  Help
SQL> CREATE OR REPLACE
  2   PACKAGE       Human_Resources AS
  3   -- we tell the package that we use a table and which procedure to expect.
  4   TYPE tbl_fnames IS TABLE OF people.first_name%TYPE
  5       INDEX BY BINARY_INTEGER;
  6   PROCEDURE first_names  (p_gender IN people.gender%TYPE, fname OUT tbl_fnames);
  7   END Human_Resources; -- it is nice to know what we have ended
  8   /

Package created.

SQL>
```

Again, you may want to do this in the Navigator. So right-click on the **Stored Program Unit** in the left window, select **New,** Then, select **Package Specification**. Enter the name of the package and select **scott** as the owner. Now press **OK** and paste the package specification code into the window. When you press **OK**, the package will compile. If there are any errors they will display in the window. Error messages are not the best, and the process is, at times, frustrating. It will become easier the more you do it.

Now it is time to build the package body:

```
PACKAGE BODY   Human_Resources IS
    PROCEDURE first_names  (p_gender IN people.gender%TYPE, fname
                          OUT tbl_fnames) IS
        CURSOR Get_people IS
            SELECT first_name from PEOPLE WHERE Gender = p_gender;
        table_index NUMBER := 1;
    BEGIN
        FOR Get_people_cur IN Get_people LOOP
            fname (table_index) := Get_people_cur.first_name;
            table_index := table_index + 1;
        END LOOP;
    END;
END;
```

Here is how it is done in SQL*PLUS:

```
Oracle SQL*Plus                                                    _ □ ×
File  Edit  Search  Options  Help

SQL> CREATE OR REPLACE
  2    PACKAGE BODY Human_Resources IS
  3      PROCEDURE first_names  (p_gender IN people.gender%TYPE, fname OUT tbl_fnames) IS
  4          CURSOR Get_people IS
  5              SELECT first_name from PEOPLE WHERE Gender = p_gender;
  6          table_index NUMBER := 1;
  7      BEGIN
  8          FOR Get_people_cur IN Get_people LOOP
  9              fname (table_index) := Get_people_cur.first_name;
 10              table_index := table_index + 1;
 11          END LOOP;
 12      END;
 13  END;
 14  /

Package body created.

SQL>
```

Because, again, this can be painful, you may do it in the Navigator. So right-click on the **Stored Program Unit** in the left window, select **New** and then select **Package Body**. Enter the name of the package and select **scott** as the owner. Now press **OK** and paste the package body code into the window. When you press **OK**, the body will compile. If there are any errors they will display in the window.

Returning PL/SQL Tables to VB

There is a great difference between the way we handle the PL/SQL table in ADO and OO4O. In ADO we use a `Command` object and a `Recordset`. With OO4O we use an `OraSQLStmt` object and a parameter array.

The ADO Way

Up till now Oracle and ADO have sometimes not been the best of partners. The method that we are forced to use here is rather inelegant.

The release of ADO 2.5 will improve matters immeasurably, as you will see in a little while.

Because we deal with Oracle we are going to have to make the call to the stored procedure as a SQL Passthrough and not as a stored procedure (`adcmdStoredProc`). Even this can only be achieved if you are using ODBC. Neither OLE DB – Oracle's or Microsoft's - allows us to use the PL/SQL table the way I describe it here. Here is the full code that will allow you to test this method:

```
Option Explicit
Private mCnn As ADODB.Connection
Private mrsSelect As ADODB.Recordset
Private mCmd As ADODB.Command
Private msSelect As String
Private mCmdPrmGender As New ADODB.Parameter
```

```
Private Sub Form_Load()

Dim sConnect As String    'Declare our connection string
sConnect = "Data Source=" & ";" & _
           "User ID=scott" & ";" & _
           "Password=tiger" & ";"

Set mCnn = New ADODB.Connection
With mCnn
    .CommandTimeout = 10
    .CursorLocation = adUseClient
    .Provider = "MSDAORA"
    .Open sConnect

End With


'resultset is a keyword, fname the name of the table in the proc.

msSelect = "{call human_resources.first_names(?, {resultset 1000, fname})}"

Set mCmd = New ADODB.Command

With mCmd
    .CommandText = msSelect
    .CommandType = adCmdText
    .ActiveConnection = mCnn

    Set mCmdPrmGender = .CreateParameter("pGender", adVarChar, _
        adParamInput, 1, "M")
    .Parameters.Append mCmdPrmGender
End With

Set mrsSelect = New ADODB.Recordset

mCmdPrmGender = "M"
Set mrsSelect = mCmd.Execute
MsgBox mrsSelect.Fields(0)
End Sub
```

Let's look at some sections the code in more detail. We have to define a Command object, a SQL string, a Recordset, a Parameter object and, of course, our Connection object. The result of the call will come back in the Recordset and we'll then span it to get the names:

```
Private mCnn As ADODB.Connection
Private mrsSelect As ADODB.Recordset
Private mCmd As ADODB.Command
Private msSelect As String
Private mCmdPrmGender As New ADODB.Parameter
```

We must call our stored procedure using placeholder syntax and the call statement. The general form is:

```
{call PackageName.ProcedureName(?, {resultset <NumberOfRows>, Table1, Table2
}}}}
```

This will allow us to combine PL/SQL tables into a single `Recordset`. You may add as many parameters or tables as you need.

Remember because the table is an output parameter, you may not be able to use more than 2 in early versions of Oracle. This limitation does not exist with OO4O.

In our case:

```
msSelect = "{call human_resources.first_names(?, {resultset 1000, fname})}"
```

We want to get the whole PL/SQL table back into the `mrsSelect Recordset` (result set). The pair (in which the comma seems to be missing and is not) `mrsSelect 1000` contains an arbitrary large number.

The way the `msSelect` is coded with the parentheses is the syntax used for SQL Passthrough in ODBC. This limits the approach to using the ODBC provider. As we have said many times before, the ODBC provider is the most stable and the most able, but it is also the slowest. Here we did not have a choice. In ADO 2.5 the story is different, as you will see when we discuss REF CURSORS further along this chapter.

We now set the `Command` object:

```
Set mCmd = New ADODB.Command

With mCmd
    .CommandText = msSelect
    .CommandType = adCmdText
    .ActiveConnection = mCnn

    Set mCmdPrmGender = .CreateParameter("pGender", adVarChar, _
        adParamInput, 1, "M")
    .Parameters.Append mCmdPrmGender
End With
```

And create the `Recordset`, set the parameter value, assign the `Recordset` to the return value from the execution of the `Command` object. We now have the first names of men in the recordset and can have a look at the first field value:

```
Set mrsSelect = New ADODB.Recordset

mCmdPrmGender = "M"
Set mrsSelect = mCmd.Execute
MsgBox mrsSelect.Fields(0)
End Sub
```

The OO4O Way

We are going to create an `OraSQLStmt` object, a parameter, and a parameter array in the database object. We are also going to create a statement for calling a stored procedure. When the call is done, we'll have the first 100 names in the parameter array.

Here is the full code, fully commented:

```
Private mOraSession As OraSession
Private mOraDatabase As OraDatabase
Private msSelect As String
Private mMyQuery As OraSqlStmt


Private Sub Form_Load()

Set mOraSession = CreateObject("OracleInProcServer.XOraSession")

'  Open the databae. Option 1 is ORA_DEFAULT
Set mOraDatabase = mOraSession.OpenDatabase("", "scott/tiger", 1)

'  Define the INPUT parameter and add it to the collecttion.
mOraDatabase.Parameters.Add "pGender", "F", 1

'  Define the OUTPUT parameter array(defined as type VARCHAR2 by
'  third argument) and addit to the collection.
mOraDatabase.Parameters.AddTable "pfnames", 2, 1, 100, 15

'  make the SQL for calling the procedure.
msSelect = "Begin Human_resources.first_names(:pGender, :pfnames); END;"

'  Execute the SQL statement and create an OraSqlStmt object from the
'  specified SQL statement and options. Option 0 is ORASQL_NO_AUTOBIND

Set mMyQuery = mOraDatabase.CreateSql(msSelect, 0)

'  Set the parameter value and refresh
mOraDatabase.Parameters("pGender").Value = "F"
mMyQuery.Refresh

'  Look at the first record.
MsgBox mOraDatabase.Parameters("pfnames").get_Value(0)
End Sub
```

Returning Recordsets from Oracle Stored Procedures

The COBOL-like cursor that we have described before, the one that mimics a sequential flat file is also known as a **REF CURSOR**. Oracle made the declaration and deployment of ref cursors relatively easy. Again, the best way to learn is doing. Here is a ref cursor way of reading the first and last names of the X (X = F or X = M) gender in the PEOPLE table. There are cases in which the cursor has already been built for our COBOL programmers and we want to use it. This is especially true if the SELECT statement that defines the cursor is very convoluted and we don't want to repeat it. The stored procedure that contains the cursor is also precompiled, so that we may get the results faster. Be it what it may, here is a new package (we could also have added this procedure to our old package) that contains a ref cursor.

```
CREATE OR REPLACE PACKAGE Personality
IS
   cursor c1 IS
      SELECT First_Name, Last_Name FROM People;
   TYPE PeopleCur IS REF CURSOR RETURN c1%rowtype;
   PROCEDURE GetNames
(
      pGender IN VARCHAR2,
      PeopleCursor in out PeopleCur
);
END Personality;
```

In the package header we declare a TYPE (PeopleCur), which is a REF CURSOR – a reference or pointer to a cursor. Here PeopleCur is declared as:

C1%rowtype

which simply states that it has the same field structure as the cursor c1, which itself is declared as a SELECT statement. PeopleCur is going to define an actual ref cursor called PeopleCursor. The definition is implicit and happens when we declare the PeopleCursor as a parameter of a stored procedure. Parameters in stored procedures are typed and thus defined. This is similar to what happens in ADA. We also declare PeopleCur as a ref cursor type.

We then declare a stored procedure within the package, which has two parameters, the first of the two is fairly straightforward – pGender is an input parameter of type VARCHAR2. The second parameter (PeopleCursor) to this procedure is an IN OUT parameter, declared as type PeopleCur, which is the TYPE we have just defined. This tells us that the third parameter will be returning a REF CURSOR with structure of c1%rowtype.

Now let's look at how we generate the package body, where the work of the procedure actually takes place. Note that there is no reference in this code to the cursor definition, as it only needs be defined once. All there is in the body is the PL/SQL code for the procedure:

```
CREATE OR REPLACE PACKAGE BODY Personality
AS
PROCEDURE GetNames
(
pGender IN VARCHAR2,
PeopleCursor in out Peoplecur
)
IS
begin
   OPEN PeopleCursor FOR
        SELECT First_Name, Last_Name FROM People WHERE gender = pGender;

END GetNames;
END Personality;
```

In the package body we actually build the stored procedure. The procedure takes in a pGender parameter. It then opens the PeopleCursor cursor and uses this parameter (specified in our WHERE clause) to get a cursor containing all the records in the People table that have field values corresponding to the value we give pGender.

That's it. Again you may do the work in the Navigator or use the CREATE OR REPLACE approach in SQL*PLUS. Here is the latter:

```
Oracle SQL*Plus                                                           _ □ X
File  Edit  Search  Options  Help
SQL> create or replace
  2   package Personality is
  3       cursor c1 is
  4           select first_name, Last_name from people;
  5       type PeopleCur is ref cursor return c1%rowtype; -- a row of first and last names
  6       -- note that in the procedure below the cursor is an in out parameter
  7       procedure GetNames(pGender IN VARCHAR2, PeopleCursor in out PeopleCur);
  8   end Personality;
  9   /

Package created.

SQL> create or replace
  2   package body Personality as
  3
  4   procedure GetNames(pGender IN VARCHAR2, PeopleCursor in out Peoplecur)
  5   is
  6   begin
  7
  8       open PeopleCursor for
  9           select first_name, last_name from people where gender = pGender;
 10
 11   end GetNames;
 12
 13   end Personality;
 14   /

Package body created.

SQL>
```

When we get ADO 2.5 we'll be able to address the REF CURSOR directly as a recordset. This will eliminate the need to use the PL/SQL table mechanism that we have described before. OO4O already has this capability and the table example only served us to learn another way to achieve the same end. Given a choice, the REF CURSOR approach is the one I prefer.

Using REF CURSORS in ADO

With ADO and OLEDB, Microsoft is making it easier for more developers to connect to Oracle databases, and do almost any common database task. There has been one feature however which has been glaringly absent. This is the ability to return a full-fledged recordset from an Oracle stored procedure's REF CURSOR parameter. With the upcoming version of ADO 2.5 and the Microsoft OLEDB provider for Oracle, this drastic limitation will finally be lifted.

> *Another set of third party ODBC and OLE DB drivers are from Merant (Formerly Intersolv and MicroFocus) that also allow us to do this. For further information refer to the Merant web site (www.Merant.com).*

It is possible with the 2.5 (Beta) version of ADO to return recordsets from Oracle stored procedures, thereby eliminating almost any need for SQL code in your Visual Basic programs. With this functionality, it is now possible to almost entirely separate your database code from your VB code.

To use this functionality, we have created a `Personality` package to house the definition of the cursor that will be returned, as well as the stored procedure itself. Now we are going to look at the VB code that calls our stored procedure.

In VB we declare the objects, set their properties and execute the command.

Declaration:

```
Private sSQL As String
Private mrsGetNames As ADODB.Recordset
Private mStoredProcCmd As ADODB.Command
Private mStoredProcPrmGender As ADODB.Parameter
```

Creation:

```
sSQL = "Personality.GetNames"
Set mStoredProcCmd = New ADODB.Command
With mStoredProcCmd
    .ActiveConnection = mADOConnection
    .CommandType = adCmdStoredProc
    .CommandText = sSQL   'the procedure name goes here.

Set mStoredProcPrmGender = .CreateParameter("pGender", adVarChar, _
adParamInput, 1)

    .Parameters.Append mStoredProcPrmGender
End With
```

Note that we can now set the `CommandType` property to `adCmdStoredProc` to indicate that we are calling a stored procedure. Since the stored procedure is in a package we specify the name as `Personality.GetNames`. When a stored procedure is in a package the MS OLEDB driver will not automatically determine the parameters for the stored procedure. We have to manually append them. Here is an important point. Our stored procedure had two parameters: `pGender` and `PeopleCursor`. Note that we do not define a parameter for the REF CURSOR.

Finally, we assign our recordset to the return value from the execution of our command. The OLEDB driver will automatically intercept our IN OUT REF CURSOR parameter and assign it to be the return from the execution:

```
mStoredProcPrmGender.Value = "M" 'set the input value
Set mrsGetNames = mStoredProcCmd.Execute 'execute
```

Voila! Remember, that you will have to wait for ADO 2.5 to be able to do this!

The time has come to do the same thing with OO4O.

Using a REF CURSOR in OO4O

Again, in VB we declare the necessary objects, create them, set their parameters and execute them. ADO (2.5) gets the REF CURSOR records (rows) into a `Recordset`. OO4O gets them into a Dynaset. This, however, is a special kind of a dynaset. It is read-only and is created using the `CreatePLSQLDynaset` method, rather than the `CreateDynaset` method of the `OraDatabase`.

The CreatePLSQLDynaset Method

You have already used the `CreateDynaset` method of `OraDatabase` to create Dynasets. Creating the cursor based dynaset is every bit as simple. Here it is:

```
Set mOraDynaset = mOraDatabase.CreatePLSQLDynaset (SQL, CursorName, Options)
```

The method has three arguments (or parameters):

❑ `SQL` – The SQL statement must be a PL/SQL stored procedure with `BEGIN` and `END` around the call

❑ `CursorName` should exactly match the cursor created inside the stored procedure

❑ `Options` – A long integer that assumes any combination (logical sum) of the following valid `Option` values:

Value	Constant	Description
0	ORADYN_DEFAULT	In a read-only Dynaset it means only that you get an Automatic `MoveFirst` (the dynaset when refreshed will already be at the first row), that blanks are stripped from the tail of a string, and that the Dynaset caches as much as it can in the client memory.
2	ORADYN_NO_BLANKSTRIP	The Dynaset normally strips trailing blanks from character fields. This option leaves the trailing blanks in.
8	ORADYN_NOCACHE	With this option, because only one record is held in memory, you can do only forward movement (`MoveNext`, but no `MovePrevious`), but you get faster results. (*)
64	ORADYN_NO_MOVEFIRST	The Dynaset is unpopulated. You have to do a `MoveFirst` to fill it.

(*) You get faster results most of the time. This is because we (the human user) usually want just one record at a time and takes his time before requesting the next record. On the other hand, if we want to do a batch process, this will make too many round trips. In such a case it is best to use a custom Dynaset (see Chapter 8) and cache as many records as we can in one round trip.

Armed with this knowledge let us proceed.

Declarations:

```
Private mDynGetNames As OraDynaset
Private sSQL As String
```

Establish our connection:

```
Private Sub Form_Load()
Set mOraSession = CreateObject("OracleInProcServer.XOraSession")
Set mOraDatabase = mOraSession.DbOpenDatabase("", "scott/tiger", 1)
```

Note the difference between this sSQL and the simpler ADO string:

```
'  make the SQL for calling the procedure.
sSQL = "Begin Personality.GetNames (:pGender,:PeopleCursor); end;"
```

Note the exact spelling of `PeopleCursor` to match the name in the stored procedure.

We have to declare the parameters before we can create the Dynaset. As was the case with ADO, we do not declare a parameter for the cursor. This was taken care of by the correct spelling of the cursor name:

```
mOraDatabase.Parameters.Add "pGender", "M", 1 'ORAPARM_INPUT

Set mDynGetNames = mOraDatabase.CreatePlsqlDynaset(sSQL, "PeopleCursor", _
    ORADYN_DEFAULT)
```

Now execute by calling the `Refresh` method and have a look at the first field value:

```
mDynGetNames.Refresh
MsgBox mDynGetNames.Fields(0)
```

Change the gender to `F`:

```
mOraDatabase.Parameters("pGender").Value = "F"
```

And refresh again to get the ladies (I wish it were that simple!):

```
mdynGetNames.Refresh
MsgBox mDynGetNames.Fields(0)
End Sub
```

That's all folks!

Writing your own Functions

What is the difference between a PL/SQL function and procedure? The same as the difference between a VB function and procedure. A function returns a result. This difference has to be reflected in the structure. Even here the difference is really minute.

Where a procedure was declared as:

```
PROCEDURE proc_name (parameterlist) IS
```

A function is declared as:

```
FUNCTION FUNC NAME (ParameterList) RETURN TYPE IS
```

The difference is the reserved word RETURN and a variable TYPE such as NUMBER or VARCHAR or DATE.

Because the function returns a value, the function will also need TO declare a variable and a RETURN variable statement.

Again it is best to show an example:

```
CREATE OR REPLACE
FUNCTION ODDITY (Num_In IN INTEGER) RETURN INTEGER
IS
Odd_out INTEGER; -- declare the return variable
BEGIN
    Odd_Out := 2 * Num_In - 1;
    RETURN Odd_Out;
EXCEPTION
    WHEN OTHERS THEN -- any error at all
        RETURN 0;
END;
```

This function apparently returns the nth odd number given n. The function may be used within you schema like any other Oracle function:

```
Oracle SQL*Plus
File  Edit  Search  Options  Help
SQL> CREATE OR REPLACE
  2  FUNCTION ODDITY (Num_In IN INTEGER) RETURN INTEGER
  3  IS
  4  Odd_out INTEGER; -- declare the return variable
  5  BEGIN
  6      Odd_Out := 2 * Num_In - 1;
  7      RETURN Odd_Out;
  8  EXCEPTION
  9      WHEN OTHERS THEN -- any error at all
 10          RETURN 0;
 11  END;
 12  /

Function created.

SQL> select ODDITY (13) FROM DUAL;

ODDITY(13)
----------
        25

SQL>
```

An Interim Summary

We have learned how to build stored procedures, even those using cursors, and how to make VB use their results. It is no wonder that we let the DBA handle this troublesome (and then some) activity, but it is good to unveil the mysteries. Next we are going to handle triggers.

Triggers

Triggers are parameter-less procedures that are triggered (fired) either before or after inserting, updating or deleting rows from a table. Because they are fired by the event and not by choice they cannot have parameters.

Triggers are used for a variety of reasons, the simplest ones are to guarantee uniqueness by using sequences. This is the reason we use them in our sample programs. Other reasons include maintaining data integrity, and doing complex cascading updates and deletes which cannot be done directly as some of us who are SQL Server aficionados prefer to do them.

We need a few triggers to make sure that our little set of tables continues with unique keys, and to verify that all the people names in the database are properly capitalized (remember, Oracle, like Unix, thinks that Athens should be sorted after Xanadu).

Let us look at a trigger that sets the PERSON_ID in the People table:

```
DECLARE X NUMBER;
BEGIN
   IF :new.PERSON_ID = 0 THEN
      SELECT PERSON_ID_SEQ.NEXTVAL INTO X FROM dual;
      :new.PERSON_ID := X;
   END IF;
END;
```

Again you can see a declaration section and a trigger body. In our trigger I wanted the user to be able to enter a unique ID of his own, or use the system-generated sequence. Thus if a non-zero ID is asked for, the system will attempt to use it. Of course, if it is not unique, it will flunk because it is a primary key. The user is actually better off letting the sequence handle the uniqueness.

Note the term :new. In a trigger you may use the word new or old in conjunction with a field name. :New.field_name is the value that will be inserted. In an UPDATE, you may also inquire about what the value was. This is found in :old.field_name.

Other than these little differences a trigger obeys all the procedural rules.

There is a shorter way to write the trigger, a way that allows you to get rid of the declaration altogether:

```
BEGIN
   IF :new.PERSON_ID = 0 THEN
SELECT PERSON_ID_SEQ.NEXTVAL INTO :new.PERSON_ID FROM DUAL;
   END IF;
END;
```

You can choose what you prefer. The first code was so written in order to show you how declarations are made in the trigger.

You can create a trigger in SQL*PLUS or in the Navigator. In both cases, I compose it in a line editor. Again, the advantage of the Navigator is getting the error messages; the disadvantage is the fixed small window.

Creating the Trigger in Navigator

Here is how we create triggers in the Navigator:

❑   Start the Oracle Navigator

❑   Click on the + next to the **Oracle 8 Personal Edition Folder**

❑   Click on the **Database** Icon

❑   Click on the + next to **Local DataBase**

❑   Click on the + next to **Table**

❑   Click on the + next to the **PEOPLE** table. You should now have a screen that looks much like the one below:

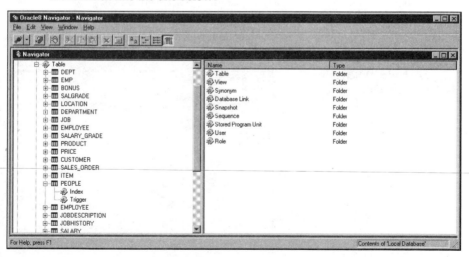

Now right-click on the trigger below **PEOPLE** and select New from the dropdown menu.

Fill in the General tab, naming the trigger, selecting the Owner scott from the dropdown combo, selecting Before, checking Insert. All this gives the trigger a meaningful name and casts it as a trigger to be run before a new row is inserted into the PEOPLE table. :

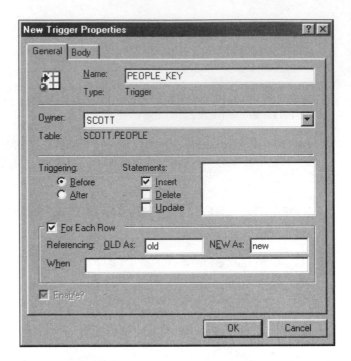

Make sure you place a tick in the For Each Row checkbox. Then in the OLD AS text box type old, in the NEW AS text box type new. This will allow you to use the words old and new in conjunction with a field name, as discussed above.

Now click the Body tab and enter the PL/SQL code that makes the trigger's body. When this is done, click OK:

That's it! You've made your first trigger! Why not do all the other triggers while we are at it?

Repeat the process this time on the EMPLOYEE table. Name the trigger EMPLOYEE_KEY and use the following code in the body:

```
DECLARE X NUMBER;
BEGIN
IF :new.EMPLOYEE_ID = 0 THEN
     SELECT EMPLOYEE_ID_SEQ.NEXTVAL INTO X FROM DUAL;
     :new.EMPLOYEE_ID := X;
  END IF;
END;
```

Now to the JOBHISTORY table. The name is (of course) JOBHISTORY_KEY and the code:

```
DECLARE X NUMBER;
BEGIN
IF :new.HISTORY_ID = 0 THEN
     SELECT HISTORY_ID_SEQ.NEXTVAL INTO X FROM DUAL;
     :new.HISTORY_ID := X;
  END IF;
END;
```

Finally SALARY:

```
DECLARE X NUMBER;
BEGIN
IF :new.SALARY_ID - 0 THEN
     SELECT SALARY_ID_SEQ.NEXTVAL INTO X FROM DUAL;
     :new.SALARY_ID := X;
END IF;
END;
```

Again, you may use the shorter code as shown in the PEOPLE_KEY trigger for all of the triggers above. If you do don't forget to remove the declaration.

In Chapter 14 we are going to encounter a problem with the sorting order. The best way to solve it is with a trigger. This trigger INITCAPS each of Last_Name, First_Name, M_I, and Gender. It works on the People table and is aptly named PEOPLE_FORMAT_NAME. This trigger should be fired before an INSERT and before an UPDATE, so you have to check both these check boxes on the form.

```
DECLARE X VARCHAR2(25);
BEGIN
  X := INITCAP(:new.LAST_NAME);
  :new.LAST_NAME := X;
  X := INITCAP(:new.FIRST_NAME);
  :new.FIRST_NAME := X;
  X := INITCAP(:new.M_I);
  :new.M_I := X;
  X := INITCAP(:new.GENDER);
  :new.GENDER := X;
END;
```

And once more, you may do a direct placement of the INIT_CAP function into the proper column without using the X intermediary. Here is how:

```
BEGIN
:new.last_name := INITCAP(:new.last_name)
:new.first_name := INITCAP(:new.first_name)
:new.M_I := INITCAP(:new.M_I)
:new.gender := INITCAP(:new.gender)
END;
```

Creating or Replacing the Trigger in SQL*PLUS

When in the Navigator we only entered the code for the trigger from the Declaration and down. We did the rest – naming and setting the triggering events – in the Navigator itself. The complete trigger structure is needed when using SQL*PLUS. Here is the complete structure:

```
TRIGGER Trigger_Name
BEFORE | AFTER
INSERT | UPDATE | DELETE OF  Column_Name ON Table_Name
FOR EACH ROW
DECLARE Variable variable_TYPE;
BEGIN
Do your Thing
END; .
```

The INSERT | UPDATE | DELETE line may contain a combination such as INSERT OR UPDATE. When this is the case the trigger will be "fired" in both cases.

Here is the PEOPLE_FORMAT_NAME in its SQL*PLUS dress:

```
TRIGGER PEOPLE_FORMAT_NAME
BEFORE
INSERT OR UPDATE OF LAST_NAME, FIRST_NAME, M_I, GENDER ON PEOPLE
FOR EACH ROW
DECLARE X VARCHAR2(25);
BEGIN .
  X := INITCAP(:new.LAST_NAME);
  :new.LAST_NAME := X;
  X := INITCAP(:new.FIRST_NAME);
  :new.FIRST_NAME := X;
  X := INITCAP(:new.M_I);
  :new.M_I := X;
  X := INITCAP(:new.GENDER);
  :new.GENDER := X;
END;
```

```
Oracle SQL*Plus                                                      _ □ ×
File  Edit  Search  Options  Help
SQL> CREATE OR REPLACE
  2  TRIGGER PEOPLE_FORMAT_NAME
  3  BEFORE
  4  INSERT OR UPDATE OF LAST_NAME, FIRST_NAME, M_I, GENDER ON PEOPLE
  5  FOR EACH ROW
  6  DECLARE X VARCHAR2(25);
  7  BEGIN
  8    X := INITCAP(:new.LAST_NAME);
  9    :new.LAST_NAME := X;
 10    X := INITCAP(:new.FIRST_NAME);
 11    :new.FIRST_NAME := X;
 12    X := INITCAP(:new.M_I);
 13    :new.M_I := X;
 14    X := INITCAP(:new.GENDER);
 15    :new.GENDER := X;
 16  END;
 17  /

Trigger created.

SQL>
```

And here is the result is reflected in the Navigator:

Error Handling

PL/SQL notifies us of a few error conditions in Oracle parlance they are named exceptions – nice euphemism. Here they are:

Exception	Description
CURSOR_ALREADY_OPEN	You can't open that cursor again!
DUP_VAL_IN_INDEX	The record was attempted with an unique key already exists.
INVALID_CURSOR	This is a misnomer if I ever heard one. You attempted an illegal operation on a cursor.
INVALID_NUMBER	The string you tried to convert does not represent a valid number.
LOGON_DENIED	You guess what that means.
NO_DATA_FOUND	The SELECT INTO statement has returned no rows.
NOT_LOGGED_ON	I really have to worry about this one!
PROGRAM_ERROR	Oracle encountered an internal error. There is nothing you can do about it, but restart and pray.
ROWTYPE_MISMATCH	You cannot use one cursor to work on a different types of row (usually different table).
STORAGE_ERROR	Server memory problems. Pray and may be you won't need to restart (fat chance!)
TIMEOUT_ON_RESOURCE	What do you think it is? Server is probably too busy.
TOO_MANY_ROWS	The SELECT INTO statement has returned more than one row.
VALUE_ERROR	Normally column size is too big. Other possibilities are arithmetic error of an undisclosed kind. Very helpful?
ZERO_DIVIDE	Just to prove that PL/SQL is a real programming language.

There is still another exception that I saved for last. It is now put in a place of honor. This is the OTHER exception. OTHER is the most important of all exceptions. It is the catch all of exceptions. If any error occurred and you have not caught it specifically by name, it falls into the OTHER category.

How do we capture these errors? A procedure may have an EXCEPTION block. This is always the last block of a procedure. It begins with the EXCEPTION keyword and in it we may write a succession of WHEN statements with instructions:

```
--This is an EXCEPTION BLOCK
EXCEPTION
WHEN NO_DATA_FOUND THEN
     r-value := 0;
WHEN ZERO_DIVIDE THEN
     r-value := 9999;
WHEN OTHER THEN
```

Once the error has been trapped, then the calling procedure is not aware that the error has occurred. We can resignal the error, using the RAISE statement, to pass the error to the calling routine (VB in our case) and notify the user via a message box.

In most procedures we just write an EXCEPTION block that rolls back and raises an error if anything at all goes awry. Here is that catchall:

```
EXCEPTION
     WHEN OTHER THEN
          ROLLBACK --Rollback changes if situation warrants it;
          RAISE --Notify the calling routine;
```

Finally, and this time I mean it, you can raise your own errors. This is done by the command:

```
RAISE_APPLICATION_ERROR (Errnum, Errmsg, Errflag)
```

Errnum must be between –20999 and –20000 (not the other way around).

Errmsg is any string you care to pass. If it is a literal, it'd better be enclosed in single quotes.

Errflag is optional. It is also a string.

You normally enclose this in an IF structure:

```
IF condition THEN
     RAISE_APPLICATION_ERROR (Errnum, Errmsg, Errflag);
END IF;
```

Summary

It is quite impossible to encompass a complete programming language in a chapter. We have barely touched on the structures involved and our sample programs are of the simplest form. Still, it is all here (except the GOTO statement). It is up to you to apply it to more complex situation. All you need is to write longer, more involved code. Because I trust that some of you will really do it -- you are hereby dubbed an accomplished PL/SQL programmer!

14

A Practical Application Using Transactions and Stored Procedures

We've come a long way in this book. We have built an application that allowed us to maintain a single HR table on the Oracle database (the `People` table). We modified this application so that we could pass parameters with our SQL and dynamically redefine our resulting dynaset or recordset.

We then refined our program further so that it would support transactions. We also improved performance by implementing a database trigger and by passing all of our class variables between form and data class in a variant array.

All of this was done for both ADO and OO4O. This, combined with the knowledge of PL/SQL and stored procedures gained from the previous chapter, puts you in a very strong position to successfully marry VB and Oracle, through either ADO or OO4O, in a real application. In this chapter we will do both, side-by-side. Our applications will be multi-form, transaction-safe and will take advantage of database stored procedures and triggers to safeguard data integrity and ensure optimum performance.

What do we want to achieve? We are going to build an application that will allow us to maintain four of the five HR tables in our database.

> *Our program only reads the `JobDescription` table - we cannot change job codes or add new ones. This also means that we cannot delete job codes that are in use (Foreign key constraints). I leave this program to the reader.*

We want to do this in a sensible manner so we are going to enforce some business rules:

❑ To add an employee, this person must exist in the `People` table.

❑ A newly added employee must have a job history and a salary

There are two ways that we can maintain our personnel tables whilst ensuring adherence to our business rules: the first way makes use of our transaction-enabled connection class. The second way uses stored procedures.

This application will also employ the triggers that we created in the previous chapter. Using the TABLE_KEY triggers simplifies the structure of the data classes because we no longer need to create an additional dynaset (OO4O) or Command object (ADO) in order to guarantee the uniqueness of the key. This saves one roundtrip per record inserted. This saving is almost a net saving, because the sequence has to be advanced in both cases.

We are going to start by looking at the user interface. You will get a feel for the sort of functionality that our program will provide and then we will look under the hood and see exactly how the program provides it.

The User Interface

Let us start by having a look at the People form. It is an offshoot of the old People maintenance program that we have used so frequently in the book. Here is how the new form looks:

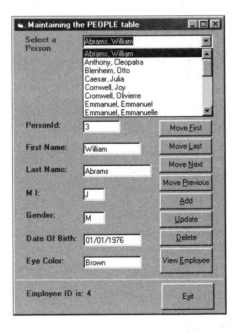

Up top we have a label and a combo box. The user may select a person from this combo box and his or her details will be displayed in the textboxes below. Alternatively they may navigate through the result set using the usual 'Move' buttons.

At the bottom of form, nicely sectioned off, we have an **Exit** button and a second label, in which we let the user know whether or not the person selected is an employee. As you can see from the previous screenshot, William Abrams is an employee and hence the label displays his `Employee_ID` number. However, when we select Jansen Janice, for example, the label informs us that he isn't an employee:

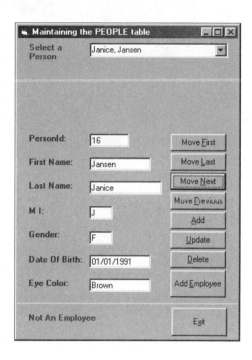

Both labels use bold font (my eyes are weak), and the ForeColor in both is set to be different (again, my eyes are weak!).

The form also has a new command button (cmdEMP). There is another difference you may have noticed in these two screenshots. The command button caption reads View **Employee** when William Abrams is displayed and **Add Employee** when Jansen Janice is displayed. We'll select another employee as an example, Ziggy Freud, and click **View Employee**:

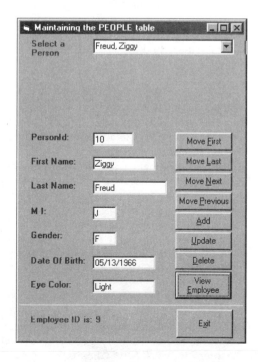

The Job and Salary History form for Ziggy Freud appears:

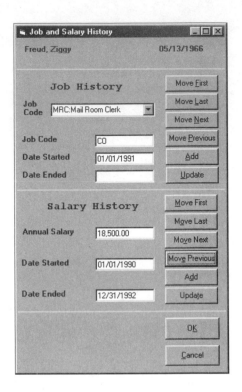

The top section of the `JobSalary` form contains two labels showing the person's name and date of birth. Below this is the **Job History** section. A combo box displays the employee's job description and textboxes display the job history details. We can navigate through the records and update or add data. The third section display records from the `Salary` table.

If we click **Add Employee** from the `People` form, the text boxes in these two sections will appear blank. We can then select the appropriate job description from the combo box and add salary and job details. Remember, according to our business rules, we must do this in order to add a new employee. Thus you must, at the minimum, enter a value in the **Job Code** box and click **Add**, then enter a value in the **Annual Salary** box and click **Add**. Finally click on **OK** and if you are successful a new employee will be added, and the newly assigned EmployeeID will be displayed at the bottom of the `People` form.

Remember also that you will not be able to create a new employee unless that person exists in the `People` table first. You must enter all the details on the `People` form (except the **PersonID** – our triggers takes care of primary key issues on all four of the tables), click **Add Employee** and proceed as before.

OK, I think that serves as a good introduction to what our application can do (it has one or two other tricks up its sleeve, as we'll discover along the way). Now let's find out how the program works. In the first instance we are going to refine and demonstrate the `clsConnection`'s transaction mechanism, which we developed in Chapter 7 for OO4O and Chapter 11 for ADO.

Sharing Objects and Information Between Forms

The application uses two forms. The VB form is a class of which the various forms in a project are objects, and our program uses this quality as a means of communications between the two forms and even for sharing the Connection object between them. In both OO4O and ADO we perform transactions at the connection level (the Connection object in ADO and the OraSession object in OO4O). This allows us to do transactions that span more than a single form. This feat requires some extra explanation. We declare a connection object in both the forms but instantiate it only in one of them. We also create a Property Let in the same form, to allow the second form to get a pointer to the connection.

Thus, in form1 (in our case the People form) we declare:

```
Private cConnection As clsConnection
Set cConnection = New clsConnection
```

And also add a Connection property:

```
Public Property Get Connection() As clsConnection
'frmJobSalary will get the connection pointer here
    Set Connection = cConnection
End Property
```

We also need a property to pass the EmployeeID between the forms:

```
Public Property Get EmployeeId() As Double
'frmJobSalary will get the employee id from here
    EmployeeId = lEmp
End Property
```

In form2 (in out case JobSalary) we declare a few data classes, and we want them to use the first form's connection. Thus, in the declaration section we have:

```
Private cJobDescription As New clsJobDescription
Private cJobHistory As New clsJobHistory
Private cSalary As New clsSalary
Private cConnection As clsConnection 'note that the word New is missing
```

And in the Form_Load routine, which is the equivalent of the Class_initialize routine in a normal class we do the following:

```
Set cConnection = frmPeople.Connection
cJobDescription.ConnectX cConnection
cJobHistory.ConnectX cConnection
cSalary.ConnectX cConnection
```

Now the data classes of form2 are using the very same connection as the data classes in form1.

We pass other pieces of information from form1 to form2 in a similar manner. We use form controls and the `EmployeeID` property. Thus in form2 we have:

```
Private Sub Form_Activate()
    lblName = frmPeople.cboPerson.Text
    lblDOB = frmPeople.txtDOB
    lEmployeeId = frmPeople.EmployeeId
    ClearScreen 'a routine that clears text boxes etc.
    If lEmployeeId <> 0 Then
        PopulateForm ' Reads the tables and populates the form controls
    End If
End Sub
```

Why the different treatment between Name, DOB and EmployeeID? All the form's controls are available to other objects, but `lEmp` is a private variable of the form and we don't want it altered by an "outsider" (it is encapsulated) so we expose it as a read only property, including just the `Property Get` procedure.

Changing the Data Classes to Accommodate Spanning the Set

Other changes needed to be made to the data classes. I want to populate a dropdown combo with the names of all the people. Another such dropdown combo (in the `frmJobSalary` form) allows us to select job codes. The way our old OO4O `MoveNext` methods work creates a problem for us. In the old programs it was beneficial to prevent the set from moving past the last row. The way we did it reset the `EOF` condition. `EOF` is set to `True` when we try to read past the last row. We did a `MoveLast` when `EOF` was detected, and `MoveLast` puts us in the last row rather than past it. This sets the `EOF` to `False`. Now, when we want to loop on the set until the end, we do not know when to stop (because `EOF` is continually reset!). This is corrected by allowing the `MoveNext` a dual behavior, depending on a parameter.

> *You should note that adding a parameter to a method or sub will break the binary compatibility of the sub to its old users (this is actually a change in the interface). You may do this – as I do here – only if the class is not a member of an already published COM/DCOM. If it is, you should add a new method to do the job.*

Here is the new `MoveNext` method from our OO4O `clsPeople` class :

```
Public Sub MoveNext(Optional ByVal bWithEOF As Boolean = False)
    If Not mdynPeople.EOF Then
        mdynPeople.MoveNext
        If Not bWithEOF Then
            If mdynPeople.EOF Then mdynPeople.MoveLast
        End If
        SetProperties
    End If
End Sub
```

When you call the method with a parameter set to `True`, you'll be able to sense the EOF and stop the loop. This is how `FillCombo` below knows when to stop (you will see the full code when we discuss the `People` form code, shortly):

```
Public Sub FillCombo ()
'This routine fills the person combo
    cboPerson.Clear
    cPeople.MoveFirst
    Do While Not cPeople.EOF
        'get a whole person
        vAll = cPeople.All

' vAll is indexed 0 to 6, 0 is the person id, 1 last name, 2 first name etc.
' we concatenate last name vAll(1) with the first name vAll (2) with
' a comma between them
        cboPerson.AddItem ("" & _
        vAll(1) & _
        ", " & _
        vAll(2))
        cPeople.MoveNext True    'Don't do the MoveLast
    Loop
    If cboPerson.ListCount > 0 Then    'did we find anybody at all?
        cboPerson.ListIndex = 0
        cmdMoveFirst_Click
    End If
End Sub
```

Other small changes are necessary as well. When reading the `JobHistory` and `Salary` tables, we only need the rows that belong to a given employee. In many cases, such as when we are entering a new employee, there are no rows. This means that the class still keeps the information for the last record shown before we switch to the current employee. I find it more convenient to set the class properties to their defaults before refreshing. This empties the class properties from any remnants left from another employee.

Here is how it is done in the refresh method of the OO4O job history data class – `clsJobHistory`.

```
Public Sub Refresh()
'** Set parameters and re-read
    SetDefaults
    mOraDatabase.Parameters("EmployeeId").Value = mlEmployeeId
    mdynJobHistory.Refresh
    SetProperties
End Sub
```

Other Design Considerations

The user can traverse the `People` table by using the various 'Move' buttons, but this is too slow if the table is even twenty persons long. To get to the seventeenth person the user would have to click `MoveNext` sixteen times. We have added a dropdown with the names. The user may click on a name and view the appropriate record immediately, but I still wanted to maintain the old approach. This requires synchronization between button and dropdown, and between the name displayed in the dropdown and the record displayed in the textboxes.

This is the most difficult feat of the program. This feat was managed by using the `MoveRel` method of the OO4O dynaset. Because we did our own 'Move' methods in the ADO classes, using the array of the `GetRows` method, we have to imitate this `MoveRel` behavior there as well. This is relatively easy, because a 'Move' on the variant array is a simple change of index.

Similar tricks are employed when we delete rows. We must remove the corresponding entry from the dropdown list, without completely reconstructing it.

We also want to know who in the `People` table are actually employees. To be able to do that, we teach the `FillCombo` sub to also handle an array in which we maintain the Employee_ID if the person is an employee, and 0 otherwise.

Traffic Management

The only time we refresh any of the sets, is when we have added a row. This is a good approach to handling network traffic and database activity.

> *Actually, if we update a first or last name - an event that should be very rare - we need to refresh then as well, in order that our combo box will also show the correct name. We will deal with this when we describe the Add method, a little later.*

We need to be able to see the changes that other users may have done in the database, but we don't want to do a refresh every second. The addition of a new row – an event that does not happen too frequently – seems to be a good compromise between refreshing constantly and not refreshing at all.

> *An additional feature that you may consider adding is a REFRESH button on the form so that the user may refresh the list at will. Otherwise, if he does not add a new person to the table, he'll never be able to see what his colleagues might (or may) have done.*

In very large entities, such as governments and international corporations, the Human Resources systems are much too large for the `People` table to be read in its whole. The common practice is for branches and departments to have their own HR sections. The practitioners normally look only for their immediate employees, and the chance of a change perpetrated by others is slim. Our decision to refresh only upon adding new rows matches the real world model well.

Brevity is the Mother of Wit

While in music and painting, minimalism makes for horribly boring results, in programming it is a noble goal. Edsger W. Dijkstra once reflected on the false pride of programmers who boasted the length and complexity of their code.

"My code for XYZ is 60,000 lines long." crowed one, soon to be outdone by another who could claim to have performed the same feat with 100,000 lines.
"You're both wrong," said Dijkstra, "I can do it in 500!"

Whose code would you rather maintain? I strive to write the briefest program still readable.

The Application

We build this personnel maintenance program on two forms and with six classes. There are five data classes – one for each table in our database – and one connection class. As you know, we have one form for maintaining the People table (frmPeople) and one for maintaining the Salary and the JobHistory tables (frmJobSalary). The Employee table is actually a linking table (alternatively called a junction table) and requires minimal maintenance, and the JobDescription is used only for input into a dropdown combo on the JobSalary form.

Before you move on and start building our new application, make sure you have created the following database triggers:

❑   PEOPLE_KEY

❑   EMPLOYEE_KEY

❑   JOBHISTORY_KEY

❑   SALARY_KEY

You may also have created the INITCAP trigger that converts M_I, Gender and the first letters of First_Name and Last_Name to capital letters. However, you will find that our program will actually perform without this trigger, because I elected to show you the VB way to deal with this functionality.

Let's start with the People form.

The People Form

Let's have another quick look at our newly designed form:

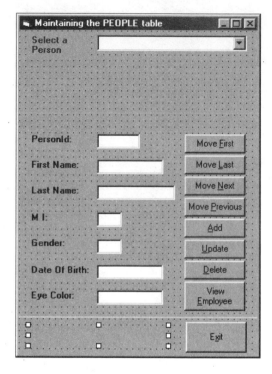

The form was made longer to accommodate the added controls, and the distance between the various controls was shrunk. As before, we have all the same labels, textboxes, and command buttons we already know and love, but we have added 2 extra labels, an extra command button, a dropdown combo, and, for a nicer, friendlier interface, a line above the exit button.

Up top we have a label (the label does not have to be named in a meaningful manner) describing the combo box that will host a list the last and first names for everybody in the People table. Name the combo box cboPeople and set its Sorted property to True.

At the bottom of form we have our second label (lblEmpStatus), in which we let the user know whether or not the person selected is an employee. The new command button is named cmdEMP and, as we know, its caption will read View Employee or Add Employee depending on whether the person is an employee or not. Clicking on View Employee will simply bring our second form into view. Clicking on Add Employee will start a transaction and add a new employee pointing to the selected (or newly added) person.

Let's start with the declaration code for this form:

```
Option Explicit
Private cConnection As New clsConnection
Private cPeople As New clsPeople
Private cEmployee As New ClsEmployee

'we use this variable as a variant array to pass a complete People row
'(one person) between clsPeople and the form
Private vAll As Variant

'the combo index of the person currently displayed
Private OldIndex As Long
'an array of employee id or 0, in the same order as the combo.

Private IsEmployee() As Double
Private lCount As Long
Private lEmp As Double
Private WithEvents fJobSalary As frmJobSalary
Private TransId As Long 'to enable secure transactions
```

The form code for our old `People` form already included a private copy of the connection class and a copy of the `People` data class. Our new form also includes a data class for the `Employee` table.

Also note the line:

```
Private WithEvents fJobSalary As frmJobSalary
```

We have declared `fJobSalary` as the main form's private copy of `frmJobSalary`. This declaration was `WithEvents`. Why is this?

We maintain the `Salary` and job history in the `JobSalary` form. As we said before, we allow new employee records to be added only after we've verified that they have a salary and history. When we exit the `JobSalary` form, it checks if we have the required rows and raises an event to be trapped by the `People` form. The `People` form will either commit the transaction or roll it back depending on the completion of the job. To allow one form to raise events that are then trapped by the other, we declare the second form – `JobSalary` with events within the first form. The events (we are going to have two of them) will be declared and raised as needed in the `JobSalary`. How do we capture these events?

Once the `fJobSalary` was declared it became an object of the `People` form. This means that we can find it in the list of objects in the dropdown list among all the other more mundane objects such as command buttons and textboxes. So find it and click on it. The dropdown on the right will now list two events: `TransAbort` and `TransComplete`.

`TransAbort` declares a Boolean variable to be used as the return value of the `RollBack` function in the connection class. Rolling back means that the new employee will not stay in the database. Have no fear, if we already had an old employee row, but without a salary or history record, rollback will not delete it. This is because it was not a part of the transaction. The way the `RollbBack` function is written, `Bdone` will be true only if we really had a transaction and successfully rolled it back. If that is the case we want to tell the user that the person now displayed is not an employee. The code below does all this.

```
Private Sub fJobSalary_TransAbort()
    Dim bDone As Boolean
    bDone = cConnection.RollBack(TransId) 'true if there was a transaction
    If bDone Then
        lEmp = 0 'after rolling back we no longer have an employee id
        lblEmpStatus = "Not An Employee"
        cmdEmp.Caption = "Add &Employee"
        IsEmployee(OldIndex) = lEmp
    End If
End Sub
```

In case of the `TransComplete` event we want to commit the transaction. Again, if we had not started a transaction (because we already had an employee, albeit without a salary or history) no harm is done.

```
Private Sub fJobSalary_TransComplete()
    Dim bDone As Boolean
    bDone = cConnection.CommitTrans(TransId) 'no need to check completion
End Sub
```

We `Commit` or `RollBack` the transaction depending on the message received from the second form. This transaction has started with the user clicking on the `cmdEMP` button when the person is not yet an employee.

```
Private Sub cmdEmp_Click()
    If lEmp = 0 Then 'not yet an employee
        TransId = cConnection.BeginTrans
    With cEmployee
        .EmployeeId = 0 'this will cause the trigger to sequence a number
        .PersonId = cPerson.PersonId
        .AddNew
        .Refresh 'read in order to get the new employee id
    End With
        lEmp = cEmployee.EmployeeId

'   mark as an employee and change the label and the command button caption
        IsEmployee(OldIndex) = lEmp
        lblEmpStatus = "Employee ID is: " &  Format$(lEmp, "#####0")
        cmdEmp.Caption = "View &Employee"
    End If
    fJobSalary.Show
End Sub
```

This mechanism also works well for employees without a corresponding `Salary` or `JobHistory`. The fact that we do not allow it to happen does not mean that it did not happen in the past. We try to make the user add these required records to the system, but we have to allow him to refuse. We are not going to remove a preexisting employee record if this information is lacking. The mechanism for that is a part of the second form, and will be discussed in detail shortly.

`IsEmployee` is an array in which we keep the `EmployeeID` of each person in the combo. It is indexed as the combo is (in other words, it is synchronized with the combo). If a person is an employee, the element in the array contains the appropriate ID, if not it contains 0. When we add an employee, we change the content of his element in the array to the new EmployeeID. When we rollback, as you have seen in the event handling routines, we change it back to 0. The array is first loaded when we load the combo, as seen in the full code of the `FillCombo` sub:

```
Public Sub FillCombo()
'This routine fills the person combo and sets the IsEmployee array
'IsEmployee is set to EmployeeId if the person is also an employee,'
'0 otherwise
    Dim lEmp As Double
    cboPerson.Clear
    ReDim IsEmployee(0)
    cPeople.MoveFirst
    Do While Not cPeople.EOF

'   get a whole person
'   vAll is indexed 0 to 6, 0 is the person id, 1 last name, 2 first name etc.
'   we concatenate last name vAll(1) wit the first name vAll (2) with
'   a comma netween them vAll = cPeople.All

    cboPerson.AddItem ("" & _
        vAll(1) & _
        ", " & _
        vAll(2))
    cEmployee.PersonId = vAll(0) 'person id
    cEmployee.Refresh
    If Not cEmployee.IsEmpty Then
        lEmp = cEmployee.EmployeeId
    Else
        lEmp = 0
    End If
    lCount = cboPerson.ListCount
    ReDim Preserve IsEmployee(0 To lCount - 1)
    IsEmployee(lCount - 1) = lEmp
    cPeople.MoveNext True 'move next with setting EOF
Loop
    If lCount > 0 Then 'did we find anybody at all?
        cboPerson.ListIndex = 0
        cmdMoveFirst_Click
    End If
End Sub
```

The following lines handle the array at the time we fill the combo:

```
ReDim Preserve IsEmployee(0 To lCount - 1)
IsEmployee(lCount - 1) = lEmp
```

This, by the way, is done the first time the form is loaded, and every time we insert a new person.

Aligning the Form and the Combo

We have seen how the combo is filled and how the `IsEmployee` array is synchronized with it. We still have to align the rest of the mechanism.

We can select a person by clicking on his name in the combo and here is what will happen:

```
Private Sub cboPerson_Click()
    Dim lDiff As Long
    lDiff = cboPerson.ListIndex - OldIndex
    OldIndex = cboPerson.ListIndex
    If cboPerson.ListIndex <> 0 Then
        cPeople.MoveRel lDiff
    Else
        cPeople.MoveFirst 'the new listindex is 0 therefore first row.
    End If
    If lDiff <> 0 Then 'not the same person
        fJobSalary.Hide 'we do not want to display the wrong person's data
    End If
    Display
End Sub
```

The last person displayed had his name in the combo. This name was held in the list in its `OldIndex` place. If we now select a new person, his name is in the `ListIndex` place. The difference between the two is how many records in the set we have to advance (positive difference) or retreat. We send that difference as a parameter to the `MoveRel` method and display the resulting record. The `MoveRel` method, when given a difference of 0, does nothing. If the difference is not 0, we know that we move to another person and therefore we no longer display the salary-history form. The `MoveRel` method is less efficient than a simple 'Move'. The `MoveFirst` method is preferred if we know that we move to the first record and the code handles the decision.

We have seen the synchronization when initiated by a selection from the combo, but what if the user clicked the `MoveNext` or the `MoveLast`? When this happens we have to repopulate the form and also change the combo's `ListIndex`. Here is how this is done:

```
Private Sub cmdMoveFirst_Click()
    cboPerson.ListIndex = 0
End Sub

Private Sub cmdMoveLast_Click()
    cboPerson.ListIndex = cboPerson.ListCount - 1
End Sub

Private Sub cmdMoveNext_Click()
    Dim lX As Long
    lX = cboPerson.ListIndex
    If lX < cboPerson.ListCount - 1 Then 'not already last
        lX = lX + 1
        cboPerson.ListIndex = lX
```

```
        End If
End Sub

Private Sub cmdMovePrevious_Click()
    Dim lX As Long
    lX = cboPerson.ListIndex
    If lX > 0 Then 'not already first
        lX = lX - 1
        cboPerson.ListIndex = lX
    End If
End Sub
```

This is a seemingly strange piece of code. Nowhere do we use a data class 'Move' method. We only change the `ListIndex` of the combo. Why? It is simply because changing the `ListIndex` in the combo generates a click event. We capture this event (`cboPerson_Click`) in its sub, as you have just seen, and that is where the work is done. Brevity means no superfluous code.

Sorting – The VB Solution

There is another little problem that hampers the synchronization effort. This stems from the difference in the way in which Oracle and VB sort data. Oracle, with its Unix mentality, uses a collating sequence in which caps precede lower case letters. The VB combo sorts alphabetically without regard to case. When I first tested this application, I was astonished to find that when I clicked the dropdown in a "barton, fink" entry, a record for "Caesar, Julia" was displayed in the text boxes. When I clicked the `MoveLast` button, the "barton, Fink" record appeared. So what's a programmer to do?

Two options came to mind. One is to correct the problem in the database with a trigger, the other to correct it in VB. Even though the latter is the lesser solution (because we have to code it in every single program rather than dealing with it in the database once and for all), I elected to implement both in our sample application, starting with the VB solution. I added the following function to the `modGeneral` module:

```
Public Function ConvertName(sName As String) As String
    ConvertName = UCase(Left$(sName, 1)) & LCase(Mid$(sName, 2))
End Function
```

This function is the equivalent of the Oracle `INITCAP`. It is used in the `Store` routine to convert the names before they are transferred to the database:

```
Private Sub Store()

'make sure names start with uppercase.
    txtLastName = ConvertName(txtLastName)

'not necessary if we use the trigger
    txtFirstName = ConvertName(txtFirstName)
    txtGender = UCase(txtGender)
    vAll(1) = txtLastName
    vAll(2) = txtFirstName
    vAll(3) = txtMI
    vAll(4) = ConvertDate(txtDOB.Text)
    vAll(5) = txtGender
    vAll(6) = txtEyeColor
    cPeople.All = vAll
End Sub
```

This leads us to the last changes we need to do. As you saw in chapters 7 and 11, one of the performance improvements is to send all the properties to and from a class in one trip. We did that using a variant array. This makes the `Store` (see above) sub move all the information from the textboxes to the elements in the variant array. The whole variant is then passed to the class at once. The reverse is true when we `Display`. Then we get the variant with all the elements, and populate the textboxes from the elements. Here is the display routine.

```
Private Sub Display()
    vAll = cPeople.All 'get all the properties in one trip
    txtPersonId = Format$(vAll(0), "#####0")
    txtLastName = vAll(1)
    txtFirstName = vAll(2)
    txtMI = vAll(3)
    txtDOB = FormatDate(vAll(4), "mm/dd/yyyy")
    txtGender = vAll(5)
    txtEyeColor = vAll(6)

'   we tell the user if the person is also an employee
    lEmp = IsEmployee(OldIndex)
    If lEmp <> 0 Then
        lblEmpStatus = "Employee ID is: " & Format$(lEmp, "#####0")
        cmdEmp.Caption = "View &Employee"
    Else
        lblEmpStatus = "Not An Employee"
        cmdEmp.Caption = "Add &Employee"
    End If
End Sub
```

We now need to look at the routines that allow us to add, delete and update data.

Modifying Data

Deleting a person also requires special action. We need to delete the person from the combo. This requires us also to remove his entry from the `IsEmployee` array. The last action means that we compress the `IsEmployee` array from the place where we deleted and up. After all, nothing has changed in the records below the point of deletion.

```
Private Sub cmdDelete_Click()
'to keep the combo and the dynaset in sync we remove deleted items
'we also need to keep the IsEmployee array in sync

    Dim lX As Long
    cPeople.Delete
    cboPerson.RemoveItem OldIndex
' compress the IsEmployee. (without redimming it, because we don't
' really 'need to)

    For lX = OldIndex To lCount - 2 'only from the point of deletion and on
        IsEmployee(lX) = IsEmployee(lX + 1)
    Next lX
    cboPerson.ListIndex = OldIndex    ' setting the index always creates
                                      ' a click event
End Sub
```

368

The basic way to code our `cmdAdd_click` event is as follows:

```
Private Sub cmdAdd_Click()
    Dim sCompare As String
    Dim lX As Long
    Store
    cPeople.AddNew
    sCompare = txtLastName & ", " & txtFirstName
    cPeople.Refresh
    FillCombo
    For lX = 0 To cboPerson.ListCount - 1
        cboPerson.ListIndex = lX
        If cboPerson.Text = sCompare Then
            Exit For
        End If
    Next lX
End Sub
```

The Update routine can be written as follows:

```
Private Sub cmdUpdate_Click()
    Store
    CPeople.Update
End Sub
```

When we add a new person, we then refresh the `Recordset` or `Oradynaset`. When this happens we want to make sure that we keep the place and display just the added person. This is a bit complex. We save the name of the new addition in the form in which it appears in the combo; we then `Store`, `AddNew`, and `Refresh`. Now, using the saved name, we loop on the new combo until we find it. When we change the index, and the person is displayed.

Unfortunately, we also have the problem of keeping the combo and textboxes in sync in the event of updating a person's name (after marriage, perhaps, or simply if we find we entered it incorrectly the first time). To deal with this we have to do similar tricks with our `cmdUpdate` routine. Thus, in order to save repeating this code in two places, we code the `Update` and `Add` routines very simply, as follows:

```
Private Sub cmdAdd_Click()
    Store
    cPeople.AddNew
    RefreshNReset    'read the table, fill the combo, and
                     'set the combo to the added name
End Sub

Private Sub cmdUpdate_Click()
    Store
    cPeople.Update
    RefreshNReset    'read the table, fill the combo, and
                     'set the combo to the changed name
End Sub
```

Both of these routines call a common new routine, `RefreshNReset`:

```
Private Sub RefreshNReset()

' we want to position the form on the new person so we keep
' the name in a string for comparison

    Dim sCompare As String
    Dim lX As Long
    sCompare = ConvertName(txtLastName) & ", " & ConvertName(txtFirstName)
    cPeople.Refresh
    FillCombo

' check the combo for a person matching the comparison string
' and stop when we found it

    For lX = 0 To cboPerson.ListCount - 1
        cboPerson.ListIndex = lX
        If cboPerson.Text = sCompare Then
            Exit For 'stop when you found it
        End If
    Next lX
End Sub
```

Almost there! We just need to have a look at the `Form_Load` routine:

```
Private Sub Form_Load()

' Note that here we do not center the forms, because we need two
' side-by-side

    Me.Left = 810
    Me.Top = 810
    cConnection.OpenDB "scott", "tiger", ""

    cPeople.ConnectX cConnection
    cEmployee.ConnectX cConnection
    FillCombo
    Set fJobSalary = New frmJobSalary
End Sub
```

All we need to do now is allow our user to gracefully exit, tidying up after them as they go:

```
Private Sub cmdExit_Click()
    Set cPeople = Nothing
    Set cConnection = Nothing
    Unload fJobSalary
    Unload Me
End Sub
```

As one final note, don't forget to include the new `Property Get` routines that we discussed earlier in the chapter ("Sharing Objects and Information between forms"):

```
Public Property Get Connection() As clsConnection
'frmJobSalary will get the connection pointer here
    Set Connection = cConnection
End Property
```

```
Public Property Get EmployeeId() As Double
'frmJobSalary will get the employee id from here
   EmployeeId = lEmp
End Property
```

That's it! The magic of the first form is explained. The complete code for the form, and that includes all the placements of the controls, may be found on the WROX site. Please download it with the rest of the program.

Sorting – The Triggered Solution

In the above code we make sure that we do not submit non-capitalized first or last names using the ConvertName routine in modGeneral, thus solving sort order problems in the database. Still, the better solution for the sort order problem is to do it with a database trigger. The trigger should be deployed before updates and inserts and should convert First_Name, Last_Name, and M_I using the INITCAP function (see Chapter 2).

Why is this solution better? Well, basically because it solves the problem once and for all. The solution in the VB program will have to be repeated with every new program we write. Using the trigger works whether or not you have corrected the problem in VB. You already know how to write triggers, but here is the trigger's body nonetheless.

```
DECLARE X VARCHAR2(25);
BEGIN
   X := INITCAP(:new.LAST_NAME);
   :new.LAST_NAME := X;
   X := INITCAP(:new.FIRST_NAME);
   :new.FIRST_NAME := X;
   X := INITCAP(:new.M_I);
   :new.M_I := X;
   X := INITCAP(:new.GENDER);
   :new.GENDER := X;
END;
```

The trigger also sets the GENDER to a capital letter.

The Job and Salary History Form

Our second form allows the user to maintain the job history and salary of the employees. Here is a reminder of how it looks:

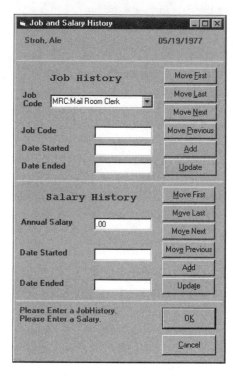

It is divided into four areas with the help of three lines that cross it from left to right. The top area has two labels: the lblName label, and the lblDOB label. They are named because we intend to change their captions. The captions, obviously, are intended to show the name and Date of Birth of the employee whose records we maintain. The same information may be viewed on the main form; the two are placed side by side, but I still display the name and DOB to give the user a warm and fuzzy feeling that everything is hunky-dory.

> *My daughter, who is a professional translator, and who lived in Japan for over six years tells me that hunky-dory is the name of a Tokyo street in the heart of the red-lantern district, and hence the term.*

The second area of the form contains the mechanism for selecting a job code and the mechanism for maintaining the job history. When a job code is selected from the combo, it is placed in txtJobCode. This way we prevent a non-existent code from creeping in.

The various controls are named according to their function. Where ambiguity with other parts of the form exists we prefix each of the names with a capital 'J'. Here are the names:

- ❑ cboJobDescription
- ❑ txtJobCode
- ❑ txtJDateStarted
- ❑ txtJDateEnded
- ❑ cmdJMoveFirst, cmdJMoveLast, cmdJMoveNext, cmdJMovePrevious, cmdJAdd and cmdJUpdate.

They are captioned as seen in the picture. The third area contains the mechanism for maintaining salaries. Again, the controls are aptly named.

- ❑ txtIncome
- ❑ txtSDateStarted
- ❑ txtSDateEnded
- ❑ cmdSMoveFirst, cmdSMoveLast, cmdSMoveNext, cmdSMovePrevious, cmdSAdd and cmdSUpdate.

Again, they are captioned as seen in the picture.

The fourth and last area contains two command buttons and a large label. They are named cmdOK, cmdCancel, and lblStatus. In cmdOK the default property is set to True. This means that pressing the **ENTER** key is akin to clicking this button. The cmdCancel has its cancel property set to true, which makes pressing the **ESC** key equivalent to clicking the command. The label is used to tell the user what still needs to be done for the employee. In the picture above the user is told to enter both a job history and a salary. If the user tries to click the **OK** button without doing so, the system will beep and nothing else will happen. If the user clicks the **Cancel** button, the TransAbort event will be raised, the form will hide, and the People form will roll the transaction back. If the **OK** button is clicked when there are at least one each of History and Salary, the TransComplete event will be raised and the People form will commit the transaction.

The form also contains a reference to the cConnection object of frmPeople, and three data classes. One is the read-only class of JobDescription, the others are updateable and are for JobHistory and Salary. As we have seen before, all use the cConnection of frmPeople.

Another important note: a bit further on we are going to find a ClearScreen routine. This routine empties the Text property of any control for which the Text property is pertinent, and where I have also set the Tag property to TEXT. When I first design a screen, I decide which textboxes I want to clear and tag them as TEXT. In this case, please fill the Tag property of every textbox to TEXT. This approach is better than just writing a routine that clears all the textboxes. Here you can be selective and clear only some.

Here is the complete code for the form. This code can also be downloaded from the Wrox site.

```
Private lEmployeeId As Double
Private cJobDescription As New ClsJobDescription
Private cJobHistory As New ClsJobHistory
Private cSalary As New ClsSalary
Private cConnection As clsConnection
'we declare two events
Event TransComplete()
Event TransAbort()

' All the columns of a single JobHistory row
Private vJAll As Variant
Private vSAll As Variant
Private bNeedsSalary As Boolean      'true if the employee is without a
                                     'salary 'record
Private bNeedsHistory As Boolean     'true if the employee is without a
                                     'history record

Private Sub cboJobDescription_Click()

'we want to change the txtJobCode to show the selected job code
'the jobcode is the part of the cbo's text that precedes the colon (:)

   Dim iX As Long
   Dim sText As String
   sText = cboJobDescription.Text
   iX = InStr(sText, ":")
   txtJobCode = Left$(sText, iX - 1)
End Sub

Private Sub cmdCancel_Click()
   RaiseEvent TransAbort
   Me.Hide
End Sub

Private Sub cmdOK_Click()
   SetStatus
   If bNeedsSalary Or bNeedsHistory Then
      Beep 'warn when incomplete employee
   Else
      RaiseEvent TransComplete
   End If
End Sub

Private Sub Form_Activate()

'even when the form was already loaded, this code will run
'whenever we do frm.show

   lblName = frmPeople.cboPerson.Text
   lblDOB = frmPeople.txtDOB
   lEmployeeId = frmPeople.EmployeeId
   ClearScreen
   If lEmployeeId <> 0 Then
      PopulateForm
   End If
End Sub
```

```
Private Sub Form_Load()
'Located to the side of frmPeople

    Me.Top = 810
    Me.Left = 6015
    Set cConnection = frmPeople.Connection
    cJobDescription.ConnectX cConnection
    cJobHistory.ConnectX cConnection
    cSalary.ConnectX cConnection
    FillCombo
End Sub

Private Sub ClearScreen()
    Dim iX As Integer
    For iX = 0 To Controls.Count - 1

'if the tag is TEXT then clear the Text property
    If Controls(iX).Tag = "TEXT" Then
        Controls(iX).Text = ""
    End If
    Next iX
End Sub

Public Sub FillCombo()
    cboJobDescription.Clear
    cJobDescription.MoveFirst
    Do While Not cJobDescription.EOF
        cboJobDescription.AddItem cJobDescription.JobCode & _
            ":" & cJobDescription.Description
        cJobDescription.MoveNext True
    Loop
    If cboJobDescription.ListCount > 0 Then
        cboJobDescription.ListIndex = 0
    End If
End Sub

Private Function PopulateForm()

'called when there is an employee id
    cSalary.EmployeeId = lEmployeeId
    cJobHistory.EmployeeId = lEmployeeId
    cSalary.Refresh
    cJobHistory.Refresh
    SetStatus
    DisplayHistory
    DisplaySalary
End Function

Private Sub DisplayHistory()
    vJAll = cJobHistory.All 'get all the properties in one trip
    txtJobCode = vJAll(2)
    txtJDateStarted = FormatDate(vJAll(3), "mm/dd/yyyy")
    txtJDateEnded = FormatDate(vJAll(4), "mm/dd/yyyy")
End Sub

Private Sub StoreHistory()
    vJAll(1) = lEmployeeId
    vJAll(2) = txtJobCode
    vJAll(3) = ConvertDate(txtJDateStarted.Text)
    vJAll(4) = ConvertDate(txtJDateEnded.Text)
    cJobHistory.All = vJAll
End Sub
```

```
Private Sub DisplaySalary()
    vSAll = cSalary.All 'get all the properties in one trip
    txtIncome = Format$(vSAll(2), "###,###.#0")
    txtSDateStarted = FormatDate(vSAll(3), "mm/dd/yyyy")
    txtSDateEnded = FormatDate(vSAll(4), "mm/dd/yyyy")
End Sub

Private Sub StoreSalary()
    vSAll(1) = lEmployeeId
    vSAll(2) = CDbl(txtIncome)
    vSAll(3) = ConvertDate(txtSDateStarted.Text)
    vSAll(4) = ConvertDate(txtSDateEnded.Text)
    cSalary.All = vSAll
End Sub

Private Sub cmdJAdd_Click()
    StoreHistory
    cJobHistory.AddNew
    cJobHistory.Refresh
    SetStatus
    End Sub

Private Sub cmdJDelete_Click()
    cJobHistory.Delete
End Sub

Private Sub cmdJMoveFirst_Click()
    cJobHistory.MoveFirst
    DisplayHistory
End Sub

Private Sub cmdJMoveLast_Click()
    cJobHistory.MoveLast
    DisplayHistory
End Sub

Private Sub cmdJMoveNext_Click()
    cJobHistory.MoveNext
    DisplayHistory
End Sub

Private Sub cmdJMovePrevious_Click()
    cJobHistory.MovePrevious
    DisplayHistory
End Sub

Private Sub cmdJUpdate_Click()
    StoreHistory
    cJobHistory.Update
End Sub

Private Sub cmdSAdd_Click()
    StoreSalary
    cSalary.AddNew
    cSalary.Refresh
    SetStatus
End Sub

Private Sub cmdSDelete_Click()
    cSalary.Delete
End Sub
```

```
Private Sub cmdSMoveFirst_Click()
   cSalary.MoveFirst
   DisplaySalary
End Sub

Private Sub cmdSMoveLast_Click()
   cSalary.MoveLast
   DisplaySalary
End Sub

Private Sub cmdSMoveNext_Click()
   cSalary.MoveNext
   DisplaySalary
End Sub

Private Sub cmdSMovePrevious_Click()
   cSalary.MovePrevious
   DisplaySalary
End Sub

Private Sub cmdSUpdate_Click()
   StoreSalary
   cSalary.Update
End Sub

Private Function SetStatus()
   If cSalary.IsEmpty Then
      bNeedsSalary = True
   Else
      bNeedsSalary = False
   End If
   If cJobHistory.IsEmpty Then
      bNeedsHistory = True
   Else
      bNeedsHistory = False
   End If
   lblStatus = ""
   If bNeedsHistory Then

'the spaces at the end of the next line
'cause the textbox to drop to the next line.
      lblStatus = lblStatus & "Please Enter a JobHistory."
   End If
   If bNeedsSalary Then
      lblStatus = lblStatus & "Please Enter a Salary."
   End If
End Function
```

All the code is pretty much as you'd expect. It is a virtual repetition of the approach we have used previously. The actions of the OK and Cancel buttons, as well as the general handling of the Status label require us to use the GetStatus function. This is the last function of the form and is listed directly above this paragraph. The bNeedsHistory and bNeedsSalary both have to be False before we can accept an employee record as complete. Again, it does not matter if the employee record is pre-existing or not. Every time a user looks at a record and something is missing, he'll be reminded. If the record is new and incomplete it will not even be allowed to stay.

All this code does not really depend on the methodology we use in the data classes. We can use ADO if our data classes use ADO, and OO4O if it happens to be the underlying methodology. I can't seem to stop singing the praise of OOP and polymorphism.

The Data and Connection Classes

Nothing much has changed in the way we do the data classes and the connection class. In fact the connection classes for OO4O and ADO remain unchanged from Chapters 7 an 11 respectively. The data classes (clsPeople and clsJobDescription) that needed the ability to span all the rows have their MoveNext methods changed as shown before. Only one additional change has been made to the clsPeople and that is the MoveRel method.

Let's start with OO4O.

OO4O clsPeople class

We have already seen the way we now code our MoveNext method. It looks as follows:

```
Public Sub MoveNext(Optional ByVal bWithEOF As Boolean = False)
    If Not mdynPeople.EOF Then
        mdynPeople.MoveNext
        If Not bWithEOF Then
            If mdynPeople.EOF Then mdynPeople.MoveLast
        End If
        SetProperties
    End If
End Sub
```

We also have to code the MoveRel method:

```
Public Sub MoveRel (lRows As Long)
    If lRows<> 0 Then
        MdynPeople.MoveRel lRows
        SetProperties
    Else
        MoveNext False
    End If
End Sub
```

We are not going to pass gender parameters in this chapter. In the code below I have disabled the WHERE clause of msSelect. There is one other minor modification you must make to this string, and the final Class_Initialize routine looks like this:

```
Private Sub Class_Initialize()

ReDim mvAll(0 To 6) 'we have 7 properties rolled into the array

'   Set the class varaibles to initial default values
SetDefaults
```

```
'    Create the mdynPeople SQL, to retrieve data from te People table
'    We've seen the initial code before.  New lines are:
msSelect = msSelect & " ORDER BY LAST_NAME, FIRST_NAME"
'msSelect = msSelect & " Where (GENDER = :pGender)"
End Sub
```

We must use the ORDER BY clause so that the combo can stay in synch with the 'Move' methods.

You have just seen the code for the two forms. They are available for download from the Wrox website. To get the full application up and running you should:

❑ Use OO4OclsPeoplePrmTrans.cls from Chapter 7, with the above alterations

❑ Use OO4OclsConnectionTrans.cls directly from Chapter 7

❑ Use modGeneralTrans from Chapter 7, but add the ConvertName routine

❑ Download OO4OclsSalary, OO4OclsEmployee, OO4OclsJobHistory and OO4OclsJobDescription from the Wrox web site (the full code can be found in Appendix E) and include these in your project.

ADO clsPeople Class

Let us now consider the changes to be made to the ADO version of clsPeople.

First, here is the MoveRel method. All we need to make it work is to advance the row index mlX by the number of rows, and check if it is not larger than the last row index (mlRows − 1) or smaller than the first row index (0):

```
Public Sub MoveRel(lDiff As Long)
    If lDiff <> 0 Then 'No need to do anyting if the number to move is 0
        mlX = mlX + lDiff
        If mlX > mlRows - 1 Then mlX = mlRows - 1
        If mlX < 0 Then mlX = 0
        SetProperties (mlX)
    End If
End Sub
```

Replace the old Refresh routine with the following:

```
Public Sub Refresh()
    Set mrsPeople = mSelectCmd.Execute
    If mrsPeople.BOF And mrsPeople.EOF Then
        SetDefaults
        mlRows = 0
        mbEOF = True
    Else
        mvRows = mrsPeople.GetRows
        mlRows = UBound(mvRows, 2) + 1    'The variants second dimension is
        mbEOF = False                     'the rows
    End If
End Sub
```

Next we need to do a small change to the MoveNext method. We teach it to notify us of the EOF condition:

```
Public Sub MoveNext()
    If mlX <> mlRows - 1 Then 'if not the last row
        mlX = mlX + 1
        SetProperties (mlX)
        mbEOF = False
    Else
        mbEOF = True
    End If
End Sub
```

EOF is set when we try to read past the last line. The reading itself is prevented. Note that EOF is raised by changing a module variable. This calls for two things. One is to declare it – this is done as the last line in the declaration section of the class:

```
'* The EOF condition
Private mbEOF As Boolean
```

Now replace the old Get EOF() routine with the following:

```
Public Property Get EOF() As Boolean
    EOF = mbEOF
End Property
```

Indeed a very simple undertaking. Similar actions need to be taken in all the other data classes.

Whenever we use the GetRows method, we get the information into mvRows and always set the mlRows – the row count. This means that regardless of the detail of the class, the code for the 'Move' routines is always identical. Once you have it done right, it is there to serve you for as long as you wish. This is another lesson of minimalism in programming. If it works, think about how it may be reused and do it!

In order to get the full ADO application up and running:

❑ Use the two forms developed in this chapter. Don't forget to connect the ADO way in the Form_Load routine of frmPeople.

❑ Use ADOclsPeoplePrmTrans.cls from Chapter 11, with the above alterations. Remember to disable parameters and add the "ORDER BY LAST_NAME, FIRST_NAME" clause to msSelect

❑ Use ADOclsConnectionTrans.cls directly from Chapter 11

❑ Use modGeneralTrans from Chapter 11, but add the ConvertName routine

❑ Download ADOclsSalary, ADOclsEmployee, ADOclsJobHistory and ADOclsJobDescription from the Wrox web site (the full code can be found in Appendix E) and include these in your project.

Next we are going to achieve the very same result with a mixture of regular data classes and stored procedure calls. Such stored procedures will insert Employee, JobHistory, and Salary in one round trip, using the parameters that we pass.

This approach to the program will teach you every possible way to combine VB and Oracle.

Using Stored Procedures

Our application is almost too simple to use stored procedures. The requirement of writing the `Employee` record only when also doing a `JobHistory` and `Salary` is, however, a good place to use a stored procedure. You have already learned how to achieve the same end with the transaction mechanism. It is time that you really finish the course with an actual stored procedure.

The stored procedure approach has an advantage. When I go into the various web user and newsgroups, I encounter many questions from people who ask how they can create a table with unique keys that are really in sequence. They mean a sequence without holes. This is theoretically impossible. One of the reasons is that a sequence never generates a number twice. If you ever delete a row, you create a hole that the sequence is not going to fill. Also if you abort (rollback) a transaction mid-way, chances are that you already advanced a few sequences – thus more holes. Our mechanism so far creates employee rows and then rolls them back. Try this a few times and watch how, without adding employee rows, the Employee ID keeps climbing. If we use a stored procedure to write all three records, and we fire it only after collecting all the pertinent data, we'll have much less discontinuity in our Employee _ID column.

The Stored Procedure

First we want to build the stored procedure. If you haven't done so yet, make sure that you read chapter 7 and follow some of its samples, then come back to the following procedure. All the parameters needed are here: job code, dates, income, and `Person _id`. They are all of type input. The `employee_id` is both input and output. We need it returned to determine the employee_ID for the form. A returned value of 0 signals an error.

```
CREATE OR REPLACE
PROCEDURE New_Employee (
    p_person_id IN NUMBER,
    p_job_code IN VARCHAR2,
    p_jstart_date IN DATE, -- start date for job
    p_jend_date IN DATE, -- end date for job
    p_income IN NUMBER,
    p_sstart_date IN DATE, -- start date for salary
    p_send_date IN DATE, -- end date for salary
    p_employee_id IN OUT NUMBER -- the system fixes the ID and sends it back
) IS
-- declare a temporary container for employee_id
    v_emp_id NUMBER;

BEGIN
-- we generate the employee_id without the trigger.
    SELECT EMPLOYEE_ID_SEQ.NEXTVAL INTO v_emp_id FROM DUAL;
-- this will insert an employee
    INSERT INTO EMPLOYEE VALUES (
        v_emp_id,
        p_person_id);
-- this will insert a job history
    INSERT INTO JOBHISTORY VALUES (
        0, -- let the trigger generate the history id
        v_emp_id,
        p_job_code,
```

```
        p_jstart_date,
        p_jend_date);
-- This will insert a salary
   INSERT INTO SALARY VALUES (
      0,  -- let the trigger generate the salary id
      v_emp_id,
      p_income,
      p_sstart_date,
      p_send_date);
-- here we set the output parameter
   p_employee_id := v_emp_id;
-- and this will commit
   COMMIT;
EXCEPTION
   WHEN OTHERS THEN -- on any error
      P_employee_id := 0;
      ROLLBACK;
END new_employee;
```

The procedure works well even without the need to raise an error. The mechanism, when successful, returns the new `employee_id` and we can insert it in the `IsEmployee` array. If unsuccessful the procedure returns a zero and we know that something went awry.

Let's make sure the procedure is in the database, this time using SQL*PLUS.

In SQL*PLUS type: CREATE OR REPLACE and hit **ENTER**. Now copy the procedure above in NotePad and cut and paste it into the SQL*PLUS window. Type a slash / and hit ENTER and the procedure will be created.

Changing the VB Program

Now it is time to change the VB to match. Again we are looking for the simplest solution. In this case it means the solution that will cause minimal change in the forms and will use the existing classes as they already are. Remember the Dijsktra principle. Do it with less, but do it elegantly.

Our stored procedure is used only when we insert a new employee. Old (existing) employees without `Salary` or `JobHistory` are not going to be inserted, so the old mechanisms of inserting `Salary` and `JobHistory` are still necessary. More than that – with the old employees I allow a partial insertion. We also do away with the transaction mechanism. It is no longer necessary. How do we achieve all that without a major operation? We hinge the firing of the stored procedure on the employee_id being 0. We also fire it only after the user has filled the screen with both salary and history. If the employee_id is not 0, we allow for a single addition of either history or salary.

Doing these changes does not depend on the way we connect to the database. It doesn't matter whether we use ADO or OO4O. In both cases we need to add a new class to the fray. This will be `clsProcedures` – named in the plural because I may put more than a single stored procedure call into it, even though in our case we only need one. In the OO4O approach we'll use an `OraSqlStmt` object, while when using ADO we'll of course use a `Command` object to fire the procedure. Let us start, as usual, with Objects for OLE.

The OO4O Version

Building clsProcedures

The procedures class is similar to a regular data class in the fact that it, too, shares the same connection. The approach is similar to the one we took in building the SQL and setting class variables. The difference is that it uses parameters rather than fields and that it contains an `OraSqlStmt` object rather than an `Oradynaset` object.

The class is a very short piece of code and is actually very simple. Let us look at it and explain the little that needs explanation. We covered all of the technical detail regarding OO4O in Chapter8.

The class starts with the declaration of the variables. It behooves us to pass all the parameters to the class in one variant array, and use the same array to get the results back. We also declare a string with the SQL statement (the procedure call) and the usual objects – `OraDatabase` and `OraSqlStmt`.

```
'Class Name is:            Procedures
Option Explicit
Private mcConnection As clsConnection    'my connection
'** The following are the OO4O objects
Private mOraDatabase As OraDatabase 'Required for connection to clsConnection
Private mProcedure As OraSqlStmt   'where the procedure is called
'** The procedure statements
Private msSQL As String
'** Class variables
Private mvAll As Variant    'where we pass all the parameters.
```

The class continues with the `Class_Initialize` routine. Here we `Redim` the variant to an array of 8 and build the procedure call statement. As you remember a procedure call is made of the word `Begin` followed by a procedure name and an open parenthesis. It continues with a comma delimited list of parameters each proceeded by a colon. The statement is ended with a semicolon and the word `End` followed by another semicolon.

```
Begin ProcName (:param1, :param2, :param3,   , :paramLast); End;
```

In the sub below I used the columnar approach to aid my poor eyes in reading the code:

```
Private Sub Class_Initialize()

'** Initialize Class Variables
    ReDim mvAll(0 To 7) 'we have 8 properties rolled into the array

' Make a parameter SQL for the reading the dynaset
    msSQL = "Begin New_Employee("
    msSQL = msSQL & ":pPersonId, "
    msSQL = msSQL & ":pJobCode, "
    msSQL = msSQL & ":pJDateStarted, "
    msSQL = msSQL & ":pJDateEnded, "
```

```
   msSQL = msSQL & ":pIncome, "
   msSQL = msSQL & ":pSDateStarted, "
   msSQL = msSQL & ":pSDateEnded, "
   msSQL = msSQL & ":pEmployeeId)"
   msSQL = msSQL & "; end;"
End Sub
```

The `ConnectX` class is where we do the actual connection. We also declare the parameters and add them to the database. Before we create the `OraSqlStmt` object, we must bind the parameters by giving them initial values.

```
Public Sub ConnectX(ByVal NewValue As clsConnection) 'Required for
                                                      'connection to
                                                      'clsConnection

   Set mcConnection = NewValue

'our class relies on an already open database.
   Set mOraDatabase = mcConnection.Database

'We ignore the errors of entering parameters twice or more
   On Error Resume Next

   'Parameters are added with: Name;  Value; and type where 1 is Input
   '                                              and  2 is output.
   '                                              and  3 is both.

   mOraDatabase.Parameters.Add "pPersonId", 0, 1
   mOraDatabase.Parameters("pPersonId").ServerType = ORATYPE_NUMBER
   mOraDatabase.Parameters.Add "pJobCode", Space(4), 1
   mOraDatabase.Parameters("pJobCode").ServerType = ORATYPE_VARCHAR2
   mOraDatabase.Parameters.Add "pJDateStarted", 0, 1
   mOraDatabase.Parameters("pJDateStarted").ServerType = ORATYPE_DATE
   mOraDatabase.Parameters.Add "pJDateEnded", 0, 1
   mOraDatabase.Parameters("pJDateEnded").ServerType = ORATYPE_DATE
   mOraDatabase.Parameters.Add "pIncome", 0, 1
   mOraDatabase.Parameters("pIncome").ServerType = ORATYPE_NUMBER
   mOraDatabase.Parameters.Add "pSDateStarted", 0, 1
   mOraDatabase.Parameters("pSDateStarted").ServerType = ORATYPE_DATE
   mOraDatabase.Parameters.Add "pSDateEnded", 0, 1
   mOraDatabase.Parameters("pSDateEnded").ServerType = ORATYPE_DATE
   mOraDatabase.Parameters.Add "pEmployeeId", 0, 3
   mOraDatabase.Parameters("pEmployeeId").ServerType = ORATYPE_NUMBER

' bind the parameters by giving them values.
' This happens only the first time

   mOraDatabase.Parameters("pPersonId").Value = 0
   mOraDatabase.Parameters("pJobCode").Value = ""
   mOraDatabase.Parameters("pJDateStarted").Value = Null
   mOraDatabase.Parameters("pJDateEnded").Value = Null
   mOraDatabase.Parameters("pIncome").Value = 0
   mOraDatabase.Parameters("pSDateStarted").Value = Null
   mOraDatabase.Parameters("pSDateEnded").Value = Null
   mOraDatabase.Parameters("pEmployeeId").Value = 0

'create the procedure
   Set mProcedure = mOraDatabase.CreateSql(msSQL, 2&) 'ORASQL_FAILEXEC
End Sub
```

`Refresh` is the `OraSqlStmt` method that fires the procedure. `mvAll(7)` returns the new Employee_ID to the calling form.

```
Public Sub Refresh()

'** Set parameters and re-run the prcedure
    mOraDatabase.Parameters("pPersonId").Value = mvAll(0)
    mOraDatabase.Parameters("pJobCode").Value = mvAll(1)
    mOraDatabase.Parameters("pJDateStarted").Value = mvAll(2)
    mOraDatabase.Parameters("pJDateEnded").Value = mvAll(3)
    mOraDatabase.Parameters("pIncome").Value = mvAll(4)
    mOraDatabase.Parameters("pSDateStarted").Value = mvAll(5)
    mOraDatabase.Parameters("pSDateEnded").Value = mvAll(6)
    mOraDatabase.Parameters("EmployeeId").Value = 0
    mProcedure.Refresh

'Get the new employee id from the 8th parameter (mvAll(7))
    mvAll(7) = mOraDatabase.Parameters("pEmployeeId").Value
End Sub

Public Property Get All() As Variant
    All = mvAll
End Property

Public Property Let All(ByVal vNewValue As Variant)
    mvAll = vNewValue
End Property
```

Changes to frmPeople

Let's consider the changes we need to effect and then go through them:

❑ Change `frmPeople` so that it passes the `Person_ID` to the `frmJobSalary`. We need this change to be able to pass the id to the stored procedure.

❑ Change `frmPeople` not to display the employee number until the stored procedure has been called and has successfully inserted the data (in the case of a new employee). In the prior version we first added the employee in an abortable transaction. Now we won't even attempt it until all the data is in.

❑ Change `frmPeople` to get the new `Employee_ID` from the `TransComplete` event. Once received display the `Employee_ID` (in case of a new employee).

❑ Remove the calls to the transaction mechanism from the form.

All this may be achieved with very little change to the form code we already have. In the declaration section remove the line defining the `TransID` and add a line declaring `lPerson` to be passed to the other form. (I commented the `TransID` line).

```
'Private TransId As Long 'to enable secure transactions
Private lPerson As Double
```

The `Display` sub of the form is where we take the variant array of the current person and format it into the various text boxes. This is the natural place to set the `lPerson` variable with the `PersonId`. We do this by inserting the following highlighted line below as the third line of the sub.

```
Private Sub Display()
    vAll = cPeople.All 'get all the properties in one trip
    lPerson = vAll(0)
```

Here is the new way we handle the click on the **Add Employee/View Employee** button. We actually remove almost all the lines. All we do is show the `frmJobSalary` form.

```
Private Sub cmdEmp_Click()
'    If lEmp = 0 Then
'        TransId = cConnection.BeginTrans
'        cEmployee.EmployeeId = 0
'        cEmployee.PersonId = cPeople.PersonId
'        cEmployee.AddNew
'        cEmployee.Refresh
'        lEmp = cEmployee.EmployeeId
'        IsEmployee(OldIndex) = lEmp
'        lblEmpStatus = "Employee ID is: " & Format$(lEmp, "#####0")
'        cmdEmp.Caption = "View &Employee"
'    End If
    fJobSalary.Show
End Sub
```

We also change the event routines. Here are the new ones.

```
Private Sub fJobSalary_TransAbort()
'in the event of an abort (the user clicked Cancel)
'lEmp is the way it was before going to frmSalary
    If lEmp = 0 Then
        lblEmpStatus = "Not An Employee"
        cmdEmp.Caption = "Add &Employee"
        IsEmployee(OldIndex) = lEmp
    End If
End Sub

Private Sub fJobSalary_TransComplete(ByVal lReturn As Long)
    IsEmployee(OldIndex) = lReturn 'set lEmp to the returned value
    lEmp = lReturn
    If lEmp <> 0 Then
        lblEmpStatus = "Employee ID is: " & Format$(lEmp, "#####0")
        cmdEmp.Caption = "View &Employee"
    End If
End Sub
```

And finally, we add another read only property to the form. This one to pass the `PersonId`:

```
Public Property Get PersonId() As Double
'frmJobSalary will get the person id from here
    PersonId = lPerson
End Property
```

Not too much, I hope. It was designed well to begin with, so it changes easily.

Changes to frmJobSalary

The changes to `frmJobSalary` have to be more extensive. Most of the work of inserting a new employee is done in here and more of the decisions have to take place here.

First we had to declare a few additional variables and also change the declaration of the `TransComplete` event to carry the new employee ID (as `lEmp`).

```
Private lPersonIdId As Double
Private cProcedures As New clsProcedures

'parameters to the clsProcedures
Private vAll As Variant

'Has the user entered salary data
Private bAddedSalary As Boolean

'Has the user entered history data
Private bAddedHistory As Boolean

'now returning employee id
Event TransComplete(ByVal lEmp As Long)
```

The `cmdOK_Click` routine has to change dramatically, even though it remains short and sweet.

As we'll see later, the `bAddedHistory` and `bAddedSalary` are set to `False` when the form loads. They are set to `True` when the user clicks the Add button in the proper areas. This is after the data has been filled. This way when the OK button is clicked we can fire the stored procedure, return the new employee_ID, and check if we succeeded by seeing a non-zero employee_ID. If failed we notify the user. Upon success, we reset all the conditions. Come what may, we send a message with the new employee_ID (zero or otherwise). `FrmPeople` takes it from there as you have already seen.

In the case of a pre-existing employee we check if we have history and salary as we did before, and warn the user of what is missing.

```
Private Sub cmdOK_Click()
    If bAddedHistory And bAddedSalary Then
        cProcedures.All = vAll
        cProcedures.Refresh
        vAll = cProcedures.All 'get it back and check if employee id <>0
        If vAll(7) = 0 Then
            MsgBox "New employee not loaded!"
Exit Sub
    Else
        lEmployeeId = vAll(7)
        bAddedHistory = False 'prevent from adding twice
        bAddedSalary = False
        bNeedsSalary = False 'no need to add records
        bNeedsHistory = False
        lblStatus = "" 'no need to prompt
    End If
    Else
        SetStatus
```

```
    If bNeedsSalary Or bNeedsHistory Then Beep 'when old employee still beep
    End If
    RaiseEvent TransComplete(lEmployeeId) '*
End Sub
```

The `Form_Activate` sub is where we get the information of `EmployeeId` and `PersonId` from `frmPeople`. This is also where we `Redim` the `vAll` variant (not redim preserve because we want to also clear it) and set the `bAddedHistory`, `bAddedSalary` to `False`. The added lines are in highlight within a highlight.

```
Private Sub Form_Activate()
    lblName = frmPeople.cboPerson.Text
    lblDOB = frmPeople.txtDOB
    lEmployeeId = frmPeople.EmployeeId
    lPersonId = frmPeople.PersonId '*
    ReDim vAll(0 To 7)
    vAll(0) = lPersonId '*
    bAddedHistory = False '*
    bAddedSalary = False '*
    ClearScreen
    If lEmployeeId <> 0 Then
        PopulateForm
    End If
End Sub
```

In the `Form_Load` sub add the following line. It will connect the `cProcedures` object to the database.

```
cProcedures.ConnectX cConnection '*
```

The `StoreSalary` and `StoreHistory` subs below were taught to work two ways: One with a pre-existing employee (non zero) and once with a new employee. In the first case they pass the info to the proper class, in the second they pass the same info into the `vAll` variant array to be passed later into the `cProcedures` object. They also set the `bAdded` conditions to `True`.

```
Private Sub StoreHistory()
    If lEmployeeId <> 0 Then
        vJAll(1) = lEmployeeId
        vJAll(2) = txtJobCode
        vJAll(3) = ConvertDate(txtJDateStarted.Text)
        vJAll(4) = ConvertDate(txtJDateEnded.Text)
        cJobHistory.All = vJAll
    Else
        vAll(1) = txtJobCode '*
        vAll(2) = ConvertDate(txtJDateStarted.Text) '*
        vAll(3) = ConvertDate(txtJDateEnded.Text) '*
        bAddedHistory = True
    End If
End Sub
```

```
Private Sub StoreSalary()
    If lEmployeeId <> 0 Then
        vSAll(1) = lEmployeeId
        vSAll(2) = CDbl(txtIncome)
        vSAll(3) = ConvertDate(txtSDateStarted.Text)
        vSAll(4) = ConvertDate(txtSDateEnded.Text)
        cSalary.All = vSAll
```

```
      Else
          vAll(4) = CDbl(txtIncome) '*
          vAll(5) = ConvertDate(txtSDateStarted.Text) '*
          vAll(6) = ConvertDate(txtSDateEnded.Text) '*
          vAll(7) = 0 '*
          bAddedSalary = True
      End If
End Sub
```

The two cmdXAdd subs (X = J and X = S) go hand-in-hand with their respective Store routines. If an old employee they use the old classes to add a JobHistory or Salary row (as the case may be). Otherwise the call to the Store routine fills the vAll for the stored procedure.

```
Private Sub cmdJAdd_Click()
    StoreHistory
    If lEmployeeId <> 0 Then '*
        cJobHistory.AddNew
        cJobHistory.Refresh
        SetStatus
    End If
End Sub
```

```
Private Sub cmdSAdd_Click()
    StoreSalary
    If lEmployeeId <> 0 Then '*
        cSalary.AddNew
        cSalary.Refresh
        SetStatus
    End If
End Sub
```

Changes to modGeneral

I've added the various Oracle OO4O constants to the modGeneral. This makes it possible to use them in the code. Here is the complete code:

```
Option Explicit
''''''''''''''''''''''''''''''
' Oracle Objects for OLE global constant file.
' This file can be loaded into a code module.
''''''''''''''''''''''''''''''

'Editmode property values
' These are intended to match similar constants in the
' Visual Basic file CONSTANT.TXT
Global Const ORADATA_EDITNONE = 0
Global Const ORADATA_EDITMODE = 1
Global Const ORADATA_EDITADD = 2

'Parameter Types
Global Const ORAPARM_INPUT = 1
Global Const ORAPARM_OUTPUT = 2
Global Const ORAPARM_BOTH = 3

'Parameter Status
Global Const ORAPSTAT_INPUT = &H1&
Global Const ORAPSTAT_OUTPUT = &H2&
```

```
Global Const ORAPSTAT_AUTOENABLE = &H4&
Global Const ORAPSTAT_ENABLE = &H8&

'CreateDynaset Method Options
Global Const ORADYN_DEFAULT = &H0&
Global Const ORADYN_NO_AUTOBIND = &H1&
Global Const ORADYN_NO_BLANKSTRIP = &H2&
Global Const ORADYN_READONLY = &H4&
Global Const ORADYN_NOCACHE = &H8&
Global Const ORADYN_ORAMODE = &H10&
Global Const ORADYN_DBDEFAULT = &H20&
Global Const ORADYN_NO_MOVEFIRST = &H40&
Global Const ORADYN_DIRTY_WRITE = &H80&

'CreateSql Method options
Global Const ORASQL_NO_AUTOBIND = &H1&
Global Const ORASQL_FAILEXEC = &H2&

'OpenDatabase Method Options
Global Const ORADB_ORAMODE = &H1&
Global Const ORADB_NOWAIT = &H2&
Global Const ORADB_DBDEFAULT = &H4&
Global Const ORADB_DEFERRED = &H8&

'Parameter Types (ServerType)
Global Const ORATYPE_VARCHAR2 = 1
Global Const ORATYPE_NUMBER = 2
Global Const ORATYPE_SINT = 3
Global Const ORATYPE_FLOAT = 4
Global Const ORATYPE_STRING = 5
Global Const ORATYPE_VARCHAR = 9
Global Const ORATYPE_DATE = 12
Global Const ORATYPE_UINT = 68
Global Const ORATYPE_CHAR = 96
Global Const ORATYPE_CHARZ = 97
Global Const ORATYPE_CURSOR = 102

Public Function FormatDate(ByVal dDate As Date, sFormat As String) As String
    If dDate = #1/1/1800# Then
        FormatDate = ""
    Else
        FormatDate = Format$(dDate, sFormat)
    End If
End Function

Public Function ConvertDate(sDate As String) As Date
    If Trim$(RemoveDashes(sDate, "/")) = "" Then
        ConvertDate = #1/1/1800#
    Else
        ConvertDate = CDate(sDate)
    End If
End Function

Public Function RemoveDashes(ByVal sIn As String, ByVal sDash As String) As
String
'Remove all hyphens from a string (SSN or USMLE_ID) or slashes from a Date
    Dim lPos As Long, sTemp As String, lLenDash As Long
    lLenDash = Len(sDash)
    sTemp = sIn
    lPos = 99
```

```
    Do Until lPos = 0
        lPos = InStr(1, sTemp, sDash)
        If lPos <> 0 Then
            sTemp = Left$(sTemp, lPos - 1) & Mid$(sTemp, lPos + lLenDash)
        End If
    Loop
    RemoveDashes = sTemp
End Function

Public Function ConvertName(sName As String) As String
    ConvertName = UCase(Left$(sName, 1)) & LCase(Mid$(sName, 2))
End Function
```

These changes do not hurt the ADO version of the modGeneral, but make it slightly bigger. I suggest you leave the ADO version as is.

That's it for the OO4O version.

The ADO Version

Again we are going to create the ADO version of clsProcedures, and make changes to the forms. The changes made to the forms are absolutely identical to those we've just finished in the OO4O version. No difference whatsoever. With this covered let us just build the class.

Again, the data class is very simple. As you have already seen in Chapter 12 (if you did not plan to read it later) all we have to do is to set parameters to the stored procedure in the exact order in which they are needed. The SQL is very simple. It does not need any place holders (?), only the procedure name. We set the parameters and in the Refresh method execute the command.

Here it is:

```
'Class Name is: Procedures
Option Explicit
Private mcConnection As clsConnection
Private mADOConnection As ADODB.Connection 'Required for connection to
clsConnection
Private mProcCmd As ADODB.Command
'** The procedure statements
Private msSQL As String
'* Parameters
'* Procedure - in order of the stored Procedure
Private mProcPrmPersonId As ADODB.Parameter
Private mProcPrmJobCode As ADODB.Parameter
Private mProcPrmJStartDate As ADODB.Parameter
Private mProcPrmJEndDate As ADODB.Parameter
Private mProcPrmIncome As ADODB.Parameter
Private mProcPrmSStartDate As ADODB.Parameter
Private mProcPrmSEndDate As ADODB.Parameter
Private mProcPrmEmployeeId As ADODB.Parameter
'** Class variables
Private mvAll As Variant
```

```
Private Sub Class_Initialize()
'** Initialize Class Variables
    ReDim mvAll(0 To 7) 'we have 8 properties rolled into the array
'Make SQL for running the proc. All you need is that procs name, no ? no ()
    msSQL = "New_Employee"
End Sub

Public Sub ConnectX(ByVal NewValue As clsConnection) 'Required for
                                                     'connection to
                                                     'clsConnection

    Set mcConnection = NewValue

'our class relies on an already open ADOConnection.

    Set mADOConnection = mcConnection.ADOConnection
    Set mProcCmd = New ADODB.Command 'needs parameters beyond cl_auth_id
    With mProcCmd
        .ActiveConnection = mADOConnection
        .CommandType = adCmdStoredProc
        .CommandText = msSQL
        Set mProcPrmPersonId = .CreateParameter("pPersonId", adDouble, _
            adParamInput)
        .Parameters.Append mProcPrmPersonId
        Set mProcPrmJobCode = .CreateParameter("pJobCode", adVarChar, _
            adParamInput, 5, "")
        .Parameters.Append mProcPrmJobCode
        Set mProcPrmJStartDate = .CreateParameter("pJStartDate", _
            adDBTimeStamp, adParamInput)
        .Parameters.Append mProcPrmJStartDate
        Set mProcPrmJEndDate = .CreateParameter("pJEndDate", adDBTimeStamp, _
            adParamInput)
        .Parameters.Append mProcPrmJEndDate
        Set mProcPrmIncome = .CreateParameter("pIncome", adDouble, _
            adParamInput)
        .Parameters.Append mProcPrmIncome
        Set mProcPrmSStartDate = .CreateParameter("pSStartDate", _
            adDBTimeStamp, adParamInput)
        .Parameters.Append mProcPrmSStartDate
        Set mProcPrmSEndDate = .CreateParameter("pSEndDate", adDBTimeStamp, _
            adParamInput)
        .Parameters.Append mProcPrmSEndDate
        Set mProcPrmEmployeeId = .CreateParameter("pEmployeeId", adDouble, _
            adParamInputOutput)
        .Parameters.Append mProcPrmEmployeeId
    End With
End Sub

Public Sub Refresh()
'** Set parameters and re-run the procedure
    mProcPrmPersonId.Value = mvAll(0)
    mProcPrmJobCode.Value = mvAll(1)
    mProcPrmJStartDate.Value = mvAll(2)
    mProcPrmJEndDate.Value = mvAll(3)
    mProcPrmIncome.Value = mvAll(4)
    mProcPrmSStartDate.Value = mvAll(5)
    mProcPrmSEndDate.Value = mvAll(6)
    mProcPrmEmployeeId.Value = 0
    mProcCmd.Execute
    mvAll(7) = mProcPrmEmployeeId.Value
End Sub
```

```
Public Property Get All() As Variant
    All = mvAll
End Property

Public Property Let All(ByVal vNewValue As Variant)
    mvAll = vNewValue
End Property
```

The whole code is on the WROX site. You'll find 4 subdirectories, one for each style: OO4O with transactions, ADO with transactions, OO4O with stored procedures, and ADO with stored procedures.

Summary

We have built an application using OO4O and then ADO. We've built it using VB controlled transactions (in both OO4O and ADO) and using a stored procedure in conjunction with standard data classes. All told, four major ways to make VB and Oracle perform the same task.

We've also seen that it is not an insurmountable task. After doing this project you'll feel a little better about the fact that you can convert a project from OO4O to ADO and vice-versa, and that it is not going to be the end of the world to do so. To me it means that even though ADO and Oracle are not yet working together fully, a fact that tilts the balance towards OO4O, I can later move to ADO and its asynchronous advantages when it learns to do all that we need. This move is not going to be as painful as you feared.

I hope that you have also learned the advantages of OOP and gained another level of expertise in using it.

The final section of the book will give you some insight into the world of VB COM data and business objects. We can host such objects on the middle-tier as part of a multi-tier application, using Oracle.

Section V

Moving on up: N-Tier Solutions

15

COM and Middle-Tier Business Objects

In this final section of the book we'll be taking a step back from our detailed discussion of working with Oracle from previous chapters, to look at the overall picture of a multi-tiered application that uses Oracle. Our example will be a fictional business, the Can Do Bancorp. In this chapter we'll see how to develop middle-tier business objects for this company, and in the next chapter we'll develop middle-tier data objects. Finally we'll bring Microsoft Transaction Server into the equation, to look at how we use MTS with middle-tier objects

This chapter is going to provide a solid foundation for business objects on the middle tier. We are going to develop middle-tier business objects for Can Do Bancorp's credit card processing application. Can Do Bancorp (CDB) does many things you would expect from a bank. They offer checking accounts, ATMs, credit cards, and loans. Our application will focus only on a subset of the credit card operations. Obviously a non-fictional bank application would do much more than the above, but for this chapter's purposes we have stuck with some basics to keep the example simple.

The application that we will write in this chapter will not be fully three-tiered at this point due to the fact that we are only focusing on half of the middle-tier. So, from a logical perspective, it would still be considered a two-tier application (Client-Server). However, we have started the process of breaking it up by creating business objects, which is a first step in re-engineering an application for multi-tiered (re-)development.

We're also going to look at a mailing list application in the later part of this chapter to see an implementation style for collection classes that Microsoft calls the "House of Bricks", due to its natural resistance to erroneous object insertions. While we will not cover collection classes in great detail in any of the remaining chapters, this exposure will give the reader a perspective as to how object hierarchies can be constructed within the middle tier.

A Little Background

Before we delve deeper into our business objects, let's take a step back and cover some ground. If you've heard colleagues talk about three-tier, n-tier, or multi-tier applications, they're all talking about the same thing. (I will use the term **multi-tier** for the rest of this discussion). It is a logical concept that breaks an application into three layers or tiers, the **presentation** or **user interface** layer, the **business services** layer, and the **data services** layer. Since it is a logical concept, then it stands to reason that the actual physical layout of the application may or may not span multiple machines.

The diagram below shows how a multi-tier application that uses Oracle would be configured:

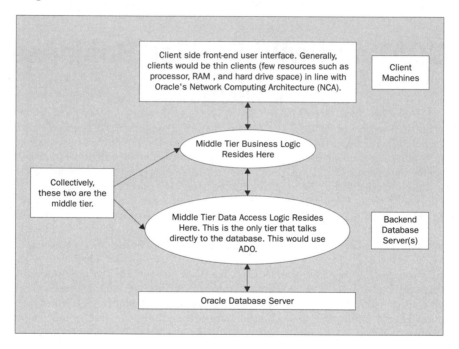

In general, the biggest overall advantage to the multi-tier architecture is **scalability**. Because the application's logic is spread out and because multiple machines can support the middle-tier services, there is no need for code changes as demand increases. Hardware alone can handle the load. While this is something that would make sense to any mainframe programmer, it is a "new" concept to PC applications.

There are other advantages as well such as availability, portability to the web, and (as machines are added) either static or dynamic load balancing.

Another big advantage, which is especially cost-effective for large companies, is the use of **thin** clients on the presentation side. Since client machines are relieved of the bulk of the processing duty, they can be less resource-intensive. This model of low-cost, resource-scarce clients is called the "thin client" architecture, versus the traditional or "fat client" architecture that permeates the business community today.

In addition to using thin clients, there is a maintainability and extensibility advantage to be gained. Since business objects and data objects reside on centrally located machines, the need to re-install "new and improved" components is greatly reduced.

There is, however, a downside to all of this. Applications developed for the multi-tier architecture usually require more time to develop. There are many reasons for this including the additional work of providing for and testing with Microsoft Transaction Server and adapting to a new technical model that requires a paradigm shift on the part of application developers. The additional resource needs associated with multi-tier development can be reduced if the business objects are re-used in later applications. The cost increase on a single application use can be significant – adding an extra 50% to the number of man-hours (and associated cost) to bring the project to completion. This chapter and the next two hope to lay a solid foundation for any developer wishing to pursue a multi-tier model.

COM vs. CORBA

Many developers, for various reasons, love to hate Microsoft. In some circles, it is quite fashionable to do so. This is not the case with me. However, despite that view, I feel that I can be objective in my review of competing technologies. The **Component Object Model** (**COM**) is an architecture for component technology that was created and is being pushed primarily by Microsoft. It specifies how *binary* code components should talk and how they should interact. It is just as much about component behavior as it is about programming and encapsulation in its effective use. Plus, because it's a binary standard, the language used by the developer is irrelevant to the application requesting a service from a code component. Many people, due to their dislike of the software refuse to objectively consider this technology coming out of Redmond.

The **Common Object Request Broker Architecture** (**CORBA**) is a competing standard. It is supported by an industry consortium (the Object Management Group or OMG) and several industry heavyweights, which include Sun, IBM, Oracle, and Sybase. It is promoted as an object standard and an alternative to COM and does many of the same things. In all honesty CORBA existed well before there was a stable COM and COM has been through many iterations. Currently, products from Oracle and Sybase continue to support CORBA as the main mechanism driving their application servers. Oracle, in fact, has made it the centerpiece of its Network Computing Architecture (NCA). Microsoft, however, owns the desktop market, and has put a goodly number of servers in corporate computer rooms, and has built MTS around its COM component architecture and operating systems.

From what I've seen the architectures, while similar in many ways, are incompatible together. As another review of CORBA prior to writing this chapter served to reinforce my original belief that COM is the better approach, I'm going to stick with that component model.

I do want to stress an important factor about the CORBA-COM debate. It is absolutely true that COM is a Windows-only solution whereas CORBA is more of a platform independent solution. Since Visual Basic is a Microsoft product, and since COM seems to me to be a better standard, and since it is my belief that over time Microsoft will win this battle, it behooves me to discuss COM in this area. But, I wanted to make it clear that there is a competing standard, and that some people believe that it is at least as good and possibly better (see my references at the end of the chapter for more about this topic) than COM. In the end, it is my strong belief that some people are not objectively (no pun intended) considering all their options.

The Can Do Bancorp Application

Now let's get to the heart of this chapter – the CDB Application and its business objects. It is interesting to note how complex even seemingly simple business concepts such as credit cards are. Some rules are obvious such as: you can't buy/use the card in excess of its limit, or accounts that have late payments are assessed a late charge. Others, though, are much more complicated such as: at what point is a person "qualified" to receive a credit card, what credit limit is appropriate, and what interest rate is the account given. All of these questions are of the type that are best solved by middle-tier business objects. Why is this? Because they are the most likely to change, and before there were code components, would require a recompile and re-installation on possibly hundreds of desktops.

One of the functions of CDB is to accept applications and potentially grant Credit Card accounts. If an account is granted, the CDB application must also set a credit limit for the individual. As you can imagine, there are a number of business rules that are tied to these actions. The process is basically as follows: a customer applies to CDB for a credit account. This customer may or may not be an existing customer of the bank. If that person is already a customer all s/he needs to do is to fill out a short questionnaire and sign a release allowing you to check his/her credit record. If the person is not a customer, they also must provide the demographic data that you need such as SSN, Name, Address, Phone, Date of Birth, etc. After this step has been completed, the business rules take over.

The requestor's credit will be checked and "scored". For those who are not in the financial services industry, this is a common practice. The bank will decide what score will automatically deny an applicant, what score will automatically grant credit to an applicant and what score may fall into the "gray zone" and be reviewed by a loan officer. For the sake of simplicity, the application takes a binary approach to whether credit is issued and so no loan officer ever needs to be involved. What scores are accepted or declined is an oft-changing rule subject to natural ebb and flow. When the economic cycle is in full swing it is easy for banks to relax their rules a little. Just as often, when the economy is in rough water or contracting, most banks will increase the requirements on all types of credit accounts.

It is also true that the interest rate(s) is often a variable. Many are now set to the prime rate or the London Interbank Rate (as published in the *Wall Street Journal*) plus some percentage. To complicate matters a little more, a fixed rate is applied to the base rate to arrive at an actual interest rate and the fixed rate is often dependent on other factors such as the income of the individual, the offer they are responding to, their credit worthiness, etc. Finally they are assigned a credit limit which is a function of both the credit score and their income. I have chosen to leave the interest rate function out as it would have proven much more complicated than needs to be covered here. But I do want you to consider why this too is a "textbook case" for a business object. I chose, instead, to focus on the "set credit limit" rule in this small "sample" application.

I have to create an Oracle Database to show how the COM objects for CDB work, and you will find the script, COM_XMPL.SQL, on the WROX site along with the rest of the code from this book. You also will need the CDB1.zip project to follow along with the examples. We'll talk a little more about that SQL script in the next chapter.

Let's start writing code. Open the application that you should have from the WROX site (CDB_1.ZIP will contain the project as it should be for this section). Open the modMain module and look at the code in the CreateOracleConnection sub. Make certain that you are using a valid username, password and data source. I chose to create a new user CanDoMan with an acceptable number of rights. You can choose to use the same system or your own. You must make sure that you have full rights to creating, deleting, and altering tables along with creating, deleting, and altering sequences; also make sure that you can create a session and select, insert, update, and delete from all your tables. If you are using a captive Oracle 8i database like I am, you can use my CreateUser.SQL script at the WROX site as long as you're logged on as SYSTEM. Security is very different in Oracle 8i than in any previous version of Oracle, so if you're not using 8i you may need to talk to your DBA to find out what privileges you need to have complete flexibility in a test area.

The user CanDoMan establishes a database connection early and holds it throughout the life of the application. This is the "standard" way that most two-tier applications work. Multi-tier objects can use MTS connection pooling in which case connections are held only long enough to extract the data and are then re-cycled into the available pool. Keep this in mind, because it is an important concept for later. Expand the zip in a clean directory and double click on the CDBCore.vbp project.

Now, with the project open, you are ready for the next step. Right now a goodly part of the UI exists, but no business rules. So, let's consider what happens when Bill Smith applies for a credit card. Bill is an existing customer, so we can bring him up in the Find dialog by clicking Find, entering Smith in the name text box and hitting tab. Several names will appear in the list box and let's double-click Bill's account (the first one). Good. Now we're looking at Bill's Customer record (presumably from another account with the bank) and he wants to apply for a credit card.

The Scoring Algorithm

Many factors are taken into account when an individual applies for credit. The scoring algorithm evaluates how long the person has lived where they are now, how long they've worked where they are now, how many accounts they have and the current balances, the individual's credit report, and even whether or not they want credit insurance. All of these factors contribute to the scoring algorithm. To save time, I have created a table in Oracle called CreditScore, which links a SSN to a bogus score. To make the call a little more realistic, you must pass in the Date of Birth since most credit reporting agencies will require this to run a report on a customer. You'll need to stop or close the application at this point, because we're going to write the ScoreApplication business function as an ActiveX "In Process" DLL server which is a COM component.

Creating the ScoreApplication Component

Click File | Add Project and you will see the Add Project Dialog shown below:

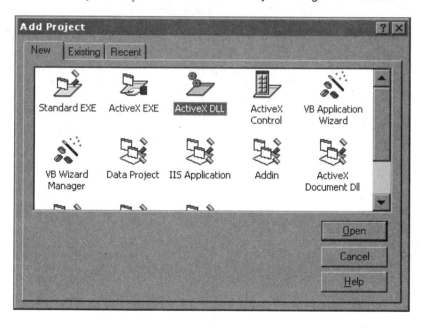

Select the ActiveX DLL icon from this box, and click Open. You will have a blank code pane in front of you. We need to create a series of module-level private variables, which serve to hold the internal, private copy of the properties, some enumerated error constants (note that in an actual application I would have used a Visual Basic Enum), and a few business-related constants.

```
Option Explicit

' Place holder for the properties
Private mdatDateOfBirth As Date
Private mstrSSN As String
Private mintScore As Integer

' Error Constants including module name
Private Const mintSSN_ERROR As Integer = 1000
Private Const mintSTATE_ERROR As Integer = 1001
Private Const mstrCLASS_NAME As String = "CreditScore"

' These are "likely to change" business constants
Private Const mcurPROG_MAXIMUM As Currency = 15000
Private Const mintMAX_SCORE As Integer = 15
Private Const mdblCUT_OFF As Double = 0.8
Private Const mintMINIMUM_SCORE As Integer = 5
```

We'll go over what these do in just a minute. Before we get ahead of ourselves, we have a little housekeeping to do. ActiveX DLL Servers are separate projects as far as VB is concerned, so the ADO 2.1 library must be checked in Project | References specifically for the DLL too. Secondly, because it is a separate project, we'll need to save soon to make sure that we have the structural changes on disk (and to make it easier to save as we move forward). However, before you save, please make sure that the following are properly set up for you new Active X DLL project:

❑ The Reference to ADO 2.1 is checked.

❑ The class is named clsCreditScore.

❑ The project containing the class is named CDB_Server.

❑ In CDB_Core go to Project | References again. Right after all the checked items, you should see CDB_Server. Check it.

❑ Right click the CDB_CORE project in the project view window and click on Set as StartUp.

❑ Finally when you're prompted to save the project group, make the name CDB_COM_PRJ. It will have the extension .vbg added automatically.

Most of the list above is pretty straightforward. If you haven't worked with project groups before, you may not have known about the reference needing to be set for each project individually or the other project being designated using the Set as StartUp option. The references line item is only needed for members of the current project group that use additional controls or components while they function as server/controls for the active, startup project. The option to Set as StartUp allows you to assign startup to a project that essentially "drives" the others. With most "in process" projects such as ActiveX DLL servers and OCX controls, you will want your core application to be the startup so that you can test your component and debug it at the same time. In fact, it is puzzling that Visual Basic will allow you to set those other projects to startup because it doesn't make much sense. They can't own process or stack space or have the startup bootstrap code attached.

Variables for our Component

Once you've completed the above task list and saved your project group, let's get back to our `CDB_server` component and examine why all these variables are needed. If you're somewhat familiar with ActiveX and COM technology, which I'm going to assume for this discussion, those lines won't look so bad. The first set of private variables is intended to hold the properties of the class/component. The second set of constants is intended to support the error messages within the class. Finally, the third set is also a series of constants and is a way to get at frequently changed business rules. I chose this approach because of its clarity, but other options included keeping the rule and constants in a table in Oracle, which is an extremely good choice, or in some kind of central file. It is just as valid to save these constants in a table or a file. The idea is to physically separate that which is likely to change from that which is not as likely to change. This overall concept is part of encapsulation which is enhanced by the use of binary components and is a large part of the focus of Object Oriented Analysis and Design (OOAD).

There also is a change that must be made in the **Apply for Credit** button on the customer form. The code is shown below and followed by an explanation:

```
Private Sub cmdApplyForCredit_Click()
    ' This will call the credit scoring mechanism
    Dim poScoreObject As clsCreditScore

    On Error GoTo ErrorHandler
    ' set aside memoryspace for the server
    Set poScoreObject = New clsCreditScore
    poScoreObject.DateOfBirth = adoPrimaryRS!BirthDate
    poScoreObject.Social = adoPrimaryRS![SSN/TaxID]

    Call poScoreObject.ScoreApplication(gcnnConnection)

    mintScore = poScoreObject.Score
    MsgBox (adoPrimaryRS!FirstName & " " & adoPrimaryRS!LastName & _
        " scored " & mintScore)
    MsgBox ("Congratulations, you've been accepted for a Can Do Bancorp" & _
        "Uranium Card" _
        & Chr$(10) & "Your credit limit will be " & _
        Str(poScoreObject.SetCreditLimit(mintScore, _
        adoPrimaryRS!AnnualIncome)))
    Exit Sub
ErrorHandler:
    MsgBox ("Scoring server failed.")
End Sub
```

We start out by declaring an object of the type of our ActiveX DLL server and using an error handler to trap unexpected errors. Then we set a few properties that will be used in the scoring and we call the `ScoreApplication` method. Note the comments about the roundtrips. This is an example of the paradigm shift involved in multi-tier applications. We, as programmers, must move away from properties and begin thinking in terms of services and methods and reducing network roundtrips. Finally we give the applicant a "Uranium" card and assign a credit limit based on the `SetCreditLimit` method of our `CreditScore` class.

Also there's an event definition that belongs after the constants we went over in the `clsCreditScore`. To explain why that was provided, imagine how, in a busy office environment, there could be problems dialing out or gathering all the data needed from the credit bureaus, etc. The idea of having the operator move forward with additional activities, perhaps even another credit application while the results are being calculated is very appealing. The event allows exactly that kind of functionality.

Sequential Operation

The problem with this idea is that an ActiveX DLL component essentially stops the processing of the application. To understand why this occurs, consider the fact that the architecture used by most computers today relies on the work of the mathematician, John Von Neumann. In his work, the architecture involves a series of sequential operations, and everything that we do on today's PC is sequential. That means that right now I think I'm running my E-mail application, but in reality this PC is "frantically" jumping back and forth between Outlook98 and MS Word (plus Windows NT, Visual Basic, Oracle SQL*Plus, etc.).

When a DLL takes a long time to execute, it essentially locks up the calling process, leaving the application in a kind of "Limbo". The thread that runs the Application is waiting for a "signal" from the thread running in the DLL, that it is complete. We will see later how the multi-tiered approach can help solve this problem, which is also called a Von Neumann Bottleneck, with connection pooling and COM instancing capabilities.

To illustrate this bottleneck concept, go to your `CDB_Server` project in the project group and add a module. Insert this code into the module:

```
Option Explicit

' API function to count X milliseconds
Public Declare Sub Sleep Lib "kernel32" _
        (ByVal lngMilliseconds As Long)
```

This references a Win32 API call that causes the caller to wait. I want to "simulate" a long-running process such as the credit scoring which might have to add up a series of questions/points, dial out on a phone line, and wait for another application on the receiving end to do some additional work.

I also added a `WaitAWhile` function in the class code module and I added a **Test** command button in the customer form. I made this the third button that you see in the screenshot below. All of these together will demonstrate the waiting concept. Go ahead and add this, run the application and click on the **test** button and see what happens. You'll end up waiting 20 seconds to see the **Wait Complete** message box:

```
' This is in clsCreditScore
Public Sub WaitAWhile(pintSeconds As Integer)
    Call Sleep(pintSeconds * 1000)
End Sub

' This is a third button in frmCustomers
Private Sub cmdTest_Click()
    Dim poScoreObject As clsCreditScore
```

```
    On Error GoTo ErrorHandler
    ' set aside memory space for the server
    Set poScoreObject = New clsCreditScore
    poScoreObject.WaitAWhile (20)
    MsgBox ("Wait Complete!")
    Exit Sub
ErrorHandler:
    MsgBox ("Problem in cmdTest_Click sub")

End Sub
```

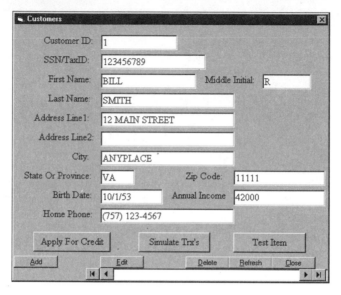

In a few minutes we'll delve further into how to deal with the waiting problem, but before we get too far off on that track, let's complete the class that we were working on.

Methods for our Component

As it stands now, there are four methods that will reside in `clsCreditScore`. They are `ScoreApplication`, `CreditLimit`, `AcceptDecline`, and `WaitAWhile`.

We've already covered `WaitAWhile` so let's look at `ScoreApplication`. This will do the "dirty work" of performing the actual scoring. The code for that is shown below. Also, I chose to pass our global connection into the method (which is just a public procedure in this class module) as opposed to making it a property of the object because of convenience.

In the real world, this call would need no connection and the function would take a tremendous amount of questionnaire data into its credit scoring system. This is another advantage of component architecture so a property would be a poor choice since this serves to illustrate yet another advantage of the multi-tiered technique. The application only cares that I get a score from the function. Other business rules will use the score but the actual calculation process is hidden (encapsulated in OO parlance) in this binary component.

```
Public Sub ScoreApplication(cnnConnection As Connection, _
                            Optional strSSN As String = "NULL", _
                            Optional strDOB As String = "NULL")

    Dim prstCreditCheck As Recordset
    Dim pstrSQL As String

    ' I have chosen to propagate the error from the property classes
    On Error GoTo ErrorHandler
    If strSSN <> "NULL" Then
        Social = strSSN
    End If
    If strSSN <> "NULL" Then
        DateOfBirth = strDOB
    End If

    pstrSQL = "SELECT * FROM CREDITSCORE " _
        & "WHERE SSN =" & Str(strSSN)

    Set prstCreditCheck = New Recordset
    prstCreditCheck.Open pstrSQL, cnnConnection, _
        adOpenDynamic, adLockReadOnly, adCmdText
    If Not prstCreditCheck.EOF Then
        prstCreditCheck.MoveFirst
        mintScore = prstCreditCheck!Score
    Else
        mintScore = 0
    End If

    Exit Sub
ErrorHandler:
        Err.Raise vbObjectError + mintSTATE_ERROR, _
            mstrCLASS_NAME, "Either SSN or DOB missing" _
& "or incorrect."

End Sub
```

Let's look at this function and what it does. First, the definition is unusual. I have two optional parameters, but for some odd reason I have defaulted them to the string value NULL. The parameters themselves were made optional as both a convenience to the coder(s) and also to illustrate some concepts later on. I take the practical view that unexpected results are "bugs", thus the NULL string is due to what I consider a "bug" in Visual Basic. I have talked to a member of Microsoft's Visual Basic testing team about this issue, although she did not consider it a "bug".

Originally, optional parameters were required to be the Visual Basic data type variant. Any good VB programmer knows the problems with variants. They are costly in terms of memory and they allow mistakes to enter the code through bad parameters (wrong type, ridiculous values, etc.). In Visual Basic 6 (and Version 5 too), you can type your optional parameters, which catches some errors "up front" when you compile, but there is a price to pay for this convenience.

The price is that you can no longer use the `IsMissing()` function. It will fail 100% of the time on optional parameters that are not `variants`. I was shocked to see the results of this discovery. So you have a couple of choices: default to something that would never occur, or use a variant. There is one other possible solution, you can check the typed variables for `vbNullString` if they are `string` and `0` if they are `long` or `integers`, but I assumed that these would be within the realm of possible values. I feel that no matter what the cost, I would much rather catch an error up front rather than in testing (either my own or that of other team members), so I use the default method. I suspect that Microsoft will eventually close the loophole in this issue, but be forewarned – you need to remember this issue.

Error Handling

Moving on in the code, you see that I have implemented an error handler. Microsoft states (and my experience tells me) that you should handle an error as close to the problem as possible, but in this case, you need to propagate an error up the chain. So, if one of the property settings fails, you will see a `STATE_ERROR` message, which is: Either SSN or DOB is missing or incorrect. Again, for this test, this is sufficient. In reality, an error could occur in data access and there would be many more parameters that could have problems. The rest of the code is basic VB and data access except for the error handler.

Error Handling is a concept that truly is not emphasized enough in the VB community. When the error handler here is triggered and handled, the error state is cleared. This can be a pivotal case if an error occurs in the handler itself – it can wipe out the original cause of the error. In fact, if you implement a global error handler for your project one of the first things you need to do is to turn error handling off (`On Error Goto 0`) or skip the bad line (`On Error Resume Next`). If you don't, you risk losing the valuable error information you are trying to access. I could have made the code "smarter" and allowed it to propagate the initial error (which would have merit in the general case that I require 10 values for scoring), but for this example producing a general, somewhat meaningful value was sufficient.

Business Rules

Let's look at the last method in the class. The code is presented below:

```
Public Function SetCreditLimit(intScore As Integer, _
                               curIncome As Currency) As Currency
    Dim pdblPercent As Double
    Dim pcurLimit As Currency


    pdblPercent = (CDbl(intScore) / CDbl(mintMAX_SCORE))
    If (pdblPercent > mdblCUT_OFF) Then
        pcurLimit = mcurPROG_MAXIMUM
    Else
        pcurLimit = pdblPercent * mcurPROG_MAXIMUM
    End If

    SetCreditLimit = pcurLimit
End Function
```

This is another good example of a business rule. What this function does is that it tries to set a reasonable credit limit based on the applicant's credit score. If s/he scored above the cut off point, s/he would get the maximum credit limit allowed. Otherwise, the applicant will get a "pro-rated" portion based on their score. From this example, you can see why a table would serve well as a repository for the fixed rules such as the maximum credit limit for the program and the cut off point.

There also is another function that is missing and in some ways it is the most important. That function is the `AcceptDecline` function. It will grade the score and "make the call" as to whether an individual is a good or bad credit risk. We need to add some code to the class module and then refine the process in the customer screen. First add the code below to the class module:

```
Public Function IsAccepted(intScore As Integer) _
        As Boolean

    If (intScore > mintMINIMUM_SCORE) Then
        IsAccepted = True
        ' generate card request
    Else
        IsAccepted = False
        ' generate declined letter in accordance
        ' with the fair credit in lending act
    End If

End Function
```

Then make sure that you modify the code in the customer form's **Apply** button as follows:

```
Private Sub cmdApplyForCredit_Click()
    ' This will call the credit scoring mechanism
    Dim poScoreObject As clsCreditScore

    On Error GoTo ErrorHandler
    ' set aside memory space for the server
    Set poScoreObject = New clsCreditScore
    poScoreObject.DateOfBirth = adoPrimaryRS!BirthDate
    poScoreObject.Social = adoPrimaryRS![SSN/TaxID]

    'The best way of handling this is to pass the B-Date and SSN in
    'the procedure to reduce roundtrips on the network
    Call poScoreObject.ScoreApplication(gcnnConnection)

    mintScore = poScoreObject.Score
    MsgBox (adoPrimaryRS!FirstName & " " & adoPrimaryRS!LastName & _
    " scored " & mintScore)
    If poScoreObject.IsAccepted(poScoreObject.Score) Then
        MsgBox ("Congratualions, you've been accepted for a Can" & _
            "Do Bancorp Uranium Card" _
            & Chr$(10) & "Your credit limit will be " & _
            Str(poScoreObject.SetCreditLimit(mintScore, _
            adoPrimaryRS!AnnualIncome)))
    Else .
        MsgBox ("We're sorry, but you were declined at this time.")
    End If
    Exit Sub
ErrorHandler:
    MsgBox ("Scoring server failed.")
End Sub
```

This enforces the rules as we have envisioned them:

❑ Apply for card supplying at least a questionnaire and release

❑ Questionnaire and credit history are scored

❑ Score is evaluated for acceptance

❑ Even if you're accepted, you may not receive the maximum credit limit

All of these are performed in one simple binary component that could be completely reworked and replaced without making changes to the client application. Let me restate because it is a critically important concept, that I can completely change the criteria for granting accounts or credit limits and expect that the client application will not change or will change only minimally. The only change would be at the client side (with this code) or at the application server (MTS) as we will see later.

Now I have one more somewhat minor point. I said earlier that there was a way around the waiting issue for in process COM components and I want to briefly cover the way. To get out of the "In Proc" limitation you need to go to an "Out of Proc" or ActiveX EXE Server. The next example will more fully address the Active X EXE approach.

Collections and Collection Classes

In the "old days" of programming, we used to talk a lot about the problems of variable memory requirements. For example, say you created a user defined type (UDT) for a person, such as the following code shows, and you know up front that you need 10 "spaces" for sure, but you might need 100 "spaces" based on uncontrollable (or unknown) factors:

```
Type Person
    FirstName As String
    LastName As String
    Address As String
    Address2 As String
    Ciy As String
    State As String
    Zip As String
End Type
```

In this situation, you wouldn't want to create a 100 element array, because for the guaranteed level of 10, that's a lot of wasted resources. In the old days this might have been solved with some sort of linked list and "on the fly" memory allocation scheme. Thankfully, we don't have to work with those kinds of data structures.

Visual Basic provides for a variable memory feature, sometimes called an associative array in other languages, but simply called a **collection** in VB. Collections are interesting because they allow you to manage a variable amount of objects in an application while using familiar array like interface. Another interesting thing is that you can manage the data using a key that is a string and not just a number.

There can be problems however with the implementation of the Collection object. For one, the collection is untyped. While this can come in handy when you want to manage all the controls on the screen, say all textboxes, checkboxes, and labels, for example or all the loaded forms, it can be devestating when you expect a certain type of object and "pop up" with the wrong one. We will examine this in more detail later.

Iterating Through Collections

There is another handy feature of collections that deserves mentioning and that is self-iteration. You can use the For Each... Next operation. Consider the case where you want to take a look at an object that contains another object. For example, recently I had a case where several files needed to be parsed. I chose to keep information about a field that needed to be broken out in an object, aptly named, FieldInfo. I created a collection called FieldInfos that was owned by a the FileInfo object which itself was a member of a FileInfos collection since I had more than one file that needed to be parsed. So the code to display some of the data for me to debug is shown below:

```
Private Sub DebugFieldInfo(oFileInfo As FileInfo)
    Dim oField As FieldInfo

    ' This is a simple function for the developer to
    ' iterate thru the collection and see what's there
    For Each oField In oFileInfo.FieldInfos
        With oField
            Debug.Print .FieldName, .Start, _
                .Length, .DataType, .RuleNumber
        End With
    Next

End Sub
```

The point of this overview was to show what a collection is and what it does and can do for you. But there are some issues that you need to consider. Microsoft uses a house analogy. There is the House of Straw (very unsafe), the House of Sticks (less unsafe), and finally, the House of Bricks (the safest and recommended method). Basically each one has features that affect its safety, and you should use the House of Bricks analogy to get the most of out your applications.

How? The idea behind it is to create a collection "container class" that allows the addition of other objects to be properly typed. In other words, with a regular collection you can add the Car Object to the Major Appliances collection. This goes back to an old concept in programming – Data Types. What sense is there in adding 25 to "hello"? In untyped languages, this can occur. In Visual Basic, in fact, if both variables are declared as variants, you will get "25hello". Never mind that it makes no sense, there is nothing to stop you. This is why Microsoft recommends using the "House of Bricks" implementation. It keeps out the undesired objects, but lets the correct ones in.

A House of Bricks

I have an ActiveX EXE Server that demonstrates a House of Bricks implementation of Mailing Labels (it doesn't actually produce the labels, just stores the info in a collection which could then be written out using the Property Bag object, which is beyond the scope of this discussion). Unzip both MailHOBExe.Zip and MailHOBUI.zip projects from the WROX web site.

This is managed by two instances of Visual Basic, so you will need to have a sufficient amount of memory to work with this. Start by opening the `customer.vbp` project which contains all the code for maintaining the customer collection class. Secondly, open another instance of Visual Basic and load `ExeUI.vbp`. Run the first instance (`customer`). Nothing will appear to happen – just what we wanted. Now go to the second instance of VB and open **Project | References** and de-select **customer**, try to run it (VB will complain about a UDT not being loaded) and then go back in and locate **customer** and re-check it and re-run. The reason for all this "Rube Goldberg" magic is that VB looks in the registry for a Class ID, yet each time we re-run the EXE Server that class ID is regenerated, so the other instance can't find what it needs so it complains. Eventually, when we write a somewhat stable customer EXE Server, we can eliminate this by checking binary compatibility in the **Project | Customer Properties | Component** Tab and selecting the customer.exe. This will keep us set unless we break the interface (by altering the calling conventions of any of the methods).

Let's consider the code from the `customer.exe` project first. There are two classes; the first is mostly shown here. I eliminated several of the property functions since I don't feel they're germane to the discussion:

```
Option Explicit

'local variable(s) to hold property value(s)
Private mvarCustomerName As String 'local copy
Private mvarCustomerAddress1 As String 'local copy
Private mvarCustomerAddress2 As String 'local copy
Private mvarCustomerCity As String 'local copy
Private mvarCustomerState As String 'local copy
Private mvarCustomerCountry As String 'local copy
'To fire this event, use RaiseEvent with the following syntax:
'RaiseEvent Changed(arg1)
Public Event Changed(intItemNumber As Integer)
'To fire this event, use RaiseEvent with the following syntax:
'RaiseEvent LoadComplete(arg1)
Public Event LoadComplete(intItemCount As Integer)
'To fire this event, use RaiseEvent with the following syntax:
'RaiseEvent SaveComplete(arg1)
Public Event SaveComplete(intItemCount As Integer)
'To fire this event, use RaiseEvent with the following syntax:
'RaiseEvent PrintComplete(arg1)
Public Event PrintComplete(intItemCount As Integer)
Private mvarCustomerZip As Long 'local copy

Public Function Search(oCustomerData As CustomerLabel) As Boolean
    'This will return a valid object based on a pattern
End Function

Public Function Sort(oCustomerData As CustomerLabel) As Boolean
    'This will sort based on a field
End Function

Public Property Let CustomerZip(ByVal vData As Long)
'used when assigning a value to the property, on the left side of an assignment.
'Syntax: X.CustomerZip = 5
    mvarCustomerZip = vData
End Property
```

```
Public Property Get CustomerZip() As Long
'used when retrieving value of a property, on the right side of an assignment.
'Syntax: Debug.Print X.CustomerZip
    CustomerZip = mvarCustomerZip
End Property

Public Function PrintCustomer(oCustomerData As CustomerLabel) As Boolean
    'This will print a mailing label
End Function

Public Function SaveCustomer(oCustomerData As CustomerLabel) As Boolean
    'This will save the customer(s) data to a file
End Function

Public Function LoadCustomer(oCustomerData As CustomerLabel) As Boolean
    'This will load the customer(s) data from a file
End Function
```

Several similar boilerplate functions have been removed:

```
Private Sub Class_ReadProperties(PropBag As PropertyBag)
    Dim pintFileNumber As Integer
    Dim pVarContents As Variant
    Dim pbytObject() As Byte

    If FileLen(App.Path & "\Customer.dat") <> 0 Then
        pintFileNumber = FreeFile
        Open App.Path & "\Customer.dat" For Binary As pintFileNumber
        Get #pintFileNumber, , pVarContents
        Close pintFileNumber

        pbytObject = pVarContents
        PropBag.Contents = pbytObject
    End If
End Sub

Private Sub Class_WriteProperties(PropBag As PropertyBag)
    Dim ppbgCustomerLabel As PropertyBag
    Dim pVarContents As Variant
    Dim pintFileNumber As Integer

    ppbgCustomerLabel.WriteProperty "Name", mvarCustomerName
    ppbgCustomerLabel.WriteProperty "Address 1", mvarCustomerAddress1
    ppbgCustomerLabel.WriteProperty "Address 2", mvarCustomerAddress2

    pVarContents = PropBag.Contents
    pintFileNumber = FreeFile
    Open App.Path & "\Customer.dat" For Binary As pintFileNumber
    Put #pintFileNumber, , pVarContents
    Close pintFileNumber
End Sub
```

Basically this is a class that defines the interface and data of the customer object. I went so far as to actually code the Read_Properties and Write_Properties function, but did not test these as they also were not why this example is here. I wanted to show how valuable a collection is. While some things may look a little unfamiliar, you will recognize this as just a class module with a few bells and whistles.

The next class module is much more valuable to our earlier discussion about the House of Bricks. Consider the following code:

```
Option Explicit

'local variable to hold collection
Private mCol As Collection

Public Function Add(CustomerName As String, _
                    CustomerAddress1 As String, _
                    CustomerAddress2 As String, _
                    CustomerCity As String, _
                    CustomerState As String, _
                    CustomerCountry As String, _
                    CustomerZip As Long, _
                    Optional sKey As String) _
                    As CustomerLabel
    'create a new object
    Dim objNewMember As CustomerLabel
    Set objNewMember = New CustomerLabel


    'set the properties passed into the method
    objNewMember.CustomerName = CustomerName
    objNewMember.CustomerAddress1 = CustomerAddress1
    objNewMember.CustomerAddress2 = CustomerAddress2
    objNewMember.CustomerCity = CustomerCity
    objNewMember.CustomerState = CustomerState
    objNewMember.CustomerCountry = CustomerCountry
    objNewMember.CustomerZip = CustomerZip
    If Len(sKey) = 0 Then
        mCol.Add objNewMember
    Else
        mCol.Add objNewMember, sKey
    End If


    'return the object created
    Set Add = objNewMember
    Set objNewMember = Nothing

End Function

Public Property Get Item(vntIndexKey As Variant) As CustomerLabel
    'used when referencing an element in the collection
    'vntIndexKey contains either the Index or Key to the collection,
    'this is why it is declared as a Variant
    'Syntax: Set foo = x.Item(xyz) or Set foo = x.Item(5)
  Set Item = mCol(vntIndexKey)
End Property

Public Property Get Count() As Long
    'used when retrieving the number of elements in the
    'collection. Syntax: Debug.Print x.Count
    Count = mCol.Count
End Property
```

```
Public Sub Remove(vntIndexKey As Variant)
    'used when removing an element from the collection
    'vntIndexKey contains either the Index or Key, which is why
    'it is declared as a Variant
    'Syntax: x.Remove(xyz)

    mCol.Remove vntIndexKey
End Sub

Public Property Get NewEnum() As IUnknown
    'this property allows you to enumerate
    'this collection with the For...Each syntax
    Set NewEnum = mCol.[_NewEnum]
End Property

Private Sub Class_Initialize()
    'creates the collection when this class is created
    Set mCol = New Collection
End Sub

Private Sub Class_Terminate()
    'destroys collection when this class is terminated
    Set mCol = Nothing
End Sub
```

In most of this code delegation is used to present information from the `Collection` object to a caller. However, by restricting the add to one function and one point, we have eliminated the potential that anyone can add objects to the collection without going through our `Add` function.

Some of you also may recognize the same boilerplate "Microsoft comments" from the Class Wizard, which I used once I had sketched out what I wanted as far as the base class and the collection class go. I highly recommend using the class wizard at least to build your foundation – that's what it's there for. Once you've become familiar with it, it can really help when you're building your own object hierarchy. If you insist on doing it the hard way, remember that the `enumerator` property, which is shown below, requires *very* special handling. You must go into **Tools | Procedure Attributes** and click on **Advanced** and make sure that the **Procedure ID** is set to -4. This is crucial – the `IUnknown` interface needs this to resolve the enumerator.

As VB programmers we're usually insulated from the details surrounding the implementation of a technology such as COM. However, all the interfaces to a COM component are derived from an initial interface, which is the only required component interface and is named `IUnkown`. Because `IUnknown`'s methods are marked as "restricted" in the type library `stdole2.tlb`, the interface is not directly exposed to us, but we can declare variables of this type as shown in the example given below. If this seems a little odd, it is. Part of the power in VB is that it abstracts these kinds of details from us so we can focus on solving the "real" business issues as opposed to spending time re-inventing existing technology. This particular example involving setting a Procedure ID to a pre-defined number is not something we come across very often. Hopefully Microsoft will come up with a cleaner way for us to get the same functionality in a future revision:

```
Public Property Get NewEnum() As IUnknown
    'this property allows you to enumerate
    'this collection with the For...Each syntax
    Set NewEnum = mCol.[_NewEnum]
End Property
```

The User Interface

Now let's look at the UI side of this example. The bulk of the code is shown here:

```
Option Explicit

' This will allow us to add chunks to the array
Private Const mintBLOCK_SIZE As Integer = 5

' Module level variable to keep track of count

Dim mintCustomerCount As Integer
Dim mstrCaption As String
Dim oCustomerLabels As CustomerLabels
Private mintRecordNumber As Integer

Private Sub cmdAddCustomer_Click()
    Dim oCustomerSingle As CustomerLabel

    If Trim(txtZip) = ""vbNullString Then
        Set oCustomerSingle = oCustomerLabels.Add(txtName, txtAddress1, _
            txtAddress2, txtCity, txtState, "USA", _
            0, Str(mintRecordNumber))
    Else
        Set oCustomerSingle = oCustomerLabels.Add(txtName, txtAddress1, _
            txtAddress2, txtCity, txtState, "USA", _
            CLng(txtZip), Str(mintRecordNumber))
    End If

    mintRecordNumber = mintRecordNumber + 1
    frmLabelManage.Caption = mstrCaption & (oCustomerLabels.Count)

    Call ClearAllTexts
End Sub

Private Sub cmdSearch_Click()
    Dim tmpCustomerLabel As CustomerLabel

    For Each tmpCustomerLabel In oCustomerLabels
        MsgBox ("Customer name " & tmpCustomerLabel.CustomerName)
    Next

End Sub

Private Sub cmdSort_Click()
    Call LoadListBox(lboHidden, oCustomerLabels)
End Sub

Private Sub Form_Load()
    mintCustomerCount = 0
    mstrCaption = frmLabelManage.Caption + " Customer # "
```

```
        Set oCustomerLabels = New CustomerLabels
        frmLabelManage.Caption = mstrCaption & "1"
        mintRecordNumber = 1
        Call ClearAllTexts
End Sub


Private Sub ClearAllTexts()
    Dim tmpControl As Control

    For Each tmpControl In Me.Controls
        If TypeOf tmpControl Is TextBox Then
            tmpControl.Text = vbNullString
        End If
    Next

End Sub

Public Sub LoadListBox(lboHidden As ListBox, _
                       oLabels As CustomerLabels)
    Dim pintCounter As Integer
    Dim poOneLabel As CustomerLabel

    lboHidden.Clear
    pintCounter = 1
    For Each poOneLabel In oLabels
        With lboHidden
            .AddItem poOneLabel.CustomerName
            .ItemData(.NewIndex) = pintCounter
            pintCounter = pintCounter + 1
        End With
    Next

    ' Now use the sort feature
    For pintCounter = 0 To lboHidden.ListCount - 1
        Debug.Print lboHidden.List(pintCounter)
    Next
End Sub
```

Nothing here should be extraordinary except for maybe the hidden list box. I was looking for a clever way to illustrate this concept without a whole lot of code to get bogged down in. I wanted to sort the customers and tried the Microsoft Knowledge Base to verify that I hadn't missed something in VB 6.0.

Well, time and time again they kept saying that sorting was a recipe for bugs – wow, it seems like sorting was the only thing I did in my first Computer Science class. So I was looking for a "clever" way to sort without all the fuss and I decided to try a hidden list box. They sort their contents as they're added, but I didn't know if that functionality required that they be visible (I could see a developer not sorting if the control was invisible). I plopped the lboHidden down, set its sorting property and then printed the customers to the immediate window with the Debug.Print command. Shazam! It worked. You can see this if you click on the sort button while the immediate window is visible.

Summary

In this chapter we've covered a lot of ground. We've seen how business objects can be developed and used on the middle tier. Although we have given it short shrift in this chapter we have mentioned how these components can be virtually re-written and have their entire logic and rules changed and then be switched out like a light bulb.

When you deal with hundreds or thousands of users, this means a terrific saving in terms of man-hours of support. Many organizations would love to have that kind of application. You've also seen a class implemented as an "Out of Proc" Server and had a brief, but thorough, introduction to collections classes. This chapter has stressed breadth over depth, because if you don't know what you have you will not use it. Now let's go forward with what we now know from this chapter and utilize this knowledge to create data objects on the middle tier.

16

COM and Middle Tier Data Objects

In the last chapter we took a look at the business type of middle-tier objects. This gave us a chance to get familiar with COM technology especially as it relates to Active X DLL servers, and to see how we might implement rules and collections. The interesting thing about business components is that you don't just have to be working in an n-tier environment to be using them and enjoying the benefits of that technology. Probably every programmer can think of a time where a binary component would have been a great thing to have such that functionality could be added or removed at will and with ease.

This chapter's focus is going to extend the middle-tier paradigm with **data objects**. These will be extremely useful when you have an n-tier application, but we'll still see some uses for general applications with these kinds of components too. One of the side benefits of working a lot with n-tier components is a kind of "Zen" component philosophy that you acquire. You don't really worry too much about any one component as long as it does its job and can be enhanced later, if need be. That peace of mind keeps you from trying to build too much functionality up-front and allows you to add more when and if you need it.

Why Use Data Components?

There are many reasons to separate data access components from the rest of an application. Anyone who's worked on a large project can tell you that they see a tremendous amount of the same work being done over and over again. First a dynamic SQL string is built, then (maybe) a connection is made, then a recordset is opened, etc. By the time you got to do any "real" work in the function, you already had what looked like a lot of code. You can forget about re-use too with the "old model ".

In general each single access is tailored to fit in the function where it is written so you can't just "make" a call and get the same effect. And just imagine how much worse it is if you are implementing any kind of referential integrity. The multi-tier approach isolates functions into discrete levels. It reduces complexity by isolating business functionality into business objects and data functionality into data objects. It also provides a common and consistent interface for business component developers. Consider the multi-tier model as depicted below. Each logical tier "insulates" the others by functioning as a service provider to the layer(s) above and below it. They layer's job is to satisfy all the needs of the layers (above and below) that it interfaces with:

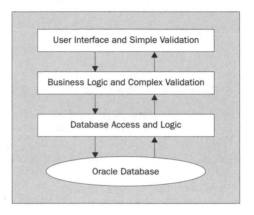

Background

I don't like to spend a lot of time on theory, and I won't in this chapter. But some fundamental concepts need to be considered. Central to the concept of data objects is the idea that there are **data providers** and **data consumers**. For example, the ADO data control (ADODC), as you've seen earlier, is a good example of a data provider. It funnels table data back and forth from the Oracle database to your User Interface. It's not the source database itself (that's Oracle) as much as it's a transit conduit through which your data can arrive at its rightful destination.

The destination in the user interface is generally what's referred to as the data consumer. It "consumes" the data from the data provider and does something with it (usually display-wise). There are two basic kinds of consumers: complex-bound and simple-bound. An example of a complex-bound control is the DataGrid or the msFlexGrid because they bind to entire rows of data. On the other hand, simple-bound controls bind to a single data element such as a single field; two good examples are a text box and a checkbox.

The introduction of VB 6.0 and ADO 2.0 gave VB programmers the ability to have classes that can function as an ADO Data Provider. This was the missing link in multi-tiered applications. The data layer is sometimes confused with the database, but it is not designed to be that way. It is an interface layer that hides the implementation of the data tables and the underlying SQL and simplifies the overall code. No code in the user interface or business layer ever directly calls the table names, field names and other database objects. They either interface with properties exposed by data-tier objects or with recordsets that are contained in ADO objects.

Consider the case of a global company that maintains customer records in multiple information systems on multiple continents. Sure, once all the systems are on Oracle 8i it should be pretty easy to pull consolidated reports, but how long will management need to wait for the consolidated capability? What about old legacy systems that are slated to be re-engineered or redeveloped? Why put time into those systems when moving the data to Oracle anyway? They can be redeveloped with that back end in mind as they become priorities. However, right now, we could implement an ADO component that pulled data from a legacy database and piped it right to our application and not worry about massive changes when we move that data to Oracle.

Finally, what about that division, department, or group, that always wants to do things their way? Or, suppose you want to pull data from a non-relational data source like the Exchange Server or Windows Directory Services? The possibilities are endless and, at each turn, you can see why data abstraction at the data provider layer comes into play.

So what exactly is the data layer? It is a set of wrappers, sometimes thin, other times fat, that insulate the application from direct access to the database. This is another crucial concept. In the well-developed multi-tier application there will never be a case where the presentation layer talks directly to the database. Why? Many of the same reasons to encapsulate the business rules. Several applications can use the same binary components thus reducing overall development costs both directly since the component should need only minor modifications and indirectly by reducing the need to test and document additional items. Applications can more easily be moved to the web since now the presentation layer is "disembodied" or compartmentalized from both the business rules and the data providers.

OK. So say I decide to follow this noble goal, how do I go about it? That is the central question -- and a tough one to boot. Many developers have strong feelings about how exactly to do it and we're going to follow what I feel will be a driving force in the next 6 to 12 months. We're going to use primarily disconnected recordsets, although I want to touch on Extensible Markup Language (XML), variant arrays, and User Defined Types (UDTs).

In a nutshell, we want to totally encapsulate the data access, so let's start by looking at our Oracle tables and see where we are headed with the data classes.

Encapsulating the Data With Disconnected Recordsets

The first concept we're going to look at is a fully disconnected Recordset. Let's start by changing the function `CreateOracle` in `modMain`. We now only want to hold one connection long enough to snag the data and disconnect from the database. This can be done over and over again and the Microsoft MTS server will pool the connections, which can, with a highly transactional system, reduce the total number of concurrent accesses. It is also possible to use the optimistic batch update with disconnected Recordsets. Right now, we're not removing that entire connection (we'll need it for our screens); all we're going to do is examine a simple case of disconnected Recordsets.

Start by creating a test form and placing three text boxes on it and a data control, as shown in the screenshot below:

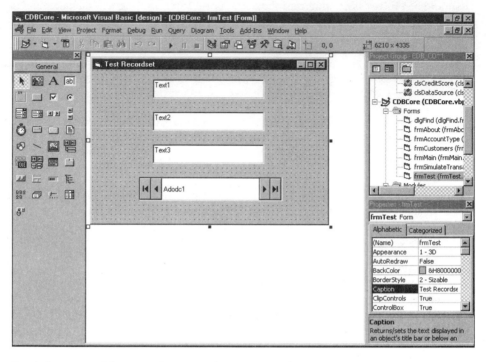

Don't forget to add a test sub to your form main such as this:

```
Private Sub mnufrmTest_Click()
    Dim frmForm As frmTest

    Set frmForm = New frmTest
    frmForm.Show vbModal

    Set frmForm = Nothing
End Sub
```

OK, so all of this is pretty basic. Go to your Active X DLL server and add a class module. This will be our home for the disconnected Recordset. Add the following code to the class module:

```
Option Explicit

Private WithEvents mrstTargetRecordset As ADODB.Recordset

Public Function GetRecordset(strConnect As String, _
        strTableName As String) As Recordset

    Set mrstTargetRecordset = New Recordset
```

```
With mrstTargetRecordset
    .CursorLocation = adUseClient
    .Open "SELECT * FROM Customers", strConnect, _
        adOpenStatic, adLockBatchOptimistic
End With

Set GetRecordset = mrstTargetRecordset

' The next step must be done to ensure that the
' recorset is disconnected (and thus local to this
' machine)
Set mrstTargetRecordset.ActiveConnection = Nothing
' "free" the memory used by the object
Set mrstTargetRecordset = Nothing

End Function
```

This is the cool part. We have a private Recordset with events here, and we tell VB that the main function is going to return a Recordset. All this is fine. We create the Recordset, connect it to Oracle, and set the Cursor Location to the Client. We open it with a straightforward line of SQL, SELECT * FROM Customers, we know there are only a few right now, and then – after we set the return – we disconnect it by setting the original Recordset to Nothing. In order to disconnect a Recordset, we are required to set the ActiveConnection property to Nothing, which we did, and since we had finished with this Recordset we closed it and set the whole thing to Nothing.

Now, I'm sure you're wondering why anyone in his/her right mind would want to do this, but there is a method to the madness. In this case we have created a Recordset that has data and, by disconnecting it, we have made the data local. This is a key concept. We have sucked that data out of Oracle and placed it in our machine running this class.

We have to make some more changes before you can see this in action. You need to place some field names in the DataField property of the textboxes and select the adodc1 as the DataSource. On my form, I left the textboxes with their default names (please don't do this in production – you will pay for it later, honestly), so change the DataField property as indicated:

- ❑ Text1.DataField = "CustomerID"

- ❑ Text2.DataField = "FirstName"

- ❑ Text3.DataField = "LastName"

- ❑ All Textboxes DataSource = "Adodc1"

Now the last step to make this magic work is a few minor changes to our Test form that we created earlier. Make the changes indicated below:

```
Option Explicit

Private Sub Form_Load()
    Dim poData As clsRstTest

    Set poData = New clsRstTest

    ' Get our dataset
    Set Adodc1.Recordset = poData.GetRecordset(gstrConnect, 'Customers')
    ' physically "remote" the data
    Set poData = Nothing

    Adodc1.Recordset.MoveFirst
End Sub
```

You may not know that the ADODC allows you to open a Recordset and use that as the Recordset property for the control. This is another really cool feature provided (mostly) by ADO. It used to be that you had to place SQL in the `RecordSource` and the Recordset was inaccessible (for writing, at least). But, now you have access to a living, breathing (oops, I'm getting carried away here) Recordset. Note that after the data class has been assigned, we need to set the object reference to `Nothing` to get the full disconnect that we want. Also realize that the table name `Customers` isn't doing anything at this point – it's just there for future additions.

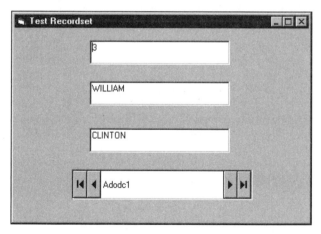

Now run the application and try the test form out. You can play around with this to your heart's content.

OK. So what we've done up to now is demonstrated that we can move a small amount of data from the Oracle Database server to a class that is potentially on another machine, and then to our User Interface and scroll through it. The power in all of this is that we can change and batch update it to the server too. For example, let's go back to the project. Let's re-run it and change one of the record's field(s). Exit the test form screen and go back in – just as you suspected, nothing happened, right? Your change went to "magnetic heaven". In fact, if you made changes to more than one record, you lost 'em all (you can lose any number of record's data for the price of one).

Making the Changes Permanent

The truth is that there's nothing telling the database that things have changed and updating them. So, when you reload the form and it calls that data class that extracts the information out of Oracle, you get the exact same results you got when you first loaded the Recordset. Of course this is unacceptable for a business application, so we're going to fix it so that the data changes are persistent.

Let's assume that we're going to cache the updates as a whole and then batch them, which is basically what our data class assumed earlier by locking with the `OptimisticBatchUpdate` option. We'll add an **Apply Changes** button and a **Cancel changes** button, which seem like meaningful names for this use. For small sets of data such as this table, especially if the data are relatively static and are only updated infrequently, this is an ideal way to manage your three-tiered system. Build classes that encapsulate the data in disconnected Recordsets and batch updates. We'll see later what needs to be done for more frequently changing data and for non-relational data, which does not follow this scheme as well.

All right, let's batch the updates. The first thing we need to do is add a `dirtyflag` as shown below:

```
Private mblnDirtyFlag As Boolean
```

This will tell us when any element of the data has changed. In the "old days", before ADO 2.0, this was not as easy as it seemed it would be, and code to keep track of whether anything had changed was prone to bugs. Now we have a really cool event that we can hook into. If we are using the Recordset directly, and as long as we declare it using the `WithEvents` keyword, we can use the `WillChangeField` event. If a field changes, this event fires. However we're not using the Recordset directly, so what do we do?

We use the `WillChangeField` event of the ADO Data Control to set the `dirtyflag`. To demonstrate the `Dirtyflag` functionality, I used the **Apply Changes** button to display a message box showing us the contents of the `dirtyflag`. I also went ahead and coded the `cancel` button, since it was just one line of code – calling `Form_Load`. Feel free to use the built in functions when you can to achieve the results you want. In this case I wanted all the functionality that `Form_Load` provided, right down to clearing the `dirtyflag`, because once the Recordset is repopulated, you have a clean state as far as what's in memory goes. The entire code for the Test form is shown below:

```
Option Explicit

Private mrstCustomers As Recordset
Private mblnDirtyFlag As Boolean

Private Sub Adodc1_WillChangeField(ByVal cFields As Long, _
Fields As Variant, _
adStatus As ADODB.EventStatusEnum, _
ByVal pRecordset As ADODB.Recordset)

    mblnDirtyFlag = True

End Sub
```

```
Private Sub cmdCancelChanges_Click()

    Call Form_Load

End Sub

Private Sub cmdApplyChanges_Click()

    Call MsgBox("Dirty flag is " & mblnDirtyFlag)

End Sub

Private Sub Form_Load()
    Dim poData As clsRstTest

    Set poData = New clsRstTest

    ' Get our dataset
    Set Adodc1.Recordset = poData.GetRecordset(gstrConnect, "Customers")
    ' physically "remote" the data
    Set poData = Nothing

    mblnDirtyFlag = False
    Adodc1.Recordset.MoveFirst
End Sub
```

Go ahead and test this out for yourself:

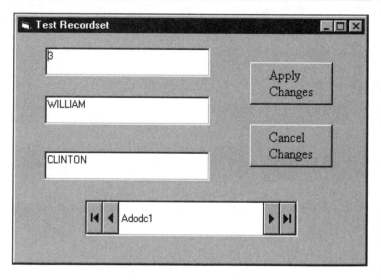

Move around in the data – change something – click the **Apply Changes** button and look at the `dirty flag`. The only time it fails is if you changed something and then change it back to what it was before – then the `dirty flag` will fail. You can even scroll through a field with your cursor and not get an erroneous `WillChange` Event.

Now let's focus on the **Apply Changes** functionality and get rid of the test code. The heart of the **Apply Changes** feature is in the data class, as you would expect. Add the `SaveEdits` function to `clsRstTest` as shown below:

```
Public Function SaveEdits(strConnect As String, _
                          strTableName As String, _
                          rstChanged As Recordset)
On Error GoTo ErrorHandler

    With rstChanged
        .UpdateBatch
    End With

    Exit Function
ErrorHandler:
    MsgBox ("An error has ocurred batching your changes" _
        & Chr$(10) & Err.Description)

End Function
```

This time we're passing in the Recordset (since it has the changes in its local copy of the data) and we're calling the `UpdateBatch` method which takes care of updating the record (by default the `UpdateBatch` method will apply changes across all the records). If an error occurs, we want to know, so we have a basic error handler in here to show us what happened. Note the use of a `with` statement for a single line of object-related code. This is here because if the operation fails (and it will, given a little time) you can interrogate the Recordset and find out what went wrong.

Consistency and Concurrency

Let's talk about data for a few minutes at this point. There's an "epic" struggle in the world of databases between **consistency** and **concurrency**. Concurrency is the ability for multiple people to have access to the same data. It can be as general as viewing records in the same table, or as specific as viewing and changing the same record. Consistency is the ability of data to reflect its true state.

I know that sounds vague, but let me illustrate what that means. Let's say that Can Do Bancorp has a credit card collections department that calls delinquent customers and gently reminds them that they are overdue. Let's also assume that the bank has a payments department that accepts payments on accounts. What happens when you disconnect a Recordset for the collectors and a few minutes later (before they've had a chance to work that account), a payment is posted? They don't have data that is consistent with the database – that's what can happen in a real life business situation and that's what I'm referring to. Now, in reality there's a lot that can be done in code to minimize this, but the bottom line is that if you don't refresh the data as frequently as needed, you can have consistency issues.

This also leads to a brief mention of the main problem with batch update. Any number of transactions within a batch can fail due to consistency. Visual Basic's Recordsets keep a "buffer" of what the data looked like when you first read it and essentially it does a compare with the data that's in the database before it writes. When it fails due to concurrency, the users have to have a way of managing this. It can be as easy as printing an exception list and having them repeat the actions on those accounts, or it can be more sophisticated. You will know what changed and its previous values.

You can "tune" a process so that you re-read the record and only change the required field or field(s). This is a very specialized process based on your business needs. In my experience, a well designed database and knowledge of likely number of transactions can help a lot, but everyone working with business transaction processing systems should consider the tradeoffs being made for the sake of concurrency and consistency.

High Transaction Systems

Let's say that you're using an On Line Transaction Processing (OLTP) system with a heavy load (i.e. the next dotcom). It doesn't really matter what you're selling, per se, but you've got a lot of hits, a million or more customers and thousands of account changes every day. How do you deal with this? One of the best ways is through **stored procedures**.

Visual Basic 6.0 comes with a poorly-described and under-utilized data environment designer. This tool was intended to give us a new way of interfacing with the database and, indeed, it does that to some degree. But what it does extremely well is give us a new window into stored procedures and provide better functionality than we ever had before.

In the "old days" it was very hard to get to specialized database functionality from within Visual Basic. This is one reason why many VB developers chose to leave out stored procedures. I've heard from a developer I know that converting from in-line Visual Basic code to stored procedures sped up his application by 400%. It makes sense to me since the database has a "local" copy of the database, and is aware of potential locking combinations before they are committed.

One the best approaches used today to manage high transaction (OLTP) systems, and still get the benefits of multi-tier architecture, is to provide a set of stored procedures that give you create, read, update, and delete (CRUD) functionality. Since this is an area that has been covered pretty well in other areas of the book, I am not going to belabor stored procedures, but here is the one I am using for insertion:

```
CREATE OR REPLACE Procedure Add_CreditScore(
      SSN number, DOB date, SCORE number) is
Begin

      Insert into CreditScore Values
            (SSN, DOB, SCORE);
      commit;

End;
```

Basically, this is a simple insertion taking only what I need to populate the table. It, in itself, does nothing fancy. If you are entering this from SQL*Plus, you will need to enter this and then hit a "/" to compile. If there are errors, the Show Errors command will display them (if you have trouble seeing the entire text of the error, use the Set CharWidth to N command to expand the size of the line).

I have written these and tested them, so you should check your typing to make sure that you have exactly what you see here. If you do, and you still have errors, check for errata at the WROX site and make sure that it is not a printing typo.

The Data Environment

OK, so let's now examine the Data Environment. Go to your instance of VB (or start it) and open the project group (CDB_COM_PRJ.VBG if you followed my naming recommendation). Go to the CDB_Server project, which is the ActiveX DLL that we worked with earlier. Click on Project | Add Data Environment and you will then see the data environment designer in front of you. Right-click on the Connection object, select Properties from the context menu, and we're going to create a connection to Oracle.

Select the Microsoft OLE DB provider for Oracle from the Provider tab and click Next. That will bring up the Connection tab. Enter your server name, which for me is TEST, your user name, which for me is CANDOMAN, and your password, in my case cdb2_test. Also, make sure that you click the Allow saving password checkbox in that tab as well. At this time you can check the connection/provider info by clicking Test Connection and you should see the screen below (note that I moved the success box to show the boxes filled out as described above):

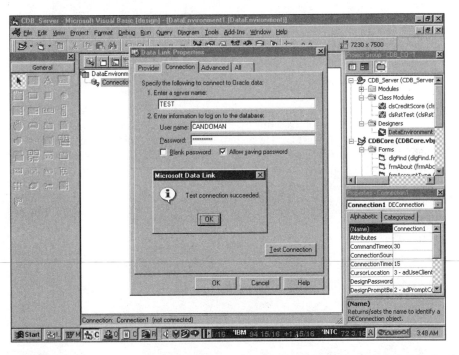

Once you get the success message box, you are ready to continue moving ahead. Click OK on the message and then OK on the Data Link Properties Tabbed dialog. Go to the standard properties for objects and change the name of the connection from Connection1 to cnnCreditScore.

Setting up a Stored Procedure

Now we're ready to add a Command object to the data environment. Once again right-click on the Connection and, this time, select **Add command** from the context menu. You will see a Command object appear right below the connection and a dotted line tying it to the Connection object. Right click on the Command object and select **Properties**. You will see the **Command Properties** dialog shown in the screenshot below:

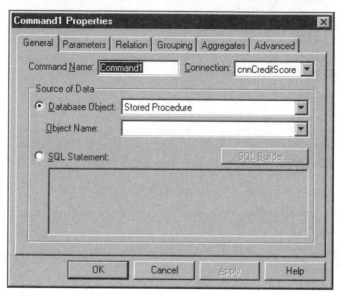

First, change the name of the Command to cmdInsert and then click on the drop down for the object name. This took a while on my system, but you should eventually see a list of stored procedures on your Oracle system. From that list select the one that says **CANDOMAN.ADD_CREDITSCORE**. This will automatically set up some parameters for you and you have your first data object. We're going to do this for two cases, but in general you'd need at least four for moderate functionality and more for extensive functionality.

Let's go ahead and close out the data environment discussion by creating the next and last stored procedure below:

```
CREATE OR REPLACE Procedure Del_CreditScore(
     SSN number) is
Begin

     delete from CreditScore
     where SSN = strSSN;
     commit;

End;
```

You will need to right click on the connection again and **Add command** plus set up the stored procedure information just like we did earlier. This time name the command cmdDelete.

Testing the Stored Procedures

Now, we're going to set up another test screen to make sure that these commands/stored procedures are working. You will need to create a new form, `DE_Test` in the `CDBCore` Project. It should have three text boxes, **SSN**, **DOB**, and **Score** on it. Add three command buttons, **Add**, **Delete**, and **Find** to the screen as shown below:

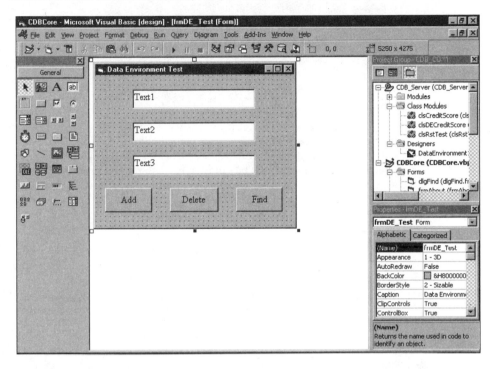

This will provide us a base from which to test the stored procedures. Please note that, if you want your data object to run under MTS all of this Data Environment work should be done in code. There are limitations built into the data environment that make it harder to scale. While this chapter uses the technique to show you what is happening, we will focus on doing essentially the same thing in Chapter 17 in code. Return to the server and add a class named `clsDECreditScore` which we will use to create the procedure for the Data Enviroment test.

```
Private WithEvents mrstTargetRecordset As ADODB.Recordset

' This is very similar to what we did in the earlier
' example, except we are getting a one-record
' disconnected recordset
Public Function GetRecordset(strConnect As String, _
        strSocial As String) As Recordset
    Dim pstrSQL As String
```

```
Set mrstTargetRecordset = New Recordset

pstrSQL = "SELECT * FROM CreditScore where SSN = " _
    & strSocial
With mrstTargetRecordset
    .CursorLocation = adUseClient
    .Open pstrSQL, strConnect, _
        adOpenStatic, adLockBatchOptimistic
End With

Set GetRecordset = mrstTargetRecordset
Set mrstTargetRecordset = Nothing

End Function
```

This code is very similar to what we did previously except that we are getting a one record disconnected Recordset. Why? To reduce the likelihood that, in a highly transactional system, we will have a consistency error. The less data we have on a local client, the less likely that a record will be out of sync with the underlying database. Also, using the Recordset this way allows us to use the familiar ADODC data binding. We will look at the form's code after we cover this class, to see how the binding is changed on the fly.

Inserting Records

Another core feature is the ability to add new records as data is entered. The following code shows how you would call a stored procedure to insert the code as data for insertion. There needs to be some validation testing done on the client side, which I have left up to the reader as it is a pretty simple VB task. The only safeguard I have at this level is the date check, which should raise an error.

```
' This is for a true insterion only.  Caller will have
' to know if it is an insertion or update.
' Ideally, we could code the two together and let
' this function figure it out (using the originalvalue
' property of a recordset that would also be passed in.
Public Function InsertRecord(strSSN As String, _
                             strDOB As String, _
                             strScore As Integer)
Dim pstrNewDOB As String
On Error GoTo ErrorHandler
    If IsDate(strDOB) Then
        pstrNewDOB = Format$(strDOB, "dd-MMM-YYYY")
    Else
        ' raise an error here -- this is a bad date
    End If
    Call DE_CDB_Server.cmdInsert(CLng(strSSN), _
        pstrNewDOB, CLng(strScore))

    Exit Function
ErrorHandler:
    MsgBox ("An error has occurred inserting your record" _
        & Chr$(10) & Err.Description)

End Function
```

None of the above should appear really unusual. I used Visual Basic's `Format` function to convert a string date into Oracle's date format. Then, using the Data Environment, I called the `cmdInsert` stored procedure which is nothing more than a thin wrapper around a SQL INSERT statement.

Let me mention this now: the other side of the coin is when the data fields change and trigger a SQL UPDATE as opposed to a SQL INSERT. This is an area where the strength of the choice to code the get as a code-based disconnected Recordset comes through. I can use the `Recordset.Fields("Target").OriginalValue` property to find out what a field was originally. Since we don't want to hold a lock across an editable screen (in most cases) we will need to do a quick compare with the database to make sure that what we have is still what is there. If so, we proceed to update, otherwise we don't.

This concept can be either coded or written as a stored procedure. A stored procedure of this nature is beyond the scope of this chapter.

Let's now take a look at the code for the DELETE functionality. As you can see below, this is a very short subroutine:

```
' This one is a breeze
Public Sub DeleteRecord(strSocial As String)
On Error GoTo ErrorHandler

    Call DE_CDB_Server.cmdDelete(strSocial)

    Exit Sub

ErrorHandler:
    MsgBox ("An error has occurred inserting your record"
        & Chr$(10) & Err.Description)

End Sub
```

All you need to do to delete a record is to call with the Social Security Number of the individual whose credit score is to be removed. In reality every delete function for any table would be the same as far as taking the primary key as the parameter. The only differences in the coding would be if and how referential integrity was maintained.

In order to test the class we've just built, we need to create another form. Add a new form to the project, call it `frmDE_Test`. Add an ADODC, three text boxes, three labels and three command buttons. I called the textboxes **txtSSN**, **txtDOB**, and **txtScore**. I followed a similar convention with the labels that served to identify the textbox information that I was displaying for each `CreditScore` record. I called the buttons **cmdAdd**, **cmdDelete**, and **cmdFind** and set the captions to **Add**, **Delete**, and **Find** respectively. The choice of which Table to Insert and Delete from/into was pretty much arbitrary, but tied in nicely with our earlier example where the score was used.

My screen for these items is shown below. It is a basic test form where a few critical values are displayed and manipulated:

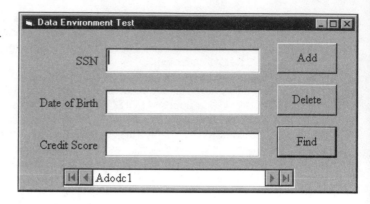

The code to drive the test form is shown below:

```
Option Explicit

Private mblnDirtyFlag As Boolean
Private mblnSearchFailure As Boolean

Private Sub cmdAdd_Click()
    Dim poData As clsDECreditScore

    On Error GoTo ErrorHandler
    If Len(Trim(txtSSN)) = 9 Then
        If Trim(txtDOB) <> vbNullString Then
            If Trim(txtScore) <> vbNullString Then
                Set poData = New clsDECreditScore
                Call poData.InsertRecord(txtSSN, _
                    txtDOB, txtScore)
                Set poData = Nothing
            Else
                MsgBox ("Bad score entered!")
            End If
        Else
            MsgBox ("Bad date entered")
        End If
    Else
        MsgBox ("Bad SSN entered!")
    End If
    Exit Sub

ErrorHandler:
    MsgBox ("Error adding record to database!")
End Sub

Private Sub cmdDelete_Click()
    Dim poData As clsDECreditScore
```

```
        On Error GoTo ErrorHandler
        If Len(Trim(txtSSN)) = 9 Then
            Set poData = New clsDECreditScore
            Call poData.DeleteRecord(txtSSN)
            Set poData = Nothing
        Else
            MsgBox ("Bad SSN entered!")
        End If

        Call ClearTextBoxes
        MsgBox ("record deleted")
        txtSSN.SelStart = 0
        txtSSN.SelLength = Len(txtSSN)
        txtSSN.SetFocus
        Exit Sub

ErrorHandler:
    MsgBox ("Error deleting record to database!")
End Sub

Private Sub cmdFind_Click()
    Dim poData As clsDECreditScore

    If (Val(txtSSN) <> 0) Then
        Set poData = New clsDECreditScore
        ' Get our dataset of one record
        Set Adodc1.Recordset = poData.GetRecordset(gstrConnect, txtSSN)
        ' physically "remote" the data
        Set poData = Nothing
        If Adodc1.Recordset.EOF Then
            mblnSearchFailure = True
            MsgBox ("No matching record, try again")
            txtSSN.SelStart = 0
            txtSSN.SelLength = Len(txtSSN)
            txtSSN.SetFocus
            Exit Sub
        Else
            txtDOB.DataField = "DOB"
            Set txtDOB.DataSource = Adodc1
            txtScore.DataField = "Score"
            Set txtScore.DataSource = Adodc1
            mblnSearchFailure = False
        End If
        mblnDirtyFlag = False
        Adodc1.Recordset.MoveFirst
    End If
End Sub

Private Sub Form_Load()
    Call ClearTextBoxes
End Sub
```

```
Private Sub txtSSN_KeyPress(KeyAscii As Integer)
    Call ClearTextBoxes
End Sub

Private Sub ClearTextBoxes()
    txtDOB.DataField = vbNullString
    Set txtDOB.DataSource = Nothing
    txtDOB = vbNullString
    txtScore.DataField = vbNullString
    Set txtScore.DataSource = Nothing
    txtScore = vbNullString
End Sub
```

Most of the code here is straightforward. The text boxes at startup do not have a `DataSource` or a `DataField`. When they need those values (as in the case of update or find), they are loaded. When they become meaningless, such as when I begin to enter a new account number or when I delete a `CreditScore` record, they are cleared. One other thing I want to bring to your attention is the `cmdAdd_Click` event, where you are seeing the beginning of the validation needed.

Data Validation

Let's briefly cover data validation. There are several kinds of validation, but I have broken them into three groups:

❑ *Simple*

❑ *Logical or Relational*

❑ *Transactional*

Simple validation verifies things such as numerics, dates, strings, and data length. **Logical** or **Relational** maintains relationships such as each X must have at least one Y and Foreign Key N must be Primary Key N in it's own table. Relational also implies maintaining relational integrity when parents of parent-child relationships go away. Finally, there's **Transactional** validation, which is intended to verify that the data makes sense. For example, in a medical information system it does not make sense to schedule a male for amniocentesis.

Communication Between Layers

Up to now we've focused on disconnected Recordsets. There are other ways to pass information between layers. For example, it is extremely efficient to pass data between layers using User Defined Types (UDTs). Consider the following example:

```
Object.LastName = "Doe"
Object.FirstName = "John"
Object.Age = 25
Object.Address = "62 Big Bear Street"
```

This is fine and adequate if we are dealing with a local object or service. Let's say, for the sake of argument, that the object was across the network at another physical site 20 miles away. The above four lines would require 4 separate round trips across the network. A UDT that contained the same data could pass it back between your application and the component in one trip.

To a great extent the same is true of Extensible Markup Language (XML). XML will be in the future of distributed applications everywhere. It is a powerful data language that excels at representing data (it was designed for that purpose exactly). There are many implications of the use of this technology. Consider the fact that the upcoming release of ADO (version 2.5) will support writing a Recordset out as XML. Also consider the fact that IE5 now has an XML parser built into the browser so that a developer can view the "raw output" directly and get a bird's-eye view of what is taking place. It also needs mentioning that it is highly likely that XML will be one of the major enabling technologies for eCommerce. Why? Because multiple businesses at various levels need to interact to get the job done and data must be interchanged between all of them. A flexible choice that can easily be added to (where the extensible comes from) makes the most sense.

Summary

In this chapter we have covered the basics of building data components for your applications including two of the most powerful concepts that are used today, disconnected recordsets and stored procedures. We have shown how you can provide functionality to your application through classes that expose the underlying data tables and how they can be modified from a static state.

We've discussed the problems of concurrency and consistency and shown how these can exist in a high transaction (OLTP) environment. Finally, we covered some of the leading edge of the field by looking at present and future technologies such as variant arrays and UDTs and what this author believes will be the future of inter-tier communication, XML.

The main goal here was to get a good feel for the underlying purpose of the approaches that were considered, including some of the implications and tradeoffs, and why one would be used over the other. While this is certainly not the only way that multi-tier applications can be built, it is an effective way that should be considered. It should become even more powerful as XML is tied more thoroughly to Visual Basic and possibly replaces recordsets. We're going to use our design understanding of these two approaches to our advantage in Chapter 17 as we begin to put these building blocks together and make components that can be hosted in Microsoft's version of the Application server, Microsoft Transaction Server.

17

Hosting COM Components on MTS

This chapter will bring together what has been covered in the previous chapters and show how Microsoft Transaction Server (MTS) can affect the performance of your application. You may already be wondering what all the fuss is about MTS. I know that I had many questions when I first heard about it, but it provides a much-needed structure for multi-tiered applications.

The power of 2-Tier (also called Client-Server) applications lies in using more than one computer to do the processing. By having one machine whose only purpose is to apply/enforce business rules and present/manage the data, we get the benefits of specialization. By having a server whose purpose is to manipulate, process, and retrieve data, we add to specialization the benefits of distributed processing, and we end up with a more powerful and flexible system than in the old days, where one machine was responsible for everything.

Essentially, just making tiers of services that can be hosted on multiple computers yields some benefits in code architecture and design. If we can later use these components on more than one machine, then we can harness the power of multiple processing, load balancing, and efficient use of resources. In short we have distributed computing. We've already seen where breaking an application up into COM components can help us to build more powerful applications; and how this level of analysis provides a better foundation upon which to rest our applications. MTS extends that functionality by providing a way for us to "host" our ActiveX ("In Proc") DLL components within it without changing a line of code (although to get the best performance and functionality you will want to change several lines here and there across the code base).

The advantages of this approach can be tremendous. For example, what are the most time-intensive things than an application must do? Well, one is loading the code for a DLL (including ActiveX DLL Servers); another is creating an object, and so is creating a database connection. MTS works to eliminate all of these. First, it keeps all your "In Proc" Servers available, so no time is wasted by client computers running initialization code and figuring out where in memory this DLL can be placed.

Secondly, MTS can create resources, and then "recycle" them, as they are needed. If you imagine a stateless component, it would be easy to recycle, because it has nothing to clear and has already been created. This ability is called **pooling objects** (note that this functionality is not presently available to Visual Basic objects in MTS, but should be available in a future revision).

Consider the full-blown MTS multi-tier environment shown below. This is a good example of what the typical multi-tier system might be supporting. Many e-commerce web sites have this kind of activity on a daily basis.

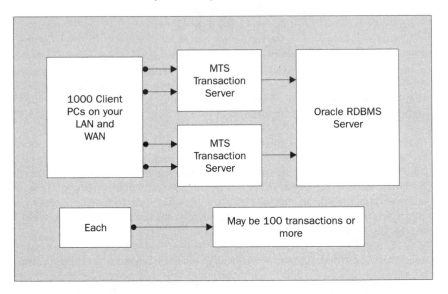

MTS Background

One of the terms that has come along with the multi-tier revolution is the concept of an **Application Server**. Most developers today consider UNIX to be the first Application server, but it seems like every vendor is redefining the standard at will in an effort to cast their offerings in the best light. Since MTS is considered to be an Application Server, and we will be using it in a way that is consistent with that concept, let's consider what it does for us.

For the most part it provides what most people consider to be middle-tier services such as managing concurrency (duplicate access to the same resource), security, resource pooling, and context issues. For the most part, the running application is unaware of any change in its services, so it appears as if it is running in "its own world", which means that clients have isolation. Its purpose in supporting all of this is to provide your application with component services as needed: to "host" components in a fail-safe environment and to provide transactional support for what Microsoft terms resource managers, including databases. Let's look at these in more detail and see how they affect an MTS application.

Component Services

Component services are how multi-tier applications get their jobs done. Some programmer, usually referred to as an author, has created a component or a set of components that will provide a needed service(s) to the application. Normally, your application would call the ActiveX DLL at the client machine. If it was in memory at the time, then there would be no delay. Generally though, Windows will keep as much out of memory as possible; so it is likely that it would have to be loaded, an object would need to be created, and only then would work commence at the client machine.

Microsoft's MTS removes both of the steps by always keeping the DLL loaded (at least in virtual memory), and by pooling objects (this feature is limited for Visual Basic programmers in MTS 2.0) so that re-creates aren't the norm. On top of that, much of the work takes place on the MTS machine(s). Please note that the MTS machine(s) may or may not include the client. Generally the idea with Microsoft's MTS is that any machine functioning as an NT System (server or workstation) can be part of a group of machines that provide application services. Plus, by placing more machines in the set of those providing application services, you can take advantage of dynamic load balancing. While an examination of load balancing is beyond the scope of this chapter, you should know that it is out there and available should you need it.

Security

I mentioned earlier that MTS provides a fail-safe environment. There are many things that can go wrong in components and most of these are unexpected. Generally, the reason to provide an error handler is to deal with unexpected circumstances (imagine your Oracle Server going down in the middle of the day because of a hardware failure). Inevitably, you will run into a circumstance that will cause your components to crash, or as I like to say "blow up". Often, because they operate in the process space of your app, this will cause a failure in your application that (often) is not recoverable. MTS will keep the component that has "blown up" from harming the application or the Operating System (mainly an issue for unprotected ones like Windows 95/98). If it's a buggy component, your application may still exit, but it will be graceful and not abrupt. Also, MTS will restart failed components for other clients so that an unexpected error doesn't cause all of your clients to lose that component's services.

Transactions

Finally, MTS provides a transactional environment. There are four things that are considered critical to a transaction and they are often remembered by the mnemonic **ACID**, which stands for **atomicity, consistency, isolation,** and **durability**.

❑   Atomicity means that the transaction either all happens or all fails – a small portion of the whole cannot complete without the whole thing going. For example, it would be awful (as far as the bank is concerned) for a bank to pay a check on your account, but then fail to debit the money from your account. Thus, atomicity means that one action cannot complete without the other.

❑   Consistency assures that if two actions are performed, then the same result is achieved. In other words, if you had $100 in your account and I subtract $50 for a check, you will have $50 left. Consistency says that every time you have $100 and I subtract $50 you will always be left with $50. In a simple example like this, it may seem trivial, but when 300 separate steps are all part of a transaction, I'd like to know that if I start out with exactly the same database that I end up with exactly the same database 100% of the time.

❑   Isolation means that no atomic transactions see any portion of an uncommitted transaction. Thus, results are "isolated" from each other and, at least while other transactions are still processing, the state of the database appears the same to any number of clients.

❑   Durability is "extreme" persistence. If I make changes to data in a table, even if the CPU and hard drive media fail, I should be able to go back in (when the system is available after repair) and expect the same results to be there. If I have a system that guarantees the four requisites of a transaction, it can be said to be transactional.

By MTS being transactional, it means that component transactions can be expected to display all four characteristics of a transactional system.

Now, you are probably wondering why you would need or even want transactions on your components. The main reason is that in order to get the most out of an Application Server, your components should be as stateless as possible. State refers to both internal and visible properties, and I am basically saying that you should try to reduce the state needs of your components. When components are simple and local, state is a good thing, but when your components are part of the Microsoft MTS system of services, you should do your best to keep state only when necessary.

This is where transactions come into play; they allow you to maintain state as least long enough to complete a task that needed the state information. Then, when state is no longer needed, the transaction should be closed with either a "completed" notification or an "abort" notification. Consider the diagram below. This graphic depicts what is needed to make sure that you have state for the components to perform the service that they provide.

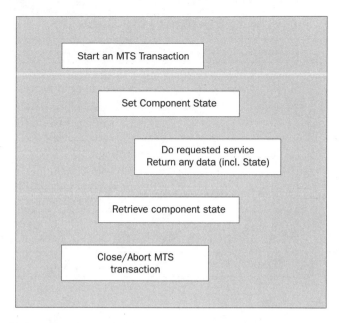

By default, every MTS object ("hosted component") has a corresponding MTS `Context` object. You can interface with MTS to get a reference to the `Context` object for the running instance of a component package. This `Context` object allows you and MTS to share information about the hosted component. By properly using the `Context` object you can easily manage transactions, security, and other component functions as shown in the tables below.

Methods for Managing Transactions

Name	Description
IsInTransaction	Determines if you are in a transaction currently
DisableCommit	Disables commits (allowing you to retain state)
EnableCommits	You can allow MTS to flush data as it is able (i.e. you're not done with the component, but the work done up to this point is internally consistent)
SetComplete	Signals MTS that the component can be deactivated when it returns and that it has completed its work normally. Also indicates that any updates performed within the transaction can be applied
Set Abort	Signals MTS that the component can be deactivated when it returns and that it has completed its work in an abnormal fashion. Thus, any updates before *or* after the call to abort must not be applied when the object returns.

Methods for Managing Security

Name	Description
IsSecurityEnabled	This is always true unless the component is running in process with the application
IsCallerInRole	Determines if the owner of the process that spawned the MTS component is a member of an assigned role
Security	Obtains a reference to a SecurityProperty object that allows you to determine who created the object, who called it, who originally created it, and who originally called it

Miscellaneous Methods for Object Contexts

Name	Description
Item	Provides another way of obtaining a property for the Context object
Count	Scalar count of the number of Context object properties
CreateInstance	Allows the developer to create additional objects from an existing MTS object context

Once you have the Context object you can manage your MTS components. Part of managing your components is deciding what level of transactional support you need. MTS provides several and we will cover what these do and why you'd want one or the other. But before we get into that, let's cover some basics.

MTS Fundamentals

Up until now, the only thing that I've mentioned about MTS is that you can host ActiveX DLLs there and this is very true. But there's more than meets the eye when you first look as MTS as an application server. MTS actually provides additional functionality to its hosted components.

We're going to start with an example project. Start up Visual Basic and start by creating a new project (**Standard EXE**) in Visual Basic. I set the name of mine to **TestDriver**. Open the standard form that VB gives you and drop two text boxes and two buttons on it as shown below:

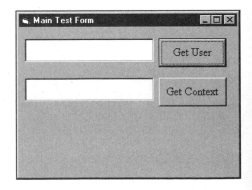

I named my text boxes **txtUserName** and **txtContextInfo**, and I named my command buttons **cmdGetUser** and **cmdGetContext**. Then go to the **Add project** and add an ActiveX DLL project. I named mine `MTS_Test` and I called the project group `Group Test`. Add a code module to your ActiveX DLL called `modAPI`. All you need in that module is an API call to get the username from the OS. Place the code shown below in that module:

```
Option Explicit

' Need this API Call for the Win32 GetUserName function
Declare Function GetUserName Lib "advapi32.dll" _
        Alias "GetUserNameA" _
        (ByVal lpBuffer As String, _
        nSize As Long) As Long
```

This is a typical API call and in this case it is aptly named, `Get User Name`.

Go into your class module, change the name to `clsSimpleTest` and set the `MTSTransactionMode` property to require transactions. There are five possible values for `TransactionMode` and the use of each is shown below:

Value	Description
`NotAnMTSObject`	Provides another way of obtaining a property for the `Context` object
`NoTransactions`	Scalar count of the number of `Context` object properties
`RequiresTransaction`	Requires a transaction
`UsesTransactions`	Supports transactions
`RequiresNewTransaction`	Requires a new transaction

We needed to have a transaction to guarantee that we would have an MTS Context. Without this, there was no guarantee that we could rely on. Also, before we get very far along, we need to add a reference to the Microsoft Transaction Server Type Library in **Project | References** for both of the projects. Once that's done, add the code shown below to the clsSimpleTest class:

```
Option Explicit

Private mctxContext As ObjectContext

Public Function GiveContext() As ObjectContext
    Set mctxContext = GetObjectContext

    Set GiveContext = mctxContext
End Function
```

```
Public Function RetUserName() As String

    Dim plngReturn As Long
    Dim strName As String * 25

    Set mctxContext = GetObjectContext

    plngReturn = GetUserName(strName, 25)

    RetUserName = strName

    mctxContext.SetComplete

End Function

Public Sub FreeContext(ctxContext As ObjectContext)

    ' Properly release this object
    Set ctxContext = Nothing

End Sub
```

The first function is very straightforward; it just grabs and returns an `ObjectContext`.

The second one is the call to our API function. It is unusual to see the `Dim strName As String * 25` notation. This creates a fixed length `string` that is 25 characters long – no matter what. Usually in Visual Basic strings are managed dynamically, if I need 25 characters, I am given 50 bytes (remember Unicode: each char = 2 bytes) not counting the memory needed to hold the "pointer", or placeholder, to that dynamically allocated space. So, if you need a fixed length string, this is how you get it. Also make sure that your username is not more than 25 characters, or you'll get to see your ActiveX DLL blow up for yourself!

Finally, the last function is the one that releases the reference to the `Context` object that was retrieved by the first.

So this is mostly basic - it's just a sample of what we can do.

Before we go onto the rest of the code, there is a very important step that needs to be done at this point. Compile the ActiveX DLL Server. Once it compiles successfully, go to the **Project | Properties | Component** Tab and, in the **version compatibility frame**, select **binary compatibility** and browse until you find the DLL you just created. This is needed to ensure that you and MTS are using the same Class `ID` for the component.

Go back to the form in your standard EXE and add the code below:

```
Private Sub cmdGetContext_Click()
    Dim poSimpleTest As Object
    Dim pctxContext As ObjectContext

    Set poSimpleTest = CreateObject("MTS_Test.clsSimpleTest")
```

```
    Set pctxContext = poSimpleTest.GiveContext
    If Not (pctxContext Is Nothing) Then
        txtContextInfo = pctxContext.IsSecurityEnabled
    Else
        txtContextInfo = "Nothing"
    End If

    Call poSimpleTest.FreeContext(pctxContext)
    Set poSimpleTest = Nothing
End Sub

Private Sub cmdGetUser_Click()
    Dim poSimpleTest As Object
    Dim pstrUserName As String

    Set poSimpleTest = CreateObject("MTS_Test.clsSimpleTest")
    pstrUserName = poSimpleTest.RetUserName
    txtUserName = pstrUserName

    Set poSimpleTest = Nothing
End Sub
```

This too is mostly straightforward. We have two buttons. One allows us to call code in
a VB class module that uses the Win32 API to get the Windows UserName from the
OS. The other one calls code in the class to retrieve the `ObjectContext` and then tells
us whether security is enabled and whether or not (indirectly) there is a valid MTS
transaction (you will see the string `Nothing` in that `txtContextInfo` textbox in that
case).

My form, after clicking both
buttons is shown below:

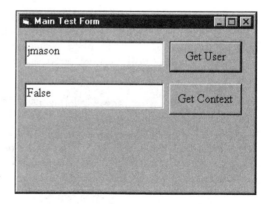

Once you've tested the code, let's move it to MTS. I am going to assume that you
performed a basic installation of the NT 4.0 option pack, which is available for free
from Microsoft as a download.

Since I have installed this multiple times and not had problems (and had very few, basic questions that were asked during installation), I am not going to cover the installation of MTS 2.0. I will highly recommend that if you are installing components from the NT option pack for the first time, that you install Microsoft Message Queue Server (MSMQ) and Internet Information Server 4.0 with the Front Page Extensions available from the same CD.

Configuring a New Package in Microsoft MTS

The bulk of what you do for MTS is done from within the MTS Explorer. MTS has three driving concepts: **Computers**, **Packages**, and **Roles**. Computers are where you install MTS packages. You can create a package from any MTS server and then move it around to any other MTS server. Packages are a set of usually related components with any number of classes and any number of interfaces for those classes. Roles, on the other hand, are a metaphor for the security that can be applied to components.

As far as Transaction Server is concerned security is applied at every level. Thus, in order to have full access to a given component and its interfaces; you must be a member of the responsible/proper roles. One nice thing is that users and groups in the NT domain may be added directly to MTS roles. This makes it easy to assign administrative interfaces and/or components to the administrators group, or a set of functionality in "special" interfaces to all managers.

Now that we have an overview of the MTS system, lets create our own MTS package. Start by copying the DLL you created earlier along with the .lib file and .exp file from the development machine to the MTS machine. Drop to DOS and TYPE regsvr32 "dllname" and wait until you see the message that says DLL Test successfully registered.

Then go to Start | Programs | Windows NT 4.0 Option Pack | Microsoft Transaction Server | Transaction Server Explorer. The MTS Explorer is based on the Microsoft Management Console, which is the way Microsoft intends to simplify administration for Networking personnel. It's loosely based on the Window's Explorer metaphor and uses a series of snap-ins to provide support for multiple products. Interestingly the snap-ins are OLE (which is a close cousin of ActiveX) "In Proc" servers.

The start-up screen for MTS Explorer is shown below. Here you get a first taste for what MTS uses to manage the system. Click on Microsoft Transaction Server to expand the tree-view control and then click again on Computers.

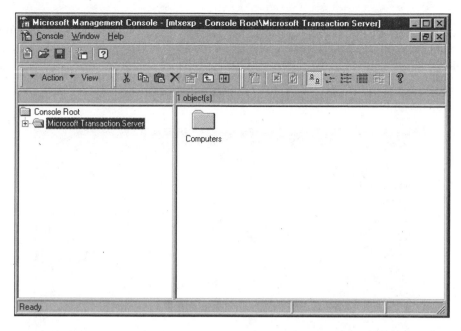

One thing that I really dislike about this interface is the extraneous number of clicks that I have to go through to do even the simplest task. You must click again on Computers just to see the machine(s) appear in the right hand window. Click on the tree-view to expand the My Computer topic. At this point your screen should resemble the screenshot below:

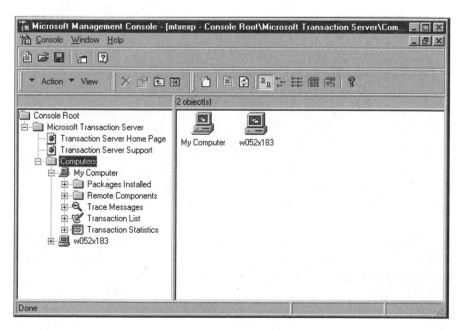

At this point, you are ready to begin the process of creating your own package. Click on **Packages Installed** and then click again on the main topic so that the control on the right synchronizes. You should see a series of "boxes" that represent installed packages. We are going to create a new one.

Right Click on the **Packages** topic and select **New Package**. You will see the screen shown below:

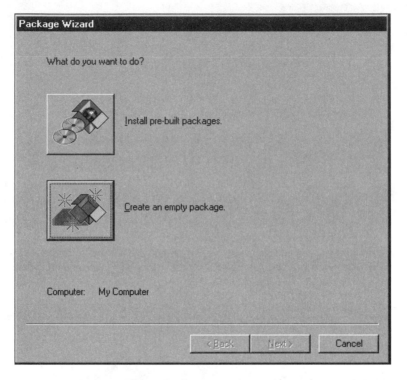

You want the second option, **Empty Package**.

You will be prompted for a name, just enter **DLL Test** and click **Next**. At this point you are prompted for **Package Identity**. This requires a little explanation. You have the ability to allow a package to log on as someone other than the user who is logged in. Why would you want this? There are numerous reasons. You may choose to expose functionality that is reserved for the database administrator; yet not want to grant full functionality to the user(s) who will have access to that interface.

At this point we do not need any special kind of functionality, so we are going to go with the **Interactive User** option which is the user logged into the NT and requesting component services. Click **Finish** and you will see the new package appear in the right side of the Explorer-like window, as shown:

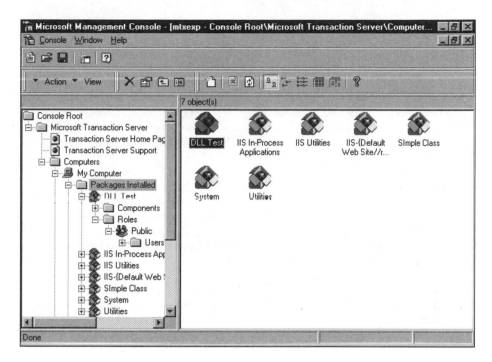

Click on the package you just created and then on Components and select New Component from the action menu. It will ask if the component is registered (it is) and you will select that and then choose from the list of registered components. By registering it ahead of time, we make sure that there are no conflicts with other component and we make it easy to find our DLL. Once you've added that component you're ready to create a role.

Assigning Roles to Your Package

Let's set up a role for our new class.

Click on the expanded topic area for our Simple Class, you will see two further expansion areas – Components and Roles. Click on Roles (it shouldn't expand) and then click again to see that there are none in the right hand windows. Right-click on the role and select New Role, you will be prompted for a name, which I just set at Public. I highly recommend that your names are more meaningful!

Click on the Public role in the right hand window, and then go to the action menu and Add User. For my test here, I added the public group Everyone and granted them access. I suggest that, while you are developing your components, you work close to the anticipated security settings to reduce the likelihood of security-related software defects.

Let me also mention that Microsoft's MTS is very strong on security. Not only can you assign roles to access packages, but you can even assign roles to interfaces. The power in this concept is that some interfaces can extend more functionality than others do and the role-based model accounts for this difference.

Exporting the Package

Once the component is built and roles are assigned, you need to "export" the package.

When MTS exports a package, it makes the package accessible to other computers and it creates an `Exe` that sets up the DCOM configuration for the MTS component. An extensive discussion of DCOM is beyond the scope of this book, however, suffice it to say that it is a way of using COM components remotely and it is the number one way of accessing MTS components (with through an Internet Browser being a close second).

Click on the **Package** icon in the left tree view to highlight it, and then right-click. In the context popup that appears will be the option to export the package. It will ask you for a destination directory. I recommend that you open Windows Explorer and create a directory for MTS packages and then a folder under that for **DLL Test**. On my system, I used the directory structure **C:\Programs\MTS Packages\DLL Test**. Then select down to the **DLL Test** folder for the export and let it go.

When the export has finished, you will find your component in the **DLL Test** folder, and also another subdirectory called **Clients**. That directory will contain one file called **DLL Test.EXE**. You will need to run that on any machine that will access the MTS component. It changes the registry so that you can get access to the component from the MTS machine but in a "remote" (as opposed to local) location.

Once we've done this, let's run our test application. At the same time, leave MTS Explorer running, and click on **Computers** in the left tree view. Once it's selected, right-click and select **Add new computer** from the resulting context popup. Add your workstation by selecting it from the network or entering its name (if you know it) or it's IP. You will need this to watch transactions for your machine. VB allows you to debug MTS components right in the IDE but, unfortunately, they run local to the machine that is the client.

Once you have done this go to your client machine and select **Transaction Monitor**. This will help you analyze what is going on. Run the application and do some testing – watch the transaction monitor and observe what happens.

One thing you may want to do is apply MTS support to our existing business and data components that we developed on the last two chapters. You should now have all the tools you need.

Summary

In this chapter you got an introduction to MTS. While it was a whirlwind tour, it is easy to see why it has become such a strong weapon in the set of technologies used for multi-tiered applications. It is a very capable Application Server and promises to have a bright future in front of it. In the version of Windows that has yet to be released, this functionality is to be built-in. That will provide another level of support for multi-tiered applications and might just hasten the pace of redevelopment to take advantage of some of the fault-tolerance and load balancing that we have missed.

While I didn't specifically mention it here, this is a pivotal technology driving quite a bit of the e-Commerce and e-Tailing that is going on today. It deserves to be considered and understood by anyone who is looking for scalable and flexible component-based solutions in the coming years.

We've now reached the end of the book, and we've come a long way. You should now have a comprehensive foundation of knowledge with which to start building your own VB Oracle solutions. All the code we've discussed in this book is available for download from the WROX web site - I hope you're keen to start implementing the technologies we've covered.

Happy Programming!

Section VI

Appendices

ADO Object Summary

The Objects

The Main Objects	Description
Command	A Command object is a definition of a specific command that you intend to execute against a data source.
Connection	A Connection object represents an open connection to a data store.
Recordset	A Recordset object represents the entire set of records from a base table or the results of an executed command. At any given time, the 'current record' of a Recordset object refers to a single record within the recordset.

The Other Objects	Description
Error	An Error object contains the details of data access errors pertaining to a single operation involving the provider.
Field	A Field object represents a column of data within a common data type.
Parameter	A Parameter object represents a parameter or argument associated with a Command object based on a parameterized query or stored procedure.
Property	A Property object represents a dynamic characteristic of an ADO object that is defined by the provider.

The Collections	Description
Errors	The Errors collection contains all of the Error objects created in response to a single failure involving the provider.
Fields	A Fields collection contains all of the Field objects of a Recordset object.
Parameters	A Parameters collection contains all the Parameter objects of a Command object.
Properties	A Properties collection contains all the Property objects for a specific instance of an object.

The Command Object

Methods of the Command Object	Return Type	Description
Cancel		Cancels execution of a pending Execute or Open call.
CreateParameter	Parameter	Creates a new Parameter object.
Execute	Recordset	Executes the query, SQL statement, or stored procedure specified in the CommandText property.

Properties of the Command Object	Return Type	Description
ActiveConnection	Variant	Indicates to which Connection object the command currently belongs.
CommandText	String	Contains the text of a command to be issued against a data provider.
CommandTimeout	Long	Indicates how long to wait, in seconds, while executing a command before terminating the command and generating an error. Default is 30.
CommandType	CommandTypeEnum	Indicates the type of command specified by the Command object.

Properties of the Command Object	Return Type	Description
Name	String	Indicates the name of the Command object.
Prepared	Boolean	Indicates whether or not to save a compiled version of a command before execution. Not relevant for Oracle.
State	Long	Describes whether the Command object is open or closed. Read only.

Collections of the Command Object	Return Type	Description
Parameters	Parameters	Contains all of the Parameter objects for a Command object.
Properties	Properties	Contains all of the Property objects for a Command object.

The Connection Object

Methods of the Connection Object	Return Type	Description
BeginTrans	Integer	Begins a new transaction.
Cancel		Cancels the execution of a pending, asynchronous Execute or Open operation.
Close		Closes an open connection and any dependent objects.
CommitTrans		Saves any changes and ends the current transaction.
Execute	Recordset	Executes the query, SQL statement, stored procedure, or provider-specific text.
Open		Opens a connection to a data source, so that commands can be executed against it.
OpenSchema	Recordset	Obtains database schema information from the provider.
RollbackTrans		Cancels any changes made during the current transaction and ends the transaction.

Properties of the Connection Object	Return Type	Description
Attributes	Long	Indicates one or more characteristics of a Connection object. Default is 0.
CommandTimeout	Long	Indicates how long, in seconds, to wait while executing a command before terminating the command and generating an error. The default is 30.
ConnectionString	String	Contains the information used to establish a connection to a data source.
ConnectionTimeout	Long	Indicates how long, in seconds, to wait while establishing a connection before terminating the attempt and generating an error. Default is 15.
CursorLocation	CursorLocationEnum	Sets or returns the location of the cursor engine.
DefaultDatabase	String	Indicates the default database for a Connection object.
IsolationLevel	IsolationLevelEnum	Indicates the level of transaction isolation for a Connection object. Write only. Oracle allows but one transaction at a time.
Mode	ConnectModeEnum	Indicates the available permissions for modifying data in a Connection.
Provider	String	Indicates the name of the provider for a Connection object.
State	Long	Describes whether the Connection object is open or closed. Read only.
Version	String	Indicates the ADO version number. Read only.

Collections of the Connection Object	Return Type	Description
Errors	Errors	Contains all of the Error objects created in response to a single failure involving the provider.
Properties	Properties	Contains all of the Property objects for a Connection object.

Events of the Connection Object	Description
BeginTransComplete	Fired after a BeginTrans operation finishes executing.
CommitTransComplete	Fired after a CommitTrans operation finishes executing.
ConnectComplete	Fired after a connection starts.
Disconnect	Fired after a connection ends.
ExecuteComplete	Fired after a command has finished executing.
InfoMessage	Fired whenever a ConnectionEvent operation completes successfully and additional information is returned by the provider. SQL Server only.
RollbackTransComplete	Fired after a RollbackTrans operation finished executing.
WillConnect	Fired before a connection starts.
WillExecute	Fired before a pending command executes on the connection.

The Error Object

Properties of the Error Object	Return Type	Description
Description	String	A description string associated with the error. Read only.
HelpContext	Integer	Indicates the ContextID in the help file for the associated error. Read only.

Table Continued on Following Page

Properties of the Error Object	Return Type	Description
HelpFile	String	Indicates the name of the help file. Read only.
NativeError	Long	Indicates the provider-specific error code for the associated error. Read only.
Number	Long	Indicates the number that uniquely identifies an Error object. Read only.
Source	String	Indicates the name of the object or application that originally generated the error. Read only.
SQLState	String	Indicates the SQL state for a given Error object. It is a five-character string that follows the ANSI SQL standard. Read only.

The Errors Collection

Methods of the Errors Collection	Return Type	Description
Clear		Removes all of the Error objects from the Errors collection.
Refresh		Updates the Error objects with information from the provider.

Properties of the Errors Collection	Return Type	Description
Count	Long	Indicates the number of Error objects in the Errors collection. Read only.
Item	Error	Allows indexing into the Errors collection to reference a specific Error object. Read only.

The Field Object

Methods of the Field Object	Return Type	Description
AppendChunk		Appends data to a large or binary Field object.
GetChunk	Variant	Returns all or a portion of the contents of a large or binary Field object.

Properties of the Field Object	Return Type	Description
ActualSize	Long	Indicates the actual length of a field's value. Read only.
Attributes	Long	Indicates one or more characteristics of a Field object.
DataFormat	Variant	Identifies the format in which data should be displayed.
DefinedSize	Long	Indicates the defined size of the Field object. Write only.
Name	String	Indicates the name of the Field object.
NumericScale	Byte	Indicates the scale of numeric values for the Field object. Write only.
OriginalValue	Variant	Indicates the value of a Field object that existed in the record before any changes were made. Read only.
Precision	Byte	Indicates the degree of precision for numeric values in the Field object. Read only.
Type	DataTypeEnum	Indicates the data type of the Field object.
UnderlyingValue	Variant	Indicates a Field object's current value in the database. Read only.
Value	Variant	Indicates the value assigned to the Field object.

Collections of the Field Object	Return Type	Description
Properties	Properties	Contains all of the Property objects for a Field object.

The Fields Collection

Methods of the Fields Collection	Return Type	Description
Append		Appends a Field object to the Fields collection.

Table Continued on Following Page

461

Methods of the Fields Collection	Return Type	Description
Delete		Deletes a `Field` object from the `Fields` collection.
Refresh		Updates the `Field` objects in the `Fields` collection.

Properties of the Fields Collection	Return Type	Description
Count	Long	Indicates the number of `Field` objects in the `Fields` collection. Read only.
Item	Field	Allows indexing into the `Fields` collection to reference a specific `Field` object. Read only.

The Parameter Object

Methods of the Parameter Object	Return Type	Description
AppendChunk		Appends data to a large or binary `Parameter` object.

Properties of the Parameter Object	Return Type	Description
Attributes	Long	Indicates one or more characteristics of a `Parameter` object.
Direction	Parameter DirectionEnum	Indicates whether the `Parameter` object represents an input parameter, an output parameter, or and input/output parameter, or if the parameter is a return value from a stored procedure.
Name	String	Indicates the name of the `Parameter` object.
NumericScale	Byte	Indicates the scale of numeric values for the `Parameter` object.
Precision	Byte	Indicates the degree of precision for numeric values in the `Parameter` object.

462

Properties of the Parameter Object	Return Type	Description
Size	Long	Indicates the maximum size (in bytes or characters) of a Parameter object.
Type	DataTypeEnum	Indicates the data type of the Parameter object.
Value	Variant	Indicates the value assigned to the Parameter object.

Collections of the Parameter Object	Return Type	Description
Properties	Properties	Contains all of the Property objects for a Parameter object.

The Parameters Collection

Methods of the Parameters Collection	Return Type	Description
Append		Appends a Parameter object to the Parameters collection.
Delete		Deletes a Parameter object from the Parameters collection.
Refresh		Updates the Parameter objects in the Parameters collection.

Properties of the Parameters Collection	Return Type	Description
Count	Long	Indicates the number of Parameter objects in the Parameters collection. Read only.
Item	Parameter	Allows indexing into the Parameters collection to reference a specific Parameter object. Read only.

The Properties Collection

Methods of the Properties Collection	Return Type	Description
Refresh		Updates the Property objects in the Properties collection with the details from the provider.

Properties of the Properties Collection	Return Type	Description
Count	Long	Indicates the number of Property objects in the Properties collection. Read only.
Item	Property	Allows indexing into the Properties collection to reference a specific Property object. Read only.

The Property Object

Properties of the Property Object	Return Type	Description
Attributes	Long	Indicates one or more characteristics of a Property object.
Name	String	Indicates the name of the Property object. Read only.
Type	DataTypeEnum	Indicates the data type of the Property object.
Value	Variant	Indicates the value assigned to the Property object.

The Recordset Object

Methods of the Recordset Object	Return Type	Description
AddNew		Creates a new record for an updateable Recordset object.

Methods of the Recordset Object	Return Type	Description
Cancel		Cancels execution of a pending asynchronous Open operation.
CancelBatch		Cancels a pending batch update.
CancelUpdate		Cancels any changes made to the current record, or to a new record prior to calling the Update method.
Clone	Recordset	Creates a duplicate Recordset object from an existing Recordset object.
Close		Closes the Recordset object and any dependent objects.
CompareBookmarks	CompareEnum	Compares two bookmarks and returns an indication of the relative values.
Delete		Deletes the current record or group of records.
Find		Searches the Recordset for a record that matches the specified criteria.
GetRows	Variant	Retrieves multiple records of a Recordset object into an array.
GetString	String	Returns a Recordset as a string.
Move		Moves the position of the current record in a Recordset.
MoveFirst		Moves the position of the current record to the first record in the Recordset.
MoveLast		Moves the position of the current record to the last record in the Recordset.
MoveNext		Moves the position of the current record to the next record in the Recordset.
MovePrevious		Moves the position of the current record to the previous record in the Recordset.
NextRecordset	Recordset	Clears the current Recordset object and returns the next Recordset by advancing to the next in a series of commands.

Table Continued on Following Page

465

Methods of the Recordset Object	Return Type	Description
Open		Opens a Recordset.
Requery		Updates the data in a Recordset object by re-executing the query on which the object is based.
Resync		Refreshes the data in the current Recordset object from the underlying database.
Save		Saves the Recordset to a file.
Seek		Searches the recordset index to locate a value
Supports	Boolean	Determines whether a specified Recordset object supports particular functionality.
Update		Saves any changes made to the current Recordset object.
UpdateBatch		Writes all pending batch updates to disk.

Properties of the Recordset Object	Return Type	Description
AbsolutePage	PositionEnum	Specifies in which page the current record resides.
AbsolutePosition	PositionEnum	Specifies the ordinal position of the Recordset object's current record.
ActiveCommand	Object	Indicates the Command object that created the associated Recordset object. Read only.
ActiveConnection	Variant	Indicates to which Connection object the Recordset object currently belongs.
BOF	Boolean	Indicates whether the record pointer is pointing before the first record in the Recordset object. Read only.

Properties of the Recordset Object	Return Type	Description
Bookmark	Variant	Returns a bookmark that uniquely identifies the current record in the Recordset object, or sets the record pointer to point to the record identified by a valid bookmark.
CacheSize	Long	Indicates the number of records from the Recordset object that are cached locally in memory. This can not be set in Oracle.
CursorLocation	CursorLocationEnum	Sets or returns the location of the cursor engine.
CursorType	CursorTypeEnum	Indicates the type of cursor used in the Recordset object.
DataMember	String	Specifies the name of the data member to be retrieved from the object referenced by the DataSource property. Write only.
DataSource	Object	Specifies an object containing data, to be represented by the Recordset object. Write only.
EditMode	EditModeEnum	Indicates the editing status of the current record. Read only.
EOF	Boolean	Indicates whether the record pointer is pointing beyond the last record in the Recordset object. Read only.
Filter	Variant	Indicates a filter for data in the Recordset.
Index	String	Identifies the name of the index currently being used.
LockType	LockTypeEnum	Indicates the type of locks placed on records during editing.
MarshalOptions	MarshalOptionsEnum	Indicates which records are to be marshaled back to the server.

Table Continued on Following Page

Properties of the Recordset Object	Return Type	Description
MaxRecords	Long	Indicates the maximum number of records that can be returned to the Recordset object from a query. Default is zero (no limit).
PageCount	Long	Indicates how many pages of data are contained in the Recordset object (and is thus dependent on the values of PageSize and RecordCount). Read only. Not supported by Oracle.
PageSize	Long	Indicates how many records constitute one page in the Recordset. Not supported by Oracle.
RecordCount	Long	Indicates the current number of records in the Recordset object. Read only. Not supported by Oracle.
Sort	String	Specifies one or more field names the Recordset is sorted on, and the direction of the sort.
Source	String	Indicates the source for the data in the Recordset object.
State	Long	Indicates whether the recordset is open, closed, or whether it is executing an asynchronous operation. Read only.
Status	Integer	Indicates the status of the current record with respect to match updates or other bulk operations. Read only.
StayInSync	Boolean	Indicates, in a hierarchical Recordset object, whether the parent row should change when the set of underlying child records changes. Read only.

Collections of the Recordset Object	Return Type	Description
Fields	Fields	Contains all of the Field objects for the Recordset object.
Properties	Properties	Contains all of the Property objects for the current Recordset object.

Events of the Recordset Object	Description
EndOfRecordset	Fired when there is an attempt to move to a row past the end of the Recordset.
FetchComplete	Fired after all the records in an asynchronous operation have been retrieved into the Recordset.
FetchProgress	Fired periodically during a length asynchronous operation, to report how many rows have currently been retrieved.
FieldChangeComplete	Fired after the value of one or more Field object has been changed.
MoveComplete	Fired after the current position in the Recordset changes.
RecordChangeComplete	Fired after one or more records change.
RecordsetChangeComplete	Fired after the Recordset has changed.
WillChangeField	Fired before a pending operation changes the value of one or more Field objects.
WillChangeRecord	Fired before one or more rows in the Recordset change.
WillChangeRecordset	Fired before a pending operation changes the Recordset.
WillMove	Fired before a pending operation changes the current position in the Recordset.

Connecting to Oracle via Access

One of the ways in which we can work with Oracle tables is the familiar interface of Microsoft Access. Many of our "Power Users" are already using it, some in very sophisticated ways. I find Access a great tool for simple tasks. For instance, I usually update code files, such as this book's `JobDescription` using Access. I'll actually do exactly this in here.

How do we connect to Oracle via Access?

Creating a New Database (New to Access)

First we start Access.

We create a **New Database** by selecting the proper radio button and clicking OK:

Then we name it properly:

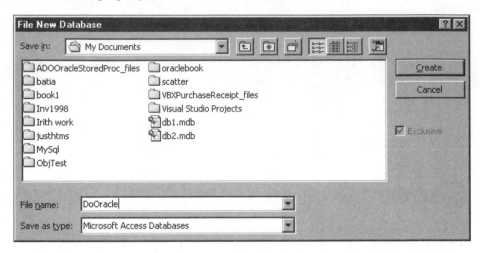

And click Create.

We now click the New button.
When the next form pops up
we select Link Table and click
OK:

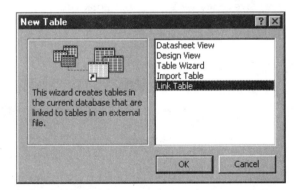

Now select
ODBC
Databases
from the
drop down
menu:

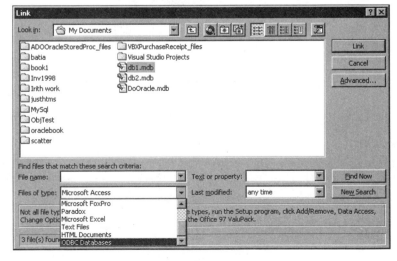

The result of this selection is the following screen, where we click the **Machine Data Source** tab and select our already prepared DSN for Oracle. This is the DSN we've been using all along with ADO:

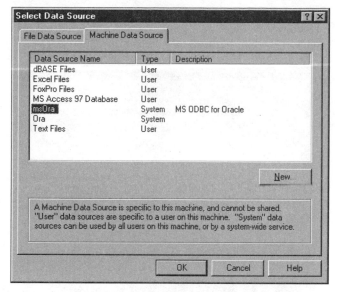

We now click **OK**. In the Input Box we enter our password (tiger) and click **OK**. Here we discover an interesting twist. Access allows us too much access (an excess of access via Access). Practically everything in the database is available to us. This is true only in the case of Personal Oracle. Whenever I connect to Oracle via Access on a client site, I only get what I am permitted to see.

Here is a normally forbidden area:

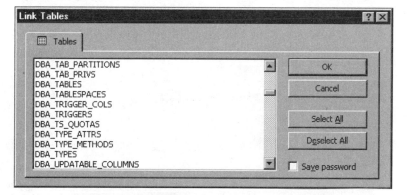

We are now in the sanctum sanctorum of the DBA area.

And here is the complete **SCOTT** schema. It includes our tables and the tables previously created by Oracle:

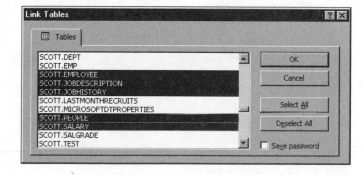

Let us have a look at our tables. We achieve this by selecting all that we want and clicking OK.

Here is the result:

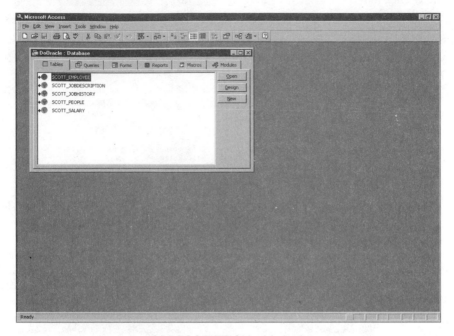

Now let us see how the JOBDESCRIPTION table looks:

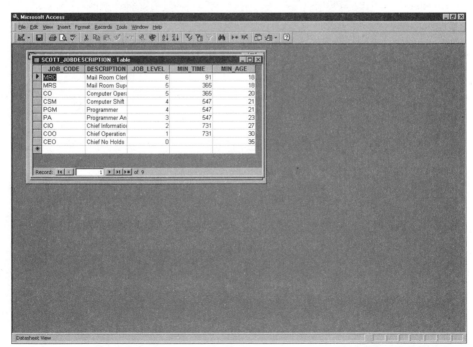

We can now add rows, update existing ones and even, god forbid delete them. Delete may actually present a problem because without cascading it creates integrity problems, and we have not set the database constraints with the ON DELETE CASCADE option. Updating JOB_CODE may present problems for the same reasons.

You can now do whatever you want. Create queries, forms, and reports, even draw the relationships map:

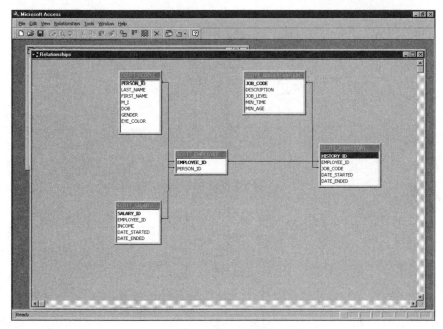

Opening an Old Database

Start Access and select the database that you created. In our case DoOracle:

Proceed as before. That's all folks!

Oracle URLs and Books

Books

❑ **Professional ADO RDS Programming with ASP**
Matt Brown, Charles Crawford Caison Jr, Peter DeBetta, John Papa, Eric Wilson
WROX. ISBN: **1861001649**

This is the only ASP book that shows how to actually connect to an Oracle database and how to get to its information.

❑ **ADO 2.1 Programmer's Reference**
David Sussman
WROX. ISBN: **1861002688**

This is the definitive ADO reference.

URLs

❑ **Large River Oracle Home Page:**

`http://www.ieighty.net/~davepamn/display.html`

A good starting point for a search.

❑ **utexas oracle documents on line:**

`http://pundit.bus.utexas.edu/oradocs/server803/index.htm`

Documentation galore - Version 8.03 is a little outdated, but every little detail is there.

❑ **Oracle assist:**

`http://www.oracleassist.com/`

General info, even jobs. Also a good starting point to further searches.

❑ **The best nonofficial Oracle site:**

`http://www.revealnet.com/`

A must for Oracle and other databases.

❑ **From LearnASP and ASPLlists (same site):**

`http://www.asplists.com/learn/FAQOraclestoredproc.asp`

`http://learnasp.com/asplists/asporaclesetup.asp`

`http://learnasp.com/asplists/asporacle.asp`

The only asp site to talk about Oracle (so far)

❑ **Oracle itself, of course:**

`http://www.Oracle.com/`

`http://technet.oracle.com/`

❑ **FAQ sites:**

`http://www.orafaq.org/faqmain.htm`

More questions than answers. Also some OO4O

❑ **SQL in general:**

`http://www.jcc.com/SQLPages/jccs_sql.htm`

❑ **SQL Tutorial:**

`http://torresoft.netmegs.com`

No www in front.

❑ **More SQL links:**

`http://dir.yahoo.com/Computers_and_Internet/`
                                    `Programming_Languages/SQL/`

Data Dictionary Tables

The DATA Dictionary

The tables of interest are:

- ❑ USER_OBJECTS - where all the objects are listed and described
- ❑ USER_TABLES- where the tables are described
- ❑ USER_SOURCE- where the code for the stored procedures is held
- ❑ USER_SEQUENCES- where all the Sequences are described
- ❑ USER_INDEXES- where the index/table relationship is kept
- ❑ USER_TAB_COLUMNS- where the columns are described

> **The data dictionary tables only describe the objects in your current schema.**

Below are the descriptions of the data dictionary tables: as well as that of the USER_ROLE_PRIVS.

Name	Null?	Type
OBJECT_NAME		VARCHAR2(128)
SUBOBJECT_NAME		VARCHAR2(30)
OBJECT_ID		NUMBER
DATA_OBJECT_ID		NUMBER

Table Continued on Following Page

Name	Null?	Type
OBJECT_TYPE		VARCHAR2(15)
CREATED		DATE
LAST_DDL_TIME		DATE
TIMESTAMP		VARCHAR2(19)
STATUS		VARCHAR2(7)
TEMPORARY		VARCHAR2(1)
GENERATED		VARCHAR2(1)

Here are the descriptions of the other 5 objects covered, starting with USER_TABLES:

Name	Null?	Type
TABLE_NAME	NOT NULL	VARCHAR2(30)
TABLESPACE_NAME		VARCHAR2(30)
CLUSTER_NAME		VARCHAR2(30)
IOT_NAME		VARCHAR2(30)
PCT_FREE		NUMBER
PCT_USED		NUMBER
INI_TRANS		NUMBER
MAX_TRANS		NUMBER
INITIAL_EXTENT		NUMBER
NEXT_EXTENT		NUMBER
MIN_EXTENTS		NUMBER
MAX_EXTENTS		NUMBER
PCT_INCREASE		NUMBER
FREELISTS		NUMBER
FREELIST_GROUPS		NUMBER
LOGGING		VARCHAR2(3)
BACKED_UP		VARCHAR2(1)
NUM_ROWS		NUMBER
BLOCKS		NUMBER
EMPTY_BLOCKS		NUMBER

Name	Null?	Type
AVG_SPACE		NUMBER
CHAIN_CNT		NUMBER
AVG_ROW_LEN		NUMBER
AVG_SPACE_FREELIST_BLOCKS		NUMBER
NUM_FREELIST_BLOCKS		NUMBER
DEGREE		VARCHAR2(10)
INSTANCES		VARCHAR2(10)
CACHE		VARCHAR2(5)
TABLE_LOCK		VARCHAR2(8)
SAMPLE_SIZE		NUMBER
LAST_ANALYZED		DATE
PARTITIONED		VARCHAR2(3)
IOT_TYPE		VARCHAR2(12)
TEMPORARY		VARCHAR2(1)
NESTED		VARCHAR2(3)
BUFFER_POOL		VARCHAR2(7)

Here is the description of the USER_SOURCE table. The rows of this table actually contain the code of the stored procedures:

Name	Null?	Type
NAME	NOT NULL	VARCHAR2(30)
TYPE		VARCHAR2(12)
LINE	NOT NULL	NUMBER
TEXT		VARCHAR2(4000)

Now a look at the description of USER_SEQUENCES:

Name	Null?	Type
SEQUENCE_NAME	NOT NULL	VARCHAR2(30)
MIN_VALUE		NUMBER

Table Continued on Following Page

Name	Null?	Type
MAX_VALUE		NUMBER
INCREMENT_BY	NOT NULL	NUMBER
CYCLE_FLAG		VARCHAR2(1)
ORDER_FLAG		VARCHAR2(1)
CACHE_SIZE	NOT NULL	NUMBER
LAST_NUMBER	NOT NULL	NUMBER

The USER_ROLE_PRIVS table:

Name	Null?	Type
USERNAME		VARCHAR2(30)
GRANTED_ROLE		VARCHAR2(30)
ADMIN_OPTION		VARCHAR2(3)
DEFAULT_ROLE		VARCHAR2(3)
OS_GRANTED		VARCHAR2(3)

The longest description goes with the USER_INDEXES table:

Name	Null?	Type
INDEX_NAME	NOT NULL	VARCHAR2(30)
INDEX_TYPE		VARCHAR2(12)
TABLE_OWNER	NOT NULL	VARCHAR2(30)
TABLE_NAME	NOT NULL	VARCHAR2(30)
TABLE_TYPE		VARCHAR2(11)
UNIQUENESS		VARCHAR2(9)
TABLESPACE_NAME		VARCHAR2(30)
INI_TRANS		NUMBER
MAX_TRANS		NUMBER
INITIAL_EXTENT		NUMBER
NEXT_EXTENT		NUMBER
MIN_EXTENTS		NUMBER
MAX_EXTENTS		NUMBER

Name	Null?	Type
PCT_INCREASE		NUMBER
PCT_THRESHOLD		NUMBER
INCLUDE_COLUMN		NUMBER
FREELISTS		NUMBER
FREELIST_GROUPS		NUMBER
PCT_FREE		NUMBER
LOGGING		VARCHAR2(3)
BLEVEL		NUMBER
LEAF_BLOCKS		NUMBER
DISTINCT_KEYS		NUMBER
AVG_LEAF_BLOCKS_PER_KEY		NUMBER
AVG_DATA_BLOCKS_PER_KEY		NUMBER
CLUSTERING_FACTOR		NUMBER
STATUS		VARCHAR2(8)
NUM_ROWS		NUMBER
SAMPLE_SIZE		NUMBER
LAST_ANALYZED		DATE
DEGREE		VARCHAR2(40)
INSTANCES		VARCHAR2(40)
PARTITIONED		VARCHAR2(3)
TEMPORARY		VARCHAR2(1)
GENERATED		VARCHAR2(1)
BUFFER_POOL		VARCHAR2(7)

And finally the description of the USER_TAB_COLUMNS table:

Name	Null?	Type
TABLE_NAME	NOT NULL	VARCHAR2(30)
COLUMN_NAME	NOT NULL	VARCHAR2(30)
DATA_TYPE		VARCHAR2(30)

Table Continued on Following Page

Name	Null?	Type
DATA_TYPE_MOD		VARCHAR2(3)
DATA_TYPE_OWNER		VARCHAR2(30)
DATA_LENGTH	NOT NULL	NUMBER
DATA_PRECISION		NUMBER
DATA_SCALE		NUMBER
NULLABLE		VARCHAR2(1)
COLUMN_ID	NOT NULL	NUMBER
DEFAULT_LENGTH		NUMBER
DATA_DEFAULT		LONG
NUM_DISTINCT		NUMBER
LOW_VALUE		RAW(32)
HIGH_VALUE		RAW(32)
DENSITY		NUMBER
NUM_NULLS		NUMBER
NUM_BUCKETS		NUMBER
LAST_ANALYZED		DATE
SAMPLE_SIZE		NUMBER
CHARACTER_SET_NAME		VARCHAR2(44)
CHAR_COL_DECL_LENGTH		NUMBER

HR Application Class Listings

When we discussed our HR application in Chapter 14, we walked through building one of the five classes we needed, clsPeople. This appendix contains the code for the other four classes used in the application:

❏ clsEmployee

❏ clsJobDescription

❏ clsJobHistory

❏ clsSalary

With the code in this appendix, you should have all the complete code you need for the HR application. It is also available to download from the WROX website after registering, at http://www.wrox.com.

clsEmployee

```
'Table name is:              EMPLOYEE
Option Explicit
Private mcConnection As clsConnection    'my connection
Private mADOConnection As ADODB.Connection 'Required for connection to clsConnection
'* Recordsets
Private mrsEmployee As ADODB.Recordset
'* Command Objects
Private mSelectCmd As ADODB.Command
Private mInsertCmd As ADODB.Command
Private mDeleteCmd As ADODB.Command
'* Parameters
'* Select
Private mSelectPrmPersonId As ADODB.Parameter
'* Insert - in order of the select statement
Private mInsertPrmEmployeeId As ADODB.Parameter
Private mInsertPrmPersonId As ADODB.Parameter
'* Delete
Private mDeletePrmEmployeeId As ADODB.Parameter
'** The sQL statements
Private msSelect As String
Private msDelete As String
```

```
Private msInsert As String
'** Class variables
Private mlPersonId As Double   'Get and Let
Private mlEmployeeId As Double   'Get and Let
'** for less round trips keep all the properties in a variant array
Private mvAll As Variant 'Get and Let
'* the recordset GetRows
Private mvRows As Variant
'* the size of the recordset (how many rows)
Private mlRows As Long
'* the index of the current row
Private mlX As Long
'* The EOF condition
Private mbEOF As Boolean


'** Class Properties
Public Property Get EOF() As Boolean
    EOF = mrsEmployee.EOF
End Property


Public Property Get IsEmpty() As Boolean
    IsEmpty = mrsEmployee.EOF And mrsEmployee.BOF
End Property


Public Property Get EmployeeId() As Double
    EmployeeId = mlEmployeeId
End Property


Public Property Let EmployeeId(ByVal NewValue As Double)
    mlEmployeeId = NewValue
End Property


Public Property Get PersonId() As Double
    PersonId = mlPersonId
End Property


Public Property Let PersonId(ByVal NewValue As Double)
    mlPersonId = NewValue
End Property


Private Sub Class_Initialize()
'** Initialize Class Variables
    SetDefaults
'Make a parameter SQL for the reading the reordset
    msSelect = "Select "
    msSelect = msSelect & "EMPLOYEE_ID, "
    msSelect = msSelect & "PERSON_ID"
    msSelect = msSelect & " FROM EMPLOYEE"
    msSelect = msSelect & " Where PERSON_ID = ?"
'Delete
    msDelete = "Delete"
    msDelete = msDelete & " FROM EMPLOYEE"
    msDelete = msDelete & " Where EMPLOYEE_ID = ?"
'Make a parameter SQL for the Inserting into the RecordSet
    msInsert = "INSERT INTO "
    msInsert = msInsert & " EMPLOYEE ("
    msInsert = msInsert & "EMPLOYEE_ID,  "
    msInsert = msInsert & "PERSON_ID) "
    msInsert = msInsert & "VALUES ("
    msInsert = msInsert & "?, "
    msInsert = msInsert & "?)"
End Sub
```

490

```
Private Sub SetDefaults()
    mlEmployeeId = 0
    mlPersonId = 0
End Sub
Public Sub ConnectX(ByVal NewValue As clsConnection) 'Required for connection to clsConnection
    Set mcConnection = NewValue
    'our class relies on an already open ADOConnection.
    Set mADOConnection = mcConnection.ADOConnection
    Set mSelectCmd = New ADODB.Command
    With mSelectCmd
        .ActiveConnection = mADOConnection
        .CommandType = adCmdText
        .CommandText = msSelect
        Set mSelectPrmPersonId = .CreateParameter("pPersonId", adDouble, adParamInput, , 0)
        .Parameters.Append mSelectPrmPersonId
    End With
    Set mrsEmployee = mSelectCmd.Execute
    Set mDeleteCmd = New ADODB.Command
    With mDeleteCmd
        .ActiveConnection = mADOConnection
        .CommandType = adCmdText
        .CommandText = msDelete
        Set mDeletePrmEmployeeId = .CreateParameter("pEmployeeId", adDouble, adParamInput)
        .Parameters.Append mDeletePrmEmployeeId
    End With
    Set mInsertCmd = New ADODB.Command 'needs parameters beyond cl_auth_id
    With mInsertCmd
        .ActiveConnection = mADOConnection
        .CommandType = adCmdText
        .CommandText = msInsert
        Set mInsertPrmEmployeeId = .CreateParameter("pEmployeeId", adDouble, adParamInput)
        .Parameters.Append mInsertPrmEmployeeId
        Set mInsertPrmPersonId = .CreateParameter("pPersonId", adDouble, adParamInput)
        .Parameters.Append mInsertPrmPersonId
    End With
End Sub

Public Sub Refresh()
'** Set parameters and re-read
    mSelectPrmPersonId.Value = mlPersonId
    Set mrsEmployee = mSelectCmd.Execute
    If mrsEmployee.EOF And mrsEmployee.BOF Then
        SetDefaults
    Else
        mvRows = mrsEmployee.GetRows
        SetProperties
    End If
End Sub

Public Sub SetProperties()
    SetDefaults
    If Not IsNull(mvRows(0, 0)) Then
        mlEmployeeId = mvRows(0, 0)
    End If
```

```
        If Not IsNull(mvRows(1, 0)) Then
            mlPersonId = mvRows(1, 0)
        End If
    End Sub

    Public Sub AddNew()
        ' Insert all the values into the parameters
        mlEmployeeId = 0
        mInsertPrmEmployeeId.Value = mlEmployeeId
        mInsertPrmPersonId.Value = mlPersonId
        mInsertCmd.Execute
    End Sub

    Public Sub Delete()
        mDeletePrmEmployeeId.Value = mlEmployeeId
        mDeleteCmd.Execute
    End Sub
```

clsJobDescription

```
'Table name is:              JOBDESCRIPTION
Option Explicit
'**
Private mcConnection As clsConnection     'my connection
Private mADOConnection As ADODB.Connection 'Required for connection to clsConnection
Private mrsJobDescription As ADODB.Recordset
'** The select statements
Private msSelect As String
'** Class variables
Private msJobCode As String  'Get Only
Private msDescription As String   'Get Only
'** The OraDynaset works faster if its field references are direct
'   For that purpose we build a field object for every column.
Private mfldJobCode As ADODB.Field
Private mfldDescription As ADODB.Field

'** Class Properties
Public Property Get EOF() As Boolean
    EOF = mrsJobDescription.EOF
End Property

Public Property Get IsEmpty() As Boolean
    IsEmpty = mrsJobDescription.EOF And mrsJobDescription.BOF
End Property

Public Property Get JobCode() As String
    JobCode = msJobCode
End Property

Public Property Get Description() As String
    Description = msDescription
End Property

Private Sub Class_Initialize()
'** Initialize Class Variables
    ReDim mvAll(0 To 1) 'we have 2 properties rolled into the array
    SetDefaults
```

```
'Make a parameter SQL for the reading the dynaset
    msSelect = "Select "
    msSelect = msSelect & "JOB_CODE, "
    msSelect = msSelect & "DESCRIPTION"
    msSelect = msSelect & " FROM JOBDESCRIPTION"
End Sub

Private Sub SetDefaults()
    msJobCode = ""
    msDescription = ""
End Sub

Public Sub ConnectX(ByVal NewValue As clsConnection) 'Required for connection to
                                                      'clsConnection

    Set mcConnection = NewValue
    'our class relies on an already open ADOConnection.
    Set mADOConnection = mcConnection.ADOConnection
    'we now create the RecordSet
    Set mrsJobDescription = New ADODB.Recordset
    mrsJobDescription.Open msSelect, mADOConnection, adOpenStatic, adLockOptimistic
    Set mfldJobCode = mrsJobDescription.Fields!JOB_CODE
    Set mfldDescription = mrsJobDescription.Fields!Description
End Sub

Public Sub Refresh()
'** Set parameters and re-read
    mrsJobDescription.Requery
    SetProperties
End Sub

Public Sub SetProperties()
    If mrsJobDescription.EOF Then Exit Sub
    SetDefaults
    If Not IsNull(mfldJobCode.Value) Then
        msJobCode = mfldJobCode.Value
    End If
    If Not IsNull(mfldDescription.Value) Then
        msDescription = mfldDescription.Value
    End If
End Sub

Public Sub MoveFirst()
    If Not mrsJobDescription.BOF Then
        mrsJobDescription.MoveFirst
        SetProperties
    End If
End Sub

Public Sub MoveLast()
    If Not mrsJobDescription.EOF Then
        mrsJobDescription.MoveLast
        SetProperties
    End If
End Sub

Public Sub MoveNext(Optional ByVal bWithEOF As Boolean = False)
    If Not mrsJobDescription.EOF Then
        mrsJobDescription.MoveNext
        If Not bWithEOF Then
```

```
                If mrsJobDescription.EOF Then mrsJobDescription.MoveLast
            End If
            SetProperties
        End If
End Sub

Public Sub MovePrevious()
    If Not mrsJobDescription.BOF Then
        mrsJobDescription.MovePrevious
        If mrsJobDescription.BOF Then mrsJobDescription.MoveFirst
        SetProperties
    End If
End Sub
```

clsJobHistory

```
'Table name is:              JOBHISTORY
'Class Name is:              JobHistory
Option Explicit
Private mcConnection As clsConnection    'Oh my Papa
Private mADOConnection As ADODB.Connection 'Required for connection to clsConnection
'* Recordsets
Private mrsHistory As ADODB.Recordset
'* Command Objects
Private mSelectCmd As ADODB.Command
Private mUpdateCmd As ADODB.Command
Private mInsertCmd As ADODB.Command
Private mDeleteCmd As ADODB.Command
'* Parameters
'* Select
Private mSelectPrmEmployeeId As ADODB.Parameter
'* Insert - in order of the select statement
Private mInsertPrmHistoryId As ADODB.Parameter
Private mInsertPrmEmployeeId As ADODB.Parameter
Private mInsertPrmJobCode As ADODB.Parameter
Private mInsertPrmDateStarted As ADODB.Parameter
Private mInsertPrmDateEnded As ADODB.Parameter
'* Update - in the order of the update statement
Private mUpdatePrmJobCode As ADODB.Parameter
Private mUpdatePrmDateStarted As ADODB.Parameter
Private mUpdatePrmDateEnded As ADODB.Parameter
Private mUpdatePrmHistoryId As ADODB.Parameter
'* Delete
Private mDeletePrmHistoryId As ADODB.Parameter
'** The sQL statements
Private msSelect As String
Private msUpdate As String
Private msDelete As String
Private msInsert As String
'** Class variables
Private mlHistoryId As Double  'Get and Let
Private mlEmployeeId As Double  'Get and Let
Private msJobCode As String  'Get and Let
Private mdDateStarted As Date  'Get and Let
Private mdDateEnded As Date  'Get and Let
'** for less round trips keep all the properties in a variant array
Private mvAll As Variant 'Get and Let
'* the recordset GetRows
```

```
Private mvRows As Variant
'* the size of the recordset (how many rows)
Private mlRows As Long
'* the index of the current row
Private mlX As Long
'* The EOF condition
Private mbEOF As Boolean
Private Sub Class_Initialize()
'** Initialize Class Variables
    ReDim mvAll(0 To 4) 'we have 5 properties rolled into the array
    SetDefaults
'Make a parameter SQL for the reading and Updating
    BuildSQL
End Sub

'** Class Properties
Public Property Get EOF() As Boolean
    EOF = mrsHistory.EOF
End Property

Public Property Get IsEmpty() As Boolean
    IsEmpty = mrsHistory.EOF And mrsHistory.BOF
End Property

Public Property Get HistoryId() As Double
    HistoryId = mlHistoryId
End Property

Public Property Let HistoryId(ByVal NewValue As Double)
    mlHistoryId = NewValue
End Property

Public Property Get EmployeeId() As Double
    EmployeeId = mlEmployeeId
End Property

Public Property Let EmployeeId(ByVal NewValue As Double)
    mlEmployeeId = NewValue
End Property

Public Property Get JobCode() As String
    JobCode = msJobCode
End Property

Public Property Let JobCode(ByVal NewValue As String)
    msJobCode = NewValue
End Property

Public Property Get DateStarted() As Date
    DateStarted = mdDateStarted
End Property

Public Property Let DateStarted(ByVal NewValue As Date)
    mdDateStarted = NewValue
End Property

Public Property Get DateEnded() As Date
    DateEnded = mdDateEnded
End Property
```

```
Public Property Let DateEnded(ByVal NewValue As Date)
    mdDateEnded = NewValue
End Property

Private Sub SetDefaults()
    mlHistoryId = 0
    'mlEmployeeId = 0
    msJobCode = ""
    mdDateStarted = #1/1/1800#
    mdDateEnded = #1/1/1800#
End Sub

Public Sub ConnectX(ByVal NewValue As clsConnection) 'Required for connection to clsConnection
    Set mcConnection = NewValue
    'our class relies on an already open ADOConnection.
    Set mADOConnection = mcConnection.ADOConnection
    Set mSelectCmd = New ADODB.Command
    With mSelectCmd
        .ActiveConnection = mADOConnection
        .CommandType = adCmdText
        .CommandText = msSelect
        Set mSelectPrmEmployeeId = .CreateParameter("pEmployeeId", adDouble, _
                                        adParamInput, , 0)
        .Parameters.Append mSelectPrmEmployeeId
    End With
    Set mrsHistory = mSelectCmd.Execute
    Set mDeleteCmd = New ADODB.Command
    With mDeleteCmd
        .ActiveConnection = mADOConnection
        .CommandType = adCmdText
        .CommandText = msDelete
        Set mDeletePrmHistoryId = .CreateParameter("pHistoryId", adDouble, adParamInput)
        .Parameters.Append mDeletePrmHistoryId
    End With
    Set mUpdateCmd = New ADODB.Command
    With mUpdateCmd
        .ActiveConnection = mADOConnection
        .CommandType = adCmdText
        .CommandText = msUpdate
        Set mUpdatePrmJobCode = .CreateParameter("pJobCode", adVarChar, _
                                        adParamInput, 25, "")
        .Parameters.Append mUpdatePrmJobCode
        Set mUpdatePrmDateStarted = .CreateParameter("pDateStarted", _
                                            adDBTimeStamp, adParamInput)
        .Parameters.Append mUpdatePrmDateStarted
        Set mUpdatePrmDateEnded = .CreateParameter("pDateEnded", adDBTimeStamp, adParamInput)
        .Parameters.Append mUpdatePrmDateEnded
        Set mUpdatePrmHistoryId = .CreateParameter("pHistoryId", adDouble, adParamInput)
        .Parameters.Append mUpdatePrmHistoryId
    End With
    Set mInsertCmd = New ADODB.Command 'needs parameters beyond cl_auth_id
    With mInsertCmd
        .ActiveConnection = mADOConnection
        .CommandType = adCmdText
        .CommandText = msInsert
        Set mInsertPrmHistoryId = .CreateParameter("pHistoryId", adDouble, adParamInput)
```

```
        .Parameters.Append mInsertPrmHistoryId
        Set mInsertPrmEmployeeId = .CreateParameter('pEmployeeId', adDouble, adParamInput)
        .Parameters.Append mInsertPrmEmployeeId
        Set mInsertPrmJobCode = .CreateParameter("pJobCode", adVarChar, _
                                    adParamInput, 25, "")
        .Parameters.Append mInsertPrmJobCode
        Set mInsertPrmDateStarted = .CreateParameter("pDateStarted", _
                                        adDBTimeStamp, adParamInput)
        .Parameters.Append mInsertPrmDateStarted
        Set mInsertPrmDateEnded = .CreateParameter("pDateEnded", adDBTimeStamp, _
                                    adParamInput)
        .Parameters.Append mInsertPrmDateEnded
    End With
End Sub

Public Sub Refresh()
'** Set parameters and re-read
    mSelectPrmEmployeeId.Value = mlEmployeeId
    Set mrsHistory = mSelectCmd.Execute
    If mrsHistory.BOF And mrsHistory.BOF Then
        SetDefaults
    Else
        mvRows = mrsHistory.GetRows
        mlRows = UBound(mvRows, 2) + 1 'The variant's second dimension is rows
        SetProperties (0)
    End If
End Sub

Public Sub SetProperties(lRow As Long)
    SetDefaults
    If Not IsNull(mvRows(0, lRow)) Then
        mlHistoryId = mvRows(0, lRow)
    End If
    If Not IsNull(mvRows(1, lRow)) Then
        mlEmployeeId = mvRows(1, lRow)
    End If
    If Not IsNull(mvRows(2, lRow)) Then
        msJobCode = mvRows(2, lRow)
    End If
    If Not IsNull(mvRows(3, lRow)) Then
        mdDateStarted = mvRows(3, lRow)
    End If
    If Not IsNull(mvRows(4, lRow)) Then
        mdDateEnded = mvRows(4, lRow)
    End If
End Sub

Public Sub MoveFirst()
    'mrsPeople.MoveFirst
    mlX = 0
    SetProperties (0)
End Sub

Public Sub MoveLast()
    mlX = mlRows - 1
    SetProperties (mlX)
End Sub
```

```
Public Sub MoveNext()
    If mlX <> mlRows - 1 Then
        mlX = mlX + 1
        SetProperties (mlX)
        mbEOF = False
    Else
        mbEOF = True
    End If
End Sub

Public Sub MovePrevious()
    If mlX <> 0 Then
        mlX = mlX - 1
        SetProperties (mlX)
    End If
End Sub

Public Sub MoveRel(lRows As Long)
    If lRows <> 0 Then
        mlX = mlX + lRows
        If mlX > mlRows - 1 Then mlX = mlRows - 1
        If mlX < 0 Then mlX = 0
        SetProperties (mlX)
    End If
End Sub
Public Sub AddNew()
    ' Insert all the values into the parameters
    mlHistoryId = 0
    mInsertPrmHistoryId.Value = mlHistoryId
    mInsertPrmEmployeeId.Value = mlEmployeeId
    mInsertPrmJobCode.Value = msJobCode
    mInsertPrmDateStarted.Value = mdDateStarted
    mInsertPrmDateEnded.Value = mdDateEnded
    mInsertCmd.Execute
End Sub

Public Sub Update()
    'mrsPeople.Edit
    'Insert all the values into the Parameters
    mUpdatePrmJobCode.Value = msJobCode
    If mdDateStarted = #1/1/1800# Then
        mUpdatePrmDateStarted.Value = Null
    Else
        mUpdatePrmDateStarted.Value = mdDateStarted
    End If
    If mdDateEnded = #1/1/1800# Then
        mUpdatePrmDateEnded.Value = Null
    Else
        mUpdatePrmDateEnded.Value = mdDateEnded
    End If
    mUpdatePrmHistoryId.Value = mlHistoryId
    mUpdateCmd.Execute
End Sub

Public Sub Delete()
    mDeletePrmHistoryId.Value = mlHistoryId
    mDeleteCmd.Execute
End Sub
```

```
Public Property Get All() As Variant
    mvAll(0) = mlHistoryId
    mvAll(1) = mlEmployeeId
    mvAll(2) = msJobCode
    mvAll(3) = mdDateStarted
    mvAll(4) = mdDateEnded
    All = mvAll
End Property

Public Property Let All(ByVal vNewValue As Variant)
    mvAll = vNewValue
    mlHistoryId = mvAll(0)
    mlEmployeeId = mvAll(1)
    msJobCode = mvAll(2)
    mdDateStarted = mvAll(3)
    mdDateEnded = mvAll(4)
End Property


Private Sub BuildSQL()
'Make a parameter SQL for the reading the RecordSet
    msSelect = "Select "
    msSelect = msSelect & "HISTORY_ID, "
    msSelect = msSelect & "EMPLOYEE_ID, "
    msSelect = msSelect & "JOB_CODE, "
    msSelect = msSelect & "DATE_STARTED, "
    msSelect = msSelect & "DATE_ENDED"
    msSelect = msSelect & " FROM JOBHISTORY"
    msSelect = msSelect & " Where EMPLOYEE_ID = ?"
'Make a parameter SQL for the Inserting into the RecordSet
    msInsert = "INSERT INTO "
    msInsert = msInsert & " JOBHISTORY ("
    msInsert = msInsert & "HISTORY_ID, "
    msInsert = msInsert & "EMPLOYEE_ID, "
    msInsert = msInsert & "JOB_CODE, "
    msInsert = msInsert & "DATE_STARTED, "
    msInsert = msInsert & "DATE_ENDED) "
    msInsert = msInsert & "VALUES ("
    msInsert = msInsert & "?, "
    msInsert = msInsert & "?, "
    msInsert = msInsert & "?, "
    msInsert = msInsert & "?, "
    msInsert = msInsert & "?)"
'Make a parameter SQL for the Updating the RecordSet
    msUpdate = "UPDATE "
    msUpdate = msUpdate & " JOBHISTORY SET"
    msUpdate = msUpdate & " JOB_CODE = ?,"
    msUpdate = msUpdate & " DATE_STARTED = ?,"
    msUpdate = msUpdate & " DATE_ENDED = ?"
    msUpdate = msUpdate & " WHERE HISTORY_ID = ?"
'Make a parameter SQL for the "deleting from the RecordSet - change status to "DELETE"
    msDelete = "DELETE "
    msDelete = msDelete & " FROM JOBHISTORY "
    msDelete = msDelete & " WHERE HISTORY_ID = ?"
End Sub
```

clsSalary

```
'Table name is:              SALARY
'Class Name is:              Salary
Option Explicit
Private mcConnection As clsConnection    'Oh my Papa
Private mADOConnection As ADODB.Connection 'Required for connection to clsConnection
'* Recordsets
Private mrsSalary As ADODB.Recordset
'* Command Objects
Private mSelectCmd As ADODB.Command
Private mUpdateCmd As ADODB.Command
Private mInsertCmd As ADODB.Command
Private mDeleteCmd As ADODB.Command
'* Parameters
'* Select
Private mSelectPrmEmployeeId As ADODB.Parameter
'* Insert - in order of the select statement
Private mInsertPrmSalaryId As ADODB.Parameter
Private mInsertPrmEmployeeId As ADODB.Parameter
Private mInsertPrmIncome As ADODB.Parameter
Private mInsertPrmDateStarted As ADODB.Parameter
Private mInsertPrmDateEnded As ADODB.Parameter
'* Update - in the order of the update statement
Private mUpdatePrmIncome As ADODB.Parameter
Private mUpdatePrmDateStarted As ADODB.Parameter
Private mUpdatePrmDateEnded As ADODB.Parameter
Private mUpdatePrmSalaryId As ADODB.Parameter
'* Delete
Private mDeletePrmSalaryId As ADODB.Parameter
'** The sQL statements
Private msSelect As String
Private msUpdate As String
Private msDelete As String
Private msInsert As String
'** Class variables
Private mlSalaryId As Double   'Get and Let
Private mlEmployeeId As Double   'Get and Let
Private mlIncome As Double   'Get and Let
Private mdDateStarted As Date   'Get and Let
Private mdDateEnded As Date   'Get and Let
'** for less round trips keep all the properties in a variant array
Private mvAll As Variant 'Get and Let
'* the recordset GetRows
Private mvRows As Variant
'* the size of the recordset (how many rows)
Private mlRows As Long
'* the index of the current row
Private mlX As Long
'* The EOF condition
Private mbEOF As Boolean

'** Class Properties
Public Property Get EOF() As Boolean
    EOF = mrsSalary.EOF
End Property

Public Property Get IsEmpty() As Boolean
    IsEmpty = mrsSalary.EOF And mrsSalary.BOF
End Property
```

```
Public Property Get SalaryId() As Double
    SalaryId = mlSalaryId
End Property

Public Property Let SalaryId(ByVal NewValue As Double)
    mlSalaryId = NewValue
End Property

Public Property Get EmployeeId() As Double
    EmployeeId = mlEmployeeId
End Property

Public Property Let EmployeeId(ByVal NewValue As Double)
    mlEmployeeId = NewValue
End Property

Public Property Get Income() As Double
    Income = mlIncome
End Property

Public Property Let Income(ByVal NewValue As Double)
    mlIncome = NewValue
End Property

Public Property Get DateStarted() As Date
    DateStarted = mdDateStarted
End Property

Public Property Let DateStarted(ByVal NewValue As Date)
    mdDateStarted = NewValue
End Property

Public Property Get DateEnded() As Date
    DateEnded = mdDateEnded
End Property

Public Property Let DateEnded(ByVal NewValue As Date)
    mdDateEnded = NewValue
End Property

Private Sub Class_Initialize()
'** Initialize Class Variables
    SetDefaults
    ReDim mvAll(0 To 4) 'we have 5 properties rolled into the array
    BuildSQL
End Sub

Private Sub SetDefaults()
    mlSalaryId = 0
    'mlEmployeeId = 0
    mlIncome = 0
    mdDateStarted = #1/1/1800#
    mdDateEnded = #1/1/1800#
End Sub

Public Sub ConnectX(ByVal NewValue As clsConnection) 'Required for connection _
                                                to clsConnection
    Set mcConnection = NewValue
```

```
        'our class relies on an already open ADOConnection.
        Set mADOConnection = mcConnection.ADOConnection
        Set mSelectCmd = New ADODB.Command
        With mSelectCmd
            .ActiveConnection = mADOConnection
            .CommandType = adCmdText
            .CommandText = msSelect
            Set mSelectPrmEmployeeId = .CreateParameter("pEmployeeId", adDouble, _
                                          adParamInput, , 0)
            .Parameters.Append mSelectPrmEmployeeId
        End With
        Set mrsSalary = mSelectCmd.Execute
        Set mDeleteCmd = New ADODB.Command
        With mDeleteCmd
            .ActiveConnection = mADOConnection
            .CommandType = adCmdText
            .CommandText = msDelete
            Set mDeletePrmSalaryId = .CreateParameter("pSalaryId", adDouble, _
                                         adParamInput)
            .Parameters.Append mDeletePrmSalaryId
        End With
        Set mUpdateCmd = New ADODB.Command
        With mUpdateCmd
            .ActiveConnection = mADOConnection
            .CommandType = adCmdText
            .CommandText = msUpdate
            Set mUpdatePrmIncome = .CreateParameter("pIncome", adVarChar, _
                                       adParamInput, 25, "")
            .Parameters.Append mUpdatePrmIncome
            Set mUpdatePrmDateStarted = .CreateParameter("pDateStarted", _
                                            adDBTimeStamp, adParamInput)
            .Parameters.Append mUpdatePrmDateStarted
            Set mUpdatePrmDateEnded = .CreateParameter("pDateEnded", _
                                          adDBTimeStamp, adParamInput)
            .Parameters.Append mUpdatePrmDateEnded
            Set mUpdatePrmSalaryId = .CreateParameter("pSalaryId", adDouble, _
                                         adParamInput)
            .Parameters.Append mUpdatePrmSalaryId
        End With
        Set mInsertCmd = New ADODB.Command 'needs parameters beyond cl_auth_id
        With mInsertCmd
            .ActiveConnection = mADOConnection
            .CommandType = adCmdText
            .CommandText = msInsert
            Set mInsertPrmSalaryId = .CreateParameter("pSalaryId", adDouble, _
                                         adParamInput)
            .Parameters.Append mInsertPrmSalaryId
            Set mInsertPrmEmployeeId = .CreateParameter("pEmployeeId", adDouble, _
                                           adParamInput)
            .Parameters.Append mInsertPrmEmployeeId
            Set mInsertPrmIncome = .CreateParameter("pIncome", adVarChar, _
                                       adParamInput, 25, "")
            .Parameters.Append mInsertPrmIncome
            Set mInsertPrmDateStarted = .CreateParameter("pDateStarted", _
                                            adDBTimeStamp, adParamInput)
            .Parameters.Append mInsertPrmDateStarted
            Set mInsertPrmDateEnded = .CreateParameter("pDateEnded", adDBTimeStamp, _
                                          adParamInput)
            .Parameters.Append mInsertPrmDateEnded
        End With
End Sub
```

```
Public Sub Refresh()
'** Set parameters and re-read
    mSelectPrmEmployeeId.Value = mlEmployeeId
    Set mrsSalary = mSelectCmd.Execute
    If mrsSalary.BOF And mrsSalary.BOF Then
        SetDefaults
    Else
        mvRows = mrsSalary.GetRows
        mlRows = UBound(mvRows, 2) + 1 'The variant's second dimension is rows
        SetProperties (0)
    End If
End Sub

Public Sub SetProperties(lRow As Long)
    SetDefaults
    If Not IsNull(mvRows(0, lRow)) Then
        mlSalaryId = mvRows(0, lRow)
    End If
    If Not IsNull(mvRows(1, lRow)) Then
        mlEmployeeId = mvRows(1, lRow)
    End If
    If Not IsNull(mvRows(2, lRow)) Then
        mlIncome = mvRows(2, lRow)
    End If
    If Not IsNull(mvRows(3, lRow)) Then
        mdDateStarted = mvRows(3, lRow)
    End If
    If Not IsNull(mvRows(4, lRow)) Then
        mdDateEnded = mvRows(4, lRow)
    End If
End Sub

Public Sub MoveFirst()
    'mrsPeople.MoveFirst
    mlX = 0
    SetProperties (0)
End Sub

Public Sub MoveLast()
    mlX = mlRows - 1
    SetProperties (mlX)
End Sub

Public Sub MoveNext()
    If mlX <> mlRows - 1 Then
        mlX = mlX + 1
        SetProperties (mlX)
        mbEOF = False
    Else
        mbEOF = True
    End If
End Sub

Public Sub MovePrevious()
    If mlX <> 0 Then
        mlX = mlX - 1
        SetProperties (mlX)
    End If
End Sub
```

```
Public Sub MoveRel(lRows As Long)
    If lRows <> 0 Then
        mlX = mlX + lRows
        If mlX > mlRows - 1 Then mlX = mlRows - 1
        If mlX < 0 Then mlX = 0
        SetProperties (mlX)
    End If
End Sub
Public Sub AddNew()
    ' Insert all the values into the parameters
    mlSalaryId = 0
    mInsertPrmSalaryId.Value = mlSalaryId
    mInsertPrmEmployeeId.Value = mlEmployeeId
    mInsertPrmIncome.Value = mlIncome
    mInsertPrmDateStarted.Value = mdDateStarted
    mInsertPrmDateEnded.Value = mdDateEnded
    mInsertCmd.Execute
End Sub

Public Sub Update()
    'mrsPeople.Edit
    'Insert all the values into the Parameters
    mUpdatePrmIncome.Value = mlIncome
    If mdDateStarted = #1/1/1800# Then
        mUpdatePrmDateStarted.Value = Null
    Else
        mUpdatePrmDateStarted.Value = mdDateStarted
    End If
    If mdDateEnded = #1/1/1800# Then
        mUpdatePrmDateEnded.Value = Null
    Else
        mUpdatePrmDateEnded.Value = mdDateEnded
    End If
    mUpdatePrmSalaryId.Value = mlSalaryId
    mUpdateCmd.Execute
End Sub

Public Sub Delete()
    mDeletePrmSalaryId.Value = mlSalaryId
    mDeleteCmd.Execute
End Sub

Public Property Get All() As Variant
    mvAll(0) = mlSalaryId
    mvAll(1) = mlEmployeeId
    mvAll(2) = mlIncome
    mvAll(3) = mdDateStarted
    mvAll(4) = mdDateEnded
    All = mvAll
End Property

Public Property Let All(ByVal vNewValue As Variant)
    mvAll = vNewValue
    mlSalaryId = mvAll(0)
    mlEmployeeId = mvAll(1)
    mlIncome = mvAll(2)
    mdDateStarted = mvAll(3)
    mdDateEnded = mvAll(4)
End Property
```

```
Private Sub BuildSQL()
'Make a parameter SQL for the reading the RecordSet
    msSelect = "Select "
    msSelect = msSelect & "SALARY_ID, "
    msSelect = msSelect & "EMPLOYEE_ID, "
    msSelect = msSelect & "INCOME, "
    msSelect = msSelect & "DATE_STARTED, "
    msSelect = msSelect & "DATE_ENDED"
    msSelect = msSelect & " FROM SALARY"
    msSelect = msSelect & " Where EMPLOYEE_ID = ?"
'Make a parameter SQL for the Inserting into the RecordSet
    msInsert = "INSERT INTO "
    msInsert = msInsert & " SALARY ("
    msInsert = msInsert & "SALARY_ID, "
    msInsert = msInsert & "EMPLOYEE_ID, "
    msInsert = msInsert & "INCOME, "
    msInsert = msInsert & "DATE_STARTED, "
    msInsert = msInsert & "DATE_ENDED) "
    msInsert = msInsert & "VALUES ("
    msInsert = msInsert & "?, "
    msInsert = msInsert & "?, "
    msInsert = msInsert & "?, "
    msInsert = msInsert & "?, "
    msInsert = msInsert & "?)"
'Make a parameter SQL for the Updating the RecordSet
    msUpdate = "UPDATE "
    msUpdate = msUpdate & " SALARY SET"
    msUpdate = msUpdate & " INCOME = ?,"
    msUpdate = msUpdate & " DATE_STARTED = ?,"
    msUpdate = msUpdate & " DATE_ENDED = ?"
    msUpdate = msUpdate & " WHERE SALARY_ID = ?"
'Make a parameter SQL for the "deleting from the RecordSet - change status to "DELETE"
    msDelete = "DELETE "
    msDelete = msDelete & " FROM SALARY "
    msDelete = msDelete & " WHERE SALARY_ID = ?"
End Sub
```

Support and Errata

One of the most irritating things about any programming book is when you find that bit of code you've just spent an hour typing simply doesn't work. You check it a hundred times to see if you've set it up correctly and then you notice the spelling mistake in the variable name on the book page. Of course, you can blame the authors for not taking enough care and testing the code, the editors for not doing their job properly, or the proofreaders for not being eagle-eyed enough, but this doesn't get around the fact that mistakes do happen.

We try hard to ensure no mistakes sneak out into the real world, but we can't promise that this book is 100% error free. What we can do is offer the next best thing by providing you with immediate support and feedback from experts who have worked on the book and try to ensure that future editions eliminate these gremlins. The following section will take you step by step through the process of posting errata to our web site to get that help. The sections that follow, therefore, are:

- ❑ Wrox Developers Membership
- ❑ Finding a list of existing errata on the web site
- ❑ Adding your own errata to the existing list
- ❑ What happens to your errata once you've posted it (why doesn't it appear immediately)?

There is also a section covering how to e-mail a question for technical support. This comprises:

- ❑ What your e-mail should include
- ❑ What happens to your e-mail once it has been received by us

So that you only need view information relevant to yourself, we ask that you register as a Wrox Developer Member. This is a quick and easy process, that will save you time in the long-run. If you are already a member, just update membership to include this book.

Wrox Developer's Membership

To get your FREE Wrox Developer's Membership click on **Membership** in the top navigation bar of our home site – http://www.wrox.com. This is shown in the following screenshot:

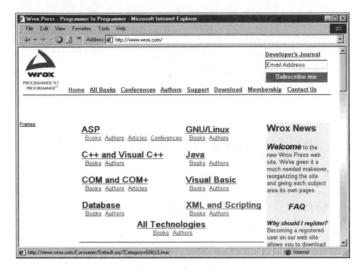

Then, on the next screen (not shown), click on **New User**. This will display a form. Fill in the details on the form and submit the details using the **Register** button at the bottom. Before you can say 'The best read books come in Wrox Red' you will get the following screen:

Type in your password once again and click **Log On**. The following page allows you to change your details if you need to, but now you're logged on, you have access to all the source code downloads and errata for the entire Wrox range of books.

Finding an Errata on the Web Site

Before you send in a query, you might be able to save time by finding the answer to your problem on our web site – http:\\www.wrox.com.

Each book we publish has its own page and its own errata sheet. You can get to any book's page by clicking on **Support** from the top navigation bar.

Halfway down the main support page is a drop down box called **Title Support**. Simply scroll down the list until you see **VB Oracle 8 Programmer's Reference**. Select it and then hit **Errata**.

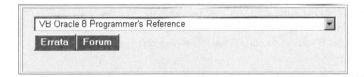

This will take you to the errata page for the book. Select the criteria by which you want to view the errata, and click the **Apply criteria** button. This will provide you with links to specific errata. For an initial search, you are advised to view the errata by page numbers. If you have looked for an error previously, then you may wish to limit your search using dates. We update these pages daily to ensure that you have the latest information on bugs and errors.

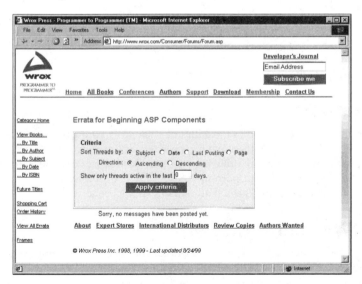

Add an Errata : E-mail Support

If you wish to point out an errata to put up on the website or directly query a problem in the book page with an expert who knows the book in detail then e-mail support@wrox.com, with the title of the book and the last four numbers of the ISBN in the subject field of the e-mail. A typical email should include the following things:

❏ The **name, last four digits of the ISBN** and **page number** of the problem in the Subject field.

❏ Your **name, contact info** and the **problem** in the body of the message.

We won't send you junk mail. We need the details to save your time and ours. If we need to replace a disk or CD we'll be able to get it to you straight away. When you send an e-mail it will go through the following chain of support:

Customer Support

Your message is delivered to one of our customer support staff who are the first people to read it. They have files on most frequently asked questions and will answer anything general immediately. They answer general questions about the book and the web site.

Editorial

Deeper queries are forwarded to the technical editor responsible for that book. They have experience with the programming language or particular product and are able to answer detailed technical questions on the subject. Once an issue has been resolved, the editor can post the errata to the web site.

The Authors

Finally, in the unlikely event that the editor can't answer your problem, s/he will forward the request to the author. We try to protect the author from any distractions from writing. However, we are quite happy to forward specific requests to them. All Wrox authors help with the support on their books. They'll mail the customer and the editor with their response, and again all readers should benefit.

What We Can't Answer

Obviously with an ever growing range of books and an ever-changing technology base, there is an increasing volume of data requiring support. While we endeavor to answer all questions about the book, we can't answer bugs in your own programs that you've adapted from our code. But do tell us if you're especially pleased with the routine you developed with our help.

How to Tell Us Exactly What You Think

We understand that errors can destroy the enjoyment of a book and can cause many wasted and frustrated hours, so we seek to minimize the distress that they can cause.

You might just wish to tell us how much you liked or loathed the book in question. Or you might have ideas about how this whole process could be improved. In which case you should e-mail `feedback@wrox.com`. You'll always find a sympathetic ear, no matter what the problem is. Above all you should remember that we do care about what you have to say and we will do our utmost to act upon it.

Index

Symbols

A